HITLER

R. H. S. STOLFI

HITLER

BEYOND EVIL AND TYRANNY

 Prometheus Books

59 John Glenn Drive
Amherst, New York 14228–2119

Published 2011 by Prometheus Books

Cover image © Library of Congress
Cover design by Grace M. Conti-Zilsberger
Dedication painting, *Honor the memory, Kathryn A. Stolfi, 1931–2010, She faced death* Sans Peur, *She lived her life* Sans Reproche, *She was a heroine for the ages,* by Sam Harris.

Inquiries should be addressed to

Prometheus Books
59 John Glenn Drive
Amherst, New York 14228–2119
VOICE: 716–691–0133 • FAX: 716–691–0137
WWW.PROMETHEUSBOOKS.COM

15 14 13 12 11   5 4 3 2 1

Library of Congress Cataloging-in-Publication Data

Stolfi, R. H. S. (Russel H. S.), 1932–
    Hitler : beyond evil and tyranny / by R. H. S. Stolfi.
        p. cm.
    Includes bibliographical references and index.
    ISBN 978-1-61614-474-6 (cloth : acid-free paper)
    ISBN 978-1-61614-475-3 (ebook)
    1. Hitler, Adolf, 1889–1945. 2. Hitler, Adolf, 1889–1945—Psychology.
3. Personality and politics—Germany—Case studies. 4. Hitler, Adolf, 1889–1945—
Childhood and youth. 5. World War, 1914–1918—Influence. 6. Heads of state—
Germany—Biography. 7. Germany—History—1933–1945. 8. Germany—History—
1918–1933. 9. National socialism—History. I. Title.

DD247.H5S777 2011
943.086092—dc23
[B]   2011023930

Honor the Memory

KATHRYN A. STOLFI
1931–2010

She faced death
Sans Peur
She lived her life
Sans Reproche
She was a heroine
for the ages

CONTENTS

CONTENTS

INTRODUCTION

After half a century, no biographer or historian has put together an adequate interpretation of Adolf Hitler. Since Hitler can be acknowledged to have been the most significant figure of the twentieth century, how is such a situation possible? The answer may be that the hunt for Hitler has been for the wrong man in the wrong historical background. The hunt has been for a political animal in the guise of a wicked man who engaged in evil deeds. But the intellectual expeditions both great and small to capture Hitler have been seeking the wrong quarry in the wrong landscape. Hitler was neither a politician nor engaged in politics. And he cannot be considered to have believed that he was a wicked man perpetrating evil deeds. Hitler had the intense psychological makeup of a prophetically styled messiah—one whose office he believed was to reveal a message of salvation to the Germans and to become the savior-hero himself. The landscape through which he moved was that of a Germany defeated in war and a European continent dominated by France. To think of Hitler as a German politician engaged in national politics would be like thinking of the quintessential Prophet Muhammad as an Arab politician engaged in similar political endeavors. Both must be comprehended as intense visionaries with their feet planted firmly several feet above the ground, in their own worlds of self-inspired revelation. Both achieved astonishing political results, but neither can be understood as a political ideologue.

Hitler brought more to the great messianic dance of the interwar period than the conventional wisdom has seen fit to accept. Underestimated by competitor and enemy contemporaneously and by biographers and historians since, he possessed traits unlike those of any other significant political figure of the era. Along with the intensity, seriousness, and earnestness that underpinned him as a self-professed messiah, he brought artistic qualities of brilliance in architecture, competence in painting, and the interest of a cognoscente in classical music. Based partly on this artistic makeup, he was characterized by extraordinary imagination and a lack of sense of proportion that would not allow him to embrace half-solutions to challenges. Thrown into this unlikely mix of traits and talents was a kind of lazy indolence that has confounded his biographers and baffled his contemporaries. In photographs that exist from World War I, he appears as dreamy visionary and fanatic adversary, pale and wrapped within an emaciated frame. Perhaps most interesting is that, in some of his photographs, his right eye seems to stare at something out of the picture and in another universe.

Writers throughout the world have put together a vast body of literature on Hitler and have used an even larger body of primary source material to buttress it. Against such a background, this book uses the following structure to extract a fresh interpretation of Hitler the person. First, because it is unlikely that any significant new primary source material will be found, this book does not search for it. Second, because another descriptive biography of Hitler would be an exercise in dullness, this book concentrates on interpretation. Overlying the literature on Hitler, there exists the great biographies that pull together most things on him that, because of their quality, comprehensiveness, and availability, dominate the worldview. The great biographers include, at least, Alan Bullock (1953), Werner Maser (1973), Joachim Fest (1974), John Toland (1976), and Ian Kershaw (1998), and their works hold the conventional wisdom on Hitler.[1] Because I have weighed the great biographies on the scales of historical reality and found them wanting, the book that follows will present a counterbalancing portrait of Hitler and a contrasting view of his times.

Virtually every literary piece written about Adolf Hitler in the more than half century since 1945 has been based on antipathy. In a seemingly boundless corpus of writing, every work from the mighty to the insignificant is fundamentally similar in its common revulsion for the man and his national movement. In the most recent great biography, Professor Ian Kershaw begins and ends with detestation. His work is skilled and often brilliant, but he fails to inform the reader of certain characteristics indispensable for true comprehension of the man, and he underestimates the importance of the postwar conditions inflicted by the Allies on Germany, which contributed to Hitler's rise. Bullock, Fest, and Kershaw ascribe criminal features to Hitler's foreign policy from 1933 through 1939, but they fail to correlate it realistically with the Allied imposition of the Versailles Treaty—the ultimate manifestation of German defeat and Allied victory following World War I. The biographers then create, during the period 1939 through 1945, an interpretation of the course of World War II and Hitler's conduct of it that fails to correspond with the German leader's actual intentions and the realistic possibilities for German victory.

In the present situation, the reading public has been served only half a portrait of the great tyrant of the twentieth century. The situation is an extraordinary one in which Hitler, as an object of biography, is portrayed as base and depraved, and the chain of foreign policy events of the 1930s leading into World War II is presented as largely the result of the machinations of this evil man. With Hitler, the perceived danger is that biography demands, or at least suggests, some empathy with its subject and a resulting understanding—and even admiration.[2] The writers on the subject of Hitler have taken the view that rehabilitation is unthinkable, and in such a situation, they have presented verbal portraits that are either half empty or but lightly sketched-in. In the former case, we glimpse the antipathetic half of the verbal canvas with the remaining half empty. In the latter, we observe the entire face but see an image with half the clarifying lines missing.

Just what do we have, therefore, with half a biographical portrait and, more specifically, the damning half? Kershaw suggests that there is no other half and that Hitler as an individual human being was base and wicked, and that most acts attributed to him were grounded in evil. A middle ground would be that half a portrait of Hitler is better than none at all, with the sense that the remaining half would little change the picture. One thesis of this book, however, is that half a portrait of Hitler tells us little about the man as a human being and presents a distorted and incredible interpretation of his actions as creator of National Socialism and leader of Germany.

One fundamental disparagement laid by biographers of Hitler is that he was an "unperson." Kershaw, for example, asks his readers: "How do we explain how someone with so few intellectual gifts and social attributes, someone no more than an empty vessel outside of his political life … could make the entire world hold its breath?"[3] He continues in an unequivocal judgment that "[Hitler] was as has been frequently said, tantamount to an 'unperson!'"[4] Biographers seem to be telling readers what Hitler ought to have been in the style of politicians in the experienced, parliamentary-styled, victorious Allied states—especially France and Britain.

Notably, however, the writers in these established democracies and others like the United States denigrate Hitler for his lack of formal education, his rude family environment, and his exaggerated dreams of success. Ironically, these characteristics read like the semi-mythical "American dream" wherein the young man with limited formal education, rude background, and dreams of success triumphs. But Hitler is noted as being an unperson because of these same characteristics, which allegedly made him incapable of embracing substantial interests beyond political propaganda and robbed him of a realistic and healthy sense of proportion. Writers on the subject of Hitler and National Socialism develop a theme that, as the most common of Germans, he resonated effectively in the hearts and minds of the German masses. This equation—Hitler's commonness equals natural empathy with the equally common German voting masses—is an enticing one. The biographers, starting with antipathy for Hitler, can scarcely be expected to search out evidence that reduces the preconceptions of commonness, evil, and neurosis. Biographers succumb to the temptation to present a mélange of denigration and demand that we accept it for a man of obvious talent in politics both domestic and foreign, talent in various fine arts and special capabilities as a frontline soldier in World War I. The denigration, which is contrived at worst and strained at best, tells much about the Hitler biographers. It shows that they have chosen to place a cloak of selective invisibility over interests and talents that conflict with their denigrating portrait. But how can one take such an interpretation seriously when, for example, in a first-hand repentance for his association with Hitler and National Socialism, the erstwhile young architect Albert Speer could comment:

> In conferring with me over plans, Hitler perpetually drew sketches of his own. They were casually tossed off but accurate in perspective; he drew outlines, cross sections, and renderings to scale. An architect could not have done better.[5]

and

> Hitler declared again and again: "How I wish I had been an architect."...I sometimes ask myself whether Hitler would have forsaken his political career if in the early twenties he had met a wealthy client willing to employ him as an architect. But at bottom, I think, his sense of political mission and his passion for architecture were always inseparable.[6]

Speer's words carry great weight. Stemming from their mutual enthusiasm for architecture, not only did Speer get as close to Hitler as any man, but he was also a formally educated professional of imagination and taste, a superb organizer of grand projects, and a winner of prestigious architectural awards including, for example, a Grand Prix at the 1937 Paris World's Fair for his model of a Nuremberg Party Day rally site. As Speer's "client," Hitler had had the taste to approve the plans for the Paris project two years earlier. His consuming passion for architecture is illustrated by the following scene recounted by Speer on the day of the approval of the plans: "That evening Adjutant Brueckner telephoned me. 'You and your goddammed plans! Couldn't they keep? The Fuehrer didn't close an eye last night, he was so excited. Next time have the goodness to ask me first?'"[7] The above picture does not sit comfortably with the *opinio communis* that alleges Hitler to have been a crude, empty vessel.

Through some similar incalculable process involving some combination of genetics and environment, he would develop an intense affinity for music—especially nineteenth century grand opera in the manner of Richard Wagner. With astonishing intensity, the young Hitler would pursue musical performances in the period 1905–1914 and during those times when he was on leave during World War I. In the interwar period he would be introduced into the Wagner household and associated with the great Bayreuth opera festivals. Hitler would also earn a modest living through landscape and cityscape painting in the period 1910–1914, carry his paints and brushes with him in a frontline infantry regiment during the Great War, and reveal an extraordinary interest in painting and sculpture after his seizure of power in 1933. He would also dictate official German taste in painting in the late 1930s.

Hitler's biographers have also broadened his historical shoulders to unrealistically large proportions. This broadening has taken place in a pattern that has prevented effective interpretation of the more important foreign policy events of the 1930s and the outbreak and course of World War II. A historical entity, "the German people," has been indicted accurately and plausibly for its role in the rise of Hitler. Another historical entity, "the German generals," has been accused by writers of having deflected blame for the loss of World War II away from itself and onto Hitler. Most important, however, yet another historical entity, "the Allies," has rendered itself historically invisible, escaping with little blame for the approach and outbreak of World War II except for the standard picture of naïveté and patient endurance of diplomatic aggression. As a noted British historian has described: "It was Hitler's war, he wanted it, planned it, and he started it."[8] This remarkable statement has lain unchallenged for decades even though it must be evident that "it was France's victorious peace, France wanted it, France planned it to dominate continental Europe and it led directly into World War II."[9]

The Germans themselves must shoulder the responsibility for the loss of World War I, and the French must acknowledge that through some combination of skill and luck, they managed to come out on the winning side in a coalition of Allies in which Britain was indispensable, Russia absorbed casualties, and the United States was responsible, in the final analysis, for tipping the balance toward victory. The point for a Hitler biography is that the loss of World War I by Germany, more than anything else, constituted the times necessary for the rise to power of a Hitler-like figure. The Allies had full freedom of political maneuver at the end of the war to bring about a stable Europe based on their military victory. They had the opportunity, initiative, and armed power to negotiate or impose a peace that would have reduced German revanchism to manageable proportions in the postwar era. But France and its allies, Britain and the United States, set no such peace in place. Instead, they inflicted one on Europe that led through its self-serving excesses to the outbreak of World War II. A recipe for disaster was drawn up, dominated by three ingredients: France, the outcome of World War I, and Hitler.

The most recent great biography of Hitler has been acclaimed by reviewers as the classic Hitler biography of our time and one of its greatest scholarly and biographical achievements.[10] It has pulled together everything preceding it and can claim to be definitive in its description. The main caveat to the latest biography's astounding descriptive breadth and depth lies in caution about the interpretive thesis that drives the work. Kershaw opens his "cool, judicious, factually reliable, and intelligently argued"[11] two-thousand-page work with an all-encompassing positioning of Hitler in world history, gracefully expressed as reflecting on Hitler the person. The reflections, however, do not place Hitler anywhere because the author posits that "the issue of 'greatness'" should be avoided altogether and holds forth that "it is a red herring," misconstrued, pointless, irrelevant, and potentially apologetic.[12] The author demands that we turn our attention to another question, one he claims to be of far greater importance. The question he poses is how an "unperson" such as Hitler made the entire world gasp. Kershaw's answer is comprehensive to the point of being definitive but, in the final analysis, lacking.

For Kershaw, the task of the Hitler biographer is to focus not on the personality of the man but on the character and the derivation of his power. The author elaborates with profound insight that Hitler's "entire being came to be subsumed within the role he played to perfection: the role of the Fuehrer."[13] Finally, Kershaw draws his arguments together by postulating that Hitler derived power from what he saw as his historic mission to save Germany. In Kershaw's view, such power depended upon the readiness of others to see heroic qualities in Hitler.[14] On the verge of developing those qualities of personality that defined Hitler and made the world hold its breath, the author perseveres unfortunately in his earlier announced intention to concentrate on the integration of the actions of Hitler "into the political structure and social forces which conditioned his acquisition and exercise of power."[15] The author, in effect, ends his reflections on Hitler by informing us that he is really going to produce an understanding of the phenomenon of Nazism, accomplish this by concentrating on the dictatorship rather than on the dictator, and also do justice to "the Hitler factor."[16]

As convoluted as this approach is to a work that has Hitler as the operative word in the title, the author nevertheless produces a magnificent portrait with special emphasis on the way in which Hitler wielded power. But why the extraordinary convolution? The answer to this question draws together the great biographies because they share antipathy for Hitler and an exaggerated fear of apologia. The great biographers take excessive liberties in denigrating his person, and, in doing so, they make it difficult to comprehend him. The common bias—contempt for the subject of the biography and a kind of arrogant fear of presenting any interpretation that might lead to greater comprehension but could also be construed as apologia— invites an analogy between biography and war fighting. The most notable soldier of the last half of the nineteenth century, Count Helmut von Moltke the Elder (1800–1891), commented that in war an error in the initial disposition of forces can never be made good. The Hitler biographers dispose of their interpretive intellectual forces with a bias that can never be made good. The result: thanks, ironically, to the historical greatness of the subject, powerful minds gripped by a preconceived picture of evil have produced brilliant biographies... and every single one falls short of producing an ade-quate understanding of Hitler as a historical person. To this point in time, the biographers have lost the biographical war.

In emphasizing Hitler as a man bent on aggrandizement of power rather than concentrating on the vision that drove his accu-mulation of power, the biographers steer us away from historical analogy as a tool for comprehending him. How can we make a potentially useful analogy between another historical figure such as a Gaius Julius Caesar and a Hitler, for example, if we expect to be scolded by writers for not emphasizing how the latter wielded power even though we might have attempted to compare them usefully in terms of similarly great achievements? In one "of the maybe half dozen books on Caesar that are worth reading,"[17] the author posits that Caesar, although an outsider to late republican Roman politics, through astounding personal achievement: added all of Gaul to Rome; seized power in the capital; defeated his opponents in a great civil war; and consolidated Roman power in a vastly extended area. Hitler was also an outsider, as an Austrian alien in Germany, and, similar to Caesar, would "seize power," add immensely to German territory from 1933 through 1942, and wield power as Fuehrer similar to the way Caesar wielded it as de facto emperor by 44 BCE. The two historical figures were also favored by social and political upheaval after World War I in Europe and in Rome during the twilight of the republic. The conditions for both men furnished opportunity for the exercise of personality.

It is difficult to imagine a Caesar or a Hitler without their surrounding heroically proportioned crises. In comparing the two for the specific purpose of comprehending the latter, we see Otto Seel in his "Essay on Caesar" remark about "the interplay between the compulsively fascinating and the disturbing, between the charisma with the *daemonia* that must have emanated from [Caesar], whom hardly anyone could resist."[18] We are compelled to see similar elements of charisma and daemonia—the presence of extraordinary genius—in Hitler and can be advised that another compelling historical figure has been branded similarly. Such observations about a historical figure with notable impact on world history are useful for comprehending Hitler, and it is evident that his achievements invite comparison.

Caesar, of course, stands as the more attractive man in terms of his family antecedents, classical learning, and towering intellect—and yet Caesar also seems to escape the shadow of mass murder that envelops Hitler. Even here, however, Caesar stands as one of the harder men in history to study, and virtually every biographer has been troubled by Caesar's ferocious determination to conquer and pacify the enormous area of Gaul and "Germany" to the Rhine River. Caesar is said to have defeated, in the ten years of the Gallic Wars, three million armed men—a third of whom were killed while another third were sold into slavery. Among the civilians—the women, the children, and the aged—casualties are estimated at one million human beings sold into slavery or killed. Although personally more attractive and accomplished than Hitler, Caesar comfortably holds his own in the balance of horror associated with the achievements of the great military and political leaders of history. Similar to Hitler, Caesar seems to have been driven by something in his personality that demanded greater achievement and higher stakes. It is blindness that destroys men, and it is stated that "there is in them an instinct, favored by their nature and strengthened by custom, which they do not resist, and which drives them on while they have any strength left."[19] Both Caesar and Hitler had a similar lack of sense of proportion. Both were afflicted by boundless ambition, revered the grandiose, defeated everyone, and yet shared endings in defeat—the one by assassination, the other by suicide in the midst of a crushing military loss.

But trying to get at Hitler by placing him alongside an allegedly similar great man has almost inherent drawbacks. How can we compare Hitler with a man who is credited with affecting a rebirth of Rome and Hellenism "by preventing the Germans from overrunning Rome and winning time for Greek culture to permeate the western half of the Mediterranean?"[20] The man who achieved this has claim to be the complete man, combining creativity and intellect with enough breadth to reconcile the Roman and Greek accomplishments within himself and communicate them to a wider world.[21] He has been called "perhaps the most gifted of mortals. Compared with him all others who have been called great were one-sided."[22] We see unparalleled human greatness in Caesar and must find it difficult even to attempt to place Hitler alongside such greatness. The lack of human or personal greatness in Hitler is deepened by the hyperbole used by his biographers in describing the "emptiness of the private person.... He was tantamount to an 'unperson'... the vulgar, uneducated upstart lacking a rounded personality, the outsider with half-baked opinions on everything under the sun, the uncultured adjudicator on culture."[23] These words are at least mildly exaggerated because they do not take account of Hitler's consuming interest and skill in the fine arts, but they picture a considerable distance between Hitler and Caesar in private, personal qualities.

We must face the reality, nevertheless, that Hitler had more impact on the course of the twentieth century than any other man. "He is one of the few individuals of whom it can be said with certainty: without him, the course of world history would have been different."[24] Faced with these interpretive truths, writers who are about to die in the arena of Hitler biography had better be prepared to come up with an adequate explanation of his greatness. Reality in the comprehending of Hitler demands that writers overcome the fear of being branded as "an apologist." Comprehension also demands that writers extricate themselves from the style of excessive disparagement to arrive at a more realistic view. Perhaps more than any other biographical vehicle, the concept of historical greatness—not personal greatness, attractiveness, and so on—permits us to sort out Hitler as a historical personage. When we see Hitler as great based on his historical achievements and their impact on the world, we can compare and contrast him with the right running mates in history for comprehension rather than criticism.

One biographer contrasts him disparagingly with such twentieth century denizens as Roosevelt, Churchill, Kennedy, and Mandela— specifically noting that these other figures symbolize the "positive values" of the century. It could be noted, though, from the perspective of historical greatness, that there must be some combination of unhistorical bias and presumption to place a Kennedy and a Mandela alongside of a Hitler, Roosevelt, or Churchill—notwithstanding the personal attractiveness of the former and the *je ne sais quoi* of the latter.[25] The whole business becomes even more intriguing when the great biographers state unequivocally that Hitler was a man of inconsequential paltriness and had no life outside of politics in the period from 1919 through 1945. The biographers do not grant a hint of personal greatness for Hitler, and we are left to discover in "politics" any claim that he may have to historical greatness. And to compound the intrigue, the biographers note that the only thing he did really well in politics was to propagandize through the spoken word.[26] We are left, as a result, with an unperson devoid of a life outside of politics. To compound this emptiness, the biographers inform us that politics for him *was* propaganda and not the vast field of action suggested by his words—namely, the art of the possible.[27]

How can we compare a man with talent largely only in political propaganda with figures such as Caesar and Napoleon with their comprehensive achievements in Rome and Europe? Hitler's historical achievements and impact remain at the level of such men, but his personality traits, dominated by seriousness, earnestness, and accompanying remoteness from all other human beings and pulled together in a distant vision of a perfect Reich, do not add up to the practice of politics. Contemporaries of Hitler in the initial stages of the movement noted behavior traits of asceticism, dysfunctional intensity, total disregard for matters of practical politics such as administration and organization, utter consistency in demands for personal control over actions and events, wildly "bohemian" work habits, the ability to inspire mass audiences with the spoken word, and so on, which do not support a view of Hitler in politics. Others around him in Germany and later in Europe were engaged in politics, but Hitler must be acknowledged, with his inimitable reserve and divorcement from the reality of others, to have been performing in the parallel universe of a prophet.

But what are the characteristics of a prophet, and do they in fact more comfortably and credibly pull together a picture of Hitler? Few can doubt that the great Arab, Muhammad "the praised," was a prophet—an inspired proclaimer of revelation—and his similarity to Hitler in style and achievement suggest that the latter was similarly driven. In Muhammad's lifetime, the people of the vast desert region of Arabia most frequently called him "the Messenger of God." The title "Prophet" came into general use after his death in 632. In those critical formative years of childhood and youth in which the indelible qualities of a man are set, observers noted the identical overriding qualities of seriousness, earnestness, and intensity. The great biographers present Hitler as incapable of calm and casual social conversation and observe that he preferred to engage in tirade and pontification with everyone from government minister and sophisticated host to his base personal entourage. The biographers elaborate that this single-minded intensity ultimately developed into unapproachable isolation and dismiss the observed behavior as egomania. The primary sources associated with the life of Muhammad are God speaking in the Quran, the revelations, and the *hadith* or table talk of the Prophet, and because of their nature they scarcely describe Muhammad as an egomaniac. It is difficult to imagine, however, that Muhammad suffered much interruption of his comments on faith and morals after the consolidation of his converts following the victories over the Quraish tribe in 622 and 623.

The great biographers of Hitler disparage him as chaste and prudish when young, use the phrase "sexual repression" to describe his lack of sexual experience, and put together a picture of unsavory oddness in the young man. In the case of Muhammad, it is pointed out that "in later life he claimed that he had never been guilty of sexual immorality in his youth."[28] The phrase "guilty of sexual immorality" is somewhat vague, but suggests reasonably that the Prophet, as a "quiet, pensive youth"[29] was at a loss about sex. Any intriguing similarity ends here, however, because, Hitler, concerned about his image as a distant, heroic leader, maintained a public image of celibacy while Muhammad had thirteen wives in the period 595 through 629.

Interpreting Hitler as a hate-filled egomaniac, the biographers underestimate the man, misjudge the disruption of the times, and prove incapable of overcoming elemental hatred for the subject of their biographies all in the presence of a man with the temperament of a modern-styled prophet. It is difficult to imagine that he would have had an assistant German messiah or felt bound by any council or counsel in interpreting his vision of new Germans and a Third Reich. The biographers do not display the self-discipline necessary to overcome their hatred of Hitler, and they adopt a morally superior position of acknowledging their fascination with the man and granting "the need of a certain shuddering admiration."[30]

Hitler himself noted in a passage in *Mein Kampf* that he "had a holy conviction of the mission and the future of his movement."[31] He elaborated that "only a storm of hot passion can turn the destinies of peoples and he alone who bears it within himself can arouse passion. [The storm] alone gives the chosen one the words which like hammer blows can open the gates to the heart of a people."[32] The biographers see in such words excessive self-adulation and, not surprisingly, call it egomania. Yet, we can take the same words that characterize the same man and see in them the description of an inspired revealer, one whose office it is to broadcast a message, and call these the words of a prophet.

The word is an emotive one, however, that can suggest different things to different people. A prophet, for example, can be seen as one who speaks in ecstasy from another world under the influence of noxious vapors, as in the case of the frantic priestess of the Pythia in ancient Greece, or in the case of Muhammad, as one who utters a God-given message. Neither noxious chemical vapors nor God seems to qualify Hitler as prophet, but his consuming earnestness, artistic and heroic sensibilities, experience of the social horror of Vienna, and stunning, unlikely survival through four years in the monastery with walls of fire, present a picture of an acolyte from an adequate preparatory school. The latest great biographer who enunciates that Hitler's entire being came to be subsumed within the role he played as Fuehrer, probably could have added with additional comprehension of the man that the Fuehrer's essential quality was that of infallible prophet rather than being a cynically adroit egomaniac good at impressing the naïve and the gullible.

Long before Hitler began to wear the trappings of power associated with the chancellorship, he had attracted around Munich the variable likes of Dietrich Eckart, Rudolf Hess, Hermann Goering, Ernst Hanfstaengl, Kurt Ludecke, et al., none particularly gullible yet all won over by Hitler's messianic-styled oratory. To comprehend Hitler and National Socialism, we must understand what attracted such men early in the movement. Ludecke agonized that he "was looking for the German soul, or rather the leader who would know how to reanimate it, and ... was resolved not to desert [Germany] again."[33] In August 1922, in a mass meeting on the *Koenigsplatz* in Munich, Ludecke, as emissary of *Bund Bayern und Reich* (the Bavarian and Imperial League), stood close to Hitler and recorded the following remarkable effects: "slight, pale man...threatening and beseeching...flaming, steel-blue eyes...the look of a fanatic... holding the masses and me with them under a hypnotic spell by the sheer force of his conviction...voice rising to passionate climaxes... then two words like the sting of a lash: '*Deutschland Erwache!*' Awake Germany...the intense will of the man, the passion of his sincerity seemed to flow into me. I experienced an exaltation that could be likened only to religious conversion."[34] Seen through Ludecke's eyes, Hitler had the appearance of a prophet, spoke the inspired words of a prophet, overwhelmed the senses as would a prophet.

The biographers have pulled together extensive documented descriptions of Hitler's life graced by sound analysis and clear prose, but we continue to face an interpretive barrier beyond which no historian or writer has been able to penetrate. The writer of a recent interpretive account of Hitler has worded the subtitle of the book as "the search for the origins of his evil," and we are left to suspect that he has selectively put together the same antipathetic half of the picture of Hitler presented by the biographers.[35] The author is searching for the origins of Hitler's evil and must reject even the conception that Hitler can be explained otherwise. He carries the reader through insight which nevertheless slips into the same morass of contempt and loathing and a nonnegotiable thesis of the dominating presence of evil. The journalist in a marvelously informative dialogue with the first great biographer, Alan Bullock, has him exclaim on the question of whether or not Hitler was consciously "evil": "If he isn't evil, who is? That's all I mean: if not he, then who?"[36] Even with Bullock we see the unarguable intonation of Hitler as evil, and the writers continue to wrestle with the frustration that somehow, someday, the key will be found to unlock the how and the why of the assumed evil resident in Hitler.

When it has become necessary at various points in most accounts of Hitler to reflect stunning achievement—successful action in the face of heavy odds—the same writers disparage the achievement and suggest that "a convincing study of Hitler" may just not be attainable at all.[37] But if it were it would almost certainly be linked with overcoming the significantly flawed assumption of pure evil that has driven Hitler biography for more than half a century after his death. We do not have to begin with a premise that Hitler was not wicked, but we do have to begin elsewhere than a premise that demands forcing everything in Hitler's life toward preconceived wickedness. The Hitler phenomenon comes into focus when its expansiveness is acknowledged rather than rendered invisible because of the notion that any unorthodoxy could lead to rehabilitation.

Hitler's fierce nationalism—which was the obvious counterbalance to his anti-Semitism, and which should be exemplified by his military service in World War I—tends to disappear from consideration as important. Instead of looking for answers to the intensity of his German nationalism and anti-Semitism, writers have claimed seriously that he welcomed the war largely as a chance to escape from a life of hopeless artistic mediocrity. No writer mentions the possibility that it may have occurred to Hitler and others in similar plights that remaining a live mediocrity would be better than becoming a dead frontline soldier. Particularly as the war developed into the grinding horror that it had become by the winter of 1915, Hitler can be seen as having steeled himself to the presence of death in the highest intensity battles of the twentieth century only through his determination to carry out his duty for the survival of the Germans. Hitler would comment that "the young regiments had not gone to their death in Flanders crying 'Long live universal suffrage and the secret ballot,' but crying *Deutschland ueber Alles in der Welt*..."[38] We could generalize that Hitler did not enter the war crying, "lift me from artistic mediocrity" but rather "test me in the sincerity of my conviction of Germany foremost."[39]

Thomas Mann, with his acute insight into Hitler in the 1930s, could pronounce that "here is a man possessed of a bottomless resentment and festering desire for revenge" and one who "rouses

the populace with images of his own insulted grandeur."[40] In such
words Mann expresses the view that Hitler was driven by some kind
of reprehensible frustration over a prior life of failure. Here we see
both the biographers and a literary giant like Mann in agreement on
a thesis of Hitler's base, hate-filled being. We must wonder thereby
if any man has comprehended the connection between Hitler and
his experience of the defeat of the Germans. Hitler could pronounce for all to read: "And so it had all been in vain...the hours in
which, with mortal fear clutching at our hearts, we nevertheless did
our duty; and in vain the death of two millions...Would not the
graves of all the hundreds of thousands open...and send the silent
mud- and blood-covered heroes back as spirits of vengeance to the
homeland which had cheated them...of the highest sacrifice which
a man can make to his people in this world."[41] Hitler reveals a combination of indignation and fury in these words, the rare combination of controlled moral condemnation and heroic rage. The words
cannot begin to be understood in terms of personal frustration and
instead support a view that an already ultraintense adolescent had
been transformed by the war into a man so earnest and serious that
he had risen above nationalism as commonly associated with politics
and had become something more.

Hitler used history to highlight the tragic grandeur of what had
happened. He called upon the example of the Aryan Dorians,
Hitler's Western man at his elite and pure best, in pointing out that
"Verily these heroes deserved a headstone: 'Thou Wanderer who
comest to Germany, tell those at home that we lie here, true to the
fatherland and obedient to duty.'"[42] Such allusion is powerful
rhetoric and does not fit a picture of whining and hate over an
unsuccessful career choice. And in a succinct follow-on, he presents
historical context by questioning, "was it only our own sacrifice that
we had to weigh in the balance? Was the Germany of the past less
precious? Was there no obligation toward our own history? Were we
worthy to relate the glory of the past to ourselves? And how could
this deed [of revolutionary villainy] be justified to future genera-

tions?"[43] With these rhetorically styled, repetitive questions that relate the German past with the present, Hitler cannot be seen as overly concerned about his own personal lot. Yet it may be that like Wagner, "*His* problems are always to be the world's problems, *his* needs the world's needs."[44] The perceived "problems" of Wagner's operas are indeed generally those of his own personality and circumstances. The similarity ends here, however, because the problem for Hitler of the salvation of the Germans was a more difficult challenge than that of combining voice, orchestra, libretto, and stage setting into musical drama.

As concerns the question of the psychological engine that drove Hitler, the conventional interpretation of lusting after power is, in final analysis, the refuge of lack of comprehension. And it is no more credible to claim that Hitler decided to save the Germans because of personal frustration than to claim that he decided to expand German space into an impregnable Reich fortress in order to satiate some lust for power, as it were, just for the evil of it. The essential qualities of Hitler's revelation include vastness, clarity, immutability, and finality that add up to the vision of a self-adjudged chosen one. The accounts from 1904 through 1908 add up to a picture of the young Hitler as consumed by interest in idealistic fantasy projects all with envisioned successful outcomes. We detect neither evil nor hate nor lust for power in these projects, and such elements should have been present even in adolescence for one interpreted as the personification of evil. Hitler instead reveals intensity and idealism. He does not introduce the word "hate" in any broad sense to his life until his ominous comment in mid-1908. It was then that he made reference to the Jews as the supreme enemy of the Germans, and that he had "gradually" begun to hate them. The operative adverb, *gradually*, provides insight because it demands that he neither hated nor was particularly concerned about Jews until after his arrival in Vienna. Then, as a result of his "objective" studies of authorities as variable as the gutter pamphlets, respected newspapers, books, and the programs of the Pan-Germans and the Christian Social Party,

Hitler claims that the Jews became revealed as the enemy. He cannot be seen as developing over a long period as a result of environmental bombardment in the home, school, and around Linz into the usual religious and crudely propagandized anti-Semite of the era. In spite of the passion with which Hitler would pursue his anti-Semitism, it would be underpinned by an extraordinary combination of objectively styled study and inspired revelation of the Germans under attack by a master enemy.

Hitler's inherent intensity and inquisitiveness and predisposition to convert his problems into those of all Germans would combine to produce his great revelation over a two-year period that centered on his nineteenth year. Hitler thereby treated the world to the unlikely picture of a nineteen-year-old who acquired a worldview that had the intensity and clarity of a prophetic vision and that developed into the political–philosophical phenomenon of the century. He would opine in *Mein Kampf* that all creative ideas appear in our youth, during which we acquire our most original and productive thoughts, and after which we are no longer able to add anything significantly more original and are faced with executing those "unchanging principles."[45] Hitler presented the picture of a self-acknowledged Romantic genius who, through concentrated self study, achieved a worldview which we can most comprehendingly liken to a single immutable revelation.

Unbeknownst to the Germans, the messiah had already experienced revelation by late 1909. The mystery, then, is why he did not begin to stalk through the streets of Vienna, staff or whip in hand, warning idolaters or flagellating modern moneylenders. The answer is that he had neither opportunity nor motive at remotely high enough levels to enter politics—perhaps appropriately from stage right. Hitler himself would be part of the problem in this realization. Thomas Mann's thesis of "the difficulty, the laziness, the pathetic formlessness in youth, the round peg in the square hole, the 'whatever *do* you want,'" would come into play for the next ten years within the framework (partly true, but significantly exaggerated) of a "lazy, vegetating existence in the depths of a moral and mental Bohemia" and an arrogance supported on a vague intuition of being reserved for something special.[46] Most significantly though, Hitler would struggle to make a living in Vienna and Munich and then struggle to stay alive on the western front with neither opportunity nor motive great enough to activate the messiah. Remarkably, the man who could display such energy post-1919 would require the stimulus of World War I and the lengthy opportunity of the 1919 barracks days in Munich to step forward.

When the time came to finally do something, he would confound the writers by claiming to wrestle mightily over entering politics. Hitler showed remarkable restraint and humility in this set of circumstances from 1910 through 1919. It would take the deaths of nearly two million sworn to duty in a losing cause to press him forward. The National Socialist cenotaph—an empty bronze tomb in Munich symbolizing the bodies of two million buried elsewhere—brings into focus the recognition of danger to the Germans and the element of revenge that must be associated with Hitler.[47] The conventional wisdom does not see such images and instead parades Hitler as a fanatic, a base self-seeker with the enlargement of his own power as his aphrodisiac; rather, he should be seen as a fanatic, base *genius* with the salvation of the *Germans* as his aphrodisiac.

Characteristically, messiahs announce themselves. No committee marches in advance to announce their arrivals. Hitler would elaborate on this theme by claiming that "In world history the man who really arises above the broad average usually announces himself personally."[48] And in a continuing apolitical and impersonal style, he would reiterate the theme that "*one* man must step forward who, with apodictic force, will form granite principles from the idea-world of the broad masses and take up the struggle for their sole correctness" all directed "toward the raising of a brazen cliff of solid unity in faith and will."[49] Although Mann would see in such verbiage histrionics in the service of a demagogue, he would admit that Hitler was an impossibly successful hysteric. He would also admit that there was absolutely no limit to the extent that Hitler could project his unconscious self on reality.[50]

In the presence of a messiah as evidenced by the words above in only two sentence fragments—*one* man, apodictic force, granite principles, idea-world, sole correctness, brazen cliff of solid unity, faith and will—the best the brilliant literatus can manage is to point out that Hitler was a contemptible hysteric. The biographers, historians, and other writers, however, comprise a literary body homogenized by its expectation to be appalled. In such a situation it is not surprising that Mann could fail to discern Hitler's dark fury over the deaths of two million soldiers. The gifted writer of the *non plus ultra* brief analysis of the Hitler phenomenon would instead elaborate on a *Death in Venice* and the challenge of the anti-intellectualism that was developing in turn-of-the-century Europe.[51] Mann would even make an analogy between Hitler and Girolamo Savonarola (1452–1498) the fiery would-be Italian messiah. He would philosophize how, in intellectually laden Florence, the sway of beauty and culture was broken by the religious and social fanaticism of a monk, and, on the verge of conceptualizing Hitler as a similar prophetic figure, would veer away from the scent. How ironic that another inspiring German writer of the century would have made available for Mann the word picture of the western front as a monastery with walls of fire and out of which Hitler would appear as warrior-monk and aspiring savior in late 1919.[52]

All of this, of course, requires imagination on the part of the interpreter, but the utter determination, the crazy fearlessness, the fanatic yet inspired will to disseminate the word of salvation—how can we miss it: "Germany Awake"—cannot be assigned to the crafty unperson of the conventional wisdom. The biographers would see in the focused, repetitive propaganda and semimystical rituals of Nazism the presence of the half-digested ideas of a junior high school dropout rather than the brilliantly clear revelation of an artistically inclined, intense, and bookish adolescent. The messiah's message must be simplicity itself. The intellectually inclined biographers stray from the point that the message is directed through the spoken word at the broad masses and not in writing to an inbred, self-adoring intellectual elite. And although the message is always simple, it does not follow that the messenger is so. The messiah is either a great simplifier or he is not the messiah.

It is a unique circumstance in the interpretation of the Hitler phenomenon that, unlike any other similarly significant political figure of the last two centuries, he was a competent artist in water-color and oils, and the measure of his competence is illustrated by his candid comments in the interwar period that his paintings were not really very good. As concerns both his abilities and his interest, he would say in Munich, to an acquaintance criticizing his work, that he painted what people would buy. In contrast, his competence in architecture would increase and be formidable by the latter half of the 1930s. Hitler would reveal impressive insight into the qualities of classical Greek, but especially Roman, structures and become aware of the centering of those civilizations on the monumental buildings which represented state power and served to unify the entire popu-lation with a sense of common destiny. In the Greek city–states and Rome, the great families lived in substantial homes but rarely palaces, as palaces would compete with the great public structures open to all—the forums, the temples, the structures of the games, the triumphal arches, the libraries, the baths. If Hitler had tri-umphed over Soviet Russia in the summer of 1941 and won World War II, his Germany would have been dominated by the aesthetic of monumental public structures in its cities. It is difficult to accept the stricture that Hitler's vast architectural projects represented per-sonal megalomania when he would repeatedly philosophize, as on the dedication in January 1939 of the new Reich Chancellery: "I stand here as representative of the German people. And whenever I receive anyone in the Chancellery, it is not the private individual Adolf Hitler who receives him, but the Leader of the German nation.... For that reason I want these rooms to be in keeping with their high mission."[53] And in support of an interpretation of himself as distant messiah and artist, he could dilate that "this is the special and wonderful property of architecture: When the work has been done, a monument remains,"[54] and "through the centuries will bear witness for all those who helped to create it."[55] Although characterized as uncultured and unread, Hitler comes off in his demands to create a monumental signature for a Greater Germany as historically and artistically gifted.

In his first significant success as the emerging dominant figure in the German Workers' Party, Hitler would move with uncanny balance among messianic idealism, political realism, and artistic imagination. Hitler argued that in 1920, in Germany, a national meeting which addressed its appeal to the masses and publicly invited attendance was "simply impossible."[56] Within this context, Hitler described the trepidation of the party committee members in the face of the mass meeting in words such as "that's impossible," "it won't work," "we can't risk that," "that's too dangerous," and so on.[57] Hitler demanded an action that was so unrealistic, idealistic, and frightening that the party chairman, Karl Harrer, resigned. Hitler faced the dangerous certainty that the Marxists would employ their street-fighting apparatus to break up the meeting and organized his "comrades" from the barracks of the Second Infantry Regiment as defensive squads to remove the agitators "with the one great thought of creating a free path for the holy mission of our movement."[58] Hitler also showed an artistic flair in the first mass meeting with the red color of the propaganda posters and the striking red banner with white disc and black swastika as the party flag, the most riveting political symbol of the century.

As such, Hitler would lead the tiny German Workers' Party to its first mass meeting in stunning success, filling the *Festsaal* of the *Hofbraeuhaus* in Munich with two thousand people on February 24, 1920. He would successfully speak in the face of physical violence by Communist meeting-breakers. In February 1921, Hitler would dare to hold a meeting in the *Zirkus Krone* and attract an overflow audience of roughly 6,500 people and successfully defend the meeting from interruption. And to illustrate his compulsive emphasis on the spoken word in politics, Hitler would unrealistically demand another meeting for the following week and again fill the hall "to the bursting point."[59] When virtually all politicians around Hitler after 1919, domestic and foreign, engaged in politics as a rewarding career, he would emerge on a higher plane as a messenger of the revealed truth of early Vienna and as the revenging angel of World War I. When the extraordinary few like the redoubtable chancellor and foreign minister Gustav Stresemann and the foreign minister Walter Rathenau acted on a plane of enlightenment well above the game of politics, Hitler stood alone on yet another plane—a higher or lower one, depending upon the bias of the observer. The issue of hate and evil resident in Hitler must also take on new meaning with Hitler as messenger of German destiny.

When Hitler entered "politics" in 1919, he had a clear goal in mind for the Germans. For a man utterly new to politics, he set a goal so optimistic and vast that it must be taken as divorced from reality both at that time and even for a distant future. To compound the implausibility of it all, he based his goal on the great revelation centered on only his nineteenth year. In the face of Hitler's achievements and his closeness to final triumph, the conventional wisdom revels in presenting a pathetic misfit who appeared from nowhere and, through some accident of history, some unlikely combinations of situation, luck, rhetorical skill, and the miraculously consistent disarray of his opponents, succeeded in everything. As far as the conventional wisdom will go, however, is perhaps summed up in the words of Kershaw: "For one thing, Hitler was certainly not unintelligent..." framed revealingly as a double negative.[60] That wisdom cannot escape its preconception of Hitler as a base nonentity or overcome its self-imposed shibboleth of no hint of rehabilitation. It cannot force itself to say: for one thing, Hitler was certainly intelligent. And the same wisdom unendingly repeats a view based on innumerable causes and personifications claimed for Hitler that there is no single or simple answer to the phenomenon.

The biographers paint themselves into an interpretive corner of denigration of Hitler from which there is no escape and which demands the unsatisfying generalization that we may never fully understand him. Yet the biographers need only admit to themselves and the reading public that he was a willful genius with extraordinarily developed qualities that, when combined, allow for adequate comprehension. The paint strokes of denigration that dominate the present biographical portrait of Hitler must be counterbalanced by admission of that genius and its associated qualities that lie strewn about the historical landscape—on ground which every biographer and historian has feared to tread. Prudence demands that we take account of the ancient admonition that fools rush in where angels fear to tread, but the time has come for some hero to save the world of Hitler interpretation by attempting comprehension rather than reveling in denigration and alleging hopeless complexity in achieving interpretation of the phenomenon.

The Nazi revolution has been interpreted variously as a product of European power politics, outgrowth of German history, tool of crisis capitalism, product of the promise and failure of socialism, nemesis of Western mass democracy, and so on, with the widely varying interpretations each having reasonable merit.[61] The writers on both Nazism and Hitler are constrained, in the face of multiple causes of Nazism, to see overwhelming complexity in relating Hitler even with what was unarguably his own revolution. Unlike a Lenin who was derived from a Marx, and a Muhammad who was derived from a vision of a monotheistic God, Hitler uniquely and single-handedly created his own revelation of the Germans in mortal danger from international Jewry and encircling French and Slavs. The situation remains muddled because writers refuse to acknowledge the existence of any superior or redeeming qualities in Hitler. How can we adequately interpret Hitler when we must wrestle with multiple causes for Nazism, which, in turn, are related with an implausibly contemptible and talentless person whose only outstanding quality was that of being evil? The only exception to this generalization is no exception at all because when the conventional wisdom acknowledges that Hitler was a propaganda genius, it undermines its own judgment by characterizing the propaganda as that of hate and evil.

Hitler can be seen as essentially amoral in his approach to any action perceived as necessary to succeed in his mission as savior of the chosen Aryans and destroyer of their archenemy—the *other*, self-appointed chosen people. In such a revision, the question of good and evil takes on a different character because instead of considering it with relation to the worn-out picture of a frustrated and hate-filled nonentity, we find ourselves in the presence of a prophet spreading a word of revealed danger and salvation. In such a picture, the equally tired thesis of Hitler as an unperson without a life outside of politics takes on a more credible glow and astonishing fullness. Being a messiah is a full-time job; as such, Hitler was not *supposed* to have had a life outside of politics. He was not only a chaste ascetic, as must be desirable for a messiah, but also possessed of an artistic talent virtually unheard of for either a practicing messiah or a professional politician. After 1945, Thomas Mann could exclaim unfettered by the straightjacket of fear of Hitler: "Alas, the artist... For must I not, however much it hurts, regard the man as an artist phenomenon? Mortifyingly it is all there."[62] Mann would unerringly discern the characteristic Bohemianism in Hitler, although he would not point out his talents in the fine arts were ignored and disparaged by the later conventional wisdom.

To comprehend the Hitler of 1919 is to comprehend the Hitler of the entire period from 1919 through 1945. Every personal characteristic and quality was in place, and nothing changed. The venues would be different and the stakes would be higher. But even the seemingly increased personal danger from assassination or incidental deadly violence in the meeting brawls, street battles, and road journeys would be less than that of the front lines of the western front. Hitler has been perceptively compared with Charles XII of Sweden, declared at age fifteen to be an adolescent genius of similar towering achievement and lack of sense of proportion, but who would be struck down by a chance shot in a no-account siege at age thirty-six.[63] Hitler would not be carried off by such a shot but would arrive in history as an adolescent prodigy with a lack of sense of proportion strikingly similar to that of "the Alexander of the North."

We should be able to approach the issue of the evil resident in Hitler and his associated anti-Semitism with more clarity and, perhaps, finality in terms of the man of 1919. For one who has come to personify evil in the twentieth century, he revealed little in the entire period of 1889 through September 1919. His friend August Kubizek and numerous acquaintances and observers present no details that support criminal or antisocial behavior or psychological instability. The associates and acquaintances of the great men's home in Vienna come up with a mixture of intensity, reserve, indolence, and a noteworthy sympathy for the lot of those less fortunate in the home. The landlords, furniture art dealers, and acquaintances of prewar Munich present a similar picture of Hitler—polite, intense, reserved, intelligent. He gave practically no evidence of anti-Semitism, with virtually no anti-Semitic conversation recounted, and polite, reserved, and functional interaction with every Jewish art and furniture dealer of the prewar period. It defies reasonable probability that the most determined anti-Semite in history could have shown such a pattern of behavior. There must have been some decisive quality in Hitler's evil and anti-Semitism which has eluded writers now into the twenty-first century.

On the question of sadism and cruelty or what might be called "advanced evil," Hitler cannot be said to have shown any during the entire period. How is it possible that Hitler gave so little evidence of such qualities in the inescapable formative years of his life or those stress-filled years up to his thirtieth year? Even a cursory reading of Hitler's account of the revelation of his worldview in Vienna shows that he had arrived at his anti-Semitism with trepidation, haltingly and through objective study. He noted that he was appalled at the exaggerated "unscientific" arguments of the religious anti-Semites and only slowly arrived at a self-revealed worldview of the Jewish menace based on ice-cold logic. Notwithstanding his messianic-style conviction in the cause of the salvation of the Germans, it seems more probable that his anti-Semitism was less emotional and more objective than has been assumed to the present.

As concerns Hitler's penchant for evil in the entire period from 1919 through 1939, we are also presented with the relatively restrained picture associated with the elimination of the upper levels of the *Sturmabteilung* (SA or storm detachment) leadership in 1934, the concentration camps of the 1930s, and the harassment of the German Jews during the same time. Not until World War II can Hitler be associated with sadism and cruelty—and then specifically in the incredible disappearance of the 3.1 million Russian prisoners of war taken in the brief period from late June through mid-October 1941 and the better-known deliberate killing of probably no fewer than 4.5 million European Jews.

The answer to the question of sadism and cruelty in Hitler can be linked with his one-time comment that he would be known as the hardest man in history. The comment was esoteric, secretive, and typical. With it, he seems to have momentarily broken the surface of studious private address to a project known only to him and to have begun to anticipate hard decisions. We can never know what decisions Hitler had begun to anticipate, but he did so with his detached solitude so similar to that which Kubizek characterized as fundamental in his makeup as an eighteen-year-old. The great question is, what was the relationship in Hitler's mind between the quality of hardness and the qualities of sadism and cruelty, which lie so closely together? This question for the ages is not unlike the one which has been asked for two millennia about the hardest men in history—the Romans. How is it possible that these impossibly serious, duty-driven, and immeasurably practical men could have been associated with the horrors of the "monstrous and inexplicable" and seemingly pointless games exemplified by the Colosseum?[64] It is difficult to accept that the Romans saw themselves as sadistic and cruel, and it is at least mildly intriguing that Hitler did not use the words: *I will be known as the most sadistic and cruel man in history.*

The seemingly obvious sadism and cruelty and apparent point-lessness in the Roman games incites us to attribute the violence to cruelty in the Roman nature. The similar qualities in the destruction of the Russian prisoners and the European Jews incite a similar attri-bution to Hitler's nature. But objections can be made because neither Roman nor Hitler can seriously be supposed to have considered himself wicked. For the noble Roman and the farmer-soldier alike, the underlying quality in them which characterized their greatness, was the Roman *gravitas*—seriousness, earnestness, sternness, grant-ing little to pleasure or extravagance. The Romans were the supreme utilitarians, realists, and practical political organizers of the ancient world. With such qualities they cannot be seen to have succumbed to vengeance, sadism, and cruelty as the motivations for the games. "Annihilation and pitiless massacre were only a last resort against an irreconcilable enemy," as seen in the annihilation of several tribes in eastern Gaul by Julius Caesar because of their unstable, mercurial, and untrustworthy savagery, which made them irreconcilable, men-acing, and useless either as allies or as slaves.[65] The Roman thereby revealed harshness of almost incredible proportion, but he did so based on realism and prudence in the face of perceived danger—scarcely sadism and cruelty.

In the case of Hitler, we see similar elements of detachment from sadism, cruelty, and even hate in the notorious harsh actions taken by him. In his first great act of overt murderous violence, Hitler personally arrested Ernst Roehm and several higher officers of the SA and made the decision to have several of them executed. In this incident, Hitler had to be goaded into taking action by Roehm's competitors in the party and found it difficult to make the decision to have Roehm shot. Faced with the menacing intransigence of Roehm with regard to what organization in Germany would be the bearer of arms, Hitler made a necessary, practical, and realistic decision to maintain the stability of the regime through support of the army. We see Hitler faced with the dangerous intransigence of the leadership of a vast, uniformed, political street-fighting organization—formerly indispensable, but then extraneous and having become a danger to the movement. Uncharacteristically prodded into action by his lieutenants Goering, Goebbels, and Himmler, who expanded the action opportunistically to eliminate competitors and enemies past, Hitler also had to work himself up into a fury to execute his friend and dismiss the fearsome storm detachment which had been instrumental in the seizure of domestic power but become a mortal danger to the holding of that power. In this action Hitler instituted bloody violence but did so as a necessary, in-house, war-fighting type of action and showed virtually nothing that can be interpreted as sadism, cruelty, or ingrained hate as opposed to temporary fury in the carrying out of the action. As in the case of the Roman extermination of some Breton tribes in around 50 BCE, Hitler took the action of pitiless massacre as a last resort in the face of a perceived irreconcilable enemy.

Hitler would comment extensively on the issue of the necessity for hard decisions. In volunteering such comments he would present two qualities ignored by the conventional wisdom, but ones that provide us with his vision of himself. Although the conventional wisdom has not taken these qualities seriously, Hitler can probably be considered an enlightening source of opinion on himself, and in the following view we could accept Hitler's authoritative comment rather than assume conscious evil. In a single sentence in late summer of 1942, he would offer the following self-analysis: "I am certainly not a brutal man and consequently it is cold reason which guides my actions."[66] This extemporaneous oral statement was made within the context of punishment for serious crimes, and he offered the following argument in support: "I say, therefore, that sentiment must play no part in these matters; we must apply a rule of iron and admit of no exceptions. This may often pain me personally, and it may lead to errors which one will later regretfully acknowledge. But any other course of action is out of the question.... The main thing is to be honest and logical with one's self."[67] Writing much earlier, in 1924, about his 1908 and 1909 revelation of the Jewish menace to the Germans and the impending necessity for them to fight for their survival, he would agonize over his struggle for objectivity. In his own words about "his greatest transformation of all" into an anti-Semite he would analyze that "it cost me the greatest inner soul struggle, and only after months of battle between my reason and my sentiments did my reason begin to emerge victorious."[68] He referred to the two-year period as a "bitter struggle between spiritual education and cold reason"[69] and summed up his anti-Semitic transformation as "the time of the greatest spiritual upheaval I have ever had to go through."[70] These unvarnished and unparaphrased words show Hitler rejecting the baser emotions associated with brutality and cruelty and embracing "cold reason" as the basis for his revelation— while simultaneously presenting the whole business as a spiritual experience! In the words above, Hitler showed an extraordinary combination of revelation and logic. He also rejected half measures and compromise and affected a pitiless hardness directed toward the realization of a Reich impregnable not only in dimension but also in the German will to seize and defend it.

The present interpretation of Hitler as an evil and insatiable force for personal political power can be challenged also as grossly unrealistic, unbalanced, and emotionally vague. Politics for Hitler must be seen as a distant, prophetic vision to be fulfilled and not as an exercise in personal power. There was no political theory for Hitler and no necessity for adherence to any political programs. There was only tactical political flexibility in the service of the seizure of power and in the establishment of a Greater Germany in Europe. We see, in effect, Hitler and Nazism as forces directed toward the realization of a vision, and, to use Hitler's own words, "force must always have ideas to support it."[71] For the first time we can comprehend Hitler's amoral flexibility in the politics of 1919–1933 more effectively as the apolitical application of force in the service of what began as a vision so distant that any suggestion of its realization would have been greeted with Thomas Mann's "peals of laughter." And for the first time, we can understand Hitler's amoral, tactical flexibility in international relations during the 1930s as the apolitical application of force in the realization of such a vision.

Hitler's storied comments—"hardest man in history," "no man will ever know what I am really thinking," "the Jews must disappear from Europe," and so on—come into focus as those of an impossibly intense and serious figure located psychologically just beyond and outside of the remainder of humanity. To search for and assign evil to such a man is to chart a course through waters more dangerous than has been acknowledged by the conventional wisdom. How do we assign evil to a bona fide messiah who was dedicated to the defeat of perceived evil and the enthronement of perceived good?

At first glance, the question seems to be answered by arguing that even if we acknowledge that Hitler were a messiah dedicated to a vision of German salvation, he affected evil in the destruction of the Russian prisoners and the European Jews. The question of intent must be evaluated, however, and Hitler cannot be considered to have believed that he had perpetrated evil in his messianic-viewed destruction of the enemies of the Germans. The enormity of the killing of 7.6 million unarmed human beings, even within the framework of a great war, nevertheless stands as a monument to evil even though intended as prudent and necessary action in the presence of an irreconcilable enemy; as it were, harsh necessity rather than conscious cruelty. Yet, the analysis cannot end here because it is necessary to consider that victors and repentant losers have dominated twentieth-century history and have failed to assign evil in cases of similar enormities. How, for example, can we accept the case for evil in Hitler from a conventional wisdom which, by conscious default, has categorically failed to assign evil to a British government that instituted a food blockade of Germany—*extended* after the close of World War I—that predominately affected German children and the elderly and resulted in the deaths through starvation of 800,000 noncombatants? And, how can the reading public be adequately informed of the quality and extent of evil in Hitler when the same wisdom has largely ignored the Winston Churchill–inspired expulsion of the Germans from eastern Europe? This act of evil is mentioned only cursorily in a few histories of the period and not at all in Hitler biography. The expulsion, however, created a staggering number of refugees and resulted in the deaths of two million of them through the inhumane circumstances of their forced flight during the winter of 1945, which echoed John Milton's poetic rejoinder, "pray not that your flight be in winter."

The present assignment of evil to Hitler leaves the impression that he was not only evil but rather *uniquely* evil. But the assignment has to provide adequate perspective to give us adequate comprehension, for after all we must be able to compare and contrast him with others of the twentieth century. Kershaw, for example, in the first paragraph of the introduction to his biography, would pronounce Winston Churchill as representative of the positive values of the century, and such may be the case. But the claim loses much in translation because the author failed to temper it by taking account of Churchill's moral frailties as a high-level British political military figure during World War I—first lord of the admiralty, munitions minister, and secretary for war and air minister—with knowledge of the policy of the starvation of the Germans. In World War II he must take significant responsibility for the policy of encouraging guerrilla war in the west, with its resulting sadistic and cruel barbarities, effecting strategic bombing so indiscriminate that it killed more than 550,000 German civilians, and, finally, being the originator of the harsh and deadly expulsion of the Germans from the east. To give the reader a realistic comprehension of Hitler as evil, the writer must present not only the qualities and extent of it but also its similarity to other figures of the era. Those factors can perhaps be compared between the British and German historical giants in an analogy that can be made between Hitler's words that the Jews must disappear from Europe and Churchill's words, which could be paraphrased that the Germans must disappear from eastern Europe.

The quality of cruelty is similar between the disappearance of the Jews and the Germans; Hitler would condone the outright killing of the former while Churchill would condone the outright expulsion of the latter and accept the resulting unintended deaths. The quality of extent or dimension is also similar. Hitler's action would result in the deaths of more than 4.5 million Jews, while Churchill's action would result in the creation of 14.5 million permanently displaced German refugees and the deaths of approximately 2 million. The quality of extravagant and cruel finality in the two acts is strikingly similar, with Hitler determined to remove from Europe a people deemed an irreconcilable menace to an envisioned Reich, and Churchill determined to remove from eastern Europe a people deemed an irreconcilable menace to the British Empire. For purposes of comprehending Hitler, the point is that the devil was loose in Europe from 1914 through 1945 and took on numerous different shapes—some well-known through the conventional wisdom and others that have been rendered invisible.

Preoccupation with perceived evil and alleged banality in Hitler, however, steers us away from adequate appreciation of the political skill and personal charisma that brought him to power in 1933. Hitler's two great political episodes of the 1920s were the Munich Putsch of November 1923 and the conceptualized strategy in its aftermath to seize power legally. Rather than being shown as driving toward a polar starlike objective and revealing consummate reality and patience in reaching it, Hitler is presented accurately but incompletely as immersed in the drab details and in-fighting associated with control of a minor and potentially ephemeral radical political party. The conventional wisdom has a chance to show how Hitler's conceptualization was on a plane above the innumerable details of a party functioning within the best days of the Weimar Republic by comparing and contrasting it with Lenin's earlier performance in seizing power in Imperial Russia. The writers in analyzing the two men suggest that Lenin was intellectually superior, by noting his formal education and brilliance in the Marxist dialectic, and present his similar success in effecting revolution in Russia between 1917 and 1921.

The great Russian, however, defied the Marxist dialectic by making the revolution in the wrong country, doing so with heavy-handed cruelty in the destruction of the middle class and so-called wealthy peasants in several years of civil war, and never transferring the revolution to its theoretical and more realistic center of Germany. The Russian Revolution as directed by Lenin, notwithstanding, or perhaps as proven by, its final consolidation under Josef Stalin, stands as clumsy, brutal, and misdirected (i.e., at the wrong time and place, but nevertheless bloodily pushed through). Hitler intended a similarly fulsome revolution and has been interpreted as a one-dimensional crude and brutal propagandist, but his seizure of power stands as a monumental address to practical reality and historical continuity. And in contrast to the Communist revolution in Russia and the Communist attempts at revolution in Germany from 1918 through 1923, Hitler's were virtually bloodless. The warrior prince of the trenches, the fanatic messiah, the destroyer of the Russian prisoners and the Jews of Europe would conceptualize outvoting the opposition in a parliamentary democracy. The conventional wisdom brands the resultant success of January 1933 as a sham "seizure of power," asserting that ignominious backstairs maneuvering and chance circumstance effected the appointment of Hitler as chancellor on January 30, 1933. But Hitler would not only almost bloodlessly (i.e., ignominiously) "seize power" but also proceed later in the year to seize power with the bloodless yet revolutionary synchronization of much of German affairs with the party.

Hitler would consolidate himself in power by late 1934 by the elimination of the internal competition from the SA in June and the assumption of the positions of chancellor, president, and Fuehrer with the support of the army and the federal bureaucracy upon the death of President Hindenburg in early August. Freed of domestic constraints, Hitler launched a foreign policy that could be characterized as resulting in the boldest and most decisive string of foreign policy victories in the history of modern diplomacy. The rapid pace of the foreign policy from 1935 through 1939 can be encapsulated in a long German word as *Blitzaussenpolitik*, the spirit of which is blitzkrieg-like foreign policy. Hitler himself, with no man comprehending the direction, urgency, and final scope, drove the policy. No general staff officer, cabinet minister, or party lieutenant was privy to his thoughts, except in the cases of ominous hints of approaching war and their involvement in the immediate actions comprising his aggressive but bloodless foreign policy moves. To comprehend this history-altering foreign policy, we must come to grips credibly with Hitler and the surrounding European historical situation. At this point, the conventional wisdom fails us on both fronts. With stubborn uniformity, it presents Hitler as a one-sidedly shabby, wicked figure who coveted power, and it presents the historical situation as one in which a legally bedecked European status quo of 1919 had come under attack by a German leader with the qualities of an international criminal.

Such an interpretation, which can be generalized as a battle between good and evil in European international relations from 1933 through 1939, is unrealistic. Hitler does not stand up to scrutiny as either intellectually inferior or consciously evil. It is challenging to consider that the foreign policy of a great power like Germany came out of the mind of a single man. At this point it would be tempting to argue that Hitler had become dictator and, like all dictators in all times and places, had become subject to the influence of cabals and court favorites in making high political policy. Perhaps uniquely in history, Hitler escaped this universal condition. He was under the influence of no other man and cannot be said to have been constrained either by democratic constitution or Communist-style central committee.

Speer would verify this extraordinary historical situation in the following casual analysis which was stimulated by his bafflement at the way in which Hitler apparently squandered time. Speer would comment: "When, I would often ask myself, did he really work?"[72]

And then Speer would note that Hitler "often allowed a problem to mature during the weeks when he seemed entirely taken up with trivial matters. Then after the 'sudden insight' came, he would spend a few days of intensive work giving final shape to his solution."[73] In this 1939 description of Hitler being Hitler, we see the adolescent style totally intact, unchanged, and projected into the great foreign policy actions of the 1930s. To make decisions, to formulate actions to solve problems, Hitler required no advisors—only listeners. Hitler's rare special companion and observer of the early 1920s, Ernst Hanfstaengl, could make the detached comment that Hitler, at his Monday evening suppers with his faithful cronies and their wives at reserved tables at Munich's Café Neumaier, "would speak *entre famille* and try out the techniques and effects of his newest ideas."[74] And earlier, his boyhood friend of four close years could claim that "our friendship endured largely for the reason that I was a good listener."[75] As a kind of precocious genius, Hitler functioned alone with intense, objectively styled conceptualizations of domestic and foreign policy in the presence of unwitting sounding boards. Hitler can be seen as moving from one self-generated revelation to another. What would have been a brilliant thought to another statesman took on the cast of revelation applicable to all of Europe with Hitler.

European foreign policy of the 1930s came to be dominated by Hitler and led into World War II with its catastrophic casualties and damage. The Germans lost that war, and it must be evident that the interpretation of that foreign policy and resulting war has been written almost exclusively by historical entities described as "the victors" and a lower number of "repentant losers." To compound this historically incestuous situation among the writers, the Germans had lost the previous war and had been handled similarly on the subject of its outbreak. These assertions may be an unusual combination of obvious, trite, superficial, and deniable, but it must nag that Germany remains saddled to this day with entire responsibility for the outbreak of World War I, and Hitler with somewhat greater responsibility for the outbreak of World War II. In the former case, entire great empires vanish from consideration in the interpretation of the outbreak of war. In the latter case, powerful states with both traditional and revolutionary aggressive political agendas crowd the scene, yet vanish in Hitler's shadow. We are left to wonder how a man painted as so uneducated, ignorant, and unsavory could have had the skill to effect the foreign policy of the 1930s. We are left with little wonder about blaming Hitler for the outbreak of World War II because, whether we subscribe to the vague but strongly held interpretation of insatiable lust for power on Hitler's part or an interpretation of messiah-styled drive for the salvation of the Germans, we are left with the same probable result of war.

Chapter 1

HITLER'S ATTRIBUTES REASSESSED

Perhaps the single most important question that we can ask about Hitler in his formative years from 1889 to 1914 is: Can we identify the fundamental, enduring temperament that had stabilized by the beginning of World War I? By about age five, Hitler had probably already developed qualities, based on a complex and indecipherable mix of heredity and environment, that would underpin his development. Those earliest qualities are beyond the reach of any man today to approximate; if Hitler himself were still alive, he would be hard-pressed to define his childhood qualities, let alone describe how he came to hold them. By the time Hitler moved through his teens, however, we can begin to see a temperament comprised of talents, interests, and predilections that can be derived from historical data. Schoolmates, friends, acquaintances, teachers, neighbors of Hitler and his family have been captured by historical researchers in enough detail to begin to assemble a picture of his personality. Although the years are early and relatively few, the temperament set within them should be similar to that which Hitler would carry largely unaltered to his grave.

In his twelfth year, Hitler would respond to an adult's question of what he would make of himself in life with the following words: "a great artist." The word, artist, linked with the fine art of painting. With remarkable consistency, he would maintain this goal until the end of World War I. Hitler had discovered early on that he could draw with pencil and paper and gradually expanded that talent into watercolor and oil painting on various surfaces. The question of exactly when and why Hitler answered the call of painting is perhaps answered in his own words: "How it happened, I myself do not know, but one day it became clear to me that I would become a painter, an artist."[1] Hitler was instinctively attracted to drawing and painting, which can be generalized as being important in his life during the period 1900–1914, along with his even stronger fascination with architecture. Similarly, in the sense of an emergent artistic temperament, Hitler would develop a strong interest in opera and classical music—particularly the heroic German tableaus of Richard Wagner, who, along with Guiseppi Verdi, was the supreme composer of opera in the talent-laden nineteenth century.

Detractors, though (and there are none other), would probably query: Can Hitler be judged to have been an artist? The question should be addressed even though it could be argued that it made no difference whether or not art critics or others judged Hitler to be one. All that is necessary is to show that he believed himself to be an artist, and historical evidence overwhelms us that Hitler thought himself to be a painter and architect. Evidence also overwhelms us that he could in fact be considered to have drawn and painted well enough to be considered one. Hitler was observed sketching as early as 1900, and by age sixteen in 1905 was continuing to comment to various listeners that his aspiration in life was to paint. Frau Pressmayer, a neighbor of the Hitlers' in Leonding, observed during the period 1905–1907 that Hitler "was busy with painting and drawing the whole day."[2] The reason why Hitler had time for painting, architectural drawing, and the opera is that he had dropped out of further formal education at age sixteen. Here we see Hitler, according to his boyhood friend August Kubizek, engaged especially in sketching architectural scenes of Linz as part of a grand scheme for the rebuilding of that city with its considerable 1911 population of 67,800, complete with municipal opera house, grand museum, electric tram lines, and major iron bridge across the Danube River. We can generalize, therefore, that

Hitler by age sixteen had become dominated by an artistic temperament. It included a self-willed aversion to formal schooling and any form of scheduled activity—a Bohemian rejection of bureaucratic regimen and bourgeois schedule.

Hitler thus embraced art as his calling in life and remarked candidly that he had no explanation for his great interest. The special intensity with which he pursued the calling, however, was so radical and divorced from the reality of his social situation that it demands interpretation. During the period 1900–1905, Hitler the previously excellent grammar school student (grades one through five), proved unwilling to cope with the Austrian junior high school system, or lower *Realschule*. He needed five years to complete the necessary four years (i.e., he had to repeat one entire year), and, if this were not enough, he compiled failing grades during four of the five years that had to be made up by special examinations immediately preceding his entry into the succeeding school year. Through strenuous efforts, Hitler improved his performance in the fourth and final grade of the lower *Realschule* but nevertheless failed geometry. Only through yet another makeup examination in September 1905 was he able to get a certificate of completion by the end of that month. Based on his poor performance, Hitler would have required a near-miracle to have made himself eligible for the Austrian high school system, or higher *Realschule*.[3] Without further education, Hitler, in late 1905, had no realistic chance to become the academic painter and artistic success that he envisioned.

As the next phase of his life unfolded from his passing out of junior high in September 1905 through his mother's death in late December 1907, the unemployed Hitler lived entirely at the expense of his nobly suffering and loving mother. During this period, Hitler led a life of leisure without apparent direction or goal. This life represented a flight from reality into a fantasy world of internal visualization of the manner in which his life would work out. His closest friend of the period 1905–1908, the talented music student August Kubizek, remarked that "he gave his whole self to his imaginary building and was carried away by it."[4] The architectural fantasizing included especially drawings based on internal visualizations inspired by attendance at Wagnerian operas—great bridges, blocks of houses, castles, villas, a monastery, and the like. One must question in retrospective wonderment how Hitler thought he would acquire the education and training to bring into being the paintings and architectural structures and cities that lay in his imagination. Here one sees Hitler lucidly visualizing his accomplishments as a great artist while apparently adrift without a notion of how to achieve anything realistic. Sometimes, however, things are not as they may seem to be.

The generalizations similar to those above embraced in the great biographies of Hitler argue that he idled away the three years after largely failing the lower *Realschule* in a kind of social and intellectual vacuum. Those generalizations do not stand up to observations by contemporaries and to the realities of his future pattern of activity. Hitler, for example, repeatedly claimed that during the years from 1905 to 1907 he engaged in serious "studies," and the complete lack of formal study in school does not necessarily add up to an unread man. Kubizek remarked, for example, that he remembered Adolf as always surrounded by books while commenting also that Hitler would make him study "this or that book which he had just read so that he could discuss it with me."[5] A similar picture emerged with a later friend, Harvard University graduate Ernst Hanfstaengl of the Munich art reproduction publishing house, who got to know him well and remarked about Hitler's life in 1923 that "he was a voracious reader and positively stormed the historical library I was building up."[6] Hitler himself would claim to have read intensively and widely in the period 1905–1914 in Linz, Vienna, and Munich, and his claims are supported by various independent sources including family friends, personal acquaintances, landlords, and the like.

The conventional wisdom has acknowledged grudgingly that Hitler read a large amount. That wisdom, however, largely cancels such acknowledgement by claiming that he read selectively to reinforce his prejudices in various fields. The conventional biographers argue that Hitler largely read the marginal (i.e., lunatic fringe) tracts and news sheets that had begun to flood Vienna by the turn of the century and suggest that such literature dominated the intellectual content of his personal "studies." With this argument, Hitler's substantial reading in Linz, which could not have been affected much by the Vienna fringe literature, his reading of respectable books in Vienna, and his continued affair with reading in Munich, tends to be ignored and slips out of his educational equation. Hitler, for example, would claim as the voracious reader that he seems to have been to have carried the works of Arthur Schopenhauer, the German pessimistic philosopher of the turn of the nineteenth century, with him into World War I in his frontline infantry regiment. Such a claim supports a view that Hitler had been inspired to master Schopenhauer's worldview and not simply confirm some prejudice.

Hitler and Schopenhauer together, under the circumstances of lengthy reading on the western front, are anathema to the conventional biographers. The following sarcastic disparagement typifies the antipathy: "[I]n the Ypres region of Flanders…he could find time to paint pictures and read (if his own account can be believed) the works of Schopenhauer that he claimed to have carried around with him."[7] Ernst Hanfstaengl, who had been on close terms with Hitler intermittently from early 1923 through 1937, remarked upon hearing Hitler expound on the need for a heroic worldview for Germany that "this was not Schopenhauer, who had been Hitler's philosophical god earlier in the Dietrich Eckart days of 1921–1924, but something new."[8] Hanfstaengl's remark supports a view that Hitler not only had carried Schopenhauer's works into the dugouts and trenches, but also that he had actually read them. It must also be evident that Hitler had had much discussion with the urbane Hanfstaengl on the subject of Schopenhauer for his intellectual patron to claim so decisively that Hitler had been a knowledgeable admirer. The presented picture is also not one of Hitler as an unperson.

The above remark by Hitler's most recent great biographer typifies the style of writing on the subject. Writers take descriptive liberties in their commentaries on Hitler that would not be tolerated by critics and readers with other similarly important historical figures. In a single sentence, the biographer quoted would sarcastically belittle Hitler's interest and talent in painting, parenthetically suggest that Hitler lied about reading Schopenhauer's works, and sarcastically call into question Hitler's comment that he carried them into the war at all. The penchant of his biographers for gratuitous sarcasm, strained skepticism, and writing from preconceived heights of antipathy has left the world with a dangerously inaccurate portrait of Hitler. In the quote above, the biographer demonstrates a dry humor by characterizing Hitler's talent in art as residing at the level "to paint pictures" in his free time with his wartime regiment. Dry humor in counterpoint could well be: Winston Churchill painted pictures; Adolf Hitler painted. Biographers practicing such sarcasm obscure the reality that an artist in spirit, talent, and style would create the most dynamic political movement of the twentieth century, seize power in Germany, lead it through the constraints of Versailles into World War II, and all but win it in August 1941. One finds here no lawyer from Columbia Law School, general studies aristocrat from Harrow and Sandhurst, political scientist from the University of Paris, or professional intellectual malcontent from the great bend of the Volga River.

In late 1907, Hitler would confront nemesis—retributive justice—during his second visit to Vienna. Hitler's dedicated, organized, and loving mother, Klara, had allowed him to withdraw his patrimony from the Mortgage Bank of Austria and travel to Vienna to apply for entrance into the painting curriculum of the Vienna Academy of Fine Arts. In October, he took the two-day examination for entrance into the first year curriculum and failed. It was the first of the five great blows in his life. These blows included the death of his mother two months later, the German loss of World War I in November 1918, the failure to limit the Danzig crisis to a war between Germany and Poland in September 1939, and the defeat in

April 1945. Hitler requested an interview with the director of the academy, who expressed the opinion that Hitler did not have the talent at that time for painting but had a surfeit of talent for architecture. Hitler would continue to have confidence in his painting but would remark in later writings that he began to realize that he would someday instead be an architect.

Notwithstanding the presence of nemesis, this great event in Hitler's life as aspiring artist has a curious twist. One writer with a perceptive interest in Hitler would publish a collection of more than seven hundred paintings and sketches attributed to Hitler, including three of the watercolors submitted during the test.[9] Those paintings are significantly and obviously below the quality of others attributed to Hitler during 1907 and 1908. He seems to have tightened on the examination and produced an effort that was not representative of his talent. We are left with the unsettling feeling that if the teenage Hitler had produced his usual and more representative work, he probably would have been accepted into the academy's painting curriculum. What is the significance of this fresh observation on the first great traumatic event in Hitler's life? Curiously enough, it supports a view that in spite of his apparent artistic death wish from 1900 through 1907, he had in his own mind, after October 1905, a "plan" embodying private immersion in art, at the end of which and at the earliest possible time—age eighteen—he would sweep into the art academy on the basis of the talent he would reveal in the yearly examination. The pattern was one of apparent drift, torpor, and self-indulgence and seemed to represent Hitler's basic temperament—artistic, Bohemian, procrastination unconstrained by ordinary consideration of time, during which he worked obliquely on developing projects until forced to act. Years later, in August 1923, when Hitler had become a leading actor in Bavarian politics, the National Socialist economic guru Gottfried Feder would criticize Hitler's lifestyle, specifically noting his anarchy in the allocation of time.[10] Here we see the "granite foundation" of Hitler's temperament laid during his teen years in Linz and the year 1908 in Vienna.

When Hitler departed by train for the Austrian capital in February 1908, he vacated Linz as a badly educated eighteen-year-old of modest social antecedents but with considerable talent in the fine arts. Looking back in time through World War II, the interwar period, and World War I, we see times of cataclysmic political violence. It is easy to forget, therefore, that Hitler went to Vienna earlier in the autumn of 1907 to take the painting admissions examination for the Vienna Academy of Fine Arts and not to prepare himself to become a German nationalist and anti-Semite. He took this great step of his formative years based on his interest in painting, and it must be jarring in the face of the present consensus of Hitler as coarse unperson that such a generalization can be made. Evidence from the years 1900 through 1907, however, shows that he thought he would become a great artist and from that lofty eminence preside over a life filled also with classical music and opera.

The biographers know this, but in their underestimation of Hitler and inability to resist the sarcastic *bon mot*, they make fun of and largely ignore what they consider to be his artistic pretensions. They do so because they are unable to rise above the unbridled hatred expressed so well by Thomas Mann that "one begins to fear lest one be pusillanimous enough to fall short in the hatred which is the only right reaction from those to whom our civilization is anyhow dear."[11] But Mann continues on to a higher plane occupied by none of the great biographers when he elaborates "that those are not my best hours, in which I hate the miserable, if also portentous phenomenon."[12] He philosophized that his better hours are those in which his hatred was overcome by the need for objective contemplation of the interest (indeed, fascination!) with Hitler. Mann generalized that people underestimate such interest and the superior morality inherent in approaching Hitler from the viewpoint of a fascination of the genius united with the limitless amoral vision in one man. The great biographers, however, do not take Hitler seriously as either an artist or as a genius who combined artistic sensibilities with other remarkable characteristics. In doing so, they underestimate his formidable artistic and messianic qualities that are the ones that largely account for Hitler's success. We are left with a caricature of a crude propagandist, a caricature that is almost valueless for comprehension of Hitler. A far better image would be a more comprehending picture of an artistic, self-educated phenomenon of vast historical breadth marching toward a final messianic vision.

Hitler entered his Vienna period in early February 1908 and exited it five years later in May 1913. Biographers of Hitler have heavily worked this period of his life based on his assertion that he laid the foundation of his political worldview during that time. Hitler's biographers, however, are in so antipathetic a hurry to tell their readers about the wicked ideas developing in the mind of a wicked man that they overemphasize the importance of politics and ignore evidence lying about that conflicts with the view that the period was dominated by Hitler's transformation into an extreme German nationalist dominated by repugnance for the Marxists, Jews, and Slavs of the empire.

The Vienna period, however, can be divided into two parts. When they are analyzed from a viewpoint of trying to comprehend what Hitler was doing contemporaneously rather than looking for evidence to project him into a known future outcome, a better understanding can be reached. For such understanding, the period can be divided into an early period ending with Hitler's fall into the abyss during late 1908 and 1909, and a later period characterized by his exit from the same depths during 1910 through 1913. That word, abyss, is a colorful one for Hitler's near social extinction around Christmas of 1909. During early 1908, Hitler developed an interest in political and social issues associated with the growing cosmopolitan center of the Austro-Hungarian Empire. His interest was characterized by concern over perceived disintegration of the Austrian part of the empire. Hitler nevertheless must be seen as far more involved in art projects including architectural drawing and planning, painting (especially cityscapes), attendance at opera and symphonic performances, and widely varied library book reading. Although these projects do not qualify as gainful employment, they do not represent the socially unredeeming, purposeless indolence emphasized by the great biographers.

In September 1908, Hitler failed for the second time the entrance examination to the academy, and from that time through December 1909 remains unknown historical terrain. Much time has to be accounted for, and the biographers (with the exception of the most recent work) work hard to denigrate Hitler and fit him into the well-known superficial reader of the newspapers and cheap political tracts of Vienna. In such a picture, they present Hitler as haunting coffee houses in the city and developing his ubiquitously described half-baked ideas on Marxists and Jews that he was beginning to assemble as his world-view. The biographers base their invariable accusation of "half-baked ideas" on the premise that an uneducated, uncultured, indolent twenty-year-old could have had none other. The biographers further claim that Hitler read especially various anti-Semitic tracts that would have supported his assumed consuming anti-Semitism by the time of his departure from Vienna in 1913. Kershaw, the latest great biographer, however, dismantles such interpretation by argument that shows that little evidence exists as to what Hitler did during the lost year.

With pitifully few eyewitness accounts of Hitler during the missing year, we can only make the modestly comfortable generalization that he continued to be attracted to heroically styled German nationalism and to pinpoint the usual suspects as the most dangerous enemies of a secure German Reich. During this year of his descent to near social obliteration, we must also conclude that his developing political enlightenment was subordinate to his practical concern over his dwindling finances, necessity to move to cheaper lodgings, continuing hope of becoming a great architect, never-ending affair with grand opera and other classical music, and concern over having to identify himself to the imperial authorities for compulsory military service.

But Kubizek's account of Hitler in Vienna earlier, from February through July 1908, establishes beyond much doubt that he immersed himself in architecture—sketching and painting buildings and planning architectural edifices such as opera houses, bridges, monumentally styled buildings, and the like. The account also shows that he read omnivorously, continued to draw and paint, and attended numberless performances of opera and classical music. The biographers agree with these generalizations but temper their remarks with so many disparaging qualifications that readers are left with the feeling that Hitler had little talent and only modest interest in the fine arts. In the case of music, for example, it is demonstrable that Hitler had an irresistible passion for it. Kubizek, the aspiring musician, had first encountered the fifteen-year-old Hitler at the Linz Opera House where the two competed for standing room to view the stage setting so important for opera. Kubizek would comment that in the Linz Opera House, "just above the promenade was the Royal Box supported by two wooden columns. These columns were...the only places with an undisturbed view of the stage...I can still see myself rushing into the theater undecided whether to choose the left- or the right-hand pillar. Often, however, one of the two columns...was already taken; someone was even more enthusiastic than I was.[13]

Adolf Hitler appears intense as always and engrossed in European grand opera of the turn of the century. Kubizek presented Hitler, even at age fifteen, as enthralled by cultural achievement and scarcely engaged in the activity of an unperson—unless we comprehend attendance at grand opera as base and unredeeming. It is possible, though, that Hitler at this young age viewed opera as a child might "read" an illustrated book, largely interested in the pictures, or, as it were, the scenery. But Kubizek elaborated that "during the interval in a performance some time later we started talking, as... neither of us approved of the casting of one of the parts. We discussed it together and rejoiced in our common adverse criticism. I marveled at the quick sure grasp of [Hitler]. In this he was undoubtedly my superior. On the other hand, when it came to talking of purely musical matters, I felt my own superiority."[14] No great biographer or any other has seen fit to add to our comprehension of Hitler by noting the quite extraordinary fact that at age fifteen he immersed himself in discussion of the casting of roles in grand opera with an aspiring and ultimately talented music student. This fragment alone hints at extraordinary qualifications for appreciation and analysis of opera and suggests that the great biographers, for whatever reason, have misleadingly exaggerated their characterization of Hitler as a personal void. The great biographers, however, level the objection at the young Kubizek that he was impressionable and willing to defer to Hitler in widely ranging matters of opinion. But no biographer can claim that Kubizek was anything but an intimate and expert commentator on Hitler and his association with music.

Kubizek gives us a brief portrait of the teenager recalled half a century later when he decided to write about his extraordinary friendship with the young Hitler. Music was the single common factor that most linked them together, and Kubizek remains superbly qualified to tell us about Hitler's interest, knowledge, and talent in music. Kubizek's account supports a view that Hitler, with or without his friend, attended an extraordinary number of opera and music performances in numerous opera houses, including the Linz Opera House, Vienna Hof Opera, and People's Opera in Waehring, a district of Vienna where performances featured the likes of Gustav Mahler and Anton Bruckner as conductors.[15] Both Kubizek and Hitler considered Richard Wagner as their *non plus ultra* composer and "just as other people quote their Goethe and Schiller, we would quote Wagner, preferably the *Meistersinger.*"[16] And, "we studied, with libretto [rendition in words] and score [rendition in music], those works we had not seen in Linz."[17] In precious firsthand detail, Kubizek recalls some of the musical performances that Adolf and he attended, and the list is impressive: In Vienna: "*The Flying Dutchmen, Lohengrin, Tannhaeuser, Tristan and Isolde, Die Meistersinger* have remained unforgettable… as has *The Ring* and even *Parsifal.*"[18] Earlier in Linz, in addition to performances of Wagner, they had seen together "a surprisingly good *Figaro*" and *The Magic Flute* by Wolfgang Amadeus Mozart and *Der Freischuetz* by Carl Maria von Weber. These details of Hitler's romance with classical music out of childhood and youth suggest that he had considerable knowledge about classical music in general and formidable knowledge of Wagnerian opera and similar grand opera by the time he was only eighteen. We must suspect that he had begun attending serious music performances earlier, around ages thirteen or fourteen.

Later, in the early stages of the Nazi movement, Hitler developed a friendly and even relaxed personal relationship and political association with the urbane, upper-class art reproduction scion Ernst Hanfstaengl who was well-educated and talented in music. Hanfstaengl noted in his memoir that he had acquired something of a reputation at Harvard University in piano. He elaborated: "My teachers in Munich had been August Schmid-Lindner and Bernhard Stavenhagen, the last pupil of Liszt, and my hands had given me a mastery of the Romantic school."[19] Hanfstaengl's son Egon commented in the 1994 afterword to the memoir that one of his father's teachers of musicology, Schmid-Lindner, had said that in his long career as a pedagogue he had "never known anyone as naturally at home on the keyboard as this Ernst Hanfstaengl."[20] Hanfstaengl commented that at his *Pienzenauerstrasse* house in Munich after a performance of *Die Meistersinger von Nuernberg* at the Hof Theater in January 1933, Hitler and he discussed the experience. Hitler was "in his most benign mood... The conductor that evening had been Hans Knuppertsbusch and Hitler had not liked his *tempi* [the rates of speed at which the passages in the music had been played] and interpretation and was expatiating on the subject. He could really do so with good sense and would hum or whistle many of the passages, the words of which he knew by heart, in order to show what he meant."[21] The most recent great biographer, however, with casual disparagement, dismisses Hitler's capabilities to understand Wagner in the following words: "Many attending the [Wagner] performances including Kubizek himself, were more skilled than Hitler, with his self-taught, amateurish, opinionated approach, in understanding and interpreting Wagner's music."[22] And the denigration does not stop here but shifts to a different plane: "Hitler, the nonentity, the mediocrity, the failure who wanted to live like a Wagnerian hero."[23] Bombarded with so critical a view of Hitler, readers might ask: How is it possible that such a man could even recognize a Wagerian hero? Yet the opinionated, amateurish nonentity would ultimately march through the vaunted Wagnerian themes of betrayal, sacrifice, redemption, and heroic death more closely and with greater effect than any man in life or myth. Hitler would make this latter-day, up-country march inspired significantly by Wagner's operas.

Hitler's two favorite operas were *Lohengrin*[24] and *Die Meistersinger von Nuernberg*, and his own character comprised elements of Lohengrin (chasteness), *Meistersinger*'s Hans Sachs (paragon of the supremacy of German song), Walter von Stolzing (artistic, noble competitor for the love of a pure and beautiful woman), and the *Flying Dutchman* (doomed to wander the world's oceans seeking the love of a special woman faithful unto death). These figures are all actors in Wagner operas and we can begin to sense the young man with the inerasable artistic temperament developing into a many-sided human being and actor in a Wagnerian-styled opera. Such a performer does not require a beautiful soul to perform beautifully, but rather "the actor must have the actor's facility for dramatization, momentary self-hypnosis."[25] Hitler, by late 1908, was becoming not only a potential lead voice in a Wagner-like opera, but also, through his ambition in architecture, the designer of the stage setting and the opera house itself. And if this were not enough, Hitler, through his "studies" of Germanic myth and history, could also be imagined as both composer and director. Finally, through some as-then undiscovered talent, he would be the lead voice in the whole drama. It would take Hitler from 1908 to 1914 to develop a more intense nationalist outlook, and a great war from 1914 through 1918 to provide motive and opportunity to project himself into German nationalist politics in 1919. But when Hitler entered the German political scene at that time, it was not so much that he entered as an actor in a Wagner-like spectacle but that he himself began to compose what could be likened to a vast German political opera.

The great biographers note that Hitler attempted to compose an opera in 1908 inspired by his discovery that Wagner had left behind an outline of a musical drama about a mythical German hero, Wieland the Smith. Hitler would embrace the project based on his driving interest in and general knowledge of opera and German mythology. To supplement his technical musical knowledge, Hitler made the effort an involuntary joint project with the gifted Kubizek. The biographers characterize the effort as contemptible, utopian, and trivial, and use it to show Hitler ineffectually scattering his efforts among chimerical schemes. In a work of over eight hundred pages, one of the great biographers would dismiss the episode of the opera in a single contemptuous sentence, noting that "he took up an idea that Wagner had dropped, and began writing an opera about Wieland the Smith, full of bloody and incestuous nonsense."[26] Kubizek spent an entire chapter on the project, however, and continued to be affected by the artistic results. He commented in 1954 that "I still have before my eyes the Wolf Lake, where the first scene of the opera was laid. From the *Edda* [old Norse epic], a book that was sacred to him, he knew Iceland, the rugged island of the north ... there he laid the scene of his opera."[27] The intense work on the opera brought the two friends closer together, and Kubizek remarked in an invaluable summary of nineteen-year-old Hitler's character that "there was an incredible earnestness in him, a true passionate interest in everything that happened, and most important, an unfailing devotion to the ... grandeur of art."[28] Pregnant with consequence for comprehending a future Hitler in politics, his friend of early manhood would point out that "when a self imposed task engrossed him completely and forced him to unceasing activity, it was as though a demon had taken possession of him. Oblivious of his surroundings, he never tired, he never slept. He ate nothing ... never before had I been so deeply impressed by this ecstatic creativeness."[29] The great biographers portray Hitler in Vienna in 1908 as indolent, lazy, and directionless—factors that apply to him but scarcely dominated his character.

Kubizek presents insights into the special imagination of the artistically tempered young Hitler in yet another remarkable paragraph ignored or missed by the biographers. Concerning music, Hitler remarked at this time in Vienna that it was not professors' wisdom in conservatories that counted for creating opera, but genius. This ambition to genius led him to a most extraordinary experiment. According to Kubizek, naturally gifted in music and with serious formal training, "Adolf harked back to the elementary possibilities of musical expression. Words seemed to him too complicated for this purpose [in opera] and he tried to discover how isolated sounds could be linked to notes of music; and with this musical language he combined certain colours."[30] Quite remarkably, Hitler conceptualized an opera in terms of sound, not words sung, and color which would be merged and would become the foundation of what would finally appear on stage. Kubizek ends this nagging remembrance by noting that he was reminded of Hitler's essays in this type of "composition" a few years later when a "Russian composer caused some sensation in Vienna by similar experiments."[31]

Kubizek claimed that Hitler suddenly realized, during a free-seat attendance at the Vienna Concert Hall, that immortal music being presented should be available to the rural masses and the urban lower classes, not given exclusively at one hall in Vienna to only five hundred people. He was listening specifically to Beethoven's *Violin Concerto in D Major* at the time. There already existed some pioneers of the idea of bringing art to "the people," but while the pioneers applied modest measures and approached their goal haltingly, Hitler, in a way that would characterize him as an adult and as leader of Germany, disdained half measures and conceptualized total solutions.

In the 1908 affair of bringing art to the people, Hitler first gave an indication that he had a fresh idea on the world of music by using a peculiar new expression with Kubizek: "that orchestra which tours the provinces." Soon Hitler used the words "mobile orchestra" because the word "touring" reminded him of second-rate theatrical companies. Finally, Hitler referred to his new instrument of mass culture as a "mobile Reichs orchestra," eerily reminiscent of his later exploitation of automobile and airplane for political campaigning and his backing of the motorization of the German army of the 1930s. The basic idea of a mobile Reichs orchestra illustrates Hitler's artistic imagination. Kubizek recalled the project in so much detail because of his own interest and technical superiority in music and commented that "Adolf's solution was both brilliant and simple: an orchestra under a gifted conductor would be organized, capable of performing classic, romantic, and modern symphonic music and sent out to the country."[32] The problem of getting beyond the span of the railway would be solved by using the newly emergent motor car. Hitler's imagination triumphed again when faced with the fundamental problem of just where such an orchestra would present its program in the numerous small towns of the empire. He informed Kubizek that there were churches everywhere with appropriate cover, variable but reasonable dimensions, and effective acoustics, therefore, the operas and symphonies should be presented in them.

Two additional confrontations between Kubizek and Hitler highlight the latter's style of action and are invaluable for understanding his future political actions. In a scene ridiculous for intense argument over a fantasy project but sublime for insight into Hitler's mindcast of final solutions and lack of ordinary sense of proportion, note the following collision over the subject of instruments for the orchestra in which Hitler outlandishly insisted on three large and expensive double-action harps:

> *Kubizek:* To what purpose? An experienced conductor can manage with only one.
> *Hitler:* Ridiculous. How can you play the Fire Music with only one double-action harp in the orchestra?
> *Kubizek:* Then the Fire Music won't be included in the repertoire.
> *Hitler:* You bet it will.[33]

It would be difficult to exaggerate the effectiveness of Hitler's future style of bold and far-reaching political action, and it is fundamental for comprehension of him to connect that style with the character recognizable in Vienna. Hitler's more important later political actions from 1919 onward have been described *ad infinitum* in the literature. But the biographers and other writers rather super-ficially characterize the later political actions of 1919–1945 using sweeping, vague, and pejorative generalizations about Hitler such as "all or nothing," "gambler," and so on, to describe his political style. In their rush to discover the science of Hitler's political thought (i.e., his knowledge about German nationalism, Marxian socialism, and world Jewry), the biographers neglect to tell their readers about the uniquely artistic approach, the creative imagination, the consuming intensity, and the heroic vision that he would bring to politics. In a word, the biographers handle Hitler as if he should have been a well-educated lawyer, social scientist, or aristocrat bred for imperial leadership rather than the informally educated but intense, willful, imaginative artist and messianic personality that he was.

*   *   *

One of the more important political actions carried out by Hitler in the 1920s was the Coburg incursion in October 1922. In Coburg, a medium-sized German town only recently included in Bavaria in 1920 as a result of postwar political trauma, the small nationalist political element had decided to organize a German Day celebration for October 14 and 15.[34] Given Hitler's growing reputation as a nationalist political figure in Munich, the organizing committee of the celebration invited him to attend and "to bring some com-pany"—or, in Hitler's words, "an escort."[35] In the ensuing adventure, Hitler acted with the imagination, the lack of any sense of propor-tion, and the all-consuming energy characteristic of most self-imposed tasks in his life.

Probably the two main circumstances that impelled Hitler to launch the daring political raid on Coburg were the following. Benito Mussolini and the black-shirted, street-fighting elements of his fascist movement—the *squadrists* or combat squads—had regained control, in 1922, of the streets and town halls of Bologna and Milan in May and early October, respectively. These areas had been formerly dominated by Marxist socialist, street-fighting bands and sympathizers. Coincidentally, Hitler had just put together an athletic street-fighting element under former naval lieutenant Hans Ulrich Klintzsch; the group was renamed in September 1921 as the *Sturmabteilung* (SA). The Marxists dominated Coburg at that time, although not to the outlandish degree as in the Italian cities where the Communists removed the Italian flag from the city halls and replaced it with red international banners. The Coburg invitation presented Hitler with a fleeting opportunity for political action similar to that in Italy using the newly formed Nazi street-fighting "storm squads" under Klintzsch.

The raid characterizes his nonpolitical style and could be generalized as theater in the form of grand opera. Hitler can be seen as composing and directing a modestly scaled, heroic political opera using Coburg as the opera house, using its streets as the stage setting, and acting in the lead role. Kurt Ludecke, the successful young investment manager who carried a spear in the drama, noted that "opportunity presented itself—or rather was manufactured by Hitler out of the slimmest materials."[36] Immediately and without any regard for normal sense of proportion, Hitler determined to produce a masterpiece of opportunistic action. Notwithstanding the words "bring some company" in his invitation, he called up six hundred SA men in Munich and two hundred more along the way as his escort. With no immediately available means to transport them, Hitler ordered the hiring of an entire *Reichsbahn* train—locomotive and third-class coaches for the large force—and without sufficient party funds to pay for the hire, convinced his followers to contribute out-of-pocket to cover costs. Upon arrival for the celebration, Hitler and his party were confronted by a Coburg police captain who ordered them not to march into town in an organized column or to unfurl any banners or to employ the large marching band that they had brought. With the same boundless, intense excess that had characterized the mobile Reichs orchestra project of his youth, Hitler ordered Klintzsch to form an SA column, positioned himself close to the front, and, with flags unfurled and band playing, marched into the menacing terrain of Communist-dominated Coburg.

Preceded only by a point element and flag bearers, Hitler advanced into an entire day and evening of street battles on October 14, 1922, in which the SA smashed the Communist street-fighting apparatus.[37] The following day at noon, Hitler and the SA conducted another march on "the great square" where the Communists had announced that they would gather ten thousand workers to throw Hitler and his party out. Hitler remarked about this Red revival in terms that characterized his determined style of political action: "Therefore, firmly resolved to dispose of the Red terror for good, I ordered the SA to line up, and set out with them on the march."[38] But few Reds appeared in the square. The Communists and Social Democrats had lost Coburg, which would become the first German city with a National Socialist mayor and city council. One thoughtful participant in the action generalized that "what seemed to others merely an insolent junket proved for us [Nazis] to be a decisive event."[39]

*   *   *

In the 1930s, on the international front, Hitler would launch another political raid that would show the same style of action as the lesser incursion at Coburg and be based on the same temperamental foundations. During 1936, Hitler began to conceptualize the reoccupation of the Rhineland necessary for an eventual armed advance east. He could make no foreign policy move of importance in any direction or under virtually any set of diplomatic circumstances because of Germany's exposure to unopposed French military invasion of an indispensable part of Germany—the Rhineland.

Hitler would carry out the armed foray into southwestern Germany as a self-imposed task. No man in the foreign office, the army, or the party advised so radical and dangerous a change in the Rhineland. We scarcely see politics in operation here. If politics can be considered as the art of the possible, we must see virtually no reasonable possibility at the turn of March 1936 that either a more conventional German government or a less erratic Adolf Hitler could have pulled off such an action. Neither politician nor statesman could have seriously conceptualized such an act, let alone have executed it, and we are driven to ask the question: What kind of man was passing by here, historically? The formidable creator of the Second Reich, Prince Otto von Bismarck, would probably have chalked off so bold a move as based on a man who sensed unique historical opportunity, closed his eyes, and grasped the hem of the garment of God as he passed by.

In the episode, of course, both the German foreign office and the army were aware of the desirability of change in the Rhineland. Hitler, with the inherent characteristics and style noted above, surprised his own foreign office and army leaders as much as the former Allies by ordering the army on Monday, March 2, 1936, to advance into the Rhineland the following Saturday. In the face of the trepidation of the professionals, Hitler launched his most daring political–military move of the interwar period. In the face of the complex international situation, the almost complete diplomatic isolation of Germany, and the enormous dangers, the foreign office counseled negotiation—an option predictably drawn out and likely inconclusive in the face of the French intransigence of the entire period from 1919 through 1935. The war minister and army commander both made it clear that Germany had no card to play if the French army moved into the area in reaction to the German advance and were categorically opposed to such an apparent escapade. Hitler, however, with vintage disregard for the realistic and the practical in self-imposed projects and playing the role of German messiah to perfection[40]—to capture the words of the first great biographer in a different context[41]— launched a new German army into the Rhineland.

The biographers characterize this foreign policy episode as Hitler's Rhineland gamble, although such a characterization is superficial and misleading. It is superficial because it does not take account of Hitler's study of the situation, his recognition of fleeting opportunity, and his impressive nerves in converting a military raid into seizure of the Rhineland. It is misleading because it implies foolish luck on Hitler's part and gives the reason for success as unwarranted weakness on the part of the French government and disarray among France and its potential allies. Hitler's understated study of potential foreign policy actions, unique willingness to take closely calculated risks (daring in both time and place), and accompanying imaginative execution, take the palm as the most important reasons for success. Those qualities derive from his artistic temperament and messianic self-image. Hitler's style, which baffled his adversaries in the 1930s, could be likened to a kind of creative unorthodoxy in a foreign-policy world inhabited largely by orthodox statesmen. Combine his Bohemian, brooding imagination with the distant vision of a messiah bent on saving the Germans, and we begin to comprehend Hitler being Hitler.

In 1940, within the framework of World War II, Hitler would conceptualize personally a military foray and time the opening of the entire western campaign to that single action. Uniquely, for a political head of state, and with extraordinary knowledge and imagination, he put together the following military masterpiece. Studying the historical literature for the means to ensure the success of an advance originally designed as a push on a broad front into Belgium, Hitler came up with the same problem of the German general staff planners of the early 1900s—the presence of powerful, newly constructed Belgian fortifications. In planning the advance into Belgium in 1939 and 1940, the Germans faced the necessity to take the extensive, ultramodern fort north of Liege opposite the so-called Dutch appendix, a peninsula of territory jutting south between Germany and Belgium. To ensure a successful attack into Belgium, the Germans had to take the large fortification located near the small village of Eben-Emael quickly in order to maintain enough momentum against the Belgian army, and the reinforcing French and British forces, to seize Belgium successfully. Just as Hitler consumed books on architecture as he designed the Linz Bridge in 1907 and books on music when faced with the necessity to acquire more knowledge for the composition of the opera Wieland the Smith, Hitler studied the challenge of Fort Eben-Emael for an unknown time period before October 27, 1939. For probably about four weeks, Hitler personally, and with no man suspecting his purpose, studied the historical literature for guide and precedent to the challenge of Eben-Emael.

Searching for historical examples of successful fort seizures in modern war, Hitler came across the example of the German capture of Fort Douaumont near Verdun in 1916 and noted perceptively that, although the literature claimed that the skill and courage of the attacking German infantry had finally forced its fall, the actual mechanism of success was the delivery of heavy German artillery projectiles on the targeted fortifications. Faced with the more modern, expertly sited, deep underground, and cupola-fortified Eben-Emael, he wrestled with the challenge of how to similarly deliver heavy enough ordnance on the small targets represented by the heavily sloped, extraordinarily thick steel of the cupola gun positions. Based on omnivorous reading parallel to the style of the 1904–1908 period noted in Kubizek's memoir, Hitler came across studies of the shaped charge principle and recognized that such charges had the destructive penetrating power necessary to destroy the armored gun positions. Hitler's further reading and consultation with unsuspecting scientists convinced him that charges big enough to penetrate and to have enough residual energy to destroy the gun positions and any other targets on the fort's surface and interior would weigh about 110 pounds and could not, at that time, be fired as artillery projectiles.[42]

Hitler had to face the technical fact that the ordnance had to be placed by hand against a target, and thus was an impossibility in the case of the super-fortification of Eben-Emael. He was already familiar as supreme commander, however, with the pioneering work of Kurt Student in the development of German parachute forces and gliders in the 1920s and 1930s. In a stroke of artistically styled imaginative genius, Hitler put together the German attack glider of 1939 with the 110-pound shape charge for final placement by combat teams out of the gliders and onto the armored cupolas. In the process noted above, the characteristic reserved brooding of the young Hitler noted by Kubizek remained indelible, and only three human beings on the face of the earth from October 27, 1939, until 0430 on May 10, 1940, were aware of the olympian mission and target of the operation: Adolf Hitler, *Generalmajor* Student, commanding the Seventh Air Landing Division of the Luftwaffe, and the task force commander, *Hauptmann Sturmabteilung* Koch. It is a telling commentary on Hitler's messianic distance from all others by 1939 that the Luftwaffe commander-in-chief, Hermann Goering, would comment on the purpose of Student's interview with Hitler: "Student, I can give you absolutely no clues. I have absolutely nothing. The whole thing is a mystery to Halder [army chief of staff] too."[43]

In this remarkable historical scene, eighty-five men in eleven canvas-covered gliders would attempt to subdue the main fortification blocking an invasion of 1940 Belgium from the east. With astounding indifference to the everyday details of running Germany, Hitler willfully concentrated on creating a tactical masterpiece with strategic ramifications. He largely dispensed with the inertia and compromise of conference, committee, and staff. He cannot be said to have put in a conventional day's work behind any desk during the period 1919–1939. Albert Speer, in his first private, formal meeting with Hitler presenting architectural plans, observed that Hitler sat cleaning the disassembled pieces of a pistol before him at his desk.[44] The *Reichschancellor* is presented as idly cleaning a pistol during regular working hours at the centerpoint of German political power. He played a role in life independent of ordinary reality.

*   *   *

As concerns Hitler's base of knowledge for running Germany, the most recent great biographer reluctantly makes the generalization that "there is no doubt that Hitler did read extensively in his Vienna period, as he himself later claimed."[45] This sentence tends to get lost, however, among accompanying belittling statements. The great biographer sarcastically adds that any reading of "literary luminaries" by Hitler must be taken with "a large pinch of salt" and adds the never-failing comment that his reading was unsystematic "and the factual knowledge that he committed to his formidable memory was used only to confirm already existing opinions."[46] And finally, the biographers fail to tell their readers about the informal studies and other considerable reading he had accomplished from 1905 to 1907 in Linz.

Since the first great biography by Alan Bullock, however, writers have presented an ambiguous picture of Hitler's knowledge as it was based on reading. The most recent great biography by Ian Kershaw, with its thesis of Hitler as nonperson and resultant necessity to paint a picture of him as intellectually uncouth, continues the ambiguity. The biographers are forced to make assertions about the base of knowledge for National Socialism, and, given Hitler's own comments that the granite foundation was laid in Vienna, they assert that it was based on the newspapers, political tracts, and campaign literature of the day. The ambiguity lies in the fact that the same biographers also assert that he read a large amount of substantial book literature. The extensive reading by Hitler would also have underlain his political thought, and readers face the following quandary: Was the intellectual foundation for National Socialism based on the trashy café literature of the day or some more substantial combination of Hitler's book and periodical reading of the period? The answer is the mildly revisionist one that the literary foundation of National Socialism combined the library books, periodicals, and political campaign literature of Vienna with the books of Linz.

All of the great biographers, from Bullock to Kershaw, acknowledge that Hitler read much—but they do so grudgingly. As previously noted, they claim that Hitler read unsystematically and only to confirm existing prejudices. Few people outside of the discipline of formal education, however, read systematically in the sense of sampling every view of a factual topic. Concerning informal reading of nonfiction, people read topics and material of interest to them but can hardly be accused of reading to reinforce existing prejudices, even though such a result may take place. The almost unique point with Hitler was that during his adolescence, which should have been dominated in school by systematic reading, he had dropped out psychologically in grades six through nine of the lower *Realschule*, never attended the higher *Realschule*, and willfully read only those things of personal interest. What suggests itself is that Hitler had formidable, underestimated knowledge of those subjects that interested him.

Hitler was interested in German history and mythology and the rather different topics of architecture, painting, drawing, and music. Dr. Leonard Poetsch, his history teacher in the lower secondary school, seems to have been a key figure in Hitler's life in its formative stage. Poetsch, for whatever the reasons, kindled in Hitler a dominating, enduring fascination with the heroic superiority of things German. Hitler acknowledged in an autobiographical comment in *Mein Kampf* the debt he owed to Poetsch for making the German past come alive as prologue to the present. The biographers cannot resist the temptation to suggest "a measure of hindsighted exaggeration" in the debt.[47] Such disparagement places a veil in front of Hitler by suggesting that he was exaggeratedly effusive in describing his history teacher's impact. If anything, Hitler comes off as an intense human being, and when he states in his autobiography that "we sat there [in Poetsch's class], often aflame with enthusiasm, and sometimes even moved to tears," he meant it.

Kershaw would state that Kubizek, although claiming to see Hitler characteristically surrounded by books, nevertheless remarked that "soon after the war, when asked about Hitler's reading

...could recall only that Hitler had two books in the room for several weeks, and owned a travel guide as well."[48] Given the chaos in Germany at the end of World War II, we can assume that if such a statement had actually been made that it was the careless and disinterested comment of a man whose life had already been ruined by World War I and who had become a desperate survivor of World War II. The statement illustrates a hunt for dry-humored disparagement, and unfortunately for even a remotely accurate measure of Hitler's base of knowledge and intellectual interests, airily dismisses his reading as having little substance. Kershaw further tells us that only one title stuck in Kubizek's mind: *Legends of Gods and Heroes: The Treasures of German Mythology.* Yet Kubizek's memoir contains more than twelve specific titles, literati, and philosophers.

During 1907, at age eighteen, Hitler created detailed architectural sketches and associated plans that showed a style similar to that described by Albert Speer as a "passion for building for eternity."[49] The Linz Museum, with its relief frieze 110 meters long, never failed to arouse his enthusiasm and characteristically he enlarged the museum and extended the frieze to make it the longest on the continent. The young Hitler considered the large train station and extensive track system as an impediment to the rebuilding of the city. His 1907 solution: move the station out of town and run the necessary tracks underground across it. Young Adolf's boldest project, however, was a great bridge designed, positioned, and proportioned to be probably the most dramatic in Europe. The project typifies his imagination and unbridled sense of proportion and can be qualified in a mixed metaphor as a deadly earnest flight of artistic fancy. Hitler did not conceptualize a large bridge conveniently located on the site of the older structure in the city. He conceptualized instead spanning the broad, eight-hundred-foot-wide river on the outskirts to the west and sited the bridge with each abutment on massive foundations high above the city on each river bank. The result was an immense structure soaring beyond sober reality above both river and city as a dramatic piece of architectural sculpture intended to inspire respect and awe. The bridge was vintage Hitler. It was divorced from the reality and proportion of most men but would represent from that point forward his characteristic style of doing. The style would confound the foreign statesmen of the 1930s and the soldiers of the 1940s.

In a sensitive and perceptive analysis of the Linz architectural projects, Kubizek would comment that they were more than nebulous fanaticism. He suggests that the "apparently absurd conceptions contained something compelling and convincing—a sort of superior logic."[50] In a jarring parallel, Hannah Arendt, in the 1970s, characterized the thinking of Kubizek's friend as "the ice cold logic of Adolf Hitler."[51] Both recognized an artful, compelling logic at work—in the case of Kubizek, the rebuilding of Linz set to the vast scenes in Wagner's operas: "architecture set to music."[52] For Arendt, Hitler's compelling logic resulted in a different sort of idealistic project—the destruction of the European Jews. And Hitler's bridge at Linz, with a suspended center span of sixteen hundred feet and roadway three hundred feet above the Danube, was only a temperamental heartbeat away from a congress hall in Berlin with a dome eight hundred feet high. No half measures, no interim or practical solutions exist here, either in architecture or politics.

When Kubizek departed for home in Linz after his end of term concert in July 1908, Hitler entered dark historical territory. After sending a letter and postcard or two to Kubizek in late July and August 1908, Hitler disappeared from the view of any witness to his activities except for a few encounters with one woman who claimed to have spoken to him occasionally in the block where he lived on the *Felberstrasse* for nine months after vacating the more expensive accommodations he had shared earlier with Kubizek. Hitler remained hidden from view from July 1908 until November 1909. This extraordinarily long period of seventeen months lies between the well-known period with Kubizek and the later period dominated by the stay in the men's home on the *Meldemannstrasse* in the northern part of Vienna. The later period, although known better than the missing one, is recounted primarily by Reinhold Hanisch (and only from late November 1909 through August 1910) and by Karl Honisch in 1913. The years 1911 and 1912, therefore, remain largely missing except for one exceedingly valuable document—Hitler's autobiography. The important part of Hitler's life during which almost all biographers assume he became the virulent anti-Marxist socialist and anti-Semite of 1919 onward is only scantily clad in supporting historical evidence.

To get at Hitler with the dearth of witnesses and hard data, we can only sketch out the high points assisted by Hitler's recollections and interpretations. As concerns the situation with German nationalism in Austria, Hitler described the only two men effectively opposed to its Marxist, Jewish, and Slavic foes as the intellectually acute Georg Ritter von Schoenerer and the master of practical mass politics Karl Lueger. Hitler commented that Schoenerer pictured the German nationalist situation more acutely than any other man but was ineffectual in creating a political movement capable of standing up to the Marxists. In contrast, Hitler described Lueger, the perennial lord mayor of Vienna, as having put together a Christian Socialist mass movement that effectively counterbalanced the Marxists. Hitler nevertheless criticized Lueger for having an ineffectually limited view of the Jews in his doctrine. Hitler took the measure of the two leading lights of the day in German nationalism in Austria and must be considered to have effectively studied, by whatever means, the nationalist situation in the heart of the empire.[53]

As concerns Marxian socialism, Hitler recognized it accurately as an international political movement dedicated to uniting the working classes of the world with no regard for ethnicity, race, or culture. As such, Marxian socialism was an inimical enemy to any national movement in any nation. Even in the ethnically polyglot Austro-Hungarian Empire, it was an inherent enemy, for example, of both German and Czech nationalists and others of the empire. The biographers accuse Hitler of not having read Marx's written works and denigrate Hitler's National Socialism as compounded of trashy opinions on international socialism. But Hitler, with impressive clarity, argued that what was important to know about Marxism was not the quasi-scientific theorizing but the practical methods used to advance political power. To illustrate the methods, he gave the vivid example of a great disciplined column of red-armbanded, grim-faced workers overawing the population of Vienna in a serpentine-like march taking two hours to complete.[54]

The Vienna period is critical for considering the questions of when, where, and why Hitler became a dedicated anti-Semite rather than a casual, fashionable one. The most important task, though, must surely be the search for the eventual intensity of his anti-Semitism. After all, there were many anti-Semites in Vienna; what separated Hitler from every one of them was the eventual intensity of his affliction. The overall question of importance becomes: When, where, and why did Hitler become not just any anti-Semite but *the* enemy of world Jewry, the anti-Semite *singularis?* The great biographers address themselves to the question, dutifully present the various simplistic interpretive theories, but never pull things together in an overarching outlook on Hitler's anti-Semitism. As it probably should be, the most recent great biographer, Ian Kershaw, presents the most convincing answer—the closest approach to probable truth. He claims that Hitler became the anti-Semite *sans égal* only by the end of 1919 and based on the impact of the loss of World War I and the chance to go into German nationalist politics. Kershaw presents convincing arguments that although Hitler had become "politicized" by the time he departed Vienna in May 1913 and was at least an ardent anti-Semite, the intensity was defused in the sense of being largely theoretical and simply not part of any practical political consideration in Vienna. Perhaps it can be generalized that Hitler's anti-Semitism was the part-time hobby of a man at the edge of bourgeois respectability. Under the impact of defeat in World War I and the opportunity to go into politics, Hitler's anti-Semitism became a full-time calling characterized by messianic intensity.

Taking the position, then, that Hitler was a politicized German nationalist and politicized racial anti-Semite by the time he left Vienna, we can agree that the grand question for humanity is, how did the aspiring architectural genius and part-time racial anti-Semite of 1913 become transformed into the most determined enemy of world Jewry in the history of mankind? Although Kershaw gives us the most convincing time for Hitler's transformation, none of the great biographers gives us an adequate explanation for the ferocity of his anti-Semitism from late 1919 onward. The question of the sources of Hitler's furious anti-Semitism is one for the ages, not only for comprehension of the man but also for the practical purpose of preventing history from repeating itself. With the exception of the great biographer John Toland, whose comprehensive descriptive work has no thesis, the interpretive biographers approach Hitler from preconceived heights of antipathy that force them to look for negative qualities that include, for example, failure, frustration, hate, and anxiety stemming from thwarted, unrealistically high expectations of a life of artistic genius. These biographers note Hitler's early hatred for his teachers in the lower *Realschule*, which later included professors at the Vienna Art Academy and a tendency to blame others for his failure to cope effectively with school and entry into the academy. As Hitler became politicized in Vienna, the biographers note the upward progression of hate with a gradual transference of most of his antipathy onto the shoulders of world Jewry. Although the biographers link the hate with failure, frustration, and anxiety, in half a century of writing since the end of World War II, none has achieved a convincing interpretation of the towering intensity in place by 1919.

The great biographers Fest and Kershaw note the self-evident importance of the question of why Hitler became the ultimate anti-Semite. They fail, however, to associate his anti-Semitism with the possibility that it could provide a fundamental comprehension *of* the man rather than just illustrate the barren and simplistic presence of hate *in* the man. For all of the significance of the question, these two great biographers treat the question with relatively mild interest and

in a surprisingly superficial manner. To compound the listlessness in
the analysis and the antipathetic approach of looking for only dark
spots in Hitler's young character, the biographers fail to consider the
possibility that some more positive factors in Hitler's vision of himself as artist-knight and savior of the Germans may be linked to his
anti-Semitism. The best Kershaw and Fest can do with a question for
all time is the reasonable but not particularly convincing argument
that he was a desperate loner in the process of politicizing his personal problems.[55] The personal problems included accumulating
failures as an aspiring academic painter and the terror of a downhill
slide into either the working class or the classless flotsam of Vienna.
In the one case, we are asked to believe that because of rejection by
the art academy and associated setbacks to his expectations in art,
Hitler set himself the mission of destroying world Jewry. The cause
and effect on display in this argument is simply not credible. In the
other case, we are asked to accept the point that he faced a terror of
plunging downward into the next lower social class. To suggest that
Hitler's anti-Semitism rested on a fear of dropping one class down
on the social scale suggests that the biographers are not genuinely
concerned with comprehending Hitler as a complex man with various motives. He was not a social scientific abstraction; he was a complex visionary, at once "banal and terrible."[56]

The great biographers present yet another standard possible
interpretation of Hitler's anti-Semitism in terms of repressed bourgeois ideas about sexual relations. In this interpretation, Hitler's anti-
Semitism is supposed to be related to and derived from his visions of
the ravishing of Aryan women by various and assorted obscenely
portrayed Jewish men. Using the term "obscenity" to characterize this
postulated repressed sexuality in Hitler and assuring his readers that
this obscenity was neither accidental nor superficial, Fest comments
that "in obscenity [Hitler's] own personality and the inner nature of
his resentment is revealed."[57] It is asking the reader too much to
accept repressed sexuality as a significant factor in explanation of
Hitler's anti-Semitism of the period 1919–1945. Finally, this factor

identified by the biographers as "obscenity" is perceived only within an iron framework of preconceived evilness; that is, it is only when the biographers have already decided that Hitler existed as an "unperson" that factors such as obscenity seem to be credible explanations for his driven anti-Semitism.

It is quite possible, however, that the reason for Hitler's intensity lies in another direction, one that would characterize him from the viewpoint of his fundamental temperament and would include not only evil but also counterbalancing elements comprising his peculiar genius. This different and more realistic direction need not result in a nicer or rehabilitating picture but one that leads to a superior comprehension of his anti-Semitism. Not surprisingly, the key to its intensity lies in the missing half of the Hitler biographical portrait. The biographers have inundated their readers with vituperative description of the hates and fears of Hitler. But one must suspect that the answer to his towering hatred of Jews lies in a counterbalancing towering esteem for something else. Here we have a kind of historical physics operating: for every action there is an opposite and equal reaction.

The biographers fail to correlate Hitler's vision of anti-Semitism with the counterbalancing vision he had of German salvation. In *Mein Kampf,* Hitler makes clear the importance of Dr. Poetsch "who as if by enchantment, carried us into past times, and out of the millennial veils of mist, molded dry historical memories into living reality." The great biographers, however, instead of taking at face value the importance of the experience—he was overwhelmed by the verbal image of German history—trivialize the whole business by suggesting that he exaggerated the experience. When he adds that history was his favorite subject, the biographers, with an outlandish display of petty disparagement, note that Poetsch did not remember Hitler as a student and point out additionally that his grades later in the fourth form of the *Realschule* in history were only "adequate" and "satisfactory."[58] The biographers suggest thereby that since Poetsch did not remember him two decades after having him as a student that Hitler could not have been so interested in history as he claims. And, in a further misreading of Hitler, they suggest that he could not have been interested in or knowledgeable about history because of his indifferent grades. The biographers thereby miss comprehension of the Hitler who had a vision of a great German historical past and began to be transformed into the most determined nationalist in modern times.

From this early calling, Hitler can be seen to have developed an exalted, ethereal vision of the German world filled with the mythic and the legendary, the chaste, the courageous, the ideal. Hitler would note that during his Vienna period he saw *Tristan and Isolde* thirty or forty times and always from the best companies,[59] and a friend would note that Hitler saw *Lohengrin* and *Die Meistersinger von Nuernberg* each about ten times in the first half of 1908. These numbers do not include the operas he attended in the four previous years in Linz and do give a measure of Hitler's enthrallment with Wagner. In Linz, Hitler discovered Wagner's prose writings and read his "thundering accusation against the *Jews in Music,* his gloomy views on *Decay and Regeneration.*"[60]

No other German nationalist would approach the tight, coherent, single-minded radicality of Hitler after 1919. In speeches made by Hitler from late 1919 through 1933, he would identify the enemy of the Germans in a manner similar to another great defender and hater, the Roman senator Marcus Porcius Cato. During the Third Punic War (149–146 BCE), Cato ended every speech, notwithstanding the topic, with the ominous words "*delenda est Carthago*" (Carthage must be destroyed).[61] Hitler brought similar intensity to bear against the Marxist enemy of the Germans. Numerous forces and "a vague sense of being reserved for something entirely indefinable" came together in Hitler to create the "perfect storm" of heroic German nationalism.[62] Such a storm interpreted as the necessary counterweight to Hitler's anti-Semitism has lain badly obscured.

To comprehend Hitler, we require some accurate adjectives that describe the factors in his character that, once identified, allow us to comprehend his radical German vision. The single best source for identifying the adjectives that defined Hitler's character lie in the memoir of the young man who knew him better than any other. August Kubizek, intelligent, talented, and humble, a man maligned by Hitler biographers for his impressionability, gives us the best single, extant picture of Hitler in terms of the adjectives we seek to capture Hitler's unparalleled nationalism and unprecedented anti-Semitism. Kubizek describes "his intense way of absorbing, scrutinizing, rejecting, [and] his terrific seriousness."[63] It was not what Hitler said but the absolute seriousness in the saying that impressed Kubizek. Subjected to Hitler's earliest "speeches," he writes that he soon realized that it was not posturing that Hitler was about: "This was not acting, not exaggeration, this was what he really felt, and I saw that he was in dead earnest."[64] One's impression was that of a serious man and "this enormous seriousness seemed to overshadow everything else."[65] He approached his self-imposed tasks, in contrast to the school assignments of his formal education, with a deadly earnestness that ill-suited a teenager.

Contrary to the drifting, hopeless butterfly image of Hitler offered up by the great biographers, Kubizek describes the young man he knew as both serious and earnest, especially when Hitler directed himself toward visionary missions. He was interested in everything, and "this extraordinary earnestness was his most striking quality."[66] Thirty years later, in 1938, Rudolf Hess would ask Kubizek whether Hitler as a young man had any sense of humor, noting that the people of his entourage felt the lack of it. The complete and deadly seriousness of Adolf Hitler was in place by 1904 and ran seamlessly through the remainder of his life. Kubizek's parting description toward the end of his memoir pulls together the potential intensity of Hitler's nationalism and anti-Semitism in the recurring theme that "there was an incredible earnestness in him, a thoroughness, a true passionate interest in everything that happened,"[67] followed by the prophetic words applied to the mobile Reichs orchestra of 1908: "While others were content to apply modest half measures to approach their goal step by step, Adolf disdained half measures and strove for a total solution regardless of when and where it could be realized."[68] Total seriousness apparently led him toward total solutions not only in the physical destruction of the European Jews but also in the realization of a thousand-year Reich.

Kubizek describes one other factor in Hitler's character that is important, though it does not lead directly to a greater comprehension of his later political intensity. There was always an element of his personality into which Hitler would not allow anyone to penetrate. Kubizek would comment that "he had his inscrutable secrets, and in many respects always remained a riddle to me." Kubizek adds that, "Adolf's plans and ideas always moved more or less on a plane above normal comprehension."[69] Hitler is noted as being reserved and even secretive by Kubizek, with the latter descriptor not presented as sinister but rather as representing unshared, secured areas of thought. A long string of Hitler's more casual acquaintances and friends from 1904 to the end of World War I would comment with remarkable consistency on his reserve. Virtually to a person, his army peers would note this remoteness—Hitler was almost always recalled as alone in a corner of the ubiquitous frontline dugout reading a newspaper or a book or wrapped in brooding private thought. Other acquaintances, including landlords, Vienna men's home denizens, art dealers, and so on, uniformly commented on his reserve and politeness. His superior officers in World War I noted characteristic seriousness and reserve, and described it as "noteworthy" for a relatively young, junior enlisted man—and particularly for an Austrian. We must add "serious" and "earnest" and "reserved" as descriptors to describe Hitler's character.

By the time of the outbreak of World War I in August 1914, Hitler had come to realize that his original aspiration to be a great painter had slipped away from him by his lack of formal education and dearth of technical schooling. Although Hitler had succeeded in 1913 and 1914 in supporting himself in Munich by painting, he lay on the margin of economic survival and respectable social status.

The scene he sets in *Mein Kampf* where he falls on his knees and thanks God for the opportunity to fight for Germany in August of 1914 has little to do with anti-Semitism, something to do with the realization that his life as a painter could continue only in obscurity, bleakness, and penury, and everything to do with German nationalism. With notable exceptions, the following four years of his life after that joyful kneeling have been covered adequately by only one writer to the present: Werner Maser.[70] The period is passed over thinly in the more prestigious general works—and done so with a hostile bias that disparages Hitler's performance, combat collegiality, and proximity to danger in the war.

No author pays much attention to the fact that Hitler survived four years of bloody and vicious trench warfare as a common soldier in a frontline infantry regiment. The great battles in 1916 and 1917 in Belgium and France, and the German offensive of March 1918 to break the trench stalemate, made considerable use of high explosives and gas bombardments that were tremendously intense. Casualties in misjudged infantry attacks frequently exceeded any other conflict in the preceding century. The most intense combat came to be centered in Belgian and French Flanders and the region to the south and west in Artois and on the Somme River. The Bavarian Reserve Infantry Regiment in which Hitler served for the entire war, after his assignment to it in early September 1914, was deployed for the duration of the war in the area of the most intense combat. Hitler's regiment found itself holding frontline positions against British and French opponents throughout the entire war, except for brief periods of rest and rearmament and shifts to adjacent sectors in Flanders, Artois, Picardy, and once in Alsace.

The intensity of the fighting is difficult to exaggerate. The young German army officer Ernst Juenger, in the most impressive account of combat in World War I by any author of any nationality, presents images of battle in the same area as Hitler's. Like Hitler, Juenger also served in a single regiment—the Seventy-Third Hanoverian Rifle Regiment—and presents some impressive scenes of "the Great War":

Everywhere we saw traces of death … there were two messengers [Hitler was a messenger] lying by a crater, from which the acrid fumes of explosive were still bubbling up. [November 1916][71]

and

As though waking from a deep dream, I saw German steel helmets approaching through the craters. They seemed to sprout from the fire-harrowed soil like some iron harvest. [March 1918][72]

Juenger wrote the above lines in his *Storm of Steel*, a copy of which he would sign and exchange with Hitler for a similarly auto-graphed copy of *Mein Kampf* at some time in the mid-1930s. The intensity of things is further illustrated by Juenger's musing to the effect that "once, I reckoned up my wounds. Leaving out trifles such as ricochets and grazes, I was hit at least 14 times, these being five bullets, two shell splinters, one shrapnel ball, four hand grenade splinters and two bullet splinters, which, with entry and exit wounds left me with an even twenty scars."[73] Hitler served in the vicinity of men such as Juenger and other even more "wild and crazy warrior princes of the trenches" and experienced violence—and not as the theoretical affair fussed over by armchair socialist political theorists. Hitler faced armed violence head-on, sequestered within the monastery with walls of fire that World War I had become.

Hitler was wounded twice by artillery fragments and once by gassing. His gassing was from the persistent agent called, variously, mustard gas, yellow cross, and Yperite, whose physiological effect is respiratory, eye, and skin irritation and blistering. Worse, mustard gas employs a diabolical delayed action for several hours (i.e., a person gassed with mustard agent does not know that he has in fact been gassed until roughly four hours after the event). In Hitler's case, he was caught in a heavy concentration that severely irritated his eyes. For Hitler, the operative effect of the gassing was temporary blindness. As somewhat of a monument to antipathy, the conventional wisdom denigrates Hitler's battle wounds by omitting his first wounding in 1914,[74] characterizing the second wounding as "lightly wounded in the left thigh" in 1916, and intimating that Hitler went blind in October 1918 as a hysterical reaction to stress as opposed to actual physical damage. The "light wound" in the left thigh, suffered at Le Barque on October 5, 1916, required evacuation to a field hospital, further evacuation to a hospital in the zone of the interior at Beelitz just southwest of Berlin, and recuperation until March 1918 (i.e., roughly five months). This hardly qualifies as a light wound. The point is that the one-sided prejudice dominating Hitler biographies has forced disparagement and belittling of his war record, thus leading to an inaccurate appreciation of his appeal to the patriotic Right in the later Weimar Republic as a genuine combat soldier.

During the war, in addition to his wound badge, Hitler received several other awards for combat achievements. The biographers of Hitler and other commentators on his life have debated these awards and his performance of duty associated with them. Characteristically, Hitler biographers—even in the face of strong evidence of exceptional soldierly qualities—attempt to deflate those achievements: the biographer Fest credits Hitler with the Iron Cross Second Class, Iron Cross First Class, and a Regimental certificate of bravery but immediately generalizes that "to this day, it has been impossible to discover the specific grounds for these decorations."[75] Fest implies by such a statement that something may have been amiss, and after repetitive disparagements, notes that "the only anecdote that was told about him [relative to his receipt of decorations]...is in fact no more than a school reader anecdote." Fest then gives up on the alleged mystery but states quite perceptively that "whatever he won them for, they proved of inestimable value for [his] future."[76] Ian Kershaw, the most recent biographer of Hitler, gives a convincing account of the winning of the two iron crosses but fails to utter a word about the salient importance of those decorations for Hitler's political success and survival from deportation in the 1920s.

Early in the war, on October 29, 1914, the rifle battalion in which

Hitler initially served in the List Regiment engaged in a violent four-day battle near Ypres, in Belgian Flanders, with elite British professional soldiers of the initial elements of the British Expeditionary Force. Hitler thereby served as a combat infantryman in one of the most intense engagements of the opening phase of World War I. The List Regiment was temporarily destroyed as an offensive force by suffering such severe casualty rates (killed, wounded, missing, and captured) that it lost approximately 70 percent of its initial strength of around 3,600 men. A bullet tore off Hitler's right sleeve in the first day of combat, and in the "batch" of men with which he originally advanced, every one fell dead or wounded, leaving him to survive as if through a miracle. On November 9, 1914, about a week after the ending of the great battle, Hitler was reassigned as a dispatch runner to regimental headquarters. Shortly thereafter, he was awarded the Iron Cross Second Class.

On about November 14, 1914, the new regimental commander, Lieutenant Colonel Philipp Engelhardt, accompanied by Hitler and another dispatch runner, moved forward into terrain of uncertain ownership. Engelhardt hoped to see for himself the regiment's tactical situation. When Engelhardt came under aimed enemy small-arms fire, Hitler and the unnamed comrade placed their bodies between their commander and the enemy fire, determined to keep him alive. The two enlisted men, who were veterans of the earlier great four-day battle around Ypres, were doubtlessly affected by the death of the regiment's first commander in that fight and were dedicated to keeping his replacement alive. Engelhardt was suitably impressed and proposed Hitler for the Iron Cross Second Class, which he was awarded on December 2. Hitler's performance was exemplary, and he began to fit into the world around him and establish the image of a combat soldier tough enough to demand the respect of anyone in right wing, *Freikorps*-style politics after the war.

Hitler evinced a genius for finding his way to forward command posts across an intricate system of routes in a lunarlike landscape of shell craters and other obstacles. Hitler appeared in situations of varying time of day or night, in rain, mud, and fog, and in frequently intense artillery concentrations. The duty was dangerous because the most important messages were those carried during the heaviest combat under the massive British and French artillery bombardments in Flanders, in Artois, and on the Somme. During the heavier Allied bombardments, German troops in the line companies entirely evacuated the deep fighting trenches, seeking relative safety in deeper "dugouts" off of and around the trenches. During those critical and almost insanely dangerous periods, Hitler and other dispatch runners would commonly be moving through and around those empty fighting and communications trenches, delivering orders from regiment. Tellingly, the German fighting trenches contained niches cut at various intervals into their deep, steep sides for the specific use of runners forced to deliver their epistles under such dangerous circumstances while the line combat troops sheltered in the dugouts.

Throughout World War I, Hitler passed through terrain permeated by "a heavy smell of death."[77] Both his division and his regiment were pulled off frontline positions for rest and retraining on several occasions, but never for very long and never very far from the front. Hitler also took leave only three times during the more than four years of the war, and during quiet periods near the front, he found time for sketching, reading newspapers and books, penning poetry, and writing and illustrating in the regimental news sheet. It is remarkable for a soldier who performed so fully as runner and bicycle dispatch rider that he had the interest and style to engage in such activity. Most young soldiers would have been idling, grousing, and engaged in lighthearted social adventures during quiet periods. The great biographers' view of Hitler as unperson during his political period should be reflected in him as unperson during his military period, but we are treated to the above activity as well as attendance at operas and visits to museums during leave in Germany. The conventional wisdom emphasizes that Hitler stood aloof from most of his comrades around him and uses the war to support the idea of Hitler as a man incapable of human feelings. The biographers equate this incapacity with the inability to form close personal relationships with his contemporaries. Unfortunately for the reader, the conventional wisdom leaves us with the feeling that forming close personal relations was the reason why he had been sent to the front and tells us little about his capabilities and adventures as a combat soldier.

On April 27, 1915, in French Flanders, while armed and making his daylight round of message deliveries, Hitler encountered and got the advantage over a French soldier in frontline country and brought him in as a prisoner, complete with rifle. A single event like this in a lifetime would be enough for most. Decades later, the room would swell with the cries of the grandchildren: "Please, please tell us again the story of how you took the French prisoner in the war." To put this incident into perspective, in World War I, frontline units made enormous efforts to take prisoners for intelligence—sifted, verified information about an enemy—but commonly the associated trench raids ended with dead prisoners and friendly casualties. But here we see Hitler returning with a prisoner and his weapon. Considerately for future historians, Hitler sketched the scene for the regimental news sheet, *Der Sandhase* [The Sand Rabbit] with the title "Corporal Hitler Back From Rounds! A Prisoner!"[78]

Later, on November 2, 1915, still in French Flanders and again as a dispatch runner on rounds, Hitler would encounter a French army patrol. The encounter would have an unusual outcome. The French patrol, moving according to some combat or reconnaissance mission, would ignominiously be overpowered by a single German runner—Adolf Hitler. He sketched the incident, probably again for publication in *Der Sandhase*, with the caption: "An enemy patrol is captured by Corporal Hitler."[79] The sketch shows him with two French soldiers in the process of being captured during daylight in a shell crater. It is possible that there were more than two enemy soldiers in the patrol and the event has an interesting tactical twist. Hitler reveals the chance and vagaries of war in his words at the bottom of the sketch: "Surprise during rounds. A shortcut on the route has its reward..." He had apparently decided to take a shortcut away from his regular route, and, while moving with increased vigilance, encountered an enemy "camped" statically in a shell crater and managed to attain the surrender of a numerically superior foe.

The war intensified in 1916. There were more battles around Verdun and 125 miles to the west on the Somme River. The division in which Hitler served fought largely in the part of French Flanders just south of the Belgian border around the towns of Fromelles and Fourness near Lille in 1916. They moved south late in the year to intervene in September in the fighting on the Somme. British artillery fire hit around the command post of the regiment on October 5, 1916, and Hitler was wounded. Almost every one of the biographers passes through this historical terrain with a single sentence similar to the preceding one while rushing on to a chapter entitled, "The Birth of Nazism."

Witness the following scene: It was night during the raw, cloud-filled, and rainy month of November in northwestern France. The regimental command post was under British artillery fire heavy enough to drive the regimental runners into a deep "dugout" built for serious protection against artillery. Hitler's locally famed immunity to gunfire was about to change. The serious dugout shelter was characterized by a set of steps sloping steeply downward into a reinforced excavation many feet below undisturbed ground level. One source indicates that Hitler was sleeping sitting up and packed together with others on the stairs. There were many ways to die under such circumstances including fragmentation, overpressure, and flame from projectiles penetrating through the top or sides of the structures. Troops in such conditions faced another horror that they were forced to imagine: being buried alive under a pile of wounded men in the case of severe explosion. The artillery projectile that wounded Hitler was probably a medium caliber shot that impacted near the entrance, driving fragments, shock wave, and debris down the stairs, killing or incapacitating those around him and seriously wounding him with a fragment in the front of the right thigh.

The year 1918 would see Hitler and his division and regiment in one engagement after another in northern France. Hitler would be in combat at the point of greatest advance in the German spring offensive of March 1918 in the area near Montdidier only fifty miles north of Paris. Hitler would receive a regimental citation on May 9, 1918, for bravery at Fontaine, located somewhere north of Soissons. Hitler was later awarded the Iron Cross First Class on August 4 of that year. Although Hitler never told anyone what the award was for, it is almost certain that it was for successfully running a message under extraordinarily dangerous circumstances from regimental headquarters to a supporting artillery command post. Information published years later claiming that Hitler received it for single-handedly capturing either a French or British patrol in Flanders was probably based on Hitler's success on two occasions earlier in 1915 in single-handedly bringing in French prisoners. Hitler likely allowed the story of the captured patrol to persist based on his personal knowledge that he had, in fact, captured a French patrol in 1915.

In addition to the conventional high explosive and fragmentation artillery bombardments of 1916 through 1918, German troops were subjected to massive attacks with various types of poison gas in 1918. Even the casual viewer of photographs of Allied and German troops near the front lines in 1918 must be struck by the presence of gas masks. The German Army introduced serious gas warfare with the experimental deployment of chlorine gas in April 1915. The chlorine was dispensed out of large metal cylinders in clouds and carried by favorable winds onto French troops in Flanders. Because the Germans had the most advanced chemical industry in the world at the beginning of the war, they maintained a continuous and significant advantage over the Allies in gas warfare. The Germans would introduce, phosgene, a deadly asphyxiator, in the fall of 1915, and the "king of the war gases," the mustard agent, in July 1917—six months ahead of the Allies in the former case and a full year ahead in the latter. They would be the first to abandon the gas cloud attacks, develop successful artillery gas projectiles, and employ the most sophisticated tactics for their use. The Allies would be close behind by June of 1918 with their first employment of mustard agent—another horror for Hitler and the troops of his division to overcome. He would sketch a German soldier with a gas mask over his face during a French counterattack near Soissons in Picardy on July 23, 1918. Two months later, Hitler was badly wounded by mustard agent and removed from the war forever.

The Greek biographer Plutarch, in his brief biography of Alexander, wrote that the most glorious exploits do not always furnish us with the closest discoveries of virtue or vice in men; sometimes a matter of less moment, an expression or a jest, informs us better of their characters and inclinations than the most famous sieges, the greatest armaments, or the bloodiest battles.[80] In the case of Hitler, a curious event and sequel of no apparent moment and seemingly only passing interest may be just such an instant. Early in the war, in January 1915, in a trench close to the front, Hitler came across a small, white terrier that had strayed across the famed no-man's-land of the day—in this case between the British and German lines south of Armentières near Fromelles. Under the circumstances, the animal's survival was problematic. The other soldiers around Hitler had their own survival to consider and ignored the creature, but Hitler, with some special conscience, patience, and compassion, would save the little dog by carrying it to the rear. Hitler would convert *Fuchsl* (Fox) into a trick-performing, ladder-climbing headquarters company mascot and note that "everybody in the trenches loved him." The little, white terrier became Hitler's constant companion as evidenced by the tactical detail: "When gas warfare started, I couldn't go on taking him into the front line. It was my comrades who fed him."[81]

Later in the war, in August 1917, Hitler's regiment made its longest lateral movement behind the western front from French Flanders to Alsace. During the deployment and under suspicious circumstances during final debarkation at a train station near Colmar, Hitler "suddenly noticed that the dog had disappeared. The column marched off, and it was impossible for me to stay behind!" Then, in words as strong as any in *Mein Kampf* pitched against the various enemies of the German fatherland, he would comment that "the swine who stole my dog doesn't realize what he did to me."[82]

Professor Ian Kershaw would take the *Fuchsl* affair and, straining it through antipathy, convert it into support for one of the conventional wisdom's fundamental tenets on Hitler, namely his limited capacity for coequal human relationships. Kershaw claims that Hitler's relationship with *Fuchsl* and other dogs later in his life were substitutes for healthy human relationships, which he was incapable of sustaining. Kershaw took a facetious comment—that Hitler liked *Fuchsl* because he would not talk back to him and would simply obey—to support the thesis. And, if this were not enough denigration, he would make the final sweeping correlation that the reason for Hitler's existence was the power to dominate others, and his relations with animals as pets exemplifies the general picture of the will to dominate:[83] "power was his aphrodisiac."[84]

There are many possibilities for explaining Hitler's interest in, or perhaps weakness for, the little, white terrier. The search for an accurate interpretation of this Plutarchian "gesture" in his life is important. Here we can get help also from the past in making a realistic appreciation of the little, white terrier; and William of Ockham, the English scholastic philosopher, comes to our aid with "Ockham's razor": *entia non sunt multiplicanda praeter ecessitatem* (no more things should be presumed to exist than are absolutely necessary). William suggests, thereby, that the simplest interpretation is always best. Hitler, conventional wisdom's ice-cold unperson, had a fondness and compassion for animals.

As a common soldier for four years, Hitler had a variety of miraculous escapes from death. As these escapes accumulated, he would have been hard-pressed not to have assumed that he was becoming bullet- and gas-proof. Analyzed less colorfully, Hitler's good fortune might easily have been mistaken for the work of some outside force, some instrument of fate determined to keep him alive. Hitler would have to have been jarred particularly by the regimental command post scene of November 1914. With his odd mixture of stiffness, discipline, and dash, he would leave the warm tent to make room for the company commanders and move into the wretched, wet cold of the beginning of winter in Flanders. Minutes later, death rode into the tent on the sibilant prow of a British artillery projectile. It would be absurd to suggest that Hitler sensed Providence had saved him for some great mission—at that point, the war could still have been won and Hitler was still the aspiring painter and architect. Once the war was over, however, and politics beckoned, Hitler could only have received enormous confidence from the realization that Providence had already chosen him for something special. Although invisible, God stood as close to him as the big vein on the side of his neck.

But the single most providential event of World War I for Hitler was one that he kept entirely to himself until years after the war. The event must have suggested to him by the early 1930s that he had been selected by fate as some kind of messenger or savior for some special purpose. In August 1934, he related in a conversation with an English correspondent, G. Ward Price, the following astonishing story: While in an area of intense combat near Arras in Picardy in autumn 1915, and under much psychological stress, he was eating dinner out of a tin can in a trench with several comrades. Then, he recounted, a voice came to him that said, *move*. It was so clear and so insistent that he obeyed mechanically as if it had been a military order. He walked about twenty yards along the trench, carrying his dinner, and sat down again, his "mind being once more at rest." Moments later came a flash and a deafening report from the vicinity of the area he had vacated. A shell had burst, killing every man he had left behind.[85]

Hitler evidently had had a vision, the genuineness of which is attested by the spare description, the recounting of it at a time in 1934 when it would have served him more practically in the years' struggle from 1919 to 1933 as a means to help lever himself into power, and its disarming plausibility. Visions have sometimes been classified as either visionary or audible, something seen or something heard, and Hitler's was the latter. The vision was significant historically because without it, Hitler would have been killed in action in 1915. Unlike his good luck in surviving numerous brushes with death, here we see Hitler directed by a vision to move and thereby survive to fulfill some purpose. Hitler probably developed some insight into the purpose because a few weeks after the incident, he cryptically prophesied to some comrades that "you will hear much about me. Just wait until my time comes."[86]

Hitler derived several things from his experience and achievements in World War I, without which his rise to power in 1933 would have been at the least problematical, and at the most inconceivable. Hitler survived the war as a combat soldier—a rifle carrier—in a frontline infantry regiment. The achievement was an extraordinary one based on some combination of near-miraculous luck and combat skill. The interpretive fussing over whether or not Hitler was a combat soldier because he spent most of the war in the part of the regiment described as regimental headquarters can be laid to rest as follows: Any soldier in an infantry regiment on an active front in the west in World War I must be considered to have been a combat soldier. Hitler's authorized regimental weapon was the Mauser bolt-action, magazine-fed rifle. This gives a basic idea of what Hitler could be called upon to do in his assignment at the front. As a regimental runner, he carried messages to the battalions and line companies of the regiment, and the more important ones had to be delivered under outrageously dangerous circumstances involving movement through artillery fire and, particularly later in the war, poison gas and the omnipresent rifle fire of the skilled British sniper detachments.

Hitler also served in a rifle company during his regiment's opening engagement in the war near Ypres in French Flanders, a four-day battle that turned into one of the most intense and casualty-filled of the entire war for both the British and the Germans. Hitler later wrote a lengthy letter to a Munich acquaintance, Ernst Hepp, in which he described the battle and his actions in it. The letter reveals an extraordinarily aggressive and dedicated soldier in action and has not been challenged by biographers for hyperbole. Ever alert for an opportunity to disparage, however, the accepted wisdom officiously criticizes his description of the same battle in a letter to his landlord, Josef Popp, with the following ineffectually rendered argument:

In his letter, Hitler stated that in the great four-day battle, his regiment fell from 3,600 to 611 men—catastrophic casualties. Pouncing on this statement, Werner Maser, one of Hitler's most respected biographers and skilled historical researchers, comments that "examination of casualty lists shows that on October 29, 1914, the day the regiment received its baptism of fire, it lost 349 dead," and during the period of October 30 to November 24, 373 more.[87] The author forgetfully fails to include missing, wounded, and captured soldiers who were also lost to the regiment. Hitler's figure is more accurate, and the point of such a critique is that the biographers feel compelled to take liberties with Hitler that are unheard of in virtually any other similarly important historical figure.

Hitler emerged from World War I as a different man from the intense, intelligent, but ineffectual and drifting painter-architect who entered it. Hitler biographers agree and dutifully state that the war hardened Hitler, but this generalization is presented perfunctorily with little conviction and with scarcely a comment on how important this new quality in Hitler would be for understanding the remainder of his life—his towering rise and his precipitous fall. The new quality tends to be ignored almost as if it were always there or should have been there because, after all, we are describing the *bête noir* of the century. Hitler adds to the seeming naturalness of the quality by his historic comments that he would be known as the hardest man in history. The biographers, however, do not tell us how Hitler became hardened. Instead, they merely add the word at the end of their relatively brief sections on World War I and give no hint of just what "hardening" was and how it would complement the temperament of the intense artist.

Hitler had already been hardened by his fall from the comfortable self-study of painting, architecture, grand opera, history, and contemporary imperial politics during the period in Linz and Vienna. When his inheritance ran out in late autumn 1909, he fell into abject poverty, sleeping on public benches and what homeless tramps would call "the green blanket" or the lawns of the Vienna parks.[88] The weather in central Europe at 48 degrees, 13 minutes north latitude, for example, approximated the climate of one hundred miles north of Quebec in Canada. Hitler faced prospects in November and December 1909 of incapacitation or death from hypothermia and frostbite. The psychological impact of these months stretching into early 1910 could have been just as important to Hitler's long-term personality as the "hardening" of war. Hitler might have lost the will to be either architect or painter, and simply succumbed to the realities of his lack of formal education and rejection by the art academy and accepted his fate as a drifter working menial jobs. As concerns the issue of the relatively soft and indolent young Hitler, he certainly was hardened by this winter of his early discontent. Strengthened with a harder disposition by the destructive poverty of late 1909 and early 1910, Hitler rose from the ashes of near-social destruction to secure a modest living and realistic appreciation of the necessities of economic survival.

World War I hardened Hitler in degree and scope far beyond that of the short but desperate privation of the middle Vienna period. The high-intensity, armed violence on the western front and the continuous presence of violent death, maiming, crippling, bloodying, battering, deafening, blinding, choking, asphyxiating, psychological unhinging, and so on, would test Hitler as no other experience. During his long war service, Hitler would see large numbers of young Germans dead on the battlefield and many others severely wounded. Altogether, the German losses would total a staggering 5.4 million young men dead or wounded.[89] They would suffer death and physical and psychological trauma while carrying out their duty in the defense of the fatherland. Based on some innate predilection reinforced by his informal studies, Hitler carried out his duty as a sacred one and served with that single-minded, aloof determination noted by his comrades and superiors. We can generalize that Hitler believed he carried the responsibility for the victory of Germany in World War I on his shoulders. With four years in the fire-swept desert, Hitler was made even more obdurate and unforgiving by the finale. He had borne firsthand witness to the sacrifice of 1.8 million lives in return for the extinction of his beloved Second Reich.

Hitler cannot be viewed as having successfully created National Socialism without bona fide credentials from World War I. No serious leader of an extreme-Right party could exist without ties with the *Freikorps* and without acceptance and respect from the rank and file of the various military units. Although Hitler was only a veteran lance corporal, his four years at the front, his Iron Cross First Class, and his wound badge in black demanded respect and acceptance from postwar *Reichsheer, Freikorps*, and the state police. The spirit and style of National Socialism is revealed in the later uniformed, heavily belted and booted political storm troops of the tough and intimidating Storm Detachment of the Nazi movement. In innumerable photographs in SA-style uniform and civilian clothes, Hitler displayed on the left breast area of shirt or jacket the Iron Cross First Class and, almost always, the wound badge. These were his most impressive pieces of visual evidence speaking to his capacity for leadership of the early National Socialists.

These personal combat decorations would help to save Hitler from deportation back to Austria in 1924. In January of that year, in anticipation of his being found guilty of treason for his earlier role in the uprising of November 1923, the Bavarian government had begun the process of deportation. The Bavarian state police enquired of the Austrian police in Linz, Hitler's home town,[90] whether they would recognize his Austrian citizenship. Two months later, in March 1924, the Bavarian police inquired again and the Austrian regional government replied on April 20, Hitler's twenty-fifth birthday, that it would recognize Hitler's citizenship and accept his deportation to Austria. The Bavarian government accordingly stood ready to eject Hitler from Germany upon his release from fortress detention by the Bavarian State Court at the end of 1924.

Hitler faced disaster because it is difficult to imagine him having any significant effect on German politics and National Socialism while deported to Austria. It is also difficult to imagine how the Bavarian authorities would have made their case against Hitler as an undesirable alien. It was true he had been tried and found guilty of treason, but he had defended himself well in the proceedings and would be released by the state court in Munich in December 1924, having fulfilled his debt to society. Hitler, however, possessed a powerful although uncertain defense against deportation as undesirable because of his distinguished combat service and his having won medals and citations from the German government as a volunteer Austrian alien. One can almost see Hitler in court holding his Iron Cross First Class in front of him in the direction of the state prosecutor, who would shrink away in its presence. In this critical situation, chance favored Hitler when, at the end of September 1924, the Austrian government reversed itself by announcing that it would not permit him to enter Austria. Hitler thereby became a *de facto* stateless individual, an ideal situation for him because deportation was no longer an option for the republic.

*   *   *

From 1889 through 1919, Hitler was unwittingly preparing for his great foray into history. As such, we should be able to get some impressions of his supposedly evil nature. It is difficult to imagine that the man who has come to personify wickedness would not be identified as such by his thirtieth birthday in 1919. Yet the entire period is largely devoid of evil that can be attributed to him—either as objective fact or as judged by the opinion of others. In his formative years, from 1889 through 1908, we see Hitler without a trace of evil in his conduct. We can find no evidence of bullying of schoolmates, no setting fire to domestic pets or other animals, no traumatic removal of the wings of insects, and so on. Neither can we find evidence of criminal behavior such as shoplifting, other theft, vandalism, or burglary—any of which would raise warning signs for the future in terms of psychological instability or evil. In the well-reported Kubizek period from late 1904 through mid-1908, with its additional data from the circumstances of failure at school, lung ailment, and tragic episode of his mother's death, the picture remains the same. Hitler's character is one of bold license for a youngster, but not directed toward dissolute behavior or activity that gives a hint of evil. Hitler devoured grand opera and classical music, painted, sketched, planned a great new Linz; he wrote sonnets, communed with nature, and exuded politeness and reserve. These are activities and qualities that suggest potential, although overblown, aspirations to artistic genius. What we see, like it or not, is morally laudable behavior and aspiration on the part of a young man in his teens. But is there a dark side somewhere in this picture?

If there were a dark side, it probably would have been the light gray of the contempt that he had for many of his school teachers and his resistance to formal education. Hitler's comments in *Mein Kampf* support such contempt and are buoyed by his indelible comment, about his tour of the customs office where his father worked, that the clerks and officials squatted about as monkeys in cages. Hitler would elaborate: "I...grew sick to my stomach at the thought of sitting in an office, deprived of my liberty; ceasing to be master of my own time and being compelled to force the contents of a whole life into blanks that had to be filled out."[91] He may have glimpsed himself as a monkey in the cage of his classroom, deprived of his liberty and forced to study things of no interest to him. Instead of accepting the reality that he must attend the lower grades of public school, Hitler bent reality to conform to his own vision of the ideal life: private reading and study. We would suspect that a youngster under such circumstance would actually engage in trivial pursuits, but Hitler confounds us with ebullient seeking after knowledge in mythology,

history, music, painting, and architecture and his extensive practice
of the latter fine arts. We see little evil in the young Hitler, but we
detect extraordinary intensity which reflects some combination of
abnormality and genius.

As concerns Hitler's worldview, in a single sentence in *Mein
Kampf* he brought together the good, the bad, and the ugly in it by
describing how his eyes had become opened to the menace that jeop-
ardized the existence of the German people (the good) by Marxism
(the bad) and Jewry (the ugly). In his words, "in this period my eyes
were opened to two menaces of which I had previously scarcely
known the names, and whose terrible importance for the existence of
the German people I certainly did not understand: Marxism and
Jewry."[92] Hitler's anti-Semitism emerged from the Vienna experience within this worldview, and it follows that it must have been
completely in place by 1913 when he departed Vienna for Munich.
Yet little can be derived from the evidence of the day that supports
a view that Hitler had become a total and uncompromising anti-
Semite by that time. "In truth, we do not know for certain why, or
even when, Hitler turned into a manic and obsessive anti-Semite," as
noted by Kershaw.[93]

Mein Kampf is probably the key, and it is not so much a conventionally rendered book as it is a speech by Hitler to whoever would
listen. The book has a rough-edged quality that makes it more effective somehow than something more polished but lacking in intensity.
Instead of being a literary sculpture likened to Michelangelo's *Pieta*
in Saint Peter's, it has a darkly different and powerful quality. It is
more similar to any one of Michelangelo's incomplete giant captives
emerging from marble, and each previously placed at one of the four
corners of the Boboli Gardens in Rome. As a rough-hewn, visionary,
and coldly logical piece, the book is Hitler, was intended to be Hitler,
and must contain the why and the how of his anti-Semitism.

Hitler maintained that he was largely unaware of the presence of
Jews or a Jewish issue in Austria during his early life in Linz. He
began his analysis of the "Jewish question" in a personal and distant

fashion, and we can almost see him staring into the distance, wondering about the whole business. The words have an eerily dreamy quality: "Today it is difficult, if not impossible, for me to say when the word 'Jew' first gave me ground for special thoughts."[94] Hitler often expressed himself in an inimitably thoughtful and earnest manner in *Mein Kampf*, and it is probably best to use his words rather than the more malleable, but always suspect, paraphrase. "At home I do not remember having heard the word during my father's lifetime [and] I believe that the old gentleman would have regarded any special emphasis on this term as cultural backwardness."[95] He went on to note that there were few Jews in Linz and that in the course of the centuries, their outward appearance had become Europeanized and that, in fact, he had even taken them for Germans—albeit with a "strange religion."

In early 1908, however, several weeks after his arrival in Vienna, he began to encounter the Jewish question though a combination of visual sightings in the streets and the existence of an organized opposition to the Jews. Hitler commented retrospectively in a remarkable picture that "the Jew was still characterized by me by nothing but his religion, and therefore, on grounds of human tolerance, I maintained my rejection of religious attacks in this case as in others. Consequently, the tone, particularly that of the Viennese anti-Semitic press, seemed to me to be unworthy of the cultural tradition of a great nation."[96] In his thoughtful and complex style of analysis, Hitler continued on to note the following: "Since the newspapers in question did not enjoy an outstanding reputation...I regarded them more as the products of anger and envy than the [representation] of a principled, though perhaps mistaken, point of view."[97] In the lines above, we see Hitler begin to wrestle with anti-Semitism, flatly reject religious anti-Semitism as unworthy of Austrian cultural tradition, and suspect that the arguments of the anti-Semitic press and gutter pamphlets were exaggerated beyond credibility by too much subjective and too little objective and principled argument. The view of virtually every Hitler biographer that he based his anti-Semitism on arguments derived from the gutter press and pamphlets of Vienna does not hold up in the face of the words above. To the contrary, we see Hitler take the measure of that literature.

Hitler painted a picture of a struggle with the vagaries of anti-Semitism, which were characterized by repeated rejection of the assertions of the anti-Semitic literature. He maintained that "the tone for the most part was such that doubts arouse in me, due in part to the dull and amazingly unscientific arguments favoring [anti-Semitism]."[98] Contrary to the view that Hitler was driven by artistic failure and accumulating hate to focus his frustrations on Jewry, he would comment that "the whole thing seemed to me to be so monstrous, the accusations so boundless, that, tormented by the fear of doing injustice, I again became anxious and uncertain."[99] Hitler faced doubts about anti-Semitism based on the repulsive excesses in its argumentation and the lack of "scientific" objectivity. The biographers assign frustration and all-consuming hate as largely the basis of his affliction. But more realistically we can see the young Hitler in his indelible pattern of discovering an issue, studying it to death, and then proceeding to create a solution that would be inspiring in its lack of sense of proportion and its finality.

There can be little doubt that the provincial, all-German student of Wagner and Poetsch experienced disquieting shock at the presence of the Slav and the Jew in cosmopolitan Vienna a few weeks after his arrival there in February 1908. Hitler stated that by two years later (i.e., roughly February 1910), he had become a convinced, objective, racial anti-Semite, and we face a sparse yet decisive picture of his conversion. Kubizek provides convincing corroboration of Hitler's developing anti-Semitism from February through July 1908, the latter month being the one in which Kubizek returned home for summer vacation from the music conservatory and did not see Hitler again until 1938. Kubizek noted the fact of Hitler's newly developing interest in the Jews of Vienna and, by extension, the whole Jewish question. Kubizek gives not a hint of any interest in

Jewry on the part of Hitler from 1904 through February 1908, and we are left with the factual impression that Hitler developed his anti-Semitic worldview in the relatively brief period between the latter month and roughly November 1909.

Although Hitler does not say exactly when he experienced his two great insights into Jewry, it is apparent that by sometime in 1909 he had come to the following conclusions. In his own words: "I could no longer very well doubt that the objects of my study were not Germans of a special religion, but a people in themselves."[100] He elaborated that in this intense study to clarify the Jewish question, "whatever doubts I may still have nourished were finally dispelled by the attitude of a portion of the Jews themselves."[101] With discerning precision, he confirmed the national rather than religious character of the Jews through the Zionist movement centered coincidentally at that time in Vienna. By 1909 a World Zionist Organization was coordinating the establishment of Jewish settlements in the Ottoman Turkish Empire that were intended to become a modern Jewish political state. The organization centered settlement in the overwhelmingly Arab administrative divisions of the Sanjaq of Jerusalem and the southern part of the Vilayet of Beirut, an area that would become part of the British Mandate of Palestine and Transjordania in April 1920 after the British conquest of the area earlier in 1917. Hitler would accurately note the development of a debate in world Jewry among Zionist and Liberal Jews over such a formulation but claim that the debate was a sham because "the so-called Liberal Jews did not reject the Zionists as non-Jews but only as Jews with an impractical … way of publicly avowing their Jewishness."[102]

Hitler thereby put together a coldly objective picture of world Jewry as a uniquely dispersed but politically coherent group of human beings. The picture became more subjective when Hitler proceeded in his analysis to formulate a conspiracy theory and "now linked the Jews with every evil he perceived."[103] Even in this subjectively tainted theory, however, in which he would blame the Jews for the disintegration of cultural life and the business of prostitution, the demonstrable presence of the Jews in tightly coherent communities in virtually every economically significant part of the world lent credence to such a theory. And similarly to the strained emphasis on the Jews as destroyers of culture, Hitler could objectively demonstrate their presence and effect in Austrian cultural life as totally out of proportion even to their relatively large numbers, for example, in Vienna. On the other hand, he could only opine that the Jews exerted pernicious and destructive effects in the arts, particularly as part of some kind of general conspiracy.

As concerns evil in Hitler's formulation, we see little of it in the fundamental tenet, as it were, the granite foundation, in which the Jews were discovered to be a people apart, camouflaged behind a religion. He could easily be comprehended as suggesting that the ancient nation of Jews invented its own religion for such a future contingency. We see a frustrating mix of objectivity with subjectivity, and to compound the frustration, we see little evil in the objective foundation of Hitler's anti-Semitism in contrast with the potential for considerable evil in the subjective superstructure. What we see here is not the usual picture of an evil, banal Hitler presented retrospectively by hostile "biographers," but an extraordinarily thoughtful and intense young provincial projected into *fin de sciècle* Vienna.

With earnestness and seriousness beyond ordinary comprehension, he had embraced a German world, German heroes, and German tribunes saving great peoples all set within impossibly expansive architectural visions. As such, by age eighteen, Hitler can be imagined to have developed a conditioned instinct to save someone from somebody under heroic circumstances. As Rienzi would save his people, Lohengrin would save Elsa, and Siegfried would save everybody, Hitler would encounter the mortal enemy of the Germans in Vienna in 1908, create an image of him that would correspond to the vastness of the danger, and begin, at least psychologically, to save the Germans.[104]

As concerns the beginning of his anti-Semitism, Hitler could state that in Vienna "I obtained the foundations for a philosophy in general and a political view in particular which later I needed only to supplement in detail, but which never left me."[105] As concerns Hitler's idealistic finality, we can tremble when he exclaims in the context of anti-Semitism that "here we are facing the question without whose solution all other attempts at a German reawakening or resurrection are and remain absolutely senseless and impossible."[106]

He would present lengthy argument that supported the concept of the Germans as Aryans without peer and a people worthy of salvation. In a supreme irony in the face of the conventional disparagement of the concept of a master race, he juxtaposed it against no less an evil in his mind than that of the chosen people—the Semitic tribe that had converted to monotheism in an ancient past and had never abandoned its claim to apartness from the rest of humanity. Acknowledged by most biographers and historians as the great simplifier, Hitler created probably his greatest simplification in the Jew as the personification of evil, not only in a European context but also worldwide.

With excruciating intensity, Hitler would argue that the basic correctness of the idea of National Socialism was decisive, and the difficulty of its execution should not be judged as guilty. "As soon as the theoretician attempts to take account of so-called 'utility' and 'reality' instead of the absolute truth, his work will cease to be a polar star [for voyaging] humanity and instead will be a prescription for everyday life"[107] He would set himself within this picture by writing that "in long periods of humanity, it may happen once that the politician is wedded to the theoretician," and continuing that "if the art of the politician is really the art of the possible, the theoretician is one of those of whom it can be said...are pleasing to the gods only if they demand and want the impossible."[108] Hitler doubtless saw himself as a unique union of both in modern times. Literally every biographer and historian who has addressed the inception of National Socialism has agreed that Hitler both created and led the movement. But in this union of theoretician and political leader, this characterization of theory as eternal truth, this vision of German resurrection, this revelation of an absolute and mortal enemy, this painting of a merciless battle between good and evil, we are forced to see the whole as greater than the sum of the parts. We can scarcely comprehend Hitler as a pathological demagogue and must see him more effectively as an astonishingly idealistic messenger of revealed truth.

In such an interpretation, Hitler does not have to be bearded, clothed in sandals and a white robe, and wandering in from an imagined Austrian desert to overwhelm the Germans with the word. A messiah must, however, possess characteristics that set him apart from all others. He must be detached from the ordinary cares of the rest of humanity yet dedicated to its salvation. He must be afflicted by a distant vision revealed to him alone yet which has universal validity and simplicity enough to be spread like a firebrand among the masses. Messiahs do not write for prizes in intellectual journals; they speak to the masses. A messiah is indispensable and irreplaceable and cannot be interchangeable. He must have a message which can be neither changed nor debated, for once the revelation has been received it represents eternal truth. And we can no more see Hitler change his vision of the Aryan German bearer of the world's culture under attack by a single supreme mortal enemy than we can comprehend Muhammad changing his message that there is "no god but God" to accommodate tactical circumstance. A messiah must combine some mixture of love and hate, and Hitler could state, for example, that as he gradually began to hate the enemy in the form of the Jew, the process "had but one good side: that in proportion as the real leaders...of Social Democracy came within my vision, my love for my people inevitably grew."[109] For a messiah as the conductor of a battle between good and evil, he must be assumed to possess the qualities of love and hate in grand dimension. The question of evil resident in messiahs and prophets must take account of precariously balanced love and hate and the conduct of an ongoing battle between good and evil in the minds of such men.

Chapter 2

HITLER AS A PRODUCT OF HIS TIMES

Perhaps the wisest characterization of Adolf Hitler is that he was a product of his times. Few could deny this generalization, although the question immediately begs: What were the times? How could "the Germans" have allowed themselves to be overwhelmed by allegedly so common a man, empty of human emotion, dedicated to politics alone—and even there, supposedly only as a propagandist? The query is typical in writings about Hitler, but it forces us to focus on Hitler and the Germans in answering it rather than on other equally important actors of the era. It must be evident that since the victors dominated the aftermath of World War I and not the vanquished, the more realistic question should be: Just what kind of peace (i.e., times) did the victors inflict? Surely the years following World War I would be the product of the will of the victors, and they would set the spirit and substance. The picture was not a pretty one, inhabited as it was by powers as imperialistically tough, aggressive, and successful as Britain and France and as naïvely self-assured and self-righteous as the United States. These powers, not Germany, set the spirit and the practice of the period of Hitler's rise to political power in Germany from 1919 through 1933.

In searching for and establishing the forces that made possible so terrible a phenomenon as Hitler, we must find that in the main he stemmed from conditions imposed by the Allies in Europe and only to a lesser extent by factors indigenous to Germany. Perhaps a more

perceptive variation of the "how is it possible" query on Hitler
would be the following redirection of thinking: How was it possible
that the British, French, and American governments produced so
dreadful a phenomenon as the peace of 1919–1933? With terrible
consequences that could have been foreseen, how could they have
instituted such a self-serving and so evil a mandate? The peace of
1919–1933 was based upon the Allied presumption, written into the
Treaty of Versailles, that "Germany and her allies" were entirely
responsible for the outbreak of World War I and the "inhumane
way" in which it was conducted. Other factors, of course, remote
from Allied control and which were the product of internal German
social and political trends, would favor Hitler—although some
might equally well have destroyed him.

Over and above the honor-style clauses in the Versailles treaty
similar to the assignment of blame, the Allies made demands and
inflicted duress so excessive that the word "outrageous" would be
reasonable to describe the condition in which Germany found itself
in 1919. The enormity of the situation imposed by the Allies is fundamental for understanding the enormity of National Socialism and
the attributes of the man who created it and became its focal point.
The Allies, especially Britain, France, and the United States,
imposed a situation distressful to most Germans but particularly to
those inclined toward the nationalist Right and extremists like
Hitler. The antidote for the helpless hand-wringing of writers who
agonize over how it was possible for Germans to succumb to this
allegedly empty man, this nonperson, is to pose this question: How
was it possible for the Allies to have created conditions so outrageous
and humiliating that they would almost certainly result in a nationalist backlash? Hitler cannot be imagined without the assistance of
the Versailles treaty and the historical excesses that came to be centered in it.

The various clauses of the treaty were so damaging and created
so much resentment among Germans that, along with the internal
situation of a powerful and dangerous Communist Party, readers are

presented with forces operating in Germany that explain the rise of Hitler. Hitler would be furnished with the opportunity to work both sides of the German political street—national and international— by credibly maintaining that the Independent Socialists and Spartacists who agitated against the war internally were responsible for Germany's defeat externally at the hands of the Allies. Marxist antiwar policies, especially in the latter half of the war, and armed revolution in Russia in late October 1918 lent credence to the claim that they stabbed the Imperial German Army in the back and were responsible for the loss of the war. Hitler could claim this because the Independent Socialists and the Spartacists had organized violent strikes in the munitions industry and undermined the war effort on the home front.

As armistice negotiations developed after September 27, 1918, the Independent Socialists and Spartacists organized revolutionary violence in Berlin, Hamburg, and Munich, Germany's three largest cities at the time. These uprisings became so threatening by November 9, 1918, that the last imperial chancellor was forced to announce, without legal authority, the abdication of the emperor. He then turned over the government of imperial Germany to the Majority, and Independent Socialists then proclaimed the formation of a German republic.

The armistice negotiations and the revolutionary actions of November 9 took place on the home front behind the field armies, which continued to present an intact front to the Allies. Two days later, the German republican armistice delegation would sign the armistice agreement that would bring the war to an end at the eleventh hour of the eleventh day of the eleventh month of 1918, but with an intact German army in the field that would be marched out of France and Belgium under the control of its officers.

Hitler would receive enormous political capital from the circumstances related. He would hammer on the theme of the "November Criminals," specifically Marxist socialists and Liberals, and the supporting theme of the German Army being stabbed in the back. The conventional wisdom in relating Hitler with the terminal stage, and immediate aftermath, of World War I agree that he would later conduct effective but unfair propaganda against the Majority Socialists who were the strongest base of support for the new republic. The conventional interpretation also affirms that Hitler made effective attacks against the republicans by representing them as traitors who had undermined the war effort. Historians argue, however, that the monarchists near war's end had opportunistically turned over the government to others, especially the Socialists and various Liberals, and saddled them with the onus of signing the armistice and being associated with the loss of the war. Historians go on to elaborate a nationalist legend of the stab in the back of the German Army, but argue that no such concept can be supported by the evidence. The consensus goes on to explain that the whole business was a device of the nationalists to destroy the republic and of Germans to blame the defeat of their army on base treachery rather than defeat in the field. The consensus flatly rejects the presence of a stab in the back.

Hitler and other nationalists benefited immensely from the concept of the stab in the back, whether it was true or not. The present consensus, however, in rejecting such an interpretation distorts reality and demands more realistic analysis. A generalization that holds for the end of the war is that by November 1918, imperial Germany had been defeated for most practical strategic purposes in World War I, but the German Army had not yet been defeated in the field. The agitation against the war by Marxists and Liberal pacifists on the home front had weakened Germany's strategic situation, and similar agitation combined with subversion of army troops in the zone of the interior directly threatened the frontline combat forces. The German field army was not only obviously intact in November but also stood in positions entirely within Belgium and France, except for a modest section of Alsace near the Swiss border. It must be acknowledged as a remarkable circumstance that the losing army occupied positions almost entirely within the territory of the victors. For the Allies to engage in armistice negotiations with the German government while German field armies lay in Belgium and France demands a conclusion that those armies were capable of combat beyond the political and military will of the Allies to evict them by force.

It is obviously not true that the main reason for the defeat of the German Army in World War I was a stab in the back through means of organized agitation and pacifism on the home front. It must be equally obvious, however, that such activities were important reasons for the collapse of the home front by October 1918, and that outright armed revolution on the home front from October 29 through November 9 was the main factor that made it impossible for the field armies to continue the fight. The accumulating armed strength of the Allies would likely have won out by no later than the spring of 1919 with the defeat of the German field armies and the forcing of their surrender. The fact remains, however, like it or not, that those armies would evacuate Belgium and France under terms of a negotiated armistice finalized and signed by a new German republican government. And the armistice would be forced by armed rebellion in Germany, as it were, in the back of the field armies and not in the face of Allied arms and resultant surrender and captivity.

*   *   *

Although Germany has remained saddled to the present day with sole responsibility for the outbreak of World War I, it can be stated unequivocally that such a consensus is unhistorical—unreal and incredible—and, in the case of Britain, France, and the United States, self-serving. Without reexamining intensively mined historical terrain, we can see the international scene of August 1914 as one in which five great powers and one lesser power with inextricably linked interrelationships confronted one another, and the reading public is asked to believe that only one of those powers, to the exclusion of all

others, was responsible for war's outbreak. The three most aggressive
and successful imperialistic powers on the face of the globe—Britain
with an overseas empire of almost 12 million square miles, France
with overseas colonies totaling 4.8 million square miles, and Imperial
Russia with a contiguous empire of almost 9 million square miles—
simply fall out of the equation. And Serbia, whose government
wanted the destruction of the Austro-Hungarian Empire, planned it,
and created the tragic act of international terrorism that started the
war that led to the empire's extinction, is dismissed with cavalier
temerity by the consensus as a valueless pawn in the outbreak of
World War I.

In the real world of international relations, it must be apparent
that blame or guilt for the outbreak of war in 1914 must be shared
among the six main actors of the moment—Germany, Austria-
Hungry, Britain, France, Russia, and Serbia. The simple device of
assigning percentages of guilt among the six powers highlights the
incredibility of the Allied assignment of total blame to Germany in
the ultimatum of June 16, 1919, to sign the Versailles treaty. The
same device illuminates the unreality of postwar writers in continuing to place most blame on Germany. Once the Allied governments, led by France, decided to justify excessive reparation by
claiming total German guilt, they painted themselves into an unenviable, irrational corner. It is difficult to accept so one-sided an
assignment given the revanchist foreign policy of France highlighted
by clamor for the "return" of Alsace and Lorraine, institution of the
first great modern arms race, formation of an anti-German diplomatic alliance system, and aggressive imperialism in Morocco,
Tunisia, and the Ottoman Turkish Empire immediately preceding
the war. The similarly aggressive international policies of Britain
and Russia and the more limited, but extraordinarily virulent, Serbian nationalism and its international terrorism also demand assignment of blame.

The conventional historical wisdom more realistically, but still
with unrealistic imbalance, assigns most blame for war's outbreak to

Germany. The concept of most blame argued mathematically gives Germany at the least 51 percent guilt and presents us with the unrealistic picture of French, British, Russian, and Serbian blame for the outbreak of war, taken together, as less than German guilt. The picture is incredible, for example, because no serious historian or writer could assign France *alone* much less guilt than Germany. The situation described above is an enormity—a study in self-deception and vindictive arrogance—on the part of the Allies and is fundamental for comprehending Hitler's appeal to Germans. Even in the more general scholarly works on European diplomatic history, authors describe Hitler as a fanatic aberration and note, for example, "the wonder is that such ranting could capture the imagination and for a time control the destinies of what for long had called itself—a claim granted by others—a great civilized nation."[1]

Biographers and other writers consistently express the theme of Hitler's "rantings" and the wonder of how the Germans could have accepted such a lack of constraint. Yet Hitler's "rantings" can scarcely be claimed to have exaggerated the actual German situation dictated by Versailles. The stiff French enforcement of the treaty can be correlated directly with the descent of republican Germany into political, economic, and social chaos, especially during 1919–1923 and then again in 1929–1933. The Allies fastened war guilt on republican Germany, split the republic into two parts territorially, squabbled among themselves over reparation, delivered an exorbitant bill two years after the treaty signing, and conducted armed incursions into Germany to force payment. It was a situation that demanded, and got, an Adolf Hitler. The great biographers and the conventional historians, however, bring Hitler and the Germans into such tight focus that Georges Clemenceau, Raymond Poincaré, and the French fade from serious consideration. The French, to the contrary, should occupy the foreground of the picture in 1919–1933 Europe, and *de rigueur* be the path along which we have to pass to get at Hitler and the Germans. If we take that path through the excesses of Versailles to get at Hitler, the wonder is that a country, which had long called itself a civilized nation, could have perpetrated a treaty so self-serving and vindictive that it fastened on Germany's political, social, and economic conditions that were indispensable in bringing to power the most terrible phenomenon of the twentieth century. And if a final wonder be in order, in the last German Reichstag election of November 1932, before the bandwagon effects of Hitler being appointed chancellor, only one German in three voted for Hitler—hardly a proportion of the voting population to support the tired generalization above that "the Germans" fell in as lemmings behind him.

Probably, though, the greatest trauma for Germans arising out of World War I was the combination of human casualties and the loss of the war. Imperial Germany suffered the combat deaths of 1,813,000 young men aged roughly seventeen to thirty (Hitler was twenty-five years old in 1914) comprising sons, husbands, brothers, and nephews killed in action or of their wounds. These losses contributed to the psychological monstrosity of the loss of the war. The numbers are staggering in an absolute sense and equally appalling relative to the contemporaneous German population of approximately sixty-five million. Adding to the carnage would be the presence of roughly one million severely wounded, their injuries characterized by noticeable, cruel, and incapacitating losses of arms, legs, hands, feet, and eyes. In the interwar period, two things characterized the streets of German cities, unlike interwar US cities but like French towns, and they were the presence of the maimed and the absence of an entire generation of young men. So what is the implication for an extremist national political movement? Hitler would begin his messianic calling in a population where virtually every citizen would have been touched by death or maiming in a cause lost.

*   *   *

To the unique advantage of Hitler and other extreme nationalists, the war would create a new man, and this man would furnish for the first time in modern Europe a political street-fighting animal to counterbalance the riotous, bourgeois, barricade mounter and socialist, working-class, street intimidator. This new man would be fearsome indeed. Witness an adolescent male at age eighteen entering the war late in 1914, surviving, and departing it at the end of 1918. This able-bodied young man's experience of life would have been four years of combat against an armed enemy, action hardly suited for a smooth transition into a postwar world. It is a monument to the times that the smoothest transition in Germany was the one from the last days of a lost war into one of the great revolutions of the modern era, followed in turn by five years of political street battles, starvation, partial military occupation, and a cruel and unusual combination of inflation and unemployment. Many of the young survivors of the war never made the transition back to the world but remained forever in the trenches. As one of them wrote:

> War, father of all things, is also our father. It has hammered us, chiseled us and hardened us into what we are.... As long as the wheel of life revolves within us, the war will be the axis around which it swirls. It has reared us for battle and we shall remain fighters as long as we live.... Under the skin of all technical and cultural progress we remain naked and raw like men of the forest and of the steppe.... [This fighter] is the new man, the pioneer of the storm, the [warrior prince] of central Europe.... This war is not the end but the new ascendancy of force...might will be seized with a hard fist.[2]

The famed and indispensable political street-fighting arm of the National Socialists represents this element of the times. Selected rougher elements in the movement were organized initially into small teams to defend, by physical force, the early political meetings. These self-defense elements quickly evolved into a larger, uniformed element designated the *Sturmabteilung* (SA), and the men within it were seen as political storm troops. Outfitted early in this process, quite by chance, in excess stocks of German army tropical brown shirts, they became the notorious Brown Shirts, who challenged for the first time in Germany the street-fighting elements of the Social Democratic Party and the Communists. Derived in spirit from the army storm companies and battalions of 1917–1918, the SA exemplified a part of the times in which Hitler would come to life politically, survive, and flourish.

*   *   *

For the Germans, the road to the Paris Peace Conference of 1919 and the Versailles treaty led through the earlier armistice negotiations of late 1918. The German Army High Command, pressed hard by the great battles on the western front in the autumn of 1918, advised the civilian imperial German government under Emperor William II of Hohenzollern on October 29, 1918, to initiate armistice negotiations with the Allies immediately while the army was still intact. The German government appealed to US president Woodrow Wilson, in his second term at the time, for peace based on the president's Fourteen Points of January 1918. During an exchange of diplomatic notes between Berlin and Washington, with Wilson speaking in the name of the Allies, the latter insisted that negotiations for both armistice and peace could proceed only through a German government that was in the process of democratizing itself and the parallel removal of "the military masters of Germany." Here we see the Allies dictating the removal of the emperor and the Prussian-dominated army high command who had led the war fighting—a questionable, propaganda-driven demand on the part of the victors. We also see the Allies dictating changes in the existing imperial German constitution that would transfer ultimate political power in the empire from the Prussian royal house of Hohenzollern to the parliament. Such a situation was only a hairbreadth from casting out centuries of princely rule in the numerous states that comprised the German Empire in 1918.

A hairbreadth proved to be too close to continue princely constitutional rule. As the loss of World War I gathered around them, the Germans faced external dictates of the Allies and internal Marxist revolutionary pressures, which led to the declaration of a German republic on November 9, 1918. On that day the leaders of the evolutionary majority wing of the Social Democratic Party created a relatively moderate republic in order to prevent the revolutionary wing of the party—the so-called Spartacists, soon to take the name Communists—from creating an internationally oriented Red republic. Germany could have suffered few more radical political changes, and a thousand years of rule by princes were swept away on that day. Based thereby on the earlier call for peace negotiations by the first quartermaster general of the army, Erich Ludendorff, Germany descended into epic chaos in the period from September 1918 through November 1923, the latter month signaling stability, finally, for the new republic. The intensity of the chaos has not been adequately correlated with the rise of Hitler.

The conventional wisdom generalizes, for example, that the feeble resistance to Hitler would be associated with alleged German inexperience with parliamentary politics, democratic government, and the like. This type of argument about German political naïveté becomes divorced from conditions in Germany that would have tried more politically sophisticated populations and were, in fact, so extreme that the more relevant question should probably be: How is it possible that so few Germans succumbed to Hitler's blandishments and that so many proved to be immune to them? It is easy to ignore the reality that close to the time of Hitler's "seizure of power" in the Reichstag election of November 6, 1932, just before Hitler was appointed chancellor through presidential fiat, that the National Socialists received only 33.1 percent of the German national vote and were supported by only 26.2 percent of eligible German voters in the last unfettered election. This fact alone obliterates conventional generalizations that the Germans offered relatively little resistance to Hitler during his rise to power.

Germans faced a black present and a bleak future in November

1918. The Second Reich of Otto von Bismarck and William I, a political edifice that was controlled ultimately by William in his alternate role as King of Prussia, was dismantled through changes in the imperial German constitution. The last imperial chancellor, Prince Max von Baden, had pushed through these changes at Allied insistence and was able to affirm on October 27 that peace negotiations were being conducted by a German government free of arbitrary and irresponsible influence. The Allied governments, in a concluding note of November 5, 1918, explicitly stated their willingness to make a just peace with the democratized German government based on President Wilson's address to the US Congress in January 1918 and principles presented in subsequent addresses. Disastrously for the future of Europe, the new German and the old Allied governments did not then conclude an armistice in the period from October 28 through November 5, 1918. The British government in particular fussed over interpretation of the words "freedom of the seas" in the American president's address of January 1918, and the German chancellor was only able to announce the abdication of William II on November 8. During the fateful period of dilatoriness, the German revolution intensified and culminated on November 9 in a new republic. The ill-timed republic was inherently less stable and no more democratic than an empire would have been with a relative of William named as a successor and a government ultimately responsible to "the people" through the earlier constitutional changes.

The so-called Majority Socialists of the Social Democratic Party, who had been handed the government by the discredited monarchists, faced revolution in turn by the Independent and Spartacist elements of the party. The Independents fell apart, gravitating to become either Majority Socialists or Spartacists, and the latter continued revolutionary activity as Communists to overthrow the new republic.

One of the grand generalizations about the entire 1918–1933 period is that Germans exaggerated the challenge from the Communists. Writers commonly note, for example, that Hitler took advantage of the burning of the Reichstag on February 27, 1933, by blaming it on them. He would claim danger so great that his new government required special emergency powers, temporarily suspending certain constitutional guarantees, in order to combat it. Writers point out with retrospective accuracy that the Communists were no longer a mortal danger to the republic. As a result, these writers brand the Germans as politically naïve for succumbing to such claims. The writers fail to counterbalance the suggested naïveté with the extreme violence and grave danger to the republic in Communist uprisings from 1918 through 1933, intimidating propaganda, and the Communist revival during the depression years of 1930 through 1933. The Communists, in self-defeating revolutionary verbiage, had actually threatened to burn the Reichstag. Faced with this background to February 27, the German people would seem to have had prudent concerns over the Communists and the possibility of another uprising under the devastating conditions of the German depression in early 1933.

The Germans had been particularly radicalized by the combination of the reparation-induced inflation of 1923 and the equally terrifying depression in place in 1933. In such a situation they had given 50 percent of the Reichstag vote in November 1932 to the parties dedicated to the destruction of the republic—33.1 percent went to the Nazis and 16.9 percent to the Communists. The times as exemplified by the Versailles treaty had created these conditions within which the Nazis had just come to power and continued to battle Ernst Thaelmann and the Communists for successful revolution. But how could a peace treaty, no matter how ill-founded, have created times so significant for understanding the success of Hitler? And is it possible that the outrageousness of the Versailles treaty can be balanced against the enormity of Hitler's actions of 1933–1945? As it were, can we balance outrageousness against enormity for superior comprehension of Hitler? The answer to these latter questions is probably yes, for as the armistice was signed on November 11, the Allied governments abandoned the principle of a just and moderate peace.

*   *   *

The Allied governments, for example, with the British as executors, maintained in place the food blockade of Germany that had been in effect since 1917. A British authority would note that "in the last two years of the war, nearly 800,000 noncombatants died in Germany from starvation or diseases attributed to undernourishment. The biggest mortality was among children between the ages of 5 and 15, where the death rate increased by 55 percent...a whole generation [the one which had been born and lived during Hitler's rise to power] grew up in an epoch of undernourishment and misery such as we [British] have never in this country experienced."[3] A distinguished American authority on United States foreign policy in the first half of the twentieth century, Stanford University professor Thomas A. Bailey, noted that "the Allied slow starvation of Germany's civilian population was quiet, unspectacular, and censored."[4] The Englishman Gilbert Murray, writing in 1933, noted that future historians would probably regard the establishment and continuation of the blockade as one of those many acts of almost incredible inhumanity which made World War I conspicuous in history.[5]

With a hint of defensiveness, the Allies noted in their June 16, 1919, ultimatum to the German government to sign the Versailles treaty that, although they had imposed on Germany an exceptionally severe blockade, they had sought consistently to conform to the principles of international law and had imposed the blockade because of "the criminal character of the war initiated by Germany and of the barbarous methods adopted by her in prosecuting it."[6] This official statement is noteworthy for its self-assured but nevertheless unhistorical assumption that Germany initiated World War I and prosecuted it in a criminal and barbarous manner. Notwithstanding, however, the self-assuredness about German guilt, the allies revealed a bad conscience about the blockade. They noted, for example, that they sought to conform with international law in the imposition of the blockade and then, straining for justification for so cruel and inhumane a policy, they claimed a criminal character to the war imposed on them by Germany.

How can this moderately complex but important issue of the blockade be summarized in order to prevent the various details from intruding on the historical interpretation of an issue so significant for the postwar German condition and the rise of Hitler? It can be generalized that the Allies inflicted a cruel wartime blockade on Germany, affecting almost entirely noncombatants. As it extended into the period of the peacetime treaty negotiations, this action became criminally inhumane. It can be further generalized that the misery and revulsion in Germany over the enormity of 800,000 human beings dying from the immediate effects (e.g., direct starvation and malnutrition-induced fatal disease) of the food blockade is indispensable for comprehending Hitler's success as the leader of an extreme nationalist political movement. Yet in the latest major biography of Hitler, we can find only understated reference to the existence of such a blockade, a troubling cloudiness that suggests acceptance of either a historical theory of a morally justifiable food blockade or the author's conscious rejection of such an action as significant for comprehending the rise of Hitler.[7]

*   *   *

The German Armistice Commission headed by the Catholic Center Party leader, Matthias Erzberger, agreed to the Allied terms for an armistice in negotiations during November 8 through 11, 1918. The fighting in World War I ended on November 11, and the two sides to the great conflict began preparations for the peace conference that would put together the various treaties that would finalize the war's outcome. The peace conference would be held in Paris, and the most important negotiations would be between Germany and the Allies at Versailles, approximately twenty-two kilometers southeast of the center of the capital. Against a complex background of national elections, political unrest, and armed revolutions in the major states in Europe, preparations moved surprisingly fast for the conference, which opened formally on January 18, 1919. Discussion centered on the provisions of a treaty between Germany and the Allies and were dominated by an Allied Supreme Council, the so-called Big Ten, and (after March 25, 1918) the Big Four—Woodrow Wilson, David Lloyd George, Georges Clemenceau, and Vittorio Orlando.

In a bizarre historical scene divorced from the reality of any previous treaty, these four men, each supported by a large staff, created a draft treaty without the presence of a single German representative. Since an international treaty is an agreement created through negotiation among two or more political entities, it is difficult to claim in the case of Versailles that a treaty as had been understood by that time in history came into existence. The draft that the Big Four created in the name of the twenty-seven Allied and Associated Powers between March 27 and May 7, 1919, was in fact built out of fiercely argued negotiations among the four principal states representing one party to the "treaty." As concerns negotiations between the Allies and the German government, none took place. The German delegation to the Paris Peace Conference was first addressed by the president of the Peace Conference, Clemenceau, on the afternoon of May 7. Clemenceau spoke *ex cathedra* the words: "You have asked for peace. We are prepared to offer you peace.... There will be no verbal discussions, and observations must be submitted in writing."[8] The Allies submitted the draft treaty to the German delegation the next day, May 8, 1919, and the German delegation submitted vigorous protesting observations in the nature of counterproposals that resulted in no changes of any substance to the draft. On June 16, 1919, the Allies responded to the earlier German counterproposals in a document that amounted to an ultimatum— ending as it did with the words: "As such the treaty in its present form must be accepted or rejected," a bare threat that if the treaty were rejected as it stood, its terms would be enforced unilaterally.

The covering letter to the Allied reply was the most important document in the exchange of notes during the Paris Peace Conference and comprised a savage, unhistorical indictment of both the German imperial government and the German people. "Never in history had such a terrible indictment been passed on a European nation as a whole."[9] In 1919 and the following years, millions of Germans would learn of the indictment through the schools and the press. The Germans became aware of the branding of an entire people as part of an international criminal conspiracy. But how could the words in a mere covering letter, notwithstanding its official sanction by the Allied governments, translate into eventual mass support for an extreme nationalist like Hitler? Witness the following excerpts from the letter:

> In General: "The conduct of Germany is almost unexampled in human history. The terrible responsibility which lies at her doors can be seen in the fact that no [fewer] than seven million dead lay buried in Europe, while more than twenty million others carry upon them the evidence of wounds and sufferings, 'because Germany saw fit to gratify her lust for tyranny by resort to war.'"
>
> In Detail: "[the Rulers of Germany] commenced the submarine campaign with its piratical challenge to international law, and its destruction of great numbers of innocent passengers and sailors in mid-ocean, far from succor, at the mercy of the winds and the waves, and the yet more ruthless submarine crews."

The above exaggerated, almost hysterical allegations in the Allied letter of June 16, 1919, and similar ones in the document, set the spirit of the times. The Allied note from which the above allegations were extracted represents the enormity of the situation about as succinctly and accurately as it can be expressed in terms of the binding accusations of the victors in World War I. The treaty forced on the Germans shortly after, on June 28, reiterated the spirit and established the times. Hitler, the artist, the architect, the would-be Wagnerian-styled Germanic hero, the already hardened, remorseless war hero, and the aspiring nemesis of German Marxism and its alter ego "European Jewry," would flourish as no other in these times.

The Allied Powers that wrote the treaty and dictated it to the Germans could not escape domination by their own wartime propaganda. The treaty has been attacked with devastating argument from many directions, but with little effect on reassessment of European history in the twentieth century. Quite astonishingly, serious and reputable historians continue as apologists for a treaty that concentrates within its articles the times that drove Europe toward World War II. The following sentences are typical of the continuing divorcement from reality about the qualities of the treaty and the dubious attempts at defense: "From a general world point of view it is difficult to see how the peacemakers, laboring under the tensions and pulls of so numerous and varied a concatenation of national interests and demands, could have done much better than they did. ...Certainly by comparison with the Treaty of Brest-Litovsk, which the Germans imposed on Bolshevik Russia, it was a model of fairness and generosity."[10]

One could reply that the treaty might have been *negotiated* with a German delegation. Leon Trotsky, in contrast, not an insignificant Bolshevik, was present at Brest to negotiate, and the contention of unfairness in the Brest-Litovsk Treaty is based largely on the German creation of client buffer states in the east. But the 2004 contemporaneous scene in Europe undermines the contention of unfairness, because the states claimed by the conventional wisdom to have been torn so unjustly from Russia under Brest-Litovsk, namely Ukraine, Belarus, Lithuania, Latvia, and Estonia, all chose independence when presented with the opportunity to escape from the latter-day Bolshevik Russia of the early 1990s.

In the treaty of June 29, 1919, there would be a pattern of excessive severity combined with unhistorical accusations impugning national honor of the Germans. The excessive severity would come from a France unable to adjust to the new reality of a recently created German state in place of the former, exorbitantly large number of tiny principalities that had made up the German-speaking area of Europe. Before 1800, the map of "Germany" consisted of 314 states and 1,475 estates, making a total of 1,789 sovereign entities.[11] As late as 1870, "Germany" comprised thirty-eight separate states, and even when the German Empire was created on January 18, 1871, it was forced to accommodate under a new imperial government a total of twenty-five states. France had reveled for centuries in this extraordinarily favorable situation and had advanced into territory inhabited by German-speaking populations including, for example, Lorraine and Alsace. Clemenceau, the patriotic, tough, and vindictive nemesis of Imperial Germany, would promise France security through annexation of German territory to the fatefully conceptualized natural boundary of the Rhine. Along with Marxism and European Jewry, Hitler would come to rank France as the great enemy of Germany— although in the quite different sense that it was a respected, cultured nation-state and as such was a dangerous foreign enemy.

The unhistorical accusations that the Allies inserted into the treaty impugning German honor came from a different direction. The major Allies, faced with the challenges of keeping their populations fighting in an unprecedented total war, embraced propaganda characterized by unrealistic exaggeration, hate, and difficult-to-fulfill promises in the event of victory. The Allies broadcast the dubious claim that the Germans wanted, planned, and started World War I, conducting it with inhuman savagery. The winning party in the British khaki elections of December 1918 would promise that German "war criminals" would be punished, and the Germans would pay the costs of the war. Buffeted by French and British propaganda-tinged insistence on German war guilt, President Wilson, who had espoused a peace of justice and fairness, collapsed in the face of French and British pressures. In a reversal of his statesman-like moderation during the armistice negotiations, he would swing to the view that the Germans had to be punished. As a result of the psychological situation of the first half of 1919, the major Allies created imperial German war guilt, and France acted to produce a treaty that embodied punishment rather than conciliation. Distinguished Allied figures of the day unambiguously recorded their views that the treaty was prologue to disaster and warned their governments of the potential for political and economic catastrophe and the onset of another war. But a miniscule nonentity in 1919, who contributed nothing to such a treaty and had little to do with the establishment of the times, would grow shoulders so large by 1939 that they would obscure entire great powers that vanish when the causes of World War II are analyzed.

But how could any treaty, even one that would emerge from the end of World War I, be ill-conceived enough to lead in only twenty years to an even greater conflict? At the very beginning of the treaty, parts two and three give concern for fairness and functionality. Those parts represent territories taken from Germany and given to various states on its frontiers. The Allies would compensate the innocent and unoffending state of Belgium, which—although neutral at war's beginning—had thoughtfully fortified its boundary against Germany. Belgium would take the German frontier districts of Eupen, Malmédy, and Moresnet as compensation for war damages. The Allies would have been better served morally and functionally to have taken almost any other action—monetary compensation or delivery of goods and services, for example. The morality of transferring German territory inhabited by approximately fifty thousand Germans and virtually no "Belgians" as compensation for damages was typical of confused thinking about punishing the former enemy. Belgium, since its modern inception in 1831, has been plagued by friction between its 60 percent Flemish-speaking and 40 percent Wallonian-speaking populations comprising two differing cultural communities, and it scarcely needed a third community of Germans. The intensity of the friction and its persistence is illustrated by the Belgian parliament's constitutional amendments of 1977, which created three separate cultural communities, namely, Flemish, Wallonian, and German.

*   *   *

In one of the most bitter struggles among the Big Four at Paris and Versailles, Clemenceau attempted to annex German territory to the west bank of the Rhine River in the name of French security. The US and British governments could not agree to so dangerous and dysfunctional an expansion of French territory but nevertheless agreed to vast changes that were both economically crippling and humiliating to Germany. As concerns the generalization "economically crippling," Germany would lose 75 percent of its iron ore production and 40 percent of its coal. For an era in which economics of the larger industrialized states pivoted around steel production—much iron, a little carbon, some alloying metals, and a large heat source— Germany would face huge adjustments in continuing to produce steel. It could be argued, of course that the iron ore taken from Germany was largely from Lorraine, which had recently been taken from France along with neighboring Alsace after the Franco–Prussian War of 1870–1871. In the end, the Germans lost World War I and should have been prepared to suffer the consequences of the loss, particularly under the circumstances noted above. Unfortunately, instead of just taking the territory, the Allies—in what would become a syndrome in the treaty—could not resist including the humiliating moral judgment that the land was being ceded "to redress the wrong done by Germany in 1870." These words have provoked little controversy among several generations of historians, who accept as obvious a view that Germany had committed a wrong against France in 1870, apparently though the immoderate territorial avarice of having torn away Alsace and Lorraine.

The entrenched wisdom would have its readers believe that the Franco–Prussian War was largely the heady scheme of the Prussian chancellor, Otto von Bismarck, to unify finally under Prussia the thirty-eight states of Germany through means of a national (i.e., all-German) fight against the traditional predator of France. Indeed, broadly stated, this was Bismarck's ambition. The entrenched wisdom rarely presents with conviction the other half of the picture, in which the emperor Napoleon III and the imperial party surrounding him required an imperial policy of territorial aggrandizement and sought to put the upstart Prussian kingdom in its proper place after its prestigious victory over Austria in 1866. The same wisdom fails to inform us that France only recently, in historical terms, had seized these ethnically and culturally German areas. Though essentially German, these states were unable to maintain their independence against a state so large and powerful as France. In a telling commentary on the concept of a wrong done to France, it could be noted that the French census of 1931 for the departments of Moselle, Haut-Rhin, and Bas-Rhin (Alsace–Lorraine) showed 10 percent of the population speaking French but with 90 percent speaking German, a statistic that does not support a case for Allied blandishment of Germany.

The Allies treated the Germans heavy-handedly in the Rhineland. The Germans lost sovereignty over the territory in the following manner: The Saarland or Saar Basin area was placed under the governing control of an international commission, and its coal mines were ceded to France as compensation for the German destruction of French coal mines in the northern areas occupied by the Germans during the war. The Allies forced the Germans to endure this economically dysfunctional situation for fifteen years until a plebiscite would be held to determine if "the inhabitants" (i.e., the Germans) living there would prefer union with France, Germany, or continuation of the international controls. The Allies also occupied the Rhineland in three zones as well as three thirty-mile deep bridgeheads centered on Cologne, Koblenz, and Mainz, with armed forces from France, Britain, the United States, and Belgium to ensure treaty enforcement. The eastern zone centered on Mainz was to be occupied by foreign troops for fifteen years. And if these conditions were not enough to help German nationalist parties gain adherents, the Allies proceeded to "demilitarize" Germany— not only on the left bank of the Rhine but also within an area thirty miles deeper into Germany along its northern bank. The Allies demilitarized the Rhineland by forbidding the presence of German troops, fortifications, mobilization installations, and maneuver areas.

The Allied military occupation of the Rhineland and the three bridgeheads east of the Rhine, combined with the demilitarization of the area, would be laden with consequence for Hitler, the Germans, the French, and even the Americans. Thwarted by the governments of Britain and the United States in attempting annexation to the west bank of the Rhine and achieving control over its own destiny, France was forced to accept the promise of a mutual defense treaty with Britain and the United States. When the government of the United States reneged on its promise and irresponsibly and immorally defected from the creation of such a treaty, and Britain, citing the US defection, refused a bilateral security treaty with France, the French government was left perched in the Rhineland to enforce the Versailles treaty largely alone. In a similar astounding vein, although the Wilson administration had signed the Versailles treaty, the US Senate rejected it terminally on March 19, 1920. And finally, although Wilson had championed a League of Nations, the United States did not join that organization during the entire interwar period. The consequences of the above situation were disastrous for the peace of Europe and for the survival of the Weimar Republic.

Deserted by the United States, of diminished foreign policy interest to Britain, and incapable of allying with Soviet Russia, France faced Germany alone. Under these circumstances, France was forced to clutch at the Versailles treaty as its main source of security. The presence of French ground troops in the Rhineland and the bridgeheads to the east until 1930 would give the French government leverage to force German adherence to the treaty. Where would Hitler begin to fit into this picture of Europe dominated by the times put in place by the Paris Peace Conference? Hitler's first nationally significant political action—the Munich Beer Hall Putsch of early November 1923—would be forced on him by the disastrous conditions created by German resistance throughout 1923 to the French military seizure of the Ruhr, the rough equivalent of the British industrial midlands and the US industrial space between Pittsburgh, Pennsylvania, and Gary, Indiana. The post-

Clemenceau *bête noir* of Germany, Prime Minister Raymond Poincaré, the tough, pitiless, strong man who had only recently "saved the franc," had ordered the invasion to force German adherence to the letter of the reparation imposed under the Versailles treaty.

*   *   *

The Allies would inflict the main territorial losses on Germany, however, in the east. There, President Wilson's thirteenth point, "an independent Poland to include territories indisputably Polish, with free and secure access to the sea," came into play with the resulting imposition of disastrous territorial conditions that would become the immediate *causus belli* for World War II. At the most general level of consideration, the Polish government census of 1931 reflects the state that Wilson and the Allies brought into existence as largely Polish but whose makeup was disastrously diverse, specifically, 22 million Poles and 9.9 million non-Polish in speech and ethnicity. The numbers do not support a view of an indisputably Polish state and suggest problems for Poland, internally and externally. The numbers, in fact, border on incomprehensibility as they are supposed to reflect the makeup of an indisputably Polish state. Poland would endure, as a result, tension with Soviet Russia over 3.2 million Ukrainians and 2.2 million Ruthenians and face further danger from 1.7 million others including especially Germans, Lithuanians, and Czechs. Poland would continue to encompass an indigestible immigrant population of 2.7 million Jews considered by the Polish government as a non-Polish racial, linguistic, and religious national minority. Here we see the Allies playing freely and loosely with ethnic reality in eastern Europe. In areas where the Allies decided to hold plebiscites, the inhabitants of the districts of Allenstein and Marienwerder, a supposedly ethnic gray area in East Prussia, voted in 1920 to remain in Germany, 460,103 to 15,927.[12]

Article eighty-eight of the Versailles treaty provided for a plebiscite to be held in Upper Silesia, which was part of Germany but inhabited by a sizeable Polish population and coveted by the Poles for its coal reserves and mines. The Allies held the plebiscite on March 20, 1921, and the Germans won—well over half the population voted to remain in Germany, specifically, 717,122 votes versus 483,154. The treaty, however, kept the final disposition of the area for the Allies to determine based on the strained but not unreasonable point that in some areas there would be significant majorities of either Poles or Germans, notwithstanding the fact that the Germans "won" the plebiscite overall. No general historical work on this part of the twentieth century has elucidated that the Allies had in fact conducted a census that would allow them (with their complete freedom of action) to partition the area to the greatest degree possible to the benefit of the Poles, who, as it turned out, had "lost" the plebiscite.

The subtlety of the Allied position was lost on the extreme Polish nationalists. Fearing after the plebiscite that Poland would "lose" all of Upper Silesia, armed irregulars under the Polish extremist Wojciech Korfanty, with the physical support of the Polish government and tacit support of the French government, moved into Upper Silesia on May 3, 1921, unopposed by the French occupying forces. The outraged moderate Weimar government protested to the Allied Supreme Council to no avail and was forced to support resurrected armed right wing volunteers, the *Freikorps*, to oppose the illegal proceedings. The enormity of the situation is illustrated by the parallel outrage of the British prime minister David Lloyd George over the situation in a speech to the House of Commons on May 13, 1921, in which he pointed out that "either the Allies ought to insist upon the treaty being respected, or they ought to allow the Germans to do it. Not merely to disarm Germany, but to say that such troops as she has got are not to be permitted to take part in restoring order [in Upper Silesia] in what, until the decision comes, is their own province—that is not fair play. Fair play is what England stands for, and I hope she will stand for it to the end."[13]

In order to assure Poland of free and unfettered "access to the sea," the Allies took the German province of West Prussia, which included the well-developed former medieval Hanseatic port of Danzig, and recast it as the Polish province of Pomerelia and the internationalized city and surrounding district of Danzig. The new Polish territory of Pomerelia held a significant number of Germans stemming from the medieval colonization of the area, especially during the period 1134–1290 under princes of the House of Anhalt and the slightly later German settlers introduced by the Teutonic Knights (the militant Order of Saint Mary's Hospital at Jerusalem), into the area of indigenous Baltic Prussian tribes and uninhabited wilderness later to be known as East Prussia.

The upshot of this complex ethnic interaction for understanding the realism of a "Polish Corridor" that divided the German Republic of 1918 into two uneven parts was the following: By 1919, the Baltic Prussian tribes had been either exterminated by the crusading Teutonic Knights or assimilated by German settlers, resulting in East Prussia, Danzig, and its expansive hinterland being over 95 percent German. The corridor between German Danzig and German Pommerania remained an area of mixed settlement balanced roughly equally between German and Pole.[14] The Danzig situation proved particularly dysfunctional because the Allies had to balance between the right of self-determination of the overwhelmingly German population to remain German, and the economic necessities of Poland to have functional access to the sea through established facilities in the port of Danzig. To solve this situation, the Allies converted Danzig and its hinterland into an international zone, thus assuring Polish access to the sea through the port. The Allies thereby solved the immediate challenges of 1919 while characteristically victimizing Germany and creating another ostensible cause for the outbreak of World War II twenty years later.

It can be generalized somewhat obviously that Hitler would be fortified, in the development of a robust national movement in domestic German politics, by such a situation. Less obviously, it could be added that in the event that he actually came to power in

Germany, he would initially have an almost inescapable path for foreign policy laid out for him in the misplaced Germans in Austria, the Sudetenland, and Danzig. The point for a more realistic picture of Hitler in 1919 and reevaluation of his foreign policy later in the 1930s is that neither Hitler nor the Germans invented a rump Austria, nationalistically abused Sudetenland, and an internationalized Danzig. With full freedom of maneuver to create a stable Europe in 1919, the Allies chose to create national moral inequities that would not only assist Hitler in his rise to power but also define the highpoints of his foreign policy once he was in control of Germany.

*   *   *

In the case of the overseas colonial settlement arrived at unilaterally by the Allies, they took every German colony on the face of the globe for redistribution among themselves. If the Allies had simply announced and carried out such action, the Germans would have been left with the unhappy but sobering fact of defeat in a great war and associated losses. The Allies, however, through some terrible combination of belief in their own wartime propaganda and yet bad conscience about the credibility of so severe an action, felt compelled to accuse the Germans of corruption and brutality. Such a quasi-gratuitous accusation impugned the honor of the German people and would have been dangerously impolitic to make even if it were supportable by evidence. German colonial administration, however, could be characterized as firm but probably fairer and more efficient than that of any other power. By the mid-1930s, however, it had become plain that a grave injustice had been done by depriving Germany of its colonies, and the British became willing to admit even Hitler's dangerously nationalist Germany into the elite group of colonial powers.[15] The British historian R. W. Seton-Watson drew up a tentative program of adjustments for the British government, noting that "the convenient thesis of Germany's unfitness to administer colonies is as untrue as it is insulting and should be recanted."[16]

This British expert thereby advised the British government as part of a policy of readjustment to repudiate formally and publicly the former opinion expressed on German colonies.

Seton-Watson's comments are particularly cogent because in the half-century in Africa prior to 1914, the Belgians, French, and British had made the greatest colonial inroads, and not surprisingly have been associated with the cruel exploitation of the natives of Congo State by the Belgians, the extraordinarily aggressive occupation of Algeria, Morocco, and Tunisia by the French, and reprehensible British wars against the South African Dutch republics. The latter imperialistically contrived aggression was linked with the strategic concept of a Cape-to-Cairo rail system and resultant probable British dominance in Africa. The concept culminated during the last Boer War in the infamous "concentration" of noncombatant Afrikaner women and children in temporary camps and the resulting deaths of approximately thirty thousand through incompetence and neglect.

In the military, naval, and air clauses of the treaty, the Allies would proceed with extraordinary convolutions—even for Versailles. With France leading, they determined to essentially disarm Germany. The situation was an enormity because it would place that country in immediate danger of foreign invasion from the east and west by tough competing national states including, of course, France, Poland, and even Czechoslovakia. The French menace was evident in a French peacetime army of approximately 800,000 professionals and conscripts in the 1920s, an associated buildup of a huge body of trained reserves, and an unrestricted weapons development. The Polish frontier was a strategic disaster area in terms of the great plain existing between the two states and a special danger because of the proximity of Berlin to the frontier. It is difficult to imagine Czechoslovakia attacking Germany, but the practical possibility in terms of a Czech peacetime army larger than the ground force of a "disarmed" Germany illustrates the extreme situation.

A question, though, is: What constituted a "disarmed" Germany, and how does it relate to the above situation? Germany was actually permitted an army of one hundred thousand officers, civilian officials, and men, with tight restrictions on weaponry including no armored vehicles, no artillery heavier than 105mm pieces, and no "heavy" machine guns. The treaty forbade any military aircraft; hence, there could be neither army air corps nor German air force. The navy was contemptuously small by the standards of Britain, France, and Italy and forbidden to have submarines. Germany, in fact, was not disarmed but nearly so. As such, it lay obviously helpless in the event of all-out attack or opportunistic border readjustment by any one of the powers noted.

The situation was an extreme one, notwithstanding writings that suggest that the Germans evaded treaty controls. The writings in general claim that the Germans clandestinely designed, produced, and tested various weapons including submarines, tanks, and aircraft in various locations. The writings note that they hid large stocks of weapons that could be used for the large numbers of young men associated with the *Freikorps* from late 1918 through 1923 and with similarly styled groups later in the 1920s. The Germans, of course, *attempted* to evade the controls, but they proved tight enough to prevent the production of significant numbers of any important weapons. The best the Germans could do until 1933 was to design various weapons for possible production upon the lifting of the quite effective Allied controls that year. The Allied disarmament of Germany had proven to be so effective, in fact, that we could postulate that the single most important technically oriented factor responsible for the German loss of World War II was the feeble rearmament in the short period from 1933 to war's outbreak in September 1939.

As concerns other effects of the disarmament clauses of the treaty on Germany, the struggling Weimar Republic would be forced to depend on the clandestinely armed *Freikorps* for protection against border incursions in the east and Communist uprisings within Germany. The army, dismantled, reassembled, reduced in numbers, and closely scrutinized by the Allies, was not up to the task. Hitler and the young National Socialist movement cannot be imagined as being successful without the atmosphere characterized by the *Freikorps* and associated with the ill-advised severity of the disarmament clauses of the treaty. Hitler would be protected by the new *Reichsheer* organized as the Seventh Infantry Division in Bavaria and responsible for aiding the local nationalists and their associated *Freikorps* groups. Captain Ernst Roehm on the division staff was responsible for secretly caching large quantities of small arms and ammunition for use by the *Freikorps* as a clandestine Bavarian light infantry reserve against left wing uprisings. This same Captain Roehm would play a crucial role in Hitler's abortive Putsch in Munich in November 1923. He would personally lead armed SA men in the seizure of the war ministry and furnish rifles and machine guns for the approximately six hundred SA men who secured the *Buergerbraeukeller* and others armed during the uprising. Hitler could not have survived the violent activity he was engaged in from 1919 through 1923 without the support and protection of a *Reichsheer* too weak to secure Germany from enemies foreign and domestic under circumstances of the disarmament.

Hitler would be aided in his expansion of the Nationalsozialistische Deutsche Arbeiterpartei (NSDAP or National Socialist German Workers' Party) by the revulsion of most Germans against Article 227 of the treaty, in which the Allies and associated powers "publicly" arraigned William II of Hohenzollern for "a supreme offense against international morality and the sanctity of treaties." Most people, German or otherwise, would consider their intelligence badly handled by the Allied statement that "a special tribunal will be constituted to try the accused, thereby assuring him the guarantees essential to the right of defense. It will be composed of five judges, one appointed by each of the following Powers; namely, the United States of America, Great Britain, France, Italy, and Japan."[17] This single sentence illustrates an almost limitless disregard for fairness and justice on the part of the Allies and characterizes the times set by them in interwar Europe.

In the same part of the treaty, the Allies would pen Article 231 with no German negotiator present to temper the wording. The article impugned the honor of the entire German nation and set in place vindictiveness as the main characteristic of the times. The article was not only psychologically calloused—a kind of glove thrown into the face of every person in the defeated nation—but also historically implausible. The article stands as a monument to a coalition of Allies that had become devoured by its own wartime propaganda. The Allies more so than the Germans employed grossly distorted images of evil in portraying their foe in order to attract allies during the war and to keep their own people in the fight. It is easy to forget, for example, that the French Army suffered a strategic-level mutiny in late 1916, which illustrated the closeness of the struggle and demanded that the Allies employ exaggerated propaganda. Faced with similar crises, the Allied governments failed to separate themselves from their own accusations of evil on the part of the Germans and reenter the world of historical reality in setting in place the times for the next twenty years in Europe. Taken by itself, Article 231 represents an enormity that significantly explains the existence and effectiveness of the parallel enormity of Hitler's strident propaganda. The article follows, necessarily, in its entirety:

> The Allied and associated Powers affirm and Germany accepts the responsibility of Germany and her allies for causing all the loss and damage to which the Allied and Associated Governments and their nationals have been subjected as a consequence of the war imposed upon them by the aggression of Germany and her allies.

Herbert Hoover, a prominent member of the American delegation, received his first copy of the draft treaty at four o'clock in the morning and was greatly disturbed by his first overall view. He later wrote that "hate and revenge" ran through the political and economic passages and that "conditions were set up upon which Europe could never be rebuilt or peace come to mankind."[18] William C. Bullitt, an officially designated expert advisor on the American commission, resigned on May 17, 1919, in protest against the draft treaty,

writing "our government [US] has consented now to deliver the suffering peoples of the world to new oppressions, subjections and dis-
memberments—a new century of war.... Unjust decisions of the
conference in regard to... the Tyrol, Thrace, Hungary, East Prussia,
Danzig the Saar Valley...make new international conflicts certain."[19] Jan Christian Smuts, distinguished and influential British
representative at the conference from the Union of South Africa,
warned in a letter to President Wilson in mid-May 1919 that the
treaty "may become an even greater disaster than the war was."[20]
These men, in these few comments, scathingly indicted the Allies for
establishing the conditions required for yet another conflict. And the
comments were prophetic. War would come in 1939 still completely
within the shadow cast by the treaty.

The German government, through its delegation at Versailles,
would present counterproposals to the Allies on May 29, 1919. The
Germans pointed out the Allied flight from a peace of justice as
espoused in the armistice agreement. The German "negotiators"
objected especially to the lack of any realistic sense of proportion in
reparation, the unsupportable allegations in the honor clauses, and
the unfairness of the territorial rectifications, especially in the east.
The plot becomes thicker here because Article 231 introduced the
section on reparation in the Versailles treaty, and we are forced to
ask the question: Just what does honor have to do with reparation?
The answer is the disturbing one, that the Allies had determined to
extract reparation so exorbitant that some equally exorbitant justification was necessary. Instead of simply pointing out *pro forma* that
the Germans, as losers in a war, would join in a long tradition of
paying the victors, the Allies would claim that Germany was like an
international armed robber, responsible for war's outbreak, and
liable for excessive reparation. The latter description is necessary
because the Allies would take away Germany's iron ore in Lorraine,
coal in the Saarland and Silesia, merchant and fishing fleets, and
internationalize its Rhine, Elbe, and Oder Rivers, leaving an
observer of the Paris Peace Conference to hold his breath in wonder

at how a state with its own national debt of over three trillion marks of 1914 value would manufacture such reparation. A member of the British delegation, Harold Nicolsen, characterized the reparation clauses as early as May 28, 1919, as the great crime in the treaty. He commented specifically that "the real crime is the reparation and indemnity chapter, which is immoral and senseless."[21] He added that because the reparations were impossible to execute, they were "sheer lunacy."[22] These are uncompromising words from a British delegate, and they bring into perspective the violent denunciations by Hitler and the support that began to gather around him— surprisingly slowly, given German desperation and revulsion.

The Allies would reject the German counterproposals and on June 16, 1919, present a reply that rises above even the various articles of the treaty to combine historically unsupportable allegations of hate and revenge that comfortably counterbalances any hate assigned to Hitler and the National Socialists by the great biographers in the political campaigns of the 1920s and 1930s in Germany. The spirit of the times resides in the words of the covering letter of the Allied reply and makes it the most important document of the Paris Peace Conference and probably the entire period of the "twenty years' crisis":

> In view of the Allied and Associated Powers the war which began on August 1, 1914, was the greatest crime against humanity and the freedom of the peoples that any nation calling itself civilized, has ever consciously committed. For many years the rulers of Germany, true to the Prussian tradition strove for a position of dominance in Europe. They required that they should be able to dictate and tyrannize to a subservient Europe, as they had dictated to and tyrannized over a subservient Germany.
>
> As soon as their preparations were complete, they encouraged a subservient ally to declare war on Serbia.... In order to make doubly sore, they refused every attempt a conciliation and conference until it was too late and the world war was inevitable for which alone among the nations they were fully equipped and prepared.

Germany's responsibility, however, is not confined to having planned and started the war. She is no less responsible for the savage and inhumane way in which it was conducted.[23]

The words above are those of the responsible governments of the United States, Britain, and France that were used to justify the refusal of any substantial changes in the treaty. They are not those of an irresponsible editorial in a Paris newspaper. The words reveal an intensity of hatred for the imperial government and the German people that demands comment. The words support a view that the Allied governments had lost touch with historical reality and were determined to demonize Germany. A terrible slide had begun by late November 1918 into a one-sided treaty and the unparalleled vituperation of the covering letter. The treaty and the following peace stemmed significantly from the traditionally practical British government becoming overwhelmed by its exaggerated propaganda and the naïve susceptibility of the US government to the same intense propaganda. The government and people of France, however, must take center stage for the spirit and word of the treaty, the ultimatum, and the peace set in place. The qualities that could be used to characterize the spirit of the French position are "arrogance" and "vindictive passion."

Unlike the treaty that placed blame for a war of aggression on "Germany and her allies," the covering letter and ultimatum of June 16, 1919, placed blame for the planning, starting, and readiness for a war of aggression on the shoulders of Germany alone. The Allies asserted in the treaty and covering letter to the ultimatum that the draft treaty was a just one that would enable the peoples of Europe to live together in friendship and equality. The articles of the treaty, the violent denunciations of Germany in the covering letter, and similar words in the ultimatum establish that no just peace could result.

Within the treaty itself, Allied interpreters would claim that Article 231 merely reaffirmed the obligation assumed by Germany when it signed the armistice on November 11 to make compensation for all damage done to the civilian population of the Allies and their properties. Such a claim is incredible in the face of the denunciations of Germany quoted above from the Allied ultimatum. The Allies had developed a fanatical belief in the total righteousness of their own cause and had determined, therefore, that the Germans would pay both war damages and costs and punctuated that determination by placing responsibility for the outbreak of war on Germany.

*   *   *

In Article 232, the Allies defined the categories of loss and damage under which they held the Germans liable. These categories included pensions to Allied military men and separation allowances to civilians, a fact that was contrary to the definition laid down in the Lansing armistice negotiation note of November 5, 1918.[24] The Allied demand for German payment of military pensions to Allied military personnel is a detail that illustrates the unfairness of the demanded reparation. Because the levying of pensions on the Germans was in defiance of the Allied armistice note, the action on pensions aggravated the situation by making it both immoral and illegal. Never in history had such a terrible indictment been passed on a European nation as a whole.[25] Since the indictment originated in the reparation part of the treaty, just what were the dimensions of *l'addition* to the Germans? After all, the purpose of examining the Allied-imposed times is to comprehend the success of Hitler's excessive propagandizing by relating it with the propagandized excesses of the times embodied in the Versailles treaty. We can generalize, for example, that few if any of Hitler's speeches, beginning in 1919, criticized German republicans and the Versailles treaty rise above the level of self-assured hate in the Allied documents. In a word, Hitler's hateful propagandizing is comfortably equaled by the hateful propagandizing carried on by Georges Clemenceau and the

French delegation officially at Versailles, echoed in the French press, and continued in 1919–1923.

Unable to agree upon a total sum, the Allies forced the German government to sign a treaty that would include an indemnity for a sum *as yet unknown* and to be determined by an Allied commission no later than May 1, 1921, almost two years later. The Allies presented the bill for reparation at that time and filled in the previously blank check with thirty-two billion dollars of relatively uninflated 1921 value. The formal German obligation was reckoned in gold marks, but payments were made largely in kind; for example, in telephone poles, coal, livestock, and so on.

The Weimar government would struggle to make payments, and as early as November 1922 the French cabinet would complete plans for a military occupation of the Ruhr to go into effect as soon as the Weimar republican government provided the necessary pretext by defaulting on reparation payments.[26] The prime minister of France, Raymond Poincaré, strong-willed and filled with vindictiveness toward the Germans, ordered French troops to seize the Ruhr area in Germany on January 11, 1923, after a German failure to deliver on time a relatively modest payment. The great biographers present Hitler's various political hatreds but fail to compare his with other contemporary political hatreds, and Hitler stomps alone through a world of more gentle figures. None point out that Prime Minister Poincaré, the man who succeed in destroying the German economy in 1923 and came close to destroying the Weimar government, was "an unreconstructed French patriot and a man whose hatred of Germany was so great that he asked to be buried [standing] facing toward the enemy in the east."[27] To comprehend Hitler, we must place him within the times set by Frenchmen of corresponding hatred, will, and determination, especially Georges Clemenceau and Raymond Poincaré. In the great biographies, the Frenchmen noted above vanish and we are left with the faceless enormity of a French and Belgian armed invasion of the Ruhr. The British government refused to take part in the action and, in a diplomatic note of August

11, 1923, declared that the "Franco–Belgian action ... was not a sanction authorized by the treaty."[28]

The armed incursion executed by Poincaré can be measured by the fact that the struggling Weimar republican government turned over its executive powers on September 26, 1923, to the minister of defense, Dr. Otto Gessler, whose final power lay with General Hans von Seeckt and the army. The president, chancellor, and cabinet were forced to do this because of accumulating danger from France, Belgium, Poland, and Lithuania externally, the Communists in Saxony, Thuringia, and Hamburg, the extreme nationalists and monarchists in Bavaria, and an impending breakaway, French-supported Rhineland Republic. To survive the mass hysterical German reaction to the invasion, the Weimar republican government was forced to resist. Unable to engage in any "active resistance," the government carried out various acts of "passive resistance," which included ordering all members of the government neither to cooperate with the occupiers nor to deliver any reparation in kind. To support this style of resistance, the government promised to pay the idle industrial workers, miners, and city service workers. Forced into uniquely desperate measures, the government could only print additional paper currency to pay the deliberately unemployed, an act that led to an inflation so great that it obliterated German finances. The runaway word, *obliterated*, is supported by the fact that the German republican government, when forced to abandon passive resistance in late November 1923, brought out a new transitional currency called the *Rentenmark*. Germans agreed to turn in the previous inflated Marks at the rate of one trillion old marks for one new *Rentenmark*. The German national debut lay at a figure of approximately 3.2 trillion old marks, and in an ironic, unintended twist, Poincaré's Ruhr occupation resulted in the Weimar republican government paying off the gigantic postwar debt of Germany with three *Rentenmarks*.

The Allies were determined, also at the expense of Germany, to secure international control over rivers that flowed through more than one country. They set up international commissions to control the Rhine, Elbe, Oder, Niemen, and Danube Rivers. The Danube and Niemen Rivers stand as monuments to the obvious in terms of the reasonableness and functionality of international controls. The Danube, for example, originates in Germany and then flows through or was shared in postwar Europe by Austria, Czechoslovakia, Hungary, Yugoslavia, Rumania, and Bulgaria. The Rhine, Elbe, and Oder Rivers must be regarded from the viewpoint of half a millennium of historical and political usage as German rivers, and the setting up of an international commission to control them simply violated the territorial integrity of even the reduced post-Versailles Germany. In a reasonable analogy, it could be noted that a great European river, the Rhone, rises in Switzerland and flows through France, but no attempt was made at internationalization even though the Allies expressed a desire to provide freer access to the sea for countries like Czechoslovakia and Switzerland.

In addition to the demilitarization of the Rhineland, the Allies provided for a military occupation with the purpose of guaranteeing the payment of reparation and carrying out other treaty terms. With the consistent excess that typified the treaty, the Allies determined that the Rhineland and three great bridgeheads across the Rhine River at Cologne, Koblenz, and Mainz were to be occupied by Allied armed forces for fifteen years from the coming into effect of the treaty on January 10, 1920. It is difficult to believe that the Allies would not correlate the outlandishly long presence of foreign ground troops in Germany with encouragement of the rise of a revanchist German government. It is true, of course, that the Allies occupied only the Rhineland and three bridgeheads, and the treaty provided for the evacuation of the bridgehead and zone of Cologne in five years, Koblenz in ten years, and Mainz in fifteen years. But the Mainz zone was slightly larger than the Cologne and Koblenz zones combined and approached the city of Frankfurt-am-Main. The Allies, therefore, considered it to be realistic and fair to occupy more than half the Rhineland and a bridgehead near Frankfurt until 1935.

Hitler would be favored in the creation of a radical nationalist movement in Bavaria by the eleven-year presence of French troops occupying German territory close by, which included all of Rhenish Bavaria. French troops, however, would evacuate the final Mainz zone of occupation by June 1930, five years ahead of the 1935 schedule. The reason for this uncharacteristic leniency was that the French and German governments—especially German foreign minister Gustav Stresemann on the one hand and French foreign minister Aristide Briand and Prime Minister Poincaré on the other hand—agreed in the latter half of 1928 to link early evacuation of the Rhineland with a final settlement of reparation. The Germans and former Allies, including the United States, then arranged a final settlement at the Hague, which was embodied in the Young Plan of June 1929. The plan included realistic payments by Germany. But less realistically, from a psychological viewpoint, the Allies secured the unconditional annual payments by a mortgage on the German state railway system; that is, the Allies would *own* the German rail system. And, in a final tour de force of lack of reality, the Young Plan established that the Germans would pay reparation for fifty-nine additional years—more than half a century. The Germans, therefore, agreed to submit to reparation until the year 1988 for a war that had ended in 1918, seventy years earlier.

In 1929, the Young Plan, as it developed from the appointment of the Young Committee on January 19, dominated European international affairs and became the most important foreign issue inside Germany. Hitler, for example, was forced to take a position on the plan. He chose to resist acceptance, and the action he took was his most important of the entire year of 1929 and would lead directly into the successes of 1930–1933, culminating in the capture of the German government. The Young Plan presented Hitler with an irresistible opportunity to gain national prominence after half a decade of intense activity that left him nevertheless languishing in Bavaria. And the opportunity was based on the Versailles treaty and Stresemann's earlier suggestion in the latter half of 1928 that the French evacuate the Rhineland ahead of the Versailles treaty schedule in return for reparation guaranties.

A question is fundamental for comprehending Hitler: Which one of the forces of 1929, Hitler or the French, was most significant in beginning to focus the effects of the loss of World War I into the obliteration of the Weimar Republic? The French government in the early 1920s, of course, could not have anticipated the Hitler of August 1929, January 1933, and September 1939, but it could and should have taken into consideration the rise of an extreme nationalist movement in Germany capable of endangering France. Dominated by hubris, the French government ignored such consideration. The answer to the question can be summarized thus: The actions of the French government in inflicting a vindictive peace on Europe led, through the secondary mechanism of Hitler and his boundlessly energetic National Socialists, to the destruction of the German republic. The thesis from this analysis is not the insipid generalization that the Versailles treaty—a distant, non-human abstraction—contributed to the fall of the German republic, but that France and its two great sons, Clemenceau and Poincaré, comprised the indispensable mechanism that enabled Hitler, with his extraordinary talents, to destroy it. Perhaps French governments euphoric over victory in World War I had come to regard themselves as foreign policy supermen and decided to live dangerously and build their diplomatic cities at the foot of Mount Vesuvius.

Chapter 3

OUT OF THE DESERT
1919–1922

Hitler was a study in improbabilities. It was improbable that he would escape near social and economic extinction similar to that in the men's home in Vienna from 1910 through 1913. It was improbable that he would survive death on the western front during the following four years. It was improbable that he would seize any position of power with the German Workers' Party after his entry into it in 1919. It was improbable that he would survive death at the point of the shattered column of the Nationalsozialistische Deutsche Arbeiterpartei (NSDAP or National Socialist German Workers' Party) on *Residenzstrasse* in Munich in November 1923. It was improbable that he would avoid political extinction after defeat, trial, conviction, and fortress detention in the aftermath. It was improbable that he would seize unconditional leadership of the party remnants in early 1925 and dictate a legal political takeover of Germany. It was improbable that his improbable strategy would ever succeed, let alone by January 1933. It was unlikely that his biographers would record and interpret this saga as other than bound by the details of Hitler's actions in Munich, Bavaria, and Germany. Their approach to the above improbabilities has been so Germano-centric that it has involved a significant flight from reality in comprehending Hitler. But how can almost exclusive emphasis on Hitler doing German things in Germany veer away from reality? Such emphasis would be a drawback if Germany could be shown to have had virtually no control over its own destiny because of the imposition of some outside force. Such force was in place in 1919.

The Allies, through the grand historical instrument of military victory in World War I, and the more immediate instrument of French power in the aftermath of the war and the simultaneous onset of World War II, would control the destiny of a disarmed Germany at least until 1933. Germany cannot be said to have had an independent foreign policy during the entire period, and its internal politics and economics moved according to the external strictures of the loss of the war and relentless French imposition of them. The biographers dutifully present the presence of Allied pressures, but only as background. Despite the elegant succinctness of some of the descriptions, they leave us with a Hitler and a Germany disembodied from the rest of Europe. With Hitler, for example, interpretive cause and effect disappear because we are presented with a picture of the times that drove his Putsch, which constitutes a canvas less than half filled-in. We see Hitler, Germans, and Germany, but little of the French, France, and the French army that had helped to set into place and then enforce the conditions that made it possible for Hitler to attempt a march on Berlin.

In Hitler's most significant action of the entire period, the Putsch of November 1923, the biographers minimize its cause: the earlier, Poincaré-led, French armed invasion of the Ruhr. Poincaré and France recede so far into the background that we are unable to formulate the necessary historical interpretation in which a heavy-handed French action was the underlying cause of the Hitler Putsch and one of the most important events that contributed to the influence of the national Right. And because the biographers are so concerned with the colorful, albeit necessary, details of the beer cellar violence and German setting, we not only miss the overall French control of events but also fail to see Hitler in the actual context of the interwar period. We miss the point that the Ruhr invasion was the earliest great action in the onset of World War II and was French-inspired.

Biographers and historians alike have placed the entire weight of the onset and outbreak of World War II onto Hitler's shoulders. As reassuring and satisfying as this situation has seemed to be for the last half century, it represents more the appearance of writers from the victorious coalition states ineffectively interpreting the outbreak of World War II and placing a cloak of selective invisibility over the actions and motives of other men and the policies of other states during 1919–1939. If we accept a thesis that the entire period was a single European crisis leading to World War II, then the onset of war must include the period so coherently periodized and vital in Hitler's life as that from 1919 through 1933.[1] As concerns Hitler in such an analysis, it must be obvious that he had no influence over the onset of war in the entire 1919–1933 period—the lion's share of the era. And it must be equally apparent that other men who directed the policies of other European states dominated the outbreak of peace in 1919 and the immediately following period that must be characterized as the onset of yet another war.

Any story of Hitler becomes, in final analysis, a story of the onset, outbreak, and course of World War II. Any credible interpretation of Hitler must address the question of how his personal characteristics, thoughts, and actions can be related with the generalization that it was Hitler's war; he wanted it, planned it, and started it. After all, World War II was the premier event of the twentieth century, and he has been interpreted as contributing more to its outbreak than any other man, indeed, as stated above, virtually the one and only man. If Hitler's greatest "contribution" to mankind was its greatest war, then his contribution should be addressed from the beginning of his political activity and dominate any biography from 1919 through 1933. Yet it cannot be claimed that any biography has adequately integrated the onset and outbreak of World War II into the ample part of most biographies that deal with Hitler's rise from political obscurity to the chancellorship of Germany—the Cinderella story of the twentieth century.

*   *   *

The story has the oddest of beginnings. On November 19, 1918, Hitler would depart Pasewalk for his regiment's garrison city of Munich, remain in the army, and have his home in a military barracks. He would thereby be in the midst of the deadly, chaotic events of November 1918 through May 1919 in that city. During that time the Bavarian monarchy, which had been associated with the princely house of Wittlesbach for almost 750 years, would fall and be succeeded by a republican government on November 8, one day before Social Democrats declared a German republic in Berlin. In a radical and bizarre course of events, the Independent Socialist Kurt Eisner, on that day and with the support of a Munich mob, took charge of events, declared a Bavarian republic, and was proclaimed minister-president by the Munich council of workers and soldiers. Hitler, the doubtless German nationalist, antisocialist, and anti-Semite; the veteran of four years of privation, fear, and the presence of violent death in the defense of the Second Reich; the participant as a front-line combat soldier in both the first and the last great offensive of the Imperial German Army on the western front; the young man who had fled cosmopolitan Vienna for German Munich; would return to that city to find it under the control of Marxists. Not one biographer points out that, in a single human being, the minister-president exemplified the enemy for Hitler: Kurt Eisner, revolutionary Marxist, Jew, internationalist, and fomenter of antiwar strikes in Germany in January 1918 while the field armies were still engaged in combat in the west. Hitler would have been presented by this apparition from hell of the destructor of a German Reich. Yet no biographer develops the Munich visions of Hitler that must have contributed to his conversion from intense, ineffectual, brooding loner into a German political phenomenon.

Hitler would relate in his autobiography that earlier, face in pillow, head burning in a Pasewalk hospital not far from the Baltic on November 10, 1918, he would collapse in the face of the news that the war had been lost as signaled by the abdication of the emperor and the declaration of a republic. "There followed terrible days and even worse nights," according to Hitler, and for his part he decided to go into politics.[2] This appropriately dramatic account of his decision has been accepted by most biographers as part of a natural progression of events that began with the nationalism and anti-Semitism in Vienna and proceeded inexorably toward entry into the German Workers' Party in September 1919. Kershaw, however, in an original analysis, points out that Hitler's Vienna anti-Semitism has probably been exaggerated by Hitler himself and other biographers and historians. The great mystery in Hitler's life (the almost inexplicable lack of action by Hitler in Munich in the midst of the tumult of November 1918 through May 1919) stares at us unexplained, particularly in the light of "the relatively large numbers of Jews among the leaders of the soviet republics [that] gave, not justification, but a rationalized basis for otherwise latent anti-Semitic feelings."[3]

In the period of November 1918 through February 1919, both Eisner and Hitler would be engulfed by further revolutions. With little support from voter and *Landtag*, Minister-President Eisner attempted to resign on February 21, 1919, but was assassinated moments before he could submit his resignation. After his death by pistol shot, political control over Bavaria would continue to be disputed among Left political groups. On April 13, 1919, Hitler would have found himself in the midst of three Left, socialist revolutionary situations comprising a Majority and Independent Socialist government removed from Munich to Bamberg for its own safety, and in Munich a soviet republic under Ernst Toller that had just been deposed on April 12 by a Bolshevik threesome who declared a real soviet republic to be developed on the Russian model. The situation suggests an enormous impact on Hitler that would have been aggravated by the loss of the war.

Unfortunately, because of its relevance to Hitler, no biographer has presented the statistically improbable historical situation relative to the anti-Semitism that followed. None pulls together the support possible

for nationalist anti-Semites by the picture of the leadership of the revolutionary Marxists (Communists) in Germany in 1918 and 1919. Karl
Liebknecht and Rosa Luxemburg, the latter Jewish, led the Communists in the most notorious and potentially successful uprising of the
entire interwar period. Kurt Eisner had seized power on November 8,
1918, in Munich and triggered the proclamation of a German-wide
republic in Berlin. He would remain minister-president until February
1919. Ernst Toller, Erich Muelhsam, and Gustav Landauer, all Jewish
intellectuals, would instigate and lead the first soviet republic in
Bavaria after Eisner's assassination. And Eugen Leviné, Towia Axelrod,
and Max Levien, all Russian Jews, would instigate and lead the second
soviet republic in Bavaria by taking over and radicalizing the previous
one. Given Hitler's coalescing anti-Semitism, we must suspect significant outrage on his part in the presence of six Jews holding the seven
top positions in the three Marxist socialist revolutions in Bavaria, the
first of which having been sparked while the Hitler and the army were
still in combat on the western front.

Yet the best the biographers can do in this situation is to present
disparagingly the question of why Hitler did not take some kind of
action against both the Majority Socialists and Communists. The biographers emphasize particularly that during the period of the Bol-
shevik-led takeover of Munich from April 12 to the entry of the
Freikorps into the city on May 1, that Hitler did nothing to resist the
Communists even though he was within the city in an army barracks.
They also note that during the entire earlier period, from November
1918 through the Communist intellectuals' takeover of Munich
through early April, that Hitler similarly took no action to resist the
Majority Socialists who would later exemplify for him the November
Criminals who had undermined the war effort through strikes and
antiwar propaganda during the last two years of the war. The biographers present, as their most damning evidence of their mini-
interpretation of Hitler as a shallow opportunist, his elections to
positions associated with the Bolshevik-inspired soldiers' councils of
war's end. Hitler, for example, on April 16, 1919, within the violent

situation of the "real" soviet republic and Communist-controlled Munich, would be elected to his battalion's soldiers' council as the second-most popular man from his company. This fact suggests that Hitler may have opportunistically embraced Marxian socialism but is more credibly explained by the high regard for Hitler on the part of his comrades and their knowledge that he was a patriot forced to conform to events.

Such generalization is supported by the scene described sparely by Hitler in *Mein Kampf* when, on April 27, he stood at the entrance to his barracks with a loaded carbine and stared down the three Red guards sent to arrest him. Hitler would have been in uniform, displaying his Iron Cross First Class, Iron Cross Second Class, and wound badge, evidence of a formidable combat soldier and a mortal danger to the three would-be arresting agents. The presence of the three Red guards also suggests that Hitler may well have done something that gave him away as a potential counterrevolutionary. However, Professor Ian Kershaw, the latest great Hitler biographer, presents the following self-confident, gratuitous denunciation of Hitler's brief description by noting that "the whole story has an air of fabrication about it."[4] The biographer generalizes that Hitler did nothing to resist the Bolshevik soviet republic in Munich and then continues sarcastically that Hitler alleged he had acted in some way that led to his attempted arrest by the Reds "but does not describe it." Who do we believe as concerns this dramatic incident?

It is difficult to accept a view that Hitler fabricated the incident. It is equally difficult to refute the biographer's point that Hitler "did nothing" during the height of the entire Marxist revolutionary crisis.[5] The biographer, however, cannot resist sarcastic disparagement: "Hitler claimed that he pondered what could be done but repeatedly realized that...he 'did not possess the least basis for any useful action.' In other words he did nothing."[6] The biographer's desire to disparage again gets in the way of comprehension of Hitler. Although a reason not to accept Hitler's story would be that it was an attempt to claim something that did not happen and cloud it in spare and vague terms, the story must almost certainly be accepted as factual. We are trying to comprehend Hitler and are presented with an incident that gives us insight, specifically his extraordinary personal courage, his combat background, his reserved style of presenting himself, his impressive resistance to exaggeration in recounting factual happenings as exemplified by his letters on his war experiences, and his tendency in *Mein Kampf* to present truth with enough vagueness to suggest many things to many readers including a bit of the heroic as seen dimly through a glass.

Kershaw, however, shrugs off the incident as prevarication. In doing so he cannot point out the similarity in style between Hitler's secretiveness that extended to his grave about the acts for which he was factually awarded the Iron Cross First Class, his ubiquitously displayed, quasi-mystical object of veneration, his uniquely German talisman. In the highly likely first action, the elusively described "it" that incurred the wrath of some Munich Red authority, he implied vaguely something heroic about the situation. In the irrefutable second action, the winning of the Iron Cross First Class, he similarly clouded the action, although we cannot doubt that it happened. But for what purpose? We are made to suspect by his silence something particularly heroic that each man must imagine separately because he is not presented with a necessarily disappointing concrete shape. Once we discern this subtle piece of myth-creation, we can connect it with yet another "mystery" that has plagued biographers and was the Vienna building site experience of Hitler.

He related this experience as a scene in *Mein Kampf* set in Vienna in 1909. He represented himself as reduced to employment as a common laborer for approximately two weeks on a building construction site. Kershaw flatly rejects the experience as "almost certainly fictional."[7] An earlier great biographer, Joachim Fest, however, accepts the scene as real.[8] The incident rings true and probably actually happened. Most importantly, however, Hitler used such a scene whether or not it actually occurred to educate his readers about Social Democracy. In it, he claimed that he "had looked for work only to avoid starvation, only to continue [his] education,"[9] and found himself in the midst of Social Democratic workers. He noted that he kept to himself but on the third or fourth day was informed that he had to join a Social Democratic trade union and become a Social Democrat. He countered that he knew nothing about trade unions and would need time to educate himself on the matter. After two weeks of studying "book after book, pamphlet after pamphlet" and debating Social Democracy with the workers, he summarized that the union representatives tired of attempting to convince him by Marxist dialectic and threatened violence if he did not embrace Social Democracy. The lesson for Hitler: the demonstrable success of Marxism as a mass movement derived not from the boring and repellent Marxist dialectic but from the practical techniques of organized physical violence. Kershaw, in his preemptory rejection of Hitler's story as a fabrication concocted to support his detestation of Social Democracy, fails to present Hitler's plainly stated lesson: "our discussions at work were often very heated. I argued back…until one day they made use of the weapon which most readily conquers reason: terror and violence. A few of the spokesmen of the other side forced me either to leave the building at once or be thrown off the scaffolding."[10]

*   *   *

By May, Hitler had survived the Munich Red soviet republic of the wandering Russian revolutionary Jews Leviné, Axelrod, and Levien in the sense of not being killed by the Reds and not having committed some unpardonable revolutionary act in the chaos of the time. Having survived both biological and political death, Hitler stood delicately poised in his inconsequential life before two paths. One path let to utter mediocrity barely at the fringes of bourgeois respectability, and the other to something else—fulfillment, perhaps, of the vague intuition of having been reserved for something special. This is the moment we can pull together what manner of man the world would be dealing with for the next quarter of a century.

The cloud of disparagement that characterizes the writing of the great biographers by the time of his entry into "politics" in 1919 continues to intrude. They take him to task in his memoir for his claim that he suffered through years of poverty and deprivation in Vienna during the initial stage of his political enlightenment. Hitler presented a picture of a young man struggling to maintain honor and dignity in the face of destructive privation in a cruel city. The biographers note to the contrary that during the period from early 1908 through 1913 he lived comfortably on his patrimony until about August 1909. They continue that he hit briefly on evil times from spring 1910 through May 1913, followed by relatively comfortable times in the men's home on the *Meldemannstrasse* and cannot be said to have suffered the privations that he claimed. Who do we believe?

Again it is Kershaw, in an inimitable, sardonic style, who notes that "Hitler was to describe his life in Vienna as one of hardship, misery, hunger, and poverty," but that "this was notably economical with the truth as regards the months spent in Stumpergasse in 1908."[11] Kershaw, with his inevitable candidness, would add that Hitler's description was "accurate enough" for the dark autumn and winter of 1909, but Kershaw does not tie together the whole Vienna experience by going on to characterize the final period 1910–1913. The biographer leaves us with a fractured picture of Hitler as a prevaricator or at least as being economical with the truth, a truth teller, and then tires of further analysis. It is worthwhile to note that during the months Hitler spent allegedly living so well in the *Stumpergasse* that the following picture existed: As concerns the potential for misery, hardship, and hunger, Hitler shared a single room with two windows having views facing a sooty brick wall, without electricity or running water, lit by a kerosene lamp. The room was so crowded that his roommate, Kubizek, noted that the space between the grand piano and the beds was roughly one foot, as was the case for the spacing between the two beds and among the table, two chairs, wash stand, wardrobe, and chest of drawers. In a fascinating commentary on Hitler, Kubizek noted that he could not exist without pacing space. Accordingly, they worked hard to provide three paces of movement for Hitler from the closed door to one side of the piano.

Hitler's room had no stove, hot plate, or even microwave, and the only warm food for him during this period of his life would be that provided by meal tickets for the canteen at the university where Kubizek was an extramural student. Hitler lived during these months largely on milk, bread, butter, and occasional "cakes," all eaten in the room. We can only imagine where drinking water came from and the distance to and the floor on which the toilet was located. Hitler would remark in anger when occasionally the circumstances got the better of him: "Isn't this a dog's life?"[12] This exclamation was appropriate because the bed clothes, mattresses, and furniture were also infested with lice. Yet, in their ubiquitous disparagement, the biographers generalize that Hitler lived under comfortable circumstances during the year 1908 in Vienna, which did not support his allegedly exaggerated claim to posterity of suffering. The conditions outlined above, however, qualify as a touch of hardship and hunger and a bit of misery sometimes associated with the life of a canine.

In this modest detail illustrating the relationship between Hitler and his biographers, however, we come upon a personal detail that gives insight into his character. Kubizek presents casually the extraordinary behavior for an eighteen-year-old of absolutely *requiring* room to pace. A female neighbor living below the Hitlers three years earlier noted the same behavior for the fifteen-year-old, as did others.[13] Pacing is a phenomenon associated with mature people under pressure and used as a thought gathering process; it is well-known but relatively rare. For a young Hitler to have affected pacing supports a view of an extraordinarily thoughtful adolescent wrestling with self-imposed projects—the great architectural and musical projects described by Kubizek.[14] And no less a literary light than Thomas Mann, wrestling over the phenomenon of an older Hitler in the mid-1930s, would remark "if genius is madness tempered with discretion, this…plotter of revenge is a genius,"[15] echoing the pacing, reserved, imaginative planner of fantasy architectural projects in Vienna.

*   *   *

The great biographers focus on the Vienna period as the one in which Hitler became an antisocialist and anti-Semite. They agonize over the derivation of his extraordinary nationalism and associate it with variously emphasized combinations of the usual suspects: in Vienna, Karl Lueger, Georg Ritter von Schoenerer, Georg Lanz von Liebenfels (Adolf Lanz), and accompanying Hitler from Linz, Professor Leonard Poetsch and Richard Wagner. Every biographer, however, throws up his or her arms in frustration over the depth of "hatred" that Hitler brought to bear against the Marxists and the Jews, and none has developed a believable interpretation of its unparalleled depth. The biographers address the same general questions in the following form: What did Hitler depart with from Vienna in 1913 in addition to his single threadbare suitcase as he headed for political greatness? The biographers agree that the foundation for a radical German national movement accompanied him, although only the latest, Kershaw, most accurately portrays the role of blind chance after World War I in ushering Hitler into politics. Notwithstanding this latter, artfully presented insight, the world remains without an adequate explanation for Hitler's violence, and the reason is probably that the wrong question has been asked. The question is not what Hitler left with from Vienna in 1913, but what he brought from Linz in 1908.

Kershaw brings into focus the lack of comprehension of Hitler in a casually penned sentence to the effect that Kubizek's recollections, for all their flaws, paint a portrait of the young Hitler whose character traits are recognizable with hindsight in the later party leader and dictator.[16] The statement, innocent enough at first glance, is a masterpiece of understatement, ignores evidence of Hitler's character traits and style of action, and contradicts the disparaging interpretation of him by all biographers. The comment, by suggesting—perhaps with an eye to scholarly moderation—that the young Hitler's character traits were recognizable in the later party leader, understates the importance of the younger years so much that it misses understanding of the subject of the biography. Kubizek's firsthand observations show that the late adolescent of 1908 was already the Hitler of 1919–1939. What is important for comprehending Hitler is not the how and when but the awe-inspiring intensity of his anti-Semitism; the not-human intensity in Hitler's character was in place before his arrival in Vienna.

Hitler's earnestness and private brooding followed by energetic action can be seen in projects described by Kubizek but ignored by biographers as curious trivia illustrating Hitler's flights from reality. The biographers handle the concept of a mobile Reichs orchestra and the planning for it in 1908, for example, as an object of derision or almost not at all. Kershaw mentions such a project only once in his two thousand pages, referring to it as a "traveling orchestra" and dismisses it contemptuously under the heading of "other utopian schemes."[17] But we see Hitler at age nineteen with artistic imagination, unbounded sense of proportion, and deadly earnestness. The same Hitler with the same attributes at age thirty would levy them on projects equally utopian in the sense of practical impossibility. But the biographers do not qualify his actions from late 1919 through 1941 as "utopian." Is it possible that the young Hitler, who had become set in ways characterized as "adrift" and "divorced from reality" from 1905 through 1908 suddenly became a different person? In his 1925 memoir, Hitler claimed that he made the conscious decision earlier in 1919 to enter a miniscule political party that had not yet ossified into an organization and to use it to save Germany.[18] If ever a man set himself a utopian task, it was Hitler assigning himself the mission to reconstitute a Reich. He intended to begin this utopian task as the seventh member of the executive committee of a political "party" with approximately fifty-five members in a country with a population of sixty-five million.

It is important to know what nationalist baggage Hitler would carry with him as he edged into the German Workers' Party over a period of several weeks in the autumn of 1919. The great biographers accurately portray the Vienna period as the one during which Hitler received the world outlook for Nazism. Hitler himself wrote that "Vienna was and remained for me the hardest, though most thorough, school of my life," and he characterized the period as dominated by study and struggle.[19] He also used the themes of study and struggle to characterize the entire period from 1904 through 1914, and through his eyes the period could be seen as one of deadly earnest study. Hitler wrote about this retrospectively in 1924 and 1925. He has been criticized accordingly by the biographers for embellishing, exaggerating, and giving the impression that he consciously maneuvered toward his entry into politics.

Hitler cannot be said to have maneuvered through this period of his life toward so specific a goal and does not actually claim as much. When he made it clear, for example, that his world outlook was put together in Vienna, he did not claim that he had begun to look at that time for an opportunity to save the Germans. In speaking retrospectively in 1924, he seems to say, rather, that when the entire scene is put together from childhood through that year, the granite foundations of the movement turned out to have been laid in Vienna—the most thorough school of his life. This is more than surmise, however, because we can state unequivocally that the chance circumstance of the German loss of World War I sensitized Hitler to the possibilities of going into politics, and this chance event must be added to his political awakening in Vienna. We now arrive at a great mystery of Hitler's odyssey into politics: the utterly chance circumstances of his first attendance, in September 1919, at a "meeting" of the German Workers' Party. After surviving behind enemy lines in the Munich Red uprisings of April and May, he was requested to comment on the presence of suspected Reds in his regiment, came to the attention of an officer putting together a counterintelligence unit, proved effective as a troop anti-Red indoctrination speaker, and was directed by that officer, Captain Karl Mayr, to observe a recently revealed tiny political group called the German Workers' Party.

Hitler's unparaphrased words present the reality of the experience. "This absurd little organization with its few members seemed to me to possess the one advantage that it had not frozen into an 'organization,' but left the individual an opportunity for real personal activity.... Here it was still possible to work.... Here the content, the goal, and the road could still be determined, which in the existing great parties was impossible from the outset."[20] We see Hitler with an idea of such originality and finality that it could be announced by him alone and disseminated, not through any conventional political party, but only by a single genius and his disciples. Hitler would elaborate "that through just such a little movement the rise of the nation could some day be organized, but never through the political parliamentary parties ... for it was a new philosophy and not a new election slogan that had to be proclaimed."[21] We sense that Hitler wrestled with the challenge of really doing something about Germany's misfortune and that the challenge was not whether to join the German Workers' Party but whether to commit himself to something from which there could be no return: "I knew that for me a decision would be for good, with no turning back."[22]

In the face of these words, Kershaw, in a work that can be considered to contain the distilled essence of the entire conventional wisdom on Hitler, maintains derisively that Hitler's account "was devised, like everything else, to serve the Fuehrer legend that was already being cultivated."[23] Kershaw elaborates that Hitler in the German Workers' Party could become a full-time political agitator and notes the theme of Hitler existing only as propagandist: "He could do for a living the only thing he was good at doing: speaking."[24] Although we are dealing with a historical figure as important as Hitler, we are told that he was good, but one-sidedly so, at only one thing. We know that he successfully seized political power in Germany, and logic demands that Hitler achieved it on the basis of his talents as a speaker. We can generalize therefore, although somewhat lamely, that

Hitler was a good speaker to mass audiences. The conventional wisdom allows us to make this generalization, but we are left with the uncomfortable feeling that we have just made the understatement of the century. The confident assertion that Hitler was devising a Fuehrer legend falters in the face of the impressions of a real Nazi like Rudolf Hess, who could comment to party critics as early as summer 1921: "Are you truly blind to the fact that this man is the leader personality who alone is able to carry through the struggle?"[25] Hess was stating bald fact and scarcely "devising" a Fuehrer legend. Thousands and, ultimately, several millions by 1933 would see Hitler as the leader personality described spontaneously by Hess in 1921; and those Germans during the intervening period cannot be claimed to have been bedazzled by a devised Fuehrer legend. After 1934 and the Nazi consolidation of power, the propaganda ministry and thousands of Nazi functionaries at various levels would contribute to the picture conveyed by the word *Fuehrer*. The propaganda ministry in particular would shower glowing praise on Hitler after 1933, but it is difficult to believe that he took some of the more exaggerated plaudits seriously except to be embarrassed by them.

As concerns the devising of a Fuehrer legend, Kershaw shows a furious will to denigrate Hitler; and his condemnations, reproaches, and abuses are legion for the 1920s: "He was above all a consummate actor."[26] "The firm handshake and 'manly' eye to eye contact which Hitler cultivated on occasions when he had to meet ordinary party members...was merely acting; it meant no more than the reinforcement of the personality cult...in reality Hitler showed remarkably little human interest in his followers."[27] But above all, Kershaw presents a hint of factually and therefore apparent objectivity: "The playacting and hypocrisy did not mean that he was solely a cynical manipulator, that he did not believe in the central tenets of his 'worldviews.'"[28] And the alternation between Hitler as empty hypocritical urge to power and Hitler as brilliant true believer beats incessantly on the reader.

Kershaw writes that, in the mid-1920s, "little or nothing had changed. Hitler was at ease only when dominating the conversation. His monologues were a cover for his half-baked knowledge. There was no doubting that he had a quick mind and a biting and destructive wit... and the combination of a domineering presence, resort to factual detail (often distorted), for which he had an exceptional memory, and utter conviction (brooking no alternative argument) based on ideological certitude was impressive... but those with knowledge and critical distance could often quickly see behind his crude arguments."[29] Kershaw personifies the conventional wisdom and seems to present an effective, reasonably balanced picture of Hitler as an intelligent ideologue, though badly educated, and a canny, shallow manipulator of those around him. Kershaw, however, is a master of depreciatory hints: Hitler's firm handshake and manly eye-to-eye contact is not only denigrated as hypocrisy but also suggested as distasteful because he had to associate with ordinary party members. We see Hitler as a petty, unprincipled tyrant aspiring to be a greater one.

Hitler's own words and those of his followers are a better guide to what he and his followers thought he was and, perhaps, who he actually was. Joseph Paul Goebbels, Hitler's educated, articulate convert of 1925 and bold, ultra-aggressive leader of the Nazi Berlin district beginning late in 1926, was effusive in praise. This extolling of Hitler is well-known, but no biographer has commented on the revealing metaphors: "Who is this man? Half plebian, half God! Actually Christ, or only John?"[30] And Goebbels would continue: "Such a sparkling mind can be my leader. I bow to the greater one, the political genius."[31] He could also note: "Adolf Hitler, I love you because you are both great and simple.... What one calls a genius."[32] And in a peculiarly mixed metaphor, Goebbels would announce to all who might someday discover his diary: "This man has everything to be a king... the born tribune of the people."[33] Others such as Dietrich Eckart, Rudolf Hess, Kurt Ludecke, Konrad Heiden, and Ernst Hanfstaengl would use similarly colored words in expressing their impressions of Hitler: messianic complex, savior, prophet, leader personality, enigma, Lohengrin, manitou—every one of which suggests that Hitler was not engaged in politics.

Hitler was a study in the rejection of the conventional rules of the game in German domestic politics. Virtually every German politician of Hitler's day viewed politics as ministerial positions, pluralities in the Reichstag and provincial legislatures, party programs, and in the case of a select few, a Germany restored to the international respectability suggested by the relaxation of the strictures of the Versailles treaty. The Communist Party, the other significant revolutionary party in Germany besides the NSDAP, stood hobbled by its internationalist subservience to the Soviet Communist Party and doctrinally bound by stiff, orthodox revolutionary thinking. In contrast, Hitler aimed to make new Germans an almost impossible challenge in human psychology and remove both from conventional politics and from what might be termed "conventional revolution." But no biographer has taken Hitler's brilliance in mass psychology, and the attracting of millions by 1933 into National Socialism, and linked it with his intent to convert each one of that mass of "supporters" into a new German. It was one thing to attract men to support of a political party and quite another to create new Germans. It is a monument to Hitler's characteristic breathtaking sweep that he conceptualized not only seizing political power in Germany largely by means of the spoken word but then also welding together all Germans into a single community dedicated to its resurrection from death in 1918. Although this outlandishly optimistic goal on Hitler's part can easily and naturally be described in terms of the seizure of political power, it can be *understood* only in terms of an apolitical savior.

The following words by Hitler at the inception of the movement are laden with apolitical pathos: "The hardest thing in this first period, when often only six, seven, or eight heads met together... was to arouse and preserve in this tiny circle faith in the mighty future of the movement. Consider that six or seven men, all nameless poor devils had joined together to succeed—where the powerful great mass parties had failed—in restoring a German Reich of greater power and glory."[34] Hitler graciously presented a picture of a handful of men totally divorced from political reality with what must be understood as an apolitical hope for the resurrection of German political influence. Hitler was gracious in his presentation because it cannot be claimed that any one of these "six or seven... all nameless poor devils," with one notable exception, had a practical expectation of the resurrection of Germany. Hitler was the notable exception and as such, the one man in the Germanic world who believed that he could convert the broad masses through the spoken word to a "*German state of the German nation*."[35] This was not politics: "Some idea of genius arises in the brain of a man who feels called upon to transmit his knowledge to the rest of humanity. He preaches his view and gradually wins a circle of adherents."[36] In such a case, a human organization must be brought into existence to transmit such an idea; according to Hitler, unparaphrased, "the best organization is... that which inserts the smallest intermediary apparatus between the leadership of a movement and its individual adherents ... the function of organization is the transmission of a definite idea—which always first arises from the brain of an individual—to a larger body of men and the supervision of its realization."[37]

It is difficult to escape the conclusion that Hitler saw Nazism as his idea of the salvation of the Germans and that the idea was unique in its comprehensiveness and finality. With a mixture of the mystical and the concrete, he would place himself in the opening scene of the grand political opera of the twentieth century: "The greatest revolutionary changes and achievements of this earth, its greatest cultural achievements, the immortal deeds in the field of statesmanship, etc., are forever inseparably bound up with a name and are represented by it."[38] In this expression of the central role of the great personality in history, Hitler obliquely but ever-so-directly demanded the presence in National Socialism of the single indispensable name. With the clearly enunciated purpose to make new Germans and to save them, Hitler can be seen clearly through a historical viewing glass as the unique, complete messiah of modern times.

This characterization that unlocks understanding of the man should not be so surprising, though, because both genetics and environment lead us to a modern savior disguised as the "leader personality" of Hess and the latter-day manufactured "Fuehrer legend" of Kershaw. In the adolescent Hitler, we have seen the overpowering intensity, seriousness, and earnestness. In the young man we have seen the ubiquitously observed correctness and politeness, and as described in an overgeneralization by a superior officer in World War I, a gravity not associated with Austrians. And in his thirties, Hitler revealed determination that was fearsome and unbending on a plane beyond the reality of others: "We must not ask if it is possible to attain this goal, but whether it is necessary. If it is impossible, we will try it anyway and be destroyed. But if it is necessary and true, we must believe that it is possible just the same. And we need this faith. A thousand years look down on us, the future demands sacrifices."[39] The words cannot be attributed to a man who was in the process of manufacturing a legend of the leader. To attempt to create a legend is to admit the absence of it. Legendary figures make themselves; they cannot and need not be created by others. Can we imagine that Alexander the Great required a body of ancient public relations men to create a legend around him? It must be acknowledged, on the other hand, that once Hitler was "in power," the propaganda apparatus of the state would extol the leader. But he would stand or fall on the aura of his vision and the substance of his achievement.

* * *

The chance projection of Hitler into counterintelligence and propaganda speaking can be seen to have intervened in his life in the period May through September 1919, and as noted by Kershaw, more than "any dramatic decision to rescue Germany from the 'November criminals,' was...to open up the path into the maelstrom of right-wing politics in Munich."[40] It can scarcely be doubted, however, that once Hitler was in politics he would be driven above everything else by a sense of mission to save the Germans from the November Criminals and several additional historical entities. At this crucial moment for the world—the entry of Hitler into politics—the biographers become bound up in the immediate details of his entry into politics and the following time through the Putsch in 1923.

Something continues to elude us, and that something becomes even more remote when the biographers characterize Hitler as a human exercise in power seeking. We are asked to believe that a drifting mediocrity consumed by lust for power entered politics in Munich in September 1919 and actually made a success of it! Yet the same biographers who characterize Hitler as noted above continue to be taken aback by him as they inform us that "in a manner difficult to describe he always stood above his banal and dull witted aspects: and that a particular source of his strength lay in his ability to build castles in the air with intrepid and acute rationality."[41] There seem to be multiple Hitlers in this interpretive landscape, and we are searching for the actual one of 1919. We need proceed no further in a Hitler biography unless we can capture the one Hitler who walked through the entrance of the Leiber Room of the former *Sterneckerbraeue* in Munich in 1919, because that Hitler was the same man who was carried out of the underground command center and into the garden of the *Reichskanzlei* a quarter of a century later. If we fail to comprehend the one who entered the beer hall in 1919, we can scarcely claim to comprehend the one who departed the bunker bereft of life in 1945.

In holding up Hitler's numerous projects from ages sixteen through nineteen for denigration as utopian, instead of heroically styled and pursued with devastating intensity, the biographers fail to show us the man who, from ages twenty through twenty-nine, set the foundation of the movement and performed so functionally in the hell of the western front. The biographers hover about the actual Hitler, making brilliantly perceptive generalizations. But, in literally every case, those perceptive insights are used to further the same tired picture of Hitler. The biographers, for example, connect Wagner and Hitler as kindred spirits: "Both Wagner and Hitler… possessed a furious will to power,"[42] both possessed a sense of being set apart from the rest of ordinary humanity by the Romantic concept of genius, and both reveled in the vision of a heroic German struggle for greatness. The biographers then proceed to represent Wagner as composing some of his music with reliance on mass effects to cover up basic weaknesses, and they quote from a distinguished detractor who called him a barber and a charlatan.[43] The two latest great biographers, John Toland and Ian Kershaw, compare Hitler with Wagner but dash the insight by belittling the musical genius of both and associating the former with the alleged frailties of the latter.

Often on the verge of giving us real insight into Hitler, the biographers fail to link their profound near-insights with an obvious, natural, and credible picture. The vast, Hitler-inspired Nazi rallies that characterized the Third Reich are noted as inconceivable without Wagner's influence through his alleged demagogical opera.[44] The biographers thereby accurately present a relationship between Wagner and Hitler, but because they are dedicated in advance to the proposition of wickedness for the latter, they characterize Wagner's art as demagogical and Hitler's politics as those of demagoguery—grand demagoguery—and hate-filled vituperation. And in a realistic perception of Hitler expressed as his theatrical, essentially nonpolitical relationship with the world, the best the biographers can do is to describe it as oppressed anxiety and belittle it as resulting in an overblown emphasis on the heroic staging of political events but little attention being paid to politics. These things continue to point to Hitler as never having been in politics but as having been involved in something else.

Hitler's explosions of oratory seem to have characterized him as much as his remarkable facility in architectural drawing and pursued him through his entry into Captain Mayr's counterintelligence speaking detachment in August 1919. During his stay in the men's home on the *Meldemannstrasse* in Vienna, various acquaintances commented on his polite manners and aloofness punctuated by outbursts of oratorical fury when aroused by strong emotions about some issue of the day being discussed by those around him. And during his service in a Bavarian reserve infantry regiment for the four years of World War I, his comrades commented consistently on his polite, reserved manner punctuated by outbursts of patriotic oratory in reaction to the grousing of those around him. Such evidence supports a view that Hitler possessed inherent predilections in grand speaking—one man speaking, all others listening—by age fifteen, and these predilections accompanied him into his army speaking course at age twenty-nine in Munich. Although the audiences would be larger in late 1919 and large indeed in the 1930s, Hitler, when stirred emotionally, must be seen as an instinctive orator. Kubizek characterized Hitler as holding forth in conversation in a manner of almost always delivering speeches to him and, on notable occasions, Kubizek's father and mother.

Kubizek gives us extraordinary insight to Hitler's qualities and style in the personal oratory that he affected around him. Kubizek came to realize that the friendship endured largely for the reason that he was a good listener and Hitler had a compulsive necessity to release his tempestuous feelings over the apparently unmemorable things that aroused his interests. Kubizek could note, for example, that "he used to give me long lectures about things that did not interest me at all... the excise duty levied at the Danube bridge or a collection in the streets for a charity lottery."[45] And as a personal witness to the events, he gives us insights into the Hitler of the *Sterneckerbraeu* noting that "these speeches... seemed like a volcano erupting. It was as though something quite apart from him was bursting out of him. Such rapture I had only witnessed so far in the theater, when an actor had to express some violent emotions."[46] Here we see intensity and seriousness in a sixteen-year-old that is difficult to fathom, and we see it combined with special fluency in the spoken word. Long before Hitler made his well-known and oft-quoted comments in *Mein Kampf* that in late 1919 he discovered he could speak, he had impressed others with impassioned oratory. For purposes of getting Hitler on stage in 1919 for his run to unparalleled historical notoriety, we can generalize that an astonishingly intense and impassioned younger Hitler had already been in place as early as 1906 and could have been characterized as, among other things, a gifted orator.

Notwithstanding the admonition of the great biographers that Hitler could be personified as craving power, we cannot claim credibly that such a picture fits either the young Hitler or the older one who took the most decisive resolve of his life in late September 1919 to enter the German Workers' Party. There is a touch of the absurd to suggest that the young Hitler was driven by some kind of lust for power in his relations with the world around him. He certainly developed a close and possessive relationship with his best friend of the period, Kubizek, who played the role of patient and attentive listener. But his friend makes it clear that the relationship was based on a similar passionate interest in art as well as Hitler's need to share his innumerable, artistically inspired projects and vision through Wagner's opera *Rienzi*. Other imaginatively and artistically inclined youngsters have undoubtedly displayed similar adolescent interests, but Kubizek remarked that, for Hitler, his seemingly imaginary perfections would be brought into existence. We simply do not see urge to power in the young Hitler of the late Vienna period and Munich and World War I. This does not mean that Hitler, in defiance of his consuming penchant for limitless, ideal, and final solutions to his projects in the formative stages of his life, would not evolve into something else, but it is unlikely.

The Hitler of 1909–1914 was one of reserved, explosive intensity and earnestness—to the young Hitler, everything was important and to be taken seriously.[47] The Hitler who strayed through Vienna after Kubizek's departure in August 1908 added the experience of a self imposed fight for social survival and fascination with the disintegration of the Austro-Hungarian Empire. He would enter World War I as the most intense personality of the twentieth century, with immense latent talents, but ineffectually drifting as an academically uneducated painter of capable landscapes and city views. We see little or no urge to power—to control those around him—and much that supports a view of culture through his freely rendered painted scenes near the various fronts, sketches and poetic contributions to the regimental news sheet, visits to museums and art galleries during his leave periods, omnivorous reading of anything available, and brooding thoughtfulness about the progress of the war. And for a high-strung young man, Hitler would display a psychological stability that defied the pressures of the most intense combat of World War I, especially in the western trenches in 1916 and 1917. He would portray his struggle for psychological equilibrium in words largely ignored by the biographers but vital for comprehending him. He noted without exaggeration or embellishment that "the enthusiasm gradually cooled and the exuberant joy was stifled by mortal fear. The time came when every man had to struggle between the instinct of self-preservation and the admonitions of duty.... Always when Death was on the hunt, a vague something tried to revolt, strove to represent itself as reason, yet it was only cowardice."[48] Hitler struggled for psychological survival for a year until the winter of 1915–1916, after which he would become master of the horror and "Fate could bring on the ultimate tests" without his nerves shattering or his reason failing.[49] This is not the picture of either a cipher or an emerging power-hungry demagogue.

*   *   *

With scarcely a ripple, this willful personality projected itself onto the German political battleground of late 1919. Having been impelled by historical circumstance and genetic predisposition to deliver a message of salvation, Hitler delivered such a message to various Germans in the period from 1919 through 1933. The message has been obscured for half a century by the circumstance of being interpreted as political propaganda. Hitler intended, naturally, that his speeches be effective political invective, but the vastness of the picture—always in grand historical perspective and always with an outsized enemy—made the "political" propaganda something more like nonnegotiable sermon. Hitler's musing in *Mein Kampf* confirms his dedication to the spoken word to influence mankind, and he did not write the work so much as dictate it to a few of his converts. The work is a speech about the granite foundation of his thought, scarcely intended for reading but rather meant for listening. Hitler's writing style in *Mein Kampf* has been criticized *ad nauseum* as turgid and rambling. Because, however, Hitler spoke out of the pages rather than wrote prose on them, the disparaging generalizations about turgid prose are non sequiturs. Hitler conceptualized that the great movements of mankind had been created and guided by the spoken word, and, for example, we do not take the measure of a Muhammad, Jesus the Christ, and Gautama Buddha as writers but rather as inspired messengers and convincing speakers. Hitler similarly was a messenger rather than a writer or a political propagandist. But how could Hitler perform such a balancing act between the moral regeneration that he envisioned and the suffocating rules of the game associated with mass parliamentary politics?

In his disguise as a politician, Hitler walked a fine line between practicing conventional politics on the one hand and presenting the sound and fury of an extreme revolutionary movement on the other. He faced this quandary from the beginning of his unannounced arrival out of the desert and succeeded in walking this line with consummate dexterity. Hitler's dexterity can be illustrated by the party's success in getting votes in the national Reichstag election of May 4, 1924. The election was the first national one in which the party entered National Socialist lists of candidates and took place after the disastrous revolutionary events of November 8–11, 1923, in which the Nazis were defeated in their attempted takeover of the Bavarian government and probable march on Berlin. At a time in which the party leadership had been dispersed and Hitler injured, tried, and placed in fortress detention, the Nazis and their *voelkisch* allies garnered almost two million votes and placed thirty-two deputies in the Reichstag.[50] Hitler had contributed to this astonishing result by his earlier speeches to large audiences in the beer cellars and meeting halls of Munich.

* * *

If we were to generalize about what Hitler was doing in this period, we would have to say that he was speaking incessantly and deploying force in the meeting halls and streets of Munich. This generalization is not particularly original, but its elaboration in an attempt to comprehend Hitler is useful. In the case of the notorious violence associated with the Nazis, he would elaborate that even in the beginning, the meeting hall protection squad "had been trained to carry out an attack blindly [i.e., without question] but not because . . . it honored the blackjack as the highest spirit, but because it understood that the greatest spirit can be eliminated when its bearer is struck down with a blackjack."[51] He noted specifically that his political combat element "did not want to set up violence as a goal, but to protect the prophets of the spiritual goal from being shoved aside by violence."[52]

In the few words above, Hitler pulled together the Nazi movement as one driven to achieve a spiritual goal announced by a prophet and which required violence to shield its messengers. The word *prophet* recurs repeatedly in *Mein Kampf* and there can be little doubt that Hitler considered himself to be *the* prophet of the movement. He would, during the early twenties, be referred to as a drummer by various observers, and in his memoir he refers to himself as one. If the word *drummer* were a metaphor for messenger of a spiritual idea, then we can see Hitler comprehended by himself and contemporaries as a prophet, or at least one who spoke prophetically rather than politically. If the word *drummer* can be comprehended more specifically as one who anticipated the arrival of a more senior prophet, messiah, or savior dedicated to the redemption of a people, then we can also see Hitler as a drummer who incidentally announced himself. The revisionist point is that Hitler cannot be considered to have understood himself as ever having been in politics. It cannot be doubted that to redeem the Germans in a modern state, he was forced to use politics as a means to the end of redemption. While all others around him practiced politics with constrained goals and the usual motives of profession, personal interest, or the like, Hitler marched toward the salvation of a great people. As such, he was understood by few, worshipped by his adherents, and feared by his opponents.

Hitler would construct the following picture of the genesis of National Socialism: "Some idea of genius arises in the brain of a man who feels called upon to transmit his knowledge to the rest of humanity. He preaches his view and gradually wins a circle of adherents. This process of the direct and personal transmittance of a man's ideas to the rest of his fellow men is the most ideal and natural."[53] Here we see no hint of practical politics or political theory. And with uncompromising logic, Hitler would continue that the ideal movement was one in which the leader—the single genius who received the vision—would spread the message to potential converts face to face by means of the spoken word. Hermann Otto Hoyer's painting of Hitler pictured at the beginning of the movement is not entitled *In the Beginning There Was the Political–Scientific Journal Article* but, unerringly, *In the Beginning Was the Word.*[54] We see Hitler in a dingy, dimly lit, windowless tavern standing on an improvised platform speaking to Germans. In an almost uncanny way, the painting brings into focus National Socialism at its inception: Hitler at a meeting speaking directly to potential adherents without the intermediary of an organization and protected in the painting by the stalwart, gray windbreaker-clad follower deployed close by. It is perhaps not too much to suggest that Hitler conceptualized the entire Nazi movement as he himself, adequately protected, preaching to Germans. If this generalization were accurate and it was evident to Hitler that he could not personally deliver the message to a growing mass of Germans, then he must be considered to have seen an organization as a necessary evil. Hitler evidently agreed with this analysis because he could remark that "the function of an organization is the transmission of a definite idea—which always first arises from the brain of an individual—to a larger body of men and the supervision of its realization. Hence, organization is in all things only a necessary evil."[55]

* * *

In his 1925 memoir, Hitler would describe the progress of the early German Workers' Party almost exclusively in terms of the numbers of Germans attending the meetings at which the apolitical idea of salvation had begun to be broadcast. He did not describe the idea as one derived from some faceless organization but an idea which had sprung from the mind of "an individual."[56] Writers on National Socialism, biographers of Hitler, and historians agree that the movement was derived uniquely from Hitler. Witness Hitler's own description in numerical detail of the beginning stages of the Movement. "I still remember how I myself in this first period once distributed about eighty [invitations] and how in the evening we sat waiting for the masses who were expected to appear. An hour later … we were again the seven men, the old seven."[57] Attendance: zero. Then, "we changed over to having the invitation slips … mimeographed…. The result at the next meeting was a few more listeners. Thus the number rose slowly from eleven to thirteen, finally to seventeen, to twenty-three to thirty-four listeners."[58] From the viewpoint of Hitler characterized as messenger, it is significant to point out that he used the word *listener* for the Germans who would attend the meetings and not attendees, observers, or invitees. Emboldened by the presence of thirty-four listeners, Hitler convinced the committee to advertise in a Munich newspaper a meeting to be held in the Munich *Hofbraeuhauskeller* "in a little room with a capacity of barely one hundred and thirty people but which seemed as a mighty edifice."[59] Success followed, for as the meeting opened at seven o'clock in the evening, "one hundred and eleven people were present."[60] National Socialism at that moment could be seen as Adolf Hitler speaking convincingly to 111 Germans.

After the success of the Munich *Hofbraeuhauskeller*, he pressed later in October 1919 for a second, larger meeting, which was held at the *Eberlbraeukeller* before an audience of 130. And two weeks later he spoke again, in the same hall, to an audience of 170. He pressed for a larger hall, which was found in the other end of town; partly for that reason, he spoke before a smaller audience of 140. The other committee members predicted doom because of excessive repetition of the "demonstrations." In the following words, Hitler would recount that "there were violent arguments in which I upheld the view that a city of seven hundred thousand inhabitants could stand not one meeting every two weeks, but ten every week...that the road we had taken was the right one, and that sooner or later, with steady perseverance, success was bound to come." The apparent lack of sense of proportion—namely, "ten every week"—and the boundless determination—namely, "sooner or later...success was bound to come"—was vintage Hitler.[61]

In 1919 and 1920 the Nazi movement would begin to embrace a rough edge of street fighters illustrated by the sparkling humor of the later *Sturmabteilung* (SA) street donation collectors of the early 1930s and their signs: *contributions, please, for the wicked Nazis.* Hostile contemporaries would superficially criticize the Nazis for their worship of the blackjack, but Hitler would make it clear in his usual apolitical sweep that "if any man wants to put into effect a bold idea whose realization seems useful in the interests of his fellow men, he will first of all have to seek supporters who are ready to fight for his intentions."[62] Hitler could scarcely have made it more clear that politics for him was conversion of Germans to an idea, and he sought followers who would be both willing and able to fight for it: "swift as greyhounds, tough as leather, hard as Krupp steel."[63] The theme of intolerantly fanatical fighters would be reinforced by his messianic-cast words that "the greatness of every mighty organization embodying an idea in this world lies in the religious fanaticism and intolerance with which, fanatically convinced of its own right, it intolerantly imposes its will against all others."[64] The words above were dictated in 1924. They carry no hint of politics.

Hitler would also conceptualize the movement as requiring a geographical focal center: "Only the presence of such a place, exerting the magic spell of a Mecca or a Rome, can in the long run give the movement a force which is based on inner unity and the recognition of a summit representing this unity."[65] With historical perspective and little regard for practical details, he would express the need for a sacrosanct geographic focus, and in choosing Mecca as an example, he expressed himself more as a holy man than a demagogue. Munich would be the focal center.

After having dipped momentarily as a speaker to 140 souls listening in the cross-town meeting in the Deutsches Reich on *Dachauerstrasse*, Hitler noted his fierce struggle with the executive committee to spread the word. The next meeting insisted upon by him, however, showed him to be right. The attendance would rise to "over two hundred." He urged preparations for another meeting and commented that "the audience rose to over two hundred and seventy heads." Then, two weeks later, toward the end of 1919, "for the seventh time, we called together the supporters and friends of the new movement and the same hall could barely hold the people who had grown to over four hundred."[66] Hitler presented the spirit of the new movement as follows: "A man who knows a thing, who is aware of a given danger, and sees the possibility of a remedy with his own eyes, has the duty and obligation by God, not to work 'silently,' but to stand up before the whole public against the evil and for its cure."[67] Hitler would use the words to reject German antiquity enthusiasts and knights of the spiritual sword, the latter being wielders of the pen in the attempt to achieve nationalist ends. Hitler would also understand the power of the German press and the "scribblers" in it to influence public opinion. He would nevertheless enforce the *Schwerpunkt* (major effort) for National Socialism in the following words: "Every last agitator who possesses the courage to stand on a tavern table among his adversaries, to defend his opinion with manly forthrightness, does more than a thousand [silent antiquity enthusiasts and knights of the spiritual sword]."

After the success of the four hundred listeners at the Deutsches Reich but after violent argument and withdrawal of Karl Harrer as first chairman of the party, Hitler forced "the first great mass meeting" after fewer than five months on the committee which would be a party. The great affair was set for February 24, 1920; based on the mild noise generated by the party, it had become noticed by the great Marxist parties, the Communist and Social Democratic. Hitler therefore had to take account of the reality for conducting politics in terms of mass meetings that the Marxists would attempt to break them up. Still living in his regimental army barracks in Munich, Hitler would put together a band of his former army comrades to defend the speaker from hecklers and those who would begin a meeting-terminating brawl. In an unrealistic appreciation of the toughness and brutality of the Marxists in a fragile postwar German republic, the Liberal press and intellectuals would harp on the theme of the brutality and violence of the Nazis. Writers would use words such as barbarous, savage, and violent to denigrate the developing movement and claim that Hitler and the Nazis embraced violence as an end in itself.

As the self-announced destroyer of Marxism in Germany, however, Hitler would point out in colorful detail that the masses could only be won back to Germany by countervailing force. Under written attack by opposing nationalist intellectuals and believers in spiritual resistance to the Marxists, he could note "the fact that in a public meeting a Demosthenes can be brought to silence if only fifty idiots, supported by their voices and their fists, refuse to let him speak."[68] Liberal intellectuals such as Thomas Mann would later castigate Hitler and the Nazis for their rejection of tolerant humanism, assuming apparently that such humanism could successfully combat the Marxists. Hitler, however, was dedicated to advancing against them head-on with the spoken word from tabletops in beer halls; and he was prepared to defend his own meetings and break up those of his enemies. When he entered the *Festsaal* of the *Hofbraeuhaus* at quarter after seven on the evening of February 24, 1920, for the first mass meeting, he observed almost two thousand people shoulder-to-shoulder, roughly half of whom appeared to be enemy Communists and Independent Socialists resolved to break it up. The resulting meeting would be easy to characterize as the essence of the Nazi style in "politics" for the entire period of the interrupted and circuitous march to power. Hitler would speak, listeners would be overwhelmed by his passion and logic, and Marxist agitators countered by force.

Hitler would reveal his métier in this situation especially in the early 1920s. The urbane, artistic, outgoing Hanfstaengl could elaborate based on the overwhelming effects of his initial exposure to Hitler's genius as a speechmaker and, within the spirit of the moment,

> he had to be reasonably careful about what he said in case the police should arrest him again as a disturber of the peace. Perhaps this is what gave such a brilliant quality to [the first speech I attended] which for innuendo and irony I have never heard matched, even by him. No one who judges his capacity as a speaker from the performances of his later years can have any true insight into his gifts.... In his early years he had a command of voice, phrase, and effect which have never been equaled.[69]

And as concerns the defensive aspects of Nazi politics in the early 1920s and early 1930s, Hanfstaengl could note that in the middle of applause toward the finale of the speech that a middle-aged man with a dark mustache would hand up to Hitler a mug of beer for a draft. Hanfstaengl looked at his bodyguard and saw that after taking the mug back "his right hand returned to the bulging pocket of his coat. From the way in which he kept his hand there, his eyes fixed on the front row, [Hanfstaengl] knew he was holding a revolver."[70] And Hitler himself was commonly armed during the period 1920–1923 with an automatic pistol positioned under his clothing on the hip and a sturdy whip heavily weighted in the handle. Kurt Ludecke, an intelligent, well-educated follower during the period could observe that "he was never without an automatic pistol which made his hip bulge as though with some deformity."[71] When not speaking at organized meetings he spent much time at various favorite cafes and beer halls and often the homes of converts to the movement and would be accompanied by a small, faithful protective element—Christian Weber, Max Amann, Hans Ulrich Klintzsch, and Ulrich Graf—well-armed and representative of the style and dangers of the movement. And Hitler could not have made the messianic nature of the whole business more clear than in words about his house guards that "like a swarm of hornets they swooped down on the disturbers of our meetings...without regard for wounds and bloody victims, filled entirely with one great thought of creating a free path for the holy mission of our movement."[72]

*   *   *

Hitler had a particular skill in sarcasm, depreciatory hints, and humor in his speechmaking, which carried over into his style of talking rather than writing in *Mein Kampf.* His sarcastic criticism of the bourgeois opposition on the matter of the mass political meeting illustrated his own energetic conception of propaganda. Concerning Hitler's characteristic urge to action, Hanfstaengl could note that it was typical of Hitler "that you could never keep him off the streets."[73] Hitler would comment that in 1919–1921, he personally attended bourgeois meetings. He noted that "they always made the same impression on me as in my youth the prescribed spoonful of cod-liver oil. You've got to take it, and it's supposed to be very good, but it tastes terrible." And in a minor sarcastic triumph, he would continue that "if the German people were tied together with cords and pulled forcibly into these bourgeois '*demonstrations*,' and the doors were locked until the end of the performance and no one allowed to leave, it might lead to success in a few centuries."[74] He could bring into perspective the divorce from reality of the parliamentary parties about the near extinction of Germany in words that "the whole thing was without any discipline, more like a yawning bridge club than a meeting of the people which had just been through their greatest revolution."[75]

Hitler feared the extinction of Germany as a state and the Germans as a people as a result of the moral erosion of Marxism and Liberal democracy. Hitler theorized that the misfortune of the Germans was not from the usual suspect of the loss of World War I.[76] He would argue that "the easiest and hence most widespread explanation of the present misfortune is that it was brought about [as a consequence] of the lost War and therefore the War is the cause of the present evil."[77] He would refute this explanation by noting that the military collapse of Germany was not the cause of Germany's "present day misfortune" but itself only an effect of other crimes. Hitler's idea of genius was recognition of the cause of the existing catastrophe as the earlier erosion of the German community by parliamentary democracy, Marxism, and particularism—the fundamental destructors of a German community. He would link these enemies with the great social force of the time, which was the expansion of the population and its redistribution from the countryside to the geometrically expanding cities. He would observe that the reality of the time was the mass conversion of the German rural population into workers in the burgeoning cities and their further conversion into internationalist Marxist socialists.[78] He would also observe that the bourgeois parliamentarians pursued party interests to the virtual exclusion of German and that, with no overarching philosophy they could not provide German leadership.

He would approach the whole business in a hopelessly idealistic manner, noting that "while the program of a solely political party is a formula for a [successful] outcome of the next election, the program of a philosophy is the formulation of a declaration of war against the existing order."[79] He could be seen as presenting a revealed message to Germans to awake in contrast to an Allied wartime propaganda ministry presenting crudely falsified and exaggerated arguments directed against a wartime enemy. But Hitler's revealed message was subject to identical rules of mass effect and crowd psychology as, for example, British wartime propaganda, so how can we differentiate between Hitler's revealed message and what we understand as political propaganda?

In the way in which we commonly understand propaganda today and the way in which wartime propaganda emerged during World War I, we cannot say that he was either a propagandist or a demagogue. Whereas Lloyd George's conventional although brilliant wartime propaganda was intended to support British munitions production, Hitler preached a new philosophy. Hitler used the spoken word with principles of mass psychology to attract men willing to fight with their fists for an idea of genius. Lloyd George was oriented to the practical result of assuring British munitions production while Hitler was oriented to the creation of a new man. If ever there were a strategy of the indirect approach, we must see it here with Hitler attracting and creating the men who would help him spread "a clearly delineated faith."[80]

Hitler would contrast the tame meetings of the bourgeois parties with Nazi gatherings and comment that "no one begged the audience graciously to permit our speech, nor was anyone granted unlimited time for discussion; it was simply stated that we were masters of the meeting... and that one who would dare to utter so much as a single cry of interruption would be mercilessly thrown out."[81] And such was not just bombast from a desk inside the walls of Landsberg Fortress. Hitler had begun personally at the beginning of the mass meetings to organize a "house guard in the form of a monitor service,"[82] which would evolve into a uniformed instrument of force conceptualized by Hitler as indispensable to achieve power through domination of meeting hall, street, and countryside in Germany. Here we see more than the charismatic leader so skillfully synthesized by the political scientist Franz Neumann. We see Hitler pull together a picture of nobility shielded by force, dictating "that we are fighting for a mighty idea, so great and noble that it well deserves to be guarded and protected with the last drop of blood. [The monitors] were imbued with the doctrine that, so long as reason was silent and violence had the last word...our monitor troop must be preceded by the reputation of not being a debating club, but a combat group determined to go to any length."[83] These words reveal Hitler being Hitler and cannot be paraphrased without becoming ineffectual.

In a peculiarly detached fashion, Hitler would give us reasons for the radicality of his early propaganda:

> As director of the party's propaganda I took much pains, not only to prepare the soil for the future greatness of the movement, but [also] by an extremely radical conception [of] this work I also strove to bring it about that the party should only obtain the best material. For the more radical and inflammatory my propaganda was, the more this frightened weaklings and hesitant characters, and prevented them from penetrating the primary core of our organization.[84]

With imaginative slants on propaganda such as these, Hitler cannot be characterized as either an ordinary or an extraordinary rabble-rouser but as a man with a sense of mission. Somehow or other in concepts such as these, Hitler stood aside from mere demagoguery. And to interpret Hitler as a kind of super demagogue is to trivialize what happened in Germany and not remotely comprehend him.

*   *   *

As concerns the violence associated with the movement, however, the conventional wisdom has taken misleading liberties in presenting violent events and the motives for them. In the epic battle during the mass meeting in the *Hofbraeuhaus* in November 1921, the Social Democratic Party in Munich had planned in advance to break up such a nationalist gathering and through the timing and effect, destroy the young Nazi movement. In his urge to emphasize the use of force by Hitler, no great biographer makes the point in this great battle of the early Nazis that the relatively mild Social Democrats had determined to break up this mass meeting. The Social Democratic Party was the strongest in the Weimar Republic and dedicated more than any other to support of the republic and law and order. This party, nevertheless, would direct several hundred fighters into the meeting and signal the start of a riot with the roar of the Social Democratic slogan, *freiheit* (freedom). Yet with wanton recklessness in interpretation, Joachim Fest would state as if it were a natural and unassailable fact that Hitler caused the riot. Within the context of the use of force by the Nazis and Hitler's comment that "the masses need something to dread," the biographer would note that "Hitler may have had this principle in mind when he instigated the so-called Battle in the Hofbraeuhaus of November, 1921."[85]

Hitler may have had many things in mind with the opening of this meeting, but it must be evident that he had been caught off guard with a small storm detachment of about forty-six "lads" and faced mortal danger to his person and severe setback to the entire movement in the event of the breaking up of the meeting. Hitler actually spoke from a beer table "in the midst of the people" and in front of him and "especially to the left...only enemies were sitting and standing." Under such circumstances Hitler cannot be seen as anxious to incite anything, and he commented that "after about an hour and a half—I was able to talk that long despite interruptions—it seemed almost as if I was going to be master of the situation."[86] Then a small psychological mistake he made in warding off an interruption gave the signal for the Social Democrats to make an end to him and his people. Pandemonium followed—roaring, screaming crowd over which beer mugs flew like howitzer shells, cracking of chair legs, and so on—and Hitler noted that he remained standing on the table in the midst of it. Frau Magdalena Schweyer, proprietress of a vegetable and fruit shop near Hitler's tiny room on *Thierschstrasse*, corroborated the scene, noting that from her safer position on the floor she glanced up curiously "to see Hitler still standing atop a table despite the barrage of heavy mugs flying past his head."[87]

This successful defense of the mass meeting of November can be used as empirical evidence to comprehend Hitler and to gauge the effectiveness of his biographers. First of all, Hitler and the Nazis had to defend themselves against numerous tough and determined Social Democrats—let alone tougher and more determined Communists illustrating the violence associated with the Left in Germany in the 1920s. We could rhapsodize, perhaps, that Weimar Germany was a tough place for conducting nationalist politics but that at least in Munich, in late 1921, a new sheriff was in town. If the early Nazis were under intimidating physical attack by Social Democrats in Munich, we must reevaluate upward the challenges presented to Hitler and the expanding movement later in population centers like Essen in the Ruhr, Leipzig in Saxony, Hamburg and finally the great urban center of Berlin. And as concerns Hitler himself, he cannot be interpreted adequately as politician. Can we feel comfortable accepting that any practicing politician would have addressed the monitor group assigned to keep order at a political meeting in the following words? "I made it clear to the lads...that not a man of us must leave the hall unless [he] were carried out dead; I myself would remain in the hall, and I did not believe that a single one of them would desert me."[88] In spite of this kind of evidence of Hitler and the Nazis on the defensive, one great biographer would state that Hitler incited the riot that followed. If anybody in the world were capable of inciting a riot in Munich of the 1920s it would have been Hitler, but apparently the inanity of Hitler inciting a riot at his own mass meeting did not occur to the biographer while the urge to portray a wicked man slipped through his critical faculty.

Chapter 4

SETBACK, PERSEVERANCE, AND INFALLIBILITY
1923–1929

On September 14, 1921, just prior to the defense of the *Festsaal* and a year later in 1922, Hitler took actions that probably help to interpret the man and the movement more than any others during the 1920s. The biographers register the events dutifully and dully as important for any descriptive rendering of Hitler and use the second event to disparage Hitler and the Nazis rather than comprehend them. The biographers describe that Hitler "had turned the original organization from discussion to action"[1] but fail to acknowledge that we see force directed toward the achievement of a distant prophetic vision. To use Hitler's own astonishing words: "force always must have ideas to support it." In late 1921, Hitler sensed momentary but immense danger to his vision of a German community from Bavarian separatism as concentrated in the party *Bayernbund* (Bavarian League) led by the engineer Otto Ballerstedt. We see little political theory operating and little attention to party program. We see much of the leader, a polar starlike consistency in his actions, and we see street fighting, meeting breaking, violence-prone disciples. Hitler had recognized Ballerstedt momentarily "as my most dangerous opponent,"[2] and decided to prevent Ballerstedt from speaking at his own mass meeting. In a well-organized attack, Hitler and his lieutenant Hermann Esser and an accompanying retinue would sweep into an opponent's meeting already packed with scores of Nazi Sport Section fighters and demand "the floor." In the ensuing riot, Hitler's fighters flooded across the speaker's stage, and, amongst other things, beat Ballerstedt. Although the wheels of justice ground slowly, Hitler would go on trial for disturbing the peace and be convicted and sentenced on January 12, 1922, to three months in prison. He would eventually serve four weeks in Munich's Stadelheim Prison, being released on July 27, 1922, on remission of the sentence, the first of only two times he would be imprisoned in his turbulent existence. But why such effort and sacrifice over a man, Ballerstedt, who was neither Jewish, nor Marxist, nor bourgeois November Criminal?

The answer to the question brings Hitler into focus nicely. Interpreting him as an intuitive, rapidly maturing German messiah, we can see that he could not permit a Ballerstedt and other Ballerstedts to fragment the Germans into the older tribes or more modern Bavarians, Saxons, Pomeranians, Silesians, Alsatians, Prussians, and the like. Although touting himself as the destroyer of Marxism in Germany, Hitler would squarely face a more immediate enemy in the form of virulent anti-Prussianism in Bavaria. Hitler instinctively sensed the danger and noted that after Bismarck's achievement of unifying by force and statesmanship, a large part of the German nation, the various tribes were at work attempting to break it up. Recognizing an enemy and with staggering disregard for practical, realistic, and legal action, Hitler would personally lead a physical attack on an opponent's mass meeting in order to prevent him from speaking. And what an insight in support of his style as messiah that he could remark doggedly, with no regrets, during the police inquiry that "it's all right.... We got what we wanted. Ballerstedt did not speak."[3] Hitler did not remark that he got what he wanted by breaking up the printing presses of an opponent's newspaper but by preventing his opponent from speaking. And as concerns the almost outlandish use of force, we see Hitler conceptualizing, organizing, and leading a physical attack on a political adversary. Could we imagine any contemporary high-level political figure during his rise to political influence, for example, a Wilson, Clemenceau, and Lloyd

George or a Churchill, Briand, and Roosevelt to have functioned similarly? And with what might seem to be exceptions in the cases of Lenin, Stalin, Trotsky, and Mussolini, we see the Russian Marxist socialists tied to their printing presses and Mussolini as the editor of the leading Marxist socialist newspaper in prewar Italy. Hitler can be comprehended in microcosm—a single characteristic action—as possessed by a vision that could only be brought into existence by conscious intention of spoken word and force.

Approximately a year later, in October 1922, Hitler concocted an action that proved to be the turning point in the early expansion of the Nationalsozialistische Deutsche Arbeiterpartei (NSDAP or National Socialist German Workers' Party) out of Munich. During the same month, Julius Streicher, leader of the Nuremberg branch of the *Deutsche Werkgemeinschaft* (German Labor Community), would bring his following into the NSDAP as a center for the expansion of Nazism into the Franconian region of Germany in the northern part of Bavaria. But in the case of Coburg, a medium-sized city on the northern fringes of Bavaria dominated by Marxists, Hitler would execute his first foray outside of Munich into enemy political terrain, terrain dominated by Reds who were accustomed to mastery over meetings and street demonstrations of the area. As a single coherent action compressed into a two-day period, it had no peer in the entire period 1919–1933 for daring, audacity, insolence, and success.

To comprehend Hitler by analysis of this single action, we can begin by pointing out that he alone—with neither committee nor gray eminence nor mistress advising him—conceptualized the action. To comprehend the action as an insolent junket by a petty tyrant who controlled a small, localized, radical political party also misses the mark. No petty political tyrant, even one who aspired to be a mammoth one, would have considered an action so daring and audacious. Not only did he lead a raid on a target 160 miles distant, but he also did so for the expressed purpose of proving that nationalists could hold mass meetings and demonstrations anywhere in Germany in the face of the pervasive "Red terror." Obviously, breaking the control of the Marxists in Coburg would not ensure success in Germany, and the point is that Hitler could be seen as having begun to create an all-German vision. Hitler would generalize that "the experience of Coburg had the significance that we now began systematically, in all places where for many years the Red terror had prevented any meeting of people with different ideas, to break this terror."[4] He issued these words in the context of the use of force and the necessity for a political street-fighting organization to ensure the spread of the spoken word. "From now on, National Socialist battalions were assembled again and again in such localities, and in Bavaria gradually one Red citadel after another fell a victim to National Socialist propaganda."[5]

In leading this foray, Hitler, who was always able to stand apart from his banal personal aspects, seems to stand apart from the biographers' approbation as a study in tyranny. It is always possible, of course, that he must be reevaluated as something else. Franz Neumann, the perceptive contemporary analyst of National Socialism, would suggest the importance of charismatic rule in the understanding of Nazism and Hitler.[6] Neumann, however, would contend that the Nazi movement was caused by the "imperialism of German monopoly capitalism," and even his suggestion of the importance of charismatic rule seems to fall short of the mark. Hitler eventually achieved authoritarian political control over Germany, but to call him a despot and a study in tyranny with the implication that he and a clique achieved absolute control over a great gray bound mass of Germans is unsatisfying. Biographer Alan Bullock's impressive title, *Hitler: A Study in Tyranny* should probably have been: *Hitler: A Study in Popular Tyranny*, or, given Hitler's mass popularity and almost unique sense of a great and final message, *Hitler: A Study in Messianic Tyranny*. The reader thus would have been alerted to the fact that he was not being treated to an ordinary, pejoratively cast tyrant who exercised power with a rigor not authorized by law or justice, but to a different phenomenon.

The existing situation by as early as 1922 and its parallel with a "movement" like Islam and a prophet like Muhammad is striking. As concerns law, messiahs, and the comprehension of Hitler, the vast structure of civil and criminal law that comprises Arabic jurisprudence derives from the Koran—the compilation of the divine messages that, according to Islamic belief, were dictated to Muhammad at irregular intervals by the archangel Gabriel as the word of God—and the tradition of the Prophet's sayings and acts known as the Hadith. There exists in the world therefore the presence of a vast code of law based on the spoken word of a man who relayed the will of God as His messenger. With a German who was identified by a contemporary of considerable intellect as having a "messianic complex," by 1922 and who launched eight hundred unquestioning street fighters into combat with the Reds in Coburg during the same year, we seem to have something more than merely a study in tyranny as demanded by unsympathetic and outraged biographers.

With Hitler interpreted as a modern messiah, it is little surprise that his word would be taken as law by many within the movement, and similar words and actions later were taken as law in Germany. In a future yet to come, Hitler in the culminating public explanation for the purge of the leadership of an expanded and turbulent SA would orate that, "If anyone reproaches me and asks why I did not resort to the regular courts of justice . . . then all I can say to him is this: in this hour I was responsible for the fate of the German people, and thereby I became the supreme Justiciar of the German people."[7] There was certainly a considerable difference between the pervasiveness of German jurisprudence in twentieth-century Germany and the tribal-based law of the 600s in Arabia, but in both cases we see the spoken word and actions of two enormously charismatic historical figures becoming the law itself. In the case of the German, the biographers see negatively cast despotism—no enlightened tyranny here—while the chroniclers of Muhammad see the messenger of God. While each preached the message of a holy mission, one is seen as having had a messianic complex, and the other is seen as the Islamic Prophet. Yet to attribute to a perfect messiah—a child and a man so earnest, so intense, so brooding, and so utterly convincing as

Adolf Hitler, the milder attributes of a messianic complex is rather like attributing a Napoleonic complex to Napoleon.

*   *   *

In January 1923, not long after the Coburg affair, the French government determined to employ armed force to bend the Germans to the will of France. The resulting French-dominated military occupation of the Ruhr district could not be understood accurately as forcing the Germans into a simple overdue payment of a large reparation of telephone poles but to force the Germans to acknowledge defeat and answer to the consequences. Prime Minister Raymond Poincaré, patriotic, vindictive, and tough, was the architect of the action that exemplified French hegemony on the European continent and was the single most important political action of the period from the signing of the Versailles treaty to the ascension of Hitler to the chancellorship of Germany in 1933. In his efforts to force the Germans to pay reparations, Poincaré destroyed German finances and destabilized the Weimar Republic to the point of mortal danger from Communist, nationalist, and separatist uprisings. The Germans experienced an inflation so extreme that even to imagine it could be likened to trying to comprehend the immensity of the universe. Hitler faced the beginning of this situation when the French invasion broke out on January 11, 1923, and he was forced to take action to exploit the republic's destabilization.

The great biographers, however, fail to relate Hitler effectively with the bad times of 1923 fastened on Germany partly by its own recalcitrance in paying excessive reparation but largely by France, "still full of hatred and suspicion of her neighbor." We see Germany traumatized in 1923 but not within the context of French initiative in bringing about the trauma. We do not see the disastrous situation correlated with the outbreak of war in the next decade. The French government would retrieve Poincaré in 1922 to save the franc and to collect reparations from the Germans. Poincaré would save France's currency from its well-developed inflation but with reckless disregard for long-term consequences, he would employ armed force to collect reparation. As a French statesman executing French foreign policy, Poincaré disregarded the fact of German power that, although presently subdued, would inexorably revive. Similarly, he disregarded the surety that the German government and people would be presented with motive for revenge. From such a perspective, Poincaré's Ruhr invasion can be interpreted as the most important political action of the 1920s, leading directly to war in the 1930s.

The French invasion inspired an immediate wave of national unity, and by March 1923, with draconian French measures against German demonstrations and sabotage, Germany experienced a sense of common purpose in resistance to the French similar to that in August 1914. The German chancellor, Wilhelm Cuno, instituted a policy of passive resistance and organized a front of national unity that included the Marxist, bourgeois, and nationalist parties. Virtually all of Germany lined up in support of the republican government against the foreign enemy. In this moment of national euphoria, Hitler would reveal his style, logic, and faith probably more than in any other action, particularly because we see him in the delicate beginning stages of his march to infamy. He would remove the NSDAP from the national front and forbid his astounded followers to engage in passive resistance against the French. Yet Hitler would view this confounding action as so plain that he would use the words with respect to those astounded that "If they haven't caught on that this idiocy about a common front is fatal for us, they're beyond help."[8] These words have a special spontaneity. They reveal Hitler willing to take an apparently inexplicable stand against the wave of patriotic enthusiasm in Germany, but to what purpose and based on what rationale?

With the biographers dedicated to an interpretation of Hitler as a shallow, wicked man dedicated to power aggrandizement, they are forced to see one of the critical decisions of his career as unscrupulous. Yet Hitler, in *Mein Kampf,* presented with excruciating clarity the reasons why his movement must not have entered the national front, and these reasons cannot be seen as those of either a dema-gogue or a propagandist. He would describe unconditionally that the real enemy of Germany was not the French but the internal Marxist enemy that had been the cause of German defeat. In vintage Hitler expression: "What we are compelled to experience around us and in us today is only the horrible, maddening, and infuriating influence of the perjuring deed of November 9, 1918." The deed of November 9 was the Social Democratic Party's declaration of a German republic while the field armies were still engaged in combat. Hitler perceived the Marxists to be the destroyers of the German Second Reich through the conversion of the growing millions of German workers to internationalism, and doing so in the face of the ineffectual poli-cies of the bourgeois political parties. This generalization, pompous as it may seem, is nonetheless accurate and reveals Hitler as neither demagogue nor propagandist but as a messenger of German salva-tion through the destruction of the Marxists. In March 1923, and with consistent logic, Hitler had ordered therefore the NSDAP not to support the policy of passive resistance against the French.

Hitler saw his stand as one of the crucial decisions of his life. The decision should provide a key for the comprehension of the man, but the biographers generalize weakly that "his particular per-spective and his sense of tactics told him that he could not line up with the others."[9] To suggest that as a shallow, tactically driven opportunist he could not allow his movement to be submerged in a government front of bourgeois Liberals, Marxists, and nationalists drifts away from comprehension of Hitler. Based on his worldview, he had determined probably by the turn of 1920 that a "basic reck-oning with Marxism" and believed that "such a reckoning of real world-historical import" required its annihilation.[10] In 1923 such a vision was vast, impractical, and apolitical. It was vast because Marxism in the 1920s was perceived as the inexorably successful political and social force in the "White world" and would soon be perceived similarly in the Yellow world (China) and Brown world (Indonesia), and Hitler was dedicated to taking it head-on. It was impractical because the bourgeoisie of the West had proven ineffectual in combating it, thus leaving Hitler alone to conceptualize and execute a successful attack. It was apolitical because Marxism, in a perversely mixed metaphor, had come to be approached as a new religion, and Hitler never varied from his inspired holy mission to save the Germans. With the finality of a messenger of fate, Hitler would declare that "regardless of what kind of resistance [to the French] was decided on, the first requirement was always the elimination of the Marxist poison from our national body."[11]

Hitler would note that the bourgeois republican cabinet of the turn of 1923, led by a nonpartisan businessman as chancellor, had the opportunity to crush the Marxists in the patriotic furor over the French invasion. Hitler would analyze with humor, scorn, and logic Cuno's policy of passive resistance through general strike in the Ruhr: "In this great hour Heaven sent the German people a great man, Herr von [sic] Cuno.... A curse for Germany because this businessman in politics regarded politics as an economic enterprise."[12] Hitler argued that Cuno believed the general strike would prevent the French from getting Ruhr coal and therefore force them to consider the invasion unprofitable and evacuate. With unerring logic, Hitler would dictate that "for a strike, of course, the Marxists were needed, for it was primarily the workers who would strike," and the result would be the recovery and strengthening of the Communists who would bolt the national front at first opportunity.[13] In fact, the Communist Party would increase in Reichstag votes from 589,500 in June 1920 to 3,693,300 in May 1924 in the aftermath of the Ruhr invasion and would launch massive, dangerous, armed uprisings that severely taxed the small treaty army and the *Freikorps* to subdue them in the Ruhr, Hamburg, and Saxony. He would summarize that Cuno's national front and passive resistance amounted to paying the Communists to conduct a strike that would destroy the German economy: "An immortal idea, to save the nation by buying a general strike" from the internationalists dedicated to the destruction of the German nation.[14]

In presenting the events of 1923, the biographers would come dangerously close to a more advanced and satisfying interpretation of Hitler. One could note, for example, that the Bavarian *Reichsheer* commander, *Generalleutnant* Otto von Lossow, "had been rather put off by Hitler's eccentric manner" in a pivotal audience with him at the beginning of the extended crisis of 1923.[15] The word *eccentric* fits Hitler well, suggests strangeness and irregularity in his personality, and indicates that Lossow detected something beyond politician and demagogue. Konrad Heiden, who often showed unmatched insight into Hitler, would comment on the earlier Vienna period that "it is safe to visualize the young Hitler of those days [1910–1913] going about like an eccentric and unkempt saint."[16] And he would continue the theme into the Munich period of 1913–1914 with the characterization of Hitler as "An eccentric... a hermit among six hundred thousand people; without wife, friend, family, or home."[17] By 1923 we can see Hitler as a resplendent eccentric with a voice, an affection for oratory, and a vision.

Heiden, as a perceptive contemporary, would describe Hitler as personally colorless to the point of invisibility and, in an indelible metaphor, suggest that the void had disguised itself as a man. In presenting Hitler as lamentable personally, Heiden was leading up to shock effect as an author because he would abruptly proclaim that "in this unlikely looking creature there dwelt a miracle. It was something unexpected.... His voice was the very epitome of power, firmness, command, and will. Even when calm, it was a guttural thunder, when agitated, it howled like a siren betokening inexorable danger. It was the roar of inanimate nature, yet accompanied by flexible human overtones of friendliness, rage, or scorn." All of the following great biographers would expatiate on Hitler's pitiable appearance and alleged human emptiness, but Heiden would pull together the banality with more zest, strength, and comprehension than all the others: "long reaches of his soul are insignificant, colored by no noteworthy qualities of intellect or will; but there are corners supercharged with strength."[18] And Heiden would place Hitler in historical context probably more realistically than any biographer with the words that "as a human figure, lamentable; as a political mind, one of the most tremendous phenomena of...world history—this is a contradiction which occurs in every man of genius, from the stuttering Moses to Bonaparte, the strange unglamorous artillery captain; but few of these historical figures united so many contradictions, such lack of distinction, and such super-human strength."[19]

*   *   *

Historians of the period and the great biographers take the position that there is no single explanation for Hitler and suggest further that we may never have one, whether simple or complex. The position is surprising because every great biographer and notable historian to the present has taken the position that Hitler was evil and dedicated to villainy, a homogeneous rendering of a man supposedly so difficult to explain. The conventional wisdom may be flawed, but it is not overly complex. The biographers and historians introduce complexity by agonizing over the causes of the Nazi revolution and the forces that produced the man who created it. It is natural, therefore, for the wisdom to maintain that there is no single or simple explanation for Hitler because of the interwoven political, social, and economic conditions ranged about him and the necessity to take account of them. We must acknowledge, for example, that the remorseless French enforcement of the Versailles treaty more than any other single factor represented the condition necessary for Hitler to maintain his radical appeal and support his rise to power. But only Adolf Hitler could have achieved the astounding success of 1919–1933. Hitler was unique, indispensable, and irreplaceable.

We are therefore less interested in the historical causes of Hitler than we are in the personality of the man, and by 1923 that personality should have been in place. Writers have presented an unattractive picture of Hitler from the beginning with descriptors such as duplicity, lying, hysteria, urge to power, contempt for the masses, pathology, and so on. These descriptors apply—although in varying degrees and as affected by historical context. In the case of power, for example, writers suggest a manic urge in Hitler to dominate all others, and Professor Ian Kershaw even extends this urge, only half-facetiously, to include his dogs. None points out that Hitler had a hyper-radical vision of a future Germany known only to him in its proportionless breadth, and since it was based on personal inspiration would hardly allow for committee debate and democratic whim of the rank and file. The conventional wisdom suggests a tyrant with a psychopathic urge to power, although we can equally sense a tribune of the people and savior of a nation. There is little balance in the existing consensus, but it has been imbued in the mind of the public, and how is it possible to establish something more realistic and illuminating?

We have the words of some remarkably articulate followers. Kurt Ludecke experienced submission to Hitler's will and its apparently political embodiment in the Nazi movement after two speeches in one day in August 1922. In the first, on a bright summer afternoon out of doors in the *Koenigsplatz* in Munich before "well over a hundred thousand" in a mixed patriotic and Nazi audience, he could comment that Hitler's "appeal to German manhood was like a call to arms, the gospel he preached a sacred truth. He seemed another Luther. I forgot everything but the man; then glancing around, I saw that his magnetism was holding these thousands as one."[20] Less well-known, Hitler spoke again that evening, indoors, in a tour de force of energy, worship of the spoken word, and a kind of holy zeal. In the *Zirkus Krone*, which was jammed to capacity with Hitler's followers, Ludecke would note that "again his power was inescapable, gripping and swaying me as it did every one [of the six thousand] within those walls."[21] The purview of politics is vast, but these effects cannot be understood in terms of propaganda and politics as carried on by a psychopathic politician.

The articulate follower could comment that he and Hitler were together a good deal and that "out of a thousand trifling incidents" he could begin to piece together the puzzling fragments of Hitler's character.[22] He had observed that early in the movement Hitler had been surrounded by associates who were, for the most part, simple souls from modest homes who knew little of the world beyond their own towns. They "were sincere, enthusiastic, loyal, looking upon Hitler as not only a genius but [also] an inspired prophet.... Night after night he sat in their homes or in the simpler cafes of Munich expounding his doctrines.... They hung on every word.... They were his circle of disciples ready to do and die for him."[23] Similar to the picture presented by the mass meetings, this one does not seem to add up to an otherwise empty propaganda adept who was practicing politics. Yet the great biographers, all of whom are accomplished historians, have buried this Hitler and certainly not come to praise him. Ludecke would not relent, however, and continued on to describe that "thousands trembled when he spoke and yet—he was simply one of them. This in itself seemed miraculous and contributed to their unreserved acceptance of him as a savior, a new Luther, a man embodying all their hopes for Germany and themselves."[24] Ludecke presented words to characterize Hitler that group themselves comfortably: genius, inspired prophet, disciples ready to do and die, a new Luther, savior, thousands trembled when he spoke. During the same period of time, the great biographers see power and "progressive megalomania" in a man who impressed his followers in words such as those above.[25]

Ludecke wrote his memoir in 1935 concerning his earlier association with Hitler, and it is probable that it would have had a different cast if written after the horrors of World War II played out. Ludecke, however, gives us a view of Hitler less encumbered by strained antipathy and more nearly as he actually was in 1922–1936, in contrast to any sketch by later writers. The latter have stood weighted by a double burden of their moral outrage over the onset, outbreak, and selected horrors of World War II and their view of the period 1914–1945 as that of the two German wars. As concerns the latter, however, it is difficult to escape a feeling that in the event of a

German victory in World War II the verdict of history would have been a period characterized as that of the two French wars.

In any event, Ludecke would continue with other trifling insights involving, for example, Hitler's saintlike yet relaxed presence with the early converts. He could remember how touched he was with the interrelationship between Hitler and the goldsmith Gahr, one of his devoted followers, a modest, quiet, dignified craftsman with whom Hitler had entrusted the execution of his design for a new standard. As the two discussed the pattern, "every word, every gesture, however reserved showed the admiration and faith that he offered the leader."[26] On yet another day, Ludecke observed Hitler in a visit with Oskar Koerner, a little merchant who had given much to the party and who would give his life on November 9, 1923. As contrasted with Gahr, "Koerner's temperament was vivacious, quick, and eager, rather than reserved; but like Gahr ... he showed that he had accepted Hitler as both a brother and leader."[27] Ludecke observed that Hitler seemed at home with both types of men. "These were the people for whose sake he meant to rescue Germany."[28] And one great biographer would comment that he was able to use phrases to his public of almost biblical ring by 1922 and add that, after the uprising of November 1923, "he had come back from [fortress detention in] Landsberg with a certain messianic aura."[29]

Probably the best authority for Hitler and propaganda is Hitler himself, and here the water runs deep. Dismissed by the great biographers as brilliantly fluent but shallow in propaganda, Hitler is made to appear brutal in nature and simplistic in his thought processes. Hitler would commit acts of brutality paralleled by only a few in the twentieth century, but to characterize thereby his propaganda as dominated by a kind of atavistic simplicity dangerously misses the mark. Hitler, with disarming objectivity, presented the Marxists and the British as the paragons of propaganda early in the twentieth century and used the Marxists in particular to illustrate the importance of propaganda for any mass movement. With breathtaking simplicity, he would take the measure of Marxism as boring but abstractly correct written law joined fortuitously by an organization of agitators who would successfully spread the idea by spoken word. Impressed by Marxist success in turning theory into a mass political movement, Hitler would unabashedly lift Marxist techniques of political action for execution by National Socialists. Hitler saw Marxist political action as conducted by agitators having the qualities of psychologists and with the ability to transmit an idea to "the broad masses."[30] Hitler would say that "out of the endless battle of words...the new Germany will be born."[31] His early associate and later paladin Ernst Roehm would agonize that "he had nothing in his head but his own propaganda."[32] The conventional wisdom would suggest that Hitler characteristically overestimated it.

In tagging Hitler as a one-sided political figure who relied excessively on propaganda, the conventional wisdom has underestimated Hitler, failed to pull together Nazism, and confounded us in most attempts to characterize him. In skilled and succinct analysis in the second volume of *Mein Kampf* and italicized to add insult to injury in the neglect of such passages, Hitler would describe the movement as it had blossomed between 1919 and 1923 and would reappear in the springtime of renewed opportunity from 1929 through 1933. Hitler reasoned that in the beginning of a political movement, when there were in essence no supporters, "it was less important to rack one's brains over organizational questions [of a practically nonexistent party] than to transmit the idea itself to a larger number of people. Propaganda had to run far in advance of and provide [the party] with the human material to be worked on.[33]

*   *   *

If then, by 1924, we can identify Hitler as the German messiah of the second half of the second millennium, how can we convince ourselves that such an interpretation accepts the historical facts more comfortably than the less savory explanation of the conventional wisdom? The question is, what man left Landsberg? Was he the creature of the great biographers—often unbelievable, sometimes sensitively and credibly drawn, but never quite pulled together into a satisfying inter-pretation? Or did someone else leave, heretofore skirted by the writers and only nibbled at interpretively? The great biographers remain pris-oners of their historical condition as either victors or repentant losers. Perhaps with the two great British biographers, Hitler's words come back from beyond some unknown grave to characterize the limits of their approach. If we posit that their biographies are a kind of histor-ical propaganda, his own words come to our assistance to tell us what we are facing. Hitler could note, for example, in context of the British wartime propaganda assignment of war guilt to Germany that "it was absolutely wrong [for the Germans] to discuss war guilt from the standpoint that Germany alone could not be held responsible for the outbreak of the catastrophe; it would have been correct to have put every bit of the blame on the shoulders of the enemy, even if this had not corresponded to the true facts."[34] He claimed that "English pro-pagandists" understood that the sentiment of the masses does not have multiple shadings but rather a positive and a negative; there is no halfway. Hitler analyzed that the English and their ruthless, one-sided atrocity propaganda "pilloried the German enemy as the sole guilty party for the outbreak of the war."[35]

We see the great English biographers paint Hitler in a single, nonnegotiable shade of dark. Analogues can be driven only so far, however, and even though British propagandists with malice, fore-thought, and distance from reality made the Germans entirely responsible for the outbreak of World War I, such a rendering does not mean that the later British biographers fell prey to the same qualifiers in applying dark shading to Hitler. We must suspect, nonetheless, that the Hitler projected out of Landsberg and into power and infamy by the great biographers would be uniquely damned. The damnation would be conditioned by the circumstances of the victors' exaggerated, spurious assignment of blame to the defeated Germans for the outbreak of World War I and the less spu-rious but still one-sided accounting of the onset of World War II.

*   *   *

During his serving of one year, thirty-two days, two hours, and ten minutes of his five-year sentence for treason, Hitler had time to take the measure of the failed march on Berlin and dictate the first volume of *Mein Kampf.* For whatever the reasons, he decided to become the sole, unfettered leader of National Socialism and absorb rather than cooperate with the other forty-two folkish organizations ineffectually fussing among themselves throughout Germany.[36] During his detention in Munich and Landsberg, Hitler would maintain an olympian detachment from the apparent necessity to hold together the NSDAP in particular and the folkish movement in general. The great biographers take Hitler's "lofty silence" and details such as his hastily scribbled note to the ineffectual Alfred Rosenberg assigning him the task of keeping together the party as evidence that we are dealing with a manic lust to keep the leadership of the party in his hands. The conventional view interprets his demand for unquestioned leadership of the party in the February 27, 1925, meeting to reconstitute it as evidence of a Hitler driven by power. This interpretation presents him as an aspiring tyrant although possessed of crafty instincts in maneuvering through the numberless forces operating in the politics of the fractured nationalist Right.

The conventional interpretation is not particularly satisfying because the man who would be the undisputed head of the NSDAP and the remainder of the folkish movement becomes drowned in the details of his craftiness. Hitler's towering sense of mission, which was there for the viewing by 1924 and which would be the rationale for his demand for unquestioned leadership, would be lost in the background noise. Hitler, however, would describe with passionate clarity the personality required to consummate the grand vision, and this synthesis of the savior and the saved could not be ignored by the biographers any more than it could be hidden from his contemporaries. "It was only in Landsberg, wrote Rudolf Hess, that he fully grasped the 'mighty significance' of Hitler's personality."[37] In such a situation, the biographers have been forced to become interpretive schizophrenics, to experience the disintegration of their interpretive personalities into two parts. One would represent Hitler as banality and evil and the other would be forced to acknowledge him as vision and genius—a human masterpiece of logical finality. But the psychological tug of war never ceases, and Kershaw at least could admit on the one hand that the idea he stood for was not a matter of short-term objectives. "It was a 'mission,' a 'vision' of long term future goals...but, incorporated into the notion of the 'heroic' leader they did amount to a dynamic 'worldview.'"[38] With unmatched insight, Kershaw would observe that the ideas that comprised the worldview were immutable and that the realization of those ideas "formed the essence of what he understood by power itself."[39]

But Hitler's broad visionary ideas are simultaneously ridiculed as "few and crude as they were" and "crude, simplistic, barbaric."[40] To make these adjectival admonitions, Kershaw had to presume that Hitler was practicing politics as a pitiable purveyor of half-digested political ideas. Hitler, with his unconstrained vision of Germany, cannot be considered to have been purveying political ideas. Were Hitler's Wagnerian heroes Rienzi, Lohengrin, Siegfried, and visionary parallels Jesus the Christ, Muhammad, Luther in politics? Can we criticize Muhammad as having crude and simplistic ideas when Islam can be distilled "simply" into the revelation that there is no god but God and one's life unfolds and completes itself through submission to his will? With Hitler, we are dealing with self-induced, incredibly clear revelation from a man with intensity and will unmatched by any other. In such a picture of Hitler as messiah, it becomes difficult to criticize as crude, simplistic, and barbaric his revelation of the impending destruction of the Germans. Messiahs are messengers, and their messages must be clear, simple, and more in tune with practical reality than the short-term programs of conventional politicians. Clear and simple need not translate into crude and simplistic; Christianity is rarely criticized in the latter sense and yet the central tenet is simplicity itself: believe in the messiah's message and achieve life eternal, an act of faith on the part of a believer. Hitler could scarcely have made it more clear than it was his intention to make new Germans who could be exemplified as true believers in a German community.

We cannot be surprised, therefore, that on February 27, a man readily conceptualized as a German messiah arrived at a long-anticipated meeting of ardent followers and announced his coming in terms that few could misunderstand. The price of the resurrection of his politically dead followers would be submission to the doctrine of political infallibility on the part of the leader. There was the possibility of a great *reductio ad absurdum* in all of this because, with seriousness that few could muster, he would make it clear that if not one man would follow him, he would reform the party by himself and apparently conquer Germany alone if necessary. These are not the words of a man in process of fastening a Fuehrer myth onto Germany. These are the words of a deadly earnest leader. He came out of the front as if out of the desert—haltingly at first, buffeted by chance, but unerringly through fate to proclaim his arrival in February 1925.

But since no messiah or prophet has come out of a desert for the last millennium and one-half, it is not surprising that the conventional wisdom should chalk off Hitler in Landsberg as "surrounded by sycophants and devotees, foremost among them the fawning Hess."[41] And to brand Hess as "fawning"—courting favor by cringing demeanor and implying servile flattery—does not fit Hess. "This flying, shooting, leaflet-distributing student, mathematician and later geographer embodied in his longing and his attitude the intellectual who is becoming the new ruler of our age," and cannot remotely be seen as some courtier seeking favor through becoming chief exponent of a Fuehrer myth.[42] Hess can be seen more realistically to have been the first to detect the presence of the German messiah, although the presence was obscured by the style of modern times and the messiah personified as the leader. Hess can be seen most accurately as fueling the accomplished fact of the infallible leader and not as attempting to create a myth as a crutch to support the image of one. And Hitler hardly comes off convincingly as a manufactured legend. He had an extraordinary sense of dramatic effect based on some natural instinct that had led him into the worship of the visual effects and heroic plots of Wagner's grand opera and an accompanying sense of being reserved for something special—Thomas Mann's accusation of "mental arrogance which thinks itself too good for any sensible and honorable activity, on the grounds of its vague intuition that it is reserved for something else."[43] By age fifteen, with his developing affair with Wagner's opera, his soaring architectural visions, his rejection of bourgeois form and function, and his impressionable Germanism, Hitler can be seen not so much as a fashionable, young rebel without a cause as a unique messiah waiting to happen.

The conventional wisdom sees in Hitler's trial and detention the development of egomania and megalomania and drive for exclusive personal control over the party in its rebirth. The great biographers see Hitler as afflicted by a kind of *folie de grandeur* based on an inwardly consolidated perception of himself as the leader of National Socialism after the 1924 treason trial.[44] They represent Hitler as continuing in the self-conscious, strained way of "a narcissistic egomaniac" to craft an image of himself in terms of the myth of the Fuehrer.[45] And based on such negatively inspired psychological analysis, the biographers project Hitler from 1919 through February 1925 into a resulting grab for domination in the refounding of the party. Yet Hitler presented a picture of agonizing over his course of action in entering "politics" in late 1919 and represented it as taking a path from which there could be no turning back. We see a millennial study in seriousness who claimed that, when presented with opportunity, embarked on a holy mission to save Germany.[46] Hitler would illustrate in his own person the apolitical intensity of the mission that unfolded along the one-way street to historical immortality by threatening at several junctures to end it all in three minutes with a bullet if he failed. It is difficult to imagine any con-

temporary German politician or statesman, even with the broad outlook of a Gustav Stresemann or Walter Rathenau, as suggesting that
if his programs miscarried, he would end his life with a bullet.

Hitler set out rather like a little German monk one-half millennium earlier on a long road in contrast to any conceivable aspiring
party chieftain on a more constrained career path in politics. The following words, although dictated retrospectively, represent the intense
renaissance adolescent, the failed artist bohemian, and the brooding
prince of the trenches, and seem to project the boy and the young man
out of a no-account existence into a great decision. "The longer I tried
to think it over, the more the conviction grew in me that through just
such a little movement the rise of the nation could some day be organized."[47] The most intense public figure of the twentieth century tells
us so. And what a mix of psychological colors we have! We are presented with towering, high-strung seriousness counterbalanced by
bedrock psychological stability not conventionally associated with
Hitler. No biographer has commented on the psychological balance
that Hitler required to endure combat in the forefront of the 1914
Schlieffen and the 1918 Ludendorff offensives of the German field
armies and in the defensive battering and almost inconceivable violence at the receiving end of the Allied ammunition-rich artillery
drum fire of the Somme in 1916 and 1917. The medical phenomenon
of shell shock appeared in World War I, and Hitler, who has been
described as an unstable hysteric, proved impervious to it. He seems
also to have been unaffected by the more recently discovered post-
traumatic stress disorder. The inconsequential social hermit who came
out of the dugout caves of the fire-swept desert of the western front
combined qualities of outrage, vision, mission, rhetoric, and will,
which translated into the seizure of the party in February 1925.

Hitler would muse in *Mein Kampf* in the third person singular
that he combined other qualities as well. He would suggest that the
great leader would more readily be an agitator than a theoretician
and elaborated that "an agitator who demonstrates the ability to
transmit an idea to the broad masses must always be a psychologist,

even if he were only a demagogue."[48] As the agitator without equal among the Nazis and as based on the words above, Hitler evidently considered himself to be a mass psychologist. Hitler also seems to have been familiar with the word *demagogue* and its negative connotation and evidently did not consider himself to be one. Because Hitler did not consider himself to be a demagogue does not mean that he was not one, but it suggests at least that he believed he was operating on some different and presumably higher plane.

Within the context of presenting the frailties of the written word, he would analyze that a speaker, if he were a brilliant, popular orator and suspected that the members of his audience did "not seem convinced of the soundness of his argument repeat it over and over in constantly new examples."[49] Similarly to his brilliant, popular orator, Hitler would repeat the themes of the genius, hero, prophet, and resulting revelational idea of the Nazi movement rather than any revolutionary political idea. Hitler would present himself repeatedly from a variety of directions from embodiment of the white-marble, distant vision of an ideal Germany through personification as the dark destructor of Marxism. The great biographers would see in the picture presented by Hitler in *Mein Kampf* and the attitude affected by him, particularly from February 1925 onward, unparalleled heights of egomania and megalomania. "He owns no ties outside his own ego.... He is in the privileged position of one who loves nothing and no one but himself... so he can dare all to preserve or magnify his power."[50]

Such an interpretation also supports the action that Hitler took to establish unconditional leadership of the movement in 1925, but it does so with little credible context. Stripped to its essentials, the interpretation demands that an uneducated youngster with delusions of being a great painter became psychologically embittered by rejection as an academic artist, discovered the Jews and Marxists, became filled with hate for both, linked them with Germany's misfortune, and decided to take over Munich, Bavaria, Germany, Europe, and yes, of course, the world. Whereas the most intense of all adolescents marveled at Wagnerian Nordic heroes, discovered that their Germanic world was under assault by Jewish-inspired Marxists, suffered his duty to defend that world in a devastating war, and then dedicated his miserable and outraged existence to retrieving Germany's misfortune. We are asked to believe that this was all driven by self-love and a craving for power. We are asked to imagine in this scene of Germany's misfortune that Hitler be heard to exclaim: I could not have loved Germany so much had I not loved myself more.

*   *   *

Later, in 1925, Hitler would make the decision as unconditional leader of the Nazi movement to come to power by legal means, and this original decision helps to sort out the question of who Hitler was and place him in historical context. The president of the republic, the Social Democrat Friedrich Ebert, died on February 28, 1925, and his death forced elections for a successor. In the first election in March, fateful chance intervened to give none of the five candidates a majority of the vote and to force a second election for April 26—in which a plurality would be sufficient to gain the presidency. The parties of the Right prevailed on Field Marshal Paul von Hindenburg to run for office in the second election, and his victory gave the economically recovering republic well nigh-unassailable stability. No man on the nationalist right in Germany could match the bona fides of Hindenburg as a German hero, and his patriotic presence, combined with the unreserved backing of the army, added almost magical strength in support of the republic. Perhaps the most revealing words uttered by Hitler during the Putsch were those shortly following the armed engagement at the *Odeonsplatz* when he asked who had fired on the Nazi column, the police or the army. Through almost incredibly good fortune for Hitler and the Nazis, the armed men who barred the way to the square were state police— the despicable "green mice"—and not soldiers, the untouchable symbol of the German nation. It is unlikely that Hitler and the Nazi movement could have recovered from the ignominious taint of being shot down by field gray–clad riflemen of the regular army. The integrity of Hitler's vision of a "German state of the German nation" lay in the identification of the Nazi movement with the mortar of the German nation—the army—the school of the nation and the defender of the faith.

Other notable contemporary Germans had recognized the truism that a continental state like Germany depended for its existence on the army to a degree so great that the integrity of the army was more important than support of transitory parliamentary-style governments. Hans von Seeckt, chief of army troop office in early 1920, could comment laconically when deciding to use force against insurgent, uniformed *Freikorps* forces: "Troops don't fire on troops."[51] Seeckt saw the German state, in contradistinction to any German government, as embodied in the army. From so fundamentally argued a viewpoint, the act of troops firing on troops would signal the destruction of the state itself. It would plunge the Germans into a long, dark civil war with an unfathomable but probably destructive outcome. Hitler, with his distant vision of an ideal German state, confronted a similar reality that his Nazis could never fire on German troops.

Hitler would react to this apparently hopeless situation so effectively in the long run, from 1925 through 1933, that his doctrines of infallibility and legality would eventually give him control of the German government. But given the trauma that Hitler suffered in the Putsch aftermath, it remains a monument to his irrepressibility that he succeeded. Not surprisingly, the great biographer John Toland, whose work on Hitler has no thesis and therefore suffers least from interpretive bias, gives us the most convincing account of the physical and psychological trauma suffered by Hitler in 1923 and 1924. The other great biographers, gripped by their interpretive preconceptions of Hitler as evil without redeeming quality, slant their description to fit that picture, leaving the thoughtful reader to wonder how any German could have believed in Hitler at all. Fest, for example, would generalize about Hitler's behavior in the skirmish at the *Odeonsplatz* that "the reports of his followers are contradictory only in small details: they agree that even while the situation was still fluid, he scrambled up from the pavement and took to his heels leaving behind him the dead and wounded." Hitler then took refuge in Hanfstaengl's country house about thirty-five miles from Munich "and nursed the painful sprained shoulder he had suffered in the course of the battle."[52]

The biographer does not tell us that Hitler was close to the front of the Nazi column, marching arm-in-arm with Max Erwin von Scheubner-Richter, who was hit and killed by the first police volley. The mortally wounded Scheubner-Richter collapsed, pulling Hitler down. Roughly simultaneously, Ulrich Graf, Hitler's personal bodyguard, in an act of magnificent faithfulness, threw himself in front of Hitler and was hit by at least six bullets while shielding him. We can assume that some or possibly all of the numerous bullets in Graf otherwise would have been in or through Hitler, and we would have to suggest to ourselves an alternate future for Europe. The most interest that the latest great biographer can generate from this scene is to philosophize that "had the bullet which killed Scheubner-Richter been a foot to the right history would have taken a different course."[53] Graf is not mentioned. Graf's formidable act of self-sacrifice for his leader and the presence of yet another brush with death by Hitler suggest that we are dealing with someone capable of earning loyalty unto death from disciples rather than an egomaniacal demagogue.

The comment that established Hitler as having come out of the fray with a "painful sprained shoulder" demands scrutiny also. Dr. Walter Schultze, the staff physician to the Munich *Sturmabteilung* (SA) regiment, observed Hitler getting up off the pavement after the brief twenty seconds of the firefight "apparently injured in the shoulder" and moving to the rear.[54] Schultze considered Hitler to be wounded and brought him to one of the SA automobiles (qua ambulances) located nearby. On Hitler's instructions, he attempted to return to the *Burgerbraeukeller* but their vehicle was fired on twice during the attempt and he decided to get Hitler out of Munich and treat him elsewhere. Ten miles south of the city, Hitler announced that he must have been shot in the left arm, and Schultze and the aid man in the vehicle undressed him to find that at least the left shoulder had been "severely dislocated."[55] Chance and Hitler's memory brought the group to Uffing, thirty-five miles south of Munich and Hanfstaengl's country villa where Schultze and the aid man needed two attempts to set the dislocated shoulder because of massive swelling. And to add psychological insult to the physical injury, two days later, on November 11, 1923, as state police arrest seemed imminent, Hitler would threaten suicide with a handgun described as a revolver. He was dissuaded, however, by some combination of second thoughts and the intervention of the attractive and firm lady of the house, Helene Hanfstaengl.

After his arraignment in Munich, the police delivered Hitler to Landsberg prison about forty miles west of Munich and into cell seven of the prison's fortress section. Hitler continued to be in excruciating pain, and the prison physician, Dr. Brinsteiner, discovered that he suffered not only a dislocation of the left shoulder but also a break in the upper left arm, "and as a result a very painful traumatic neurosis," or nervous collapse resulting from the extended physical exhaustion and pain.[56] Dr. Brinsteiner opined that Hitler would "most likely suffer permanently a partial rigidity and pain in the left shoulder."[57] Added to all of this, a despondent Hitler would attempt suicide by starvation during the first weeks in the fortress, and when Anton Drexler visited him, he found an emaciated Hitler "sitting like a frozen thing at the barred window of his cell." Brinsteiner warned Drexler that the prisoner would die if the fast continued.[58] We have come a long way from a Hitler with a sprained shoulder taking to his heels and, what appears to be more realistically, a severely injured Hitler being assisted rearward to a makeshift ambulance by a combat surgeon. Similarly styled denigration of

Hitler by the great biographers throughout his life accumulates and tends to deflect us from the irrepressibility of Hitler the man and his not-human determination to save the Germans. It is difficult if not impossible to imagine the sordid creature of the biographers rebounding from the trauma of November 1923.

Hans Ehard, an assistant prosecutor from Munich, arrived early in the morning on November 12, 1923, to interrogate the prisoner. At first Hitler refused to give a statement, but when Ehard dismissed the accompanying stenographer and ostensibly off-the-record asked for Hitler's views on the German situation, Hitler spoke. "On this day his supply of sentences was truly inexhaustible: not stopping to eat, never going to the bathroom, Hitler spoke from early morning until early evening," for approximately twelve hours.[59] Kubizek could recall Hitler in 1908 working "feverishly" on his Wolf Lake grand opera project and, in eerily similar words, present a picture that "when a self imposed task engrossed him completely . . . it was as though a demon had taken possession of him. Oblivious to his surroundings, he never tired, he never slept. He ate nothing, he hardly drank."[60] And in 1923, Hitler would persevere in a similar self-imposed task and apply his talents to the salvation of the Germans.

The biographers, including the great, insightful, pedestrian, and superficial, have commented on Hitler in prophetic or similarly half-mystical terms. Hitler as his own biographer demanded that the young movement "from the first day" put forward its idea spiritually and noted in his prophetic style and within the context of the battle against Marxism that "it is an eternal experience of world history that a terror represented by a philosophy of life [Marxism] can never be broken by a formal state power, but at all times can be defeated only by another new philosophy of life [National Socialism] proceeding with the same boldness and determination."[61] These words are not those of a historical figure who can be interpreted as having been manufactured into "the leader" by a latter-day propaganda ministry or his own affectation of a stern face. And although we do not see the white flowing robes *de rigueur* for the earlier great Messiah and the parched landscape background, we detect a modern savior. Both Kershaw, as Hitler's most recent great biographer, and Heiden, as an earlier articulate and a personal observer, agree on his elevated charisma. Kershaw could claim that "Hitler's entire being came to be subsumed within the role he played to perfection: the role of 'Fuehrer.'"[62] Heiden could physically observe that "the image of the great man always hovers like a model and catchword before his inner eye. He always tries to act as in his opinion the image would act."[63] But in the entire period of 1919 through the trial of 1924, we see Hitler as the embodiment of the spoken word—a fiery, passionate orator requiring no party apparatus to tout him as the premier figure of the German folkish movement.

*   *   *

The conventional wisdom has characterized Hitler as the great simplifier, and he possessed a unique facility for reducing complex historical issues to manageable proportions. He would take the measure of the entire Pan-German and Christian Social movements in Austria, for example, in an almost incredibly brief analysis that illustrated his grasp of the overall historical picture: The Pan-German movement was right in its theoretical view about having the aim of a German reawakening but unfortunate in its choice of methods to accomplish it. The Christian Social movement erred in not having the aim of a German reawakening but had intelligence, luck, and resulting success in its methods as a party.[64] And he would note that the Pan-Germans with the political program of the Christian Socialists, or the latter with the correct view of the importance of the Jewish Marxist question, "would have resulted in a movement even then in my opinion which might have successfully intervened in German destiny."[65] There is a boldness, simplicity, and finality in such analysis that does not seem to be motivated by the personal frustration and hate that the conventional wisdom has assigned to Hitler.

During the entire period, Hitler could be seen as expounding a new "philosophy of life" and developing and using the Nazi party as a means to an end of realizing a philosophy. He would note emphatically (italicized in *Mein Kampf*) that "*political parties are inclined to compromise; philosophies never. Political parties even reckon with opponents; philosophies proclaim their infallibility.*"[66] From Hitler's own words, we can comprehend his movement as infallible, uncompromising philosophy disguised as political party doctrine. And Hitler's successful seizure of the leadership of the Nazi party in 1925 can be understood in terms, also of his own words (stated obliquely in the third person): "It is not necessary that every individual fighting for this philosophy should obtain a full insight and precise knowledge of the ultimate ideas and thought processes of the leaders of the movement. What is necessary is that some few, really great ideas be made clear to him and that the essential fundamental lines be burned inextinguishably into him."[67] By early 1925, Hitler had become the originator of an infallible historical philosophy and had announced that an infallible philosophy must be led by an infallible leader.

The great biographers nevertheless interpret Hitler as tyrant and egomaniac although they note the presence of some messianic quality that seemed to surround him in the 1920s, appearing and disappearing according to circumstance. Kershaw could generalize, for example, that in the wake of the trial of early 1924, "[Hitler] began to see himself, as his followers had begun to portray him from the end of 1922 onwards, as Germany's savior."[68] With perceptive insight into Hitler and on the verge of breaking the code of explanation for the man, Kershaw would claim that "his almost mystical faith in himself as walking with destiny, with a 'mission' to rescue Germany, dates from this time."[69] Apparently, others besides Nazis cast Hitler in the light of savior-hero; for an earlier biographer, Toland could note how he was buoyed in detention by a copy of the satirical weekly *Simplissimus* which had on its front page a cartoon showing Hitler in armor entering Berlin on a white horse as if he were Sir Galahad.[70] Biographer Fest would argue that by the end of the Munich trial he "boldly came forth as the divinely appointed and only Fuehrer" and earlier had already developed "delusions of grandeur, his 'messiah' complex."[71]

Bullock, as the first of the great biographers, however, would interpret Hitler as "a study in tyranny" and would relate the quality of tyranny with Hitler's will to power and ambition. In a modest two sentences within the context of describing Hitler as a dictator, Bullock summarized the conventional view of him that predominates to the present:

> To say that Hitler was ambitious scarcely describes the intensity of the lust for power and the craving to dominate which consumed him. It was the will to power in its crudest form, not identifying itself with the triumph of a principle as with Lenin or Robespierre —for the only principle of Nazism was power and domination for its own sake.[72]

This one-sided historical verdict has a ring of propaganda about it—similar to the tone of British propaganda in World War I in which Germany was represented as exclusively responsible for the outbreak of war. Hitler as master propagandist and mass psychologist would extol the virtuosity of the British in the conduct of wartime propaganda and their conformance with the "first axiom of all propagandist activity to wit the basically subjective and one-sided attitude it must take toward every question it deals with."[73] British wartime propagandists loaded all of the blame for the outbreak of World War I on the shoulders of Germany. More recent peacetime historians have similarly heaped exclusive blame on Hitler for the outbreak of World War II, although, of course, this does not prove that the historians have been conducting propaganda. Such a situation suggests, however, that the biographers have looked upon Hitler as an enemy to be attacked and scarcely as a credible object for biography.

It is a supreme irony—a result opposite to that which was intended—that Bullock, who gave us the first great interpretation of Hitler that has remained unchallenged, should have presented unintended the most coherent picture of who Hitler thought he was.

Calling on the early-nineteenth-century German philosopher Georg W. F. Hegel, Bullock would point out the concept of world-historical individuals as the agents by which the plan of Providence is carried out. Hegel would conceptualize in his lectures at the University of Berlin, where he occupied a professorial chair from 1818 through 1831, the phenomenon of the world-historical man and a theory of the unfolding of history in terms of his passion and will. Such men "are *great* men, because they willed and accomplished something great; not a mere fancy, a mere intention, but that which met the case and fell in with the needs of an age."[74] For the moral objections of how men such as Alexander the Great, Julius Caesar, and Napoleon could be considered great in view of the monstrous carnage associated with them, Hegel could at least attempt to smooth ruffled feathers by noting that so mighty a form must necessarily trample down many an innocent flower and crush to pieces many an object in its path. For Hegel, the morality associated with individuals and the laws associated with societies were irrelevant for purposes of criticizing the actions of the world-historical individual.

He would philosophize that the comprehensive relations of history present "those momentous collisions between existing acknowledged duties, laws, and rights and those contingencies which are adverse to this fixed system; which assail and even destroy its foundations and existence."[75] Those contingencies realize themselves in history and involve a general principle different from that on which the permanence of an already existing state depends. "Historical men—world-historical individuals—are those in whose aims such a general principle lies."[76] We can imagine Nazism as a contingency that represented a principle different from that which underlay the existing Weimar system. And we can similarly see Hitler as a world-historical personality in whose aims lay the idea of Nazism. Hitler, of course, could hardly have paraded himself by Germans and Europeans as Hegel's world spirit, but he would come off convincingly to Germans as a savior. And he could be interpreted as a world-historical personality dressed for the occasion as a messiah.

The conventional wisdom in interpreting Hitler as crude unperson would seem to be describing an outer shell surrounding him. Hitler's biographers, both great and otherwise, have elaborated Hitler's various peculiarities as they applied to him as a private person. With preconceptions of Hitler's banality and in order to emphasize his common and unredeeming qualities, they have emphasized his ability to relax among his chauffeurs, bodyguards, and adjutants, to enjoy insipid light opera, and so on. Such emphasis on off-duty relaxation detracts dangerously from comprehension of the world-historical "supercharged corners in various parts of his personality." In the presence of a man who has reasonable claim to have been a world-historical personality—the hero in history—the biographers steer us away from understanding the qualities that made him lift the world off its hinges and bombard us with his personal commonness. "No man is a hero to his valet-de-chambre" is a well-known proverb, and the biographical valets of Hitler handle him similarly. Hegel, however, added to the well-known proverb the words "but not because the hero is not a hero, but because the latter is a valet."[77]

We must suspect that the biographical valets have brought Hitler down to their level of contempt for him; although he must remain great in history based upon achievement. Hitler's greatness was his passion in the pursuit of his mission, and the banality of the man in certain personal features remains a red herring in the path of comprehending that passion. Hegel could assert that nothing has been accomplished without interest on the part of the great catalysts in history and "if interest be called passion, inasmuch as the whole individuality, to the neglect of all other actual or possible interests and claims, is devoted to an object with every fiber of volition, concentrating all its desires and powers upon it—we may affirm absolutely that *nothing great in the world* has been accomplished without passion."[78] Hitler was passion incarnate. During the period 1919–1933 he was consumed by his self-anointed mission to seize power in order to save the Germans from the Marxists. "A world-historical individual is not so unwise as to indulge in a variety of wishes to divide his interests. He is devoted to the one aim, regardless of all else."[79] The great interpretive question in the case of Hitler would seem to be whether or not his single-minded passion was directed by a morbid craving for power, as demanded by the great biographers, or a somewhat loftier craving for the salvation of the Germans. In either interpretation, Hitler would seem to fit as a world-historical individual, but the paths to historical immortality would have been as different as the darkness of power and the light of salvation.

For Hitler to have seized power over the party in 1925, power over Germany in 1934, and near-power over Europe in August 1941 based exclusively on an insatiable urge to dominate all things and every man around him strains our credulity. The conventional wisdom, for example, in alleging this drive for power gives as its proof the fact that he did that which resulted in power. Faced with Hitler's determined propagandizing about the resurrection of Germany, however, that wisdom has acknowledged that he was a convinced ideologue and actually believed his own tenets of Nazism: "All consuming though power was for Hitler, it was not a matter of power for its own sake...he was also an ideologue of unshakeable convictions."[80] Here we face the great contradiction in the existing interpretation, or perhaps more accurately, uninterpretation of Hitler: the uncertain confrontation between the historical figure consumed exclusively by lust for power and the same historical figure consumed exclusively by unshakeable convictions.

In the former case we have a wicked man, an interpretation that must remain a comfort to the great biographers and reading public alike. In the latter case we have an individual who could be described variously as a fanatic, patriot, savior, visionary, and so on, none of whom would necessarily qualify as evil or engaged in evil deeds. Kershaw partly escaped the contradiction by suggesting that Hitler's worldview was so repellent that Hitler's acknowledged sense of mission was morally defunct. And Kershaw simply lived with the contradiction by noting that Hitler was dedicated entirely to the pursuit of power while simultaneously maintaining that "cynical though he was, Hitler's cynicism stopped short of his own person; he came to believe that he was a man with a mission marked out by Providence and therefore exempt from the ordinary canons of human conduct."[81] And if Hegel had been available to discuss the contradiction with the biographers and had decided that based on Hitler's accomplishments he embodied world-historical change, Hegel would have rejected their moralizing as irrelevant to the comprehension of Hitler and of the course of history.

*   *   *

With Hitler in one prison or another from November 1923 through December 1924 and the economic stabilization of the Weimar Republic during the same period, he and the NSDAP hit on hard times in the quest for power from 1925 through 1929. In the Reichstag elections of May 20, 1928, the Nazis would bottom out at 810,100 votes and twelve deputies, and these numbers are often used to generalize about the misfortune of the movement. The Nazis garnered only twelve seats out of a total of 491, and that number qualifies as a disaster and supports a generalization that they had become impotent in German politics, let alone any other kinds of politics in Europe by 1928. Yet, in a seldom-made observation, we could see that the Nazis got 810,100 Germans to vote for them. Since it would be difficult to suggest any bandwagon effect for the Nazis in 1928, we could observe that Hitler had managed to hold on to a number of followers who, in turn, could be described as genuine Nazis. The number is large enough to suggest that if conditions were to improve after 1928, that the Nazis would have a cadre capable of levering them into power.

The situation becomes more accurately rendered, however, when we consider that Hitler conceptualized his followers as supporters of the movement on one hand and active fighters on the other. Hitler believed that his followers could be subdivided into about 85 percent supporters and 15 percent fighters—"to ten supporters there will at most be one or two [fighters]"—the latter who could perhaps be qualified as the real Nazis.[82] Those Nazis would be the core of the movement, and as the party expanded after 1928, they would be the ones to "complete the victory of the original idea."[83] We can generalize therefore that Hitler and an elite band of about 120,000 fighters for the faith that had clustered around him went on during the next five years to attract so large an additional number of supporters, fighters, and opportunists that the original band and latter-day followers took over a great modern state.

It is difficult to believe that the creature of the great biographers could have refused to participate in the battles among the various factions over control of the shambles of the banned NSDAP and could have formally resigned from leadership of the party. How could the conventionally cast tyrant resist the obvious necessity to maintain his power? The conventional wisdom would maintain that Hitler, with canny, wicked genius, would remove himself from the factional struggle and thereby deliberately set the various factions fighting among themselves. Such an interpretation is natural for hostile biographers and satisfying to a reading public that expects wicked genius, but it weakens in the face of the situation and Hitler's personality. Hitler announced simply that he was unable to run the movement from inside a prison cell in a fortress. Here we see the biographers transform the obvious and the practical into a malicious strategy to hold on to power when the simplest interpretation is the best: Hitler meant what he said. It must be evident that Hitler faced the practical impossibility of effectively controlling a shattered movement under such circumstances.

A messiah cannot take sides in a struggle among his disciples because there can be no sides in the case of his message. Disciples cannot argue with the messiah about the content of the message. Can we imagine Muhammad's tribal followers debating his word as God's messenger? Weimar Germany was a different place from the

Arabian Desert of the 600s, but Hitler can be seen as one who had synthesized a worldview by 1913 that he translated into a message of German destiny. The messiah announced his arrival in 1925, but the biographers see in this announcement the unfolding of the famed leadership principle. It is easy to see such a principle arriving, albeit dry as dust and contributing to the picture of a man driven by a quest for power. Upon momentary reflection, however, we cannot see how real Germans would have embraced such a political scientific abstraction. It is not credible that so many Nazis could have been fooled by a manipulative tyrant into accepting his total authority over their own popular mass movement. Though wisdom suggests that you cannot fool all of your followers all of the time, Hitler seems to have defied the dictum. Within the spirit of the movement, Hitler cannot be seen to have attempted to fool anybody—to manipulate in order to accrue power. We see, rather, a will to deliver a nonnegotiable message.

*   *   *

In the live-or-die initial stage of the expansion of the party from late 1919 through 1923, Hitler claimed in passages of *Mein Kampf* ill-digested by his biographers that he faced hostile audiences that could be converted to the developing Nazi outlook only by supreme effort and practiced skill. In vital passages disguised from his biographers as being important by such boring subject areas for Hitler biography as the Treaty of Brest-Litovsk and the South Tyrol, Hitler would describe the essence of the movement as the conversion of Germans —all Germans in every audience, however hostile—to the new thinking. Concerning Brest-Litovsk, he could describe "at that time I spoke on this theme at meetings of two thousand people, and often I was struck by the glances of three thousand six hundred hostile eyes. And three hours later I had before me a surging mass full of the holiest indignation and boundless wrath. Again a great lie had been torn out of the hearts and brains of a crowd numbering thousands, and a truth implanted in its place."[84] In this case, for Hitler, the lie was the "adroit propaganda" of the Marxist and bourgeois parties that had convinced "millions of Germans" to regard "the peace treaty of Versailles as nothing more than just retribution for the crime committed by us at Brest-Litovsk."[85] In defiance of the picture presented by the conventional wisdom of Hitler playing on the baser emotions of receptive audiences, we see Hitler often reveling in a perilous battle to convert hostile Germans to the new thinking.

Hitler consistently took dangerously unpopular positions in the face of popular opinion, including the initial mindset on Brest-Litovsk, popular support for passive resistance to the French, and the clamor of republican governments over injustice to Germans in South Tyrol. He would comment that in such cases that "supreme energy was necessary to keep the ship of the movement from drifting with the artificially aroused general current or [even] from being driven by it."[86] The dangers to Hitler personally in such situations and the possibilities for the ruination of the movement have been missed with the conventional interpretation of Hitler. He would analyze that to resist capitulation to public opinion it was necessary "to shake the movement with an iron fist to preserve it from ruin" and that such a stand "sometimes puts the venturesome leader in almost mortal peril. But not a few men in history have at such moments been stoned for an action which posterity...had every cause to thank them on its knees."[87] It is difficult to miss the messianic tone in such expression, and if such words were not enough he could summarize that "in such hours the individual [leader] feels afraid; but he must not forget that after every such hour salvation comes at length, and that a movement that wants to renew a world must serve, not the moment, but the future."[88] The collection of words in these brief dictations—iron fist, mortal peril, men stoned for taking an action, posterity, thank them on its knees, the leader feels afraid, salvation comes, renew a world—presents a picture of a man in another universe of idealistic intensity.

A cruder part of the conventional wisdom nevertheless has cast

Hitler as the most common of Germans and hence most capable of playing on their most prevalent hopes and fears. In making such a claim, the wisdom has desperately confused Hitler's characteristics as a private individual as being the basis for his appeal—the ultimate common man reverberates best among the common masses. Hitler, however, was scarcely common, and he appealed to many Germans as a kind of other-worldly mystic. His intelligent, tough, and independent chief of the SA from 1926 through 1930, Franz Pfeffer von Salomon, "took Hitler to be a genius, something the world might experience only once in a thousand years."[89] For a man who had face-to-face dealings with Hitler for four years and who suffered an eventual falling out, to summarize as such, suggests that Hitler reverberated among Germans as an extremely uncommon and irresistible messenger of glittering hope. Salomon was a no-nonsense Prussian who, in an unguarded moment, had referred to Hitler as "a flabby Austrian," yet he could make the estimate of his brilliance noted above and do so hardly as a sycophant.

In the period following his successful demand for uncontested leadership of the movement, Hitler created extraordinary cohesiveness among Nazis because of the removal of the usual policy debates of a parliamentary party. In May 1928, for example, elections took place to the Reichstag, and the most inflammatory issue was the one of the forced Italianization of the German minority in South Tyrol, an area which had in 1919 been ceded to Italy. The various parliamentary parties would take the opportunity to appeal to voters' patriotism by taking an exaggerated stand in support of the Germans and against the Mussolini government. In defiance of the conventional wisdom that would demand that Hitler be seen as courting followers for a mass movement, he would reject the republican policy of support for the Germans of South Tyrol. He would take the stand that the existing republican government of November Criminals had placed the Germans in so unfortunate a situation. The real enemy was the republican government and not Mussolini, who was merely riding with an accomplished fact. Hitler revealed here an extraordinary adherence to principle, rivaling his refusal five years earlier to support parallel November Criminals over passive resistance in the Ruhr. The explanation for this political behavior by the conventional wisdom is that Hitler could neither allow his movement to be submerged in the other parties nor accept the reduction of his own personal power. We are left thereby with the uncomfortable feeling that we are being asked to believe that Hitler effected two unfulfilled political death wishes in fits of pique over lessened political power in common fronts and reduced personal power over his own movement.

Hitler's Marxist foes in Bavaria would make political capital out of his refusal to line up patriotically with the other parties against the Italian government by claiming that Hitler was being paid by the Italians to take his otherwise inexplicable stance. Outraged by the outlandish Social Democratic claims, annoyed by the uncritical and opportunistic positions of the bourgeois parties, and suspicious of the discernment of his own followers, he would actually dictate his "second book" to describe the real enemies of the Germans as concerned South Tyrol. As Hitler got immersed in the book, he extended the latter part to include a far-reaching exposition of Nazi foreign policy. The point for comprehending Hitler is that based on principle he took an unpopular position during a Reichstag election battle.

In the face of such adherence to principle, Kershaw claims nevertheless with one-sided propagandistic certitude that Hitler was, at bottom, an actor who played the role of leader to perfection and did so for the accretion of power. With contemptuous brevity, Kershaw would note that the "firm handshake and 'manly' eye to eye contact... when he had to meet ordinary party members was, for the awestruck lowly activist, a moment never to be forgotten. For Hitler it was merely acting: it meant no more than the reinforcement of the personality cult."[90]

We could just as readily see him revealing his true nature with a kind of fearlessness of the consequences of looking strained to effete bourgeois Liberals or see him appearing as if he were attempting to upstage tougher Marxists. We could also see the unfailingly deadly, uncontrived earnestness of the adolescent of Linz and combat soldier of World War I. Was the young Hitler acting out some contrived role when he seized the pillar alongside of which was the best standing room in the Linz Municipal Opera House? Did Hitler contrive to present the image of lofty isolation among his life and death comrades in his frontline infantry regiment? For the biographer, the firm handshake and fixed glance are taken as cheap playacting to be ridiculed. His choice of the word *manly* suggests a picture of infantile male posturing, and his scarcely disguised hint that Hitler looked with distaste on his own rank and file is spun into the interpretation with the derogation: "when he had to meet ordinary party members." The word *manly*, although excellent for the intended humorous disparagement of Hitler, is ill-suited for comprehension suggesting the presence of the unmanly. It is as difficult to accept that Hitler was imitating manliness in his encounters with his political troops as it is to imagine Siegfried from Wagner's *The Ring* feeling that he was being manly in his encounters with dragons, giants, and Nordic gods. We see a Romantic Hitler, soldierly, fearless, the scourger of temples. We see followers faithful unto death but scarcely those who could be adequately described as manly.

By 1929, the man who would seize power in 1933 was in place and ready for characterization. Since Hitler would be successful, it is difficult to resist accepting his own description of himself. Hitler, for example, would reply to the anti-Catholic Nazi Artur Dinter, who would challenge him openly in late 1929 by proposing an advisory senate that "as leader of the National Socialist Movement and as the person who possesses the blind faith of somebody belonging to those who make history, I have [as a politician] the boldness to claim in this sphere the same infallibility that you reserve for yourself in your [religious] reformationist area."[91] And the second most important man in National Socialism at this time, the self-confident, independent Gregor Strasser, would support Hitler with the written position agreed to by at least eighteen district leaders that any attempt to establish even the smallest difference of opinion between Adolf Hitler and his fellow workers, in any question of principle, would be impossible to tolerate. Hitler cannot be claimed to be padding a cult of the Fuehrer with words such as those above but rather presenting the reality that he was infallible in the Nazi version of politics and the seizure of power in Germany. Gregor Strasser also cannot be claimed to be producing a cult but rather running with the necessity for a seamless front to be presented to Germans—a brazen cliff of unshakeable unity. And, in a grudging admission of Hitler's emanation of genius, even the hard-headed Strasser was forced to acknowledge that "the man has a prophetic talent for reading great political problems correctly and doing the right thing at the opportune moment despite apparently insuperable difficulties."[92]

Kershaw is aware of these words but instead of acknowledging that Hitler had the talent to match his pretensions to greatness, he veers off into forced and sometimes irrelevant disparagement. Faced with the words of a high-level, tough-minded political associate who defined Hitler's political genius during the march to internal political power and even threw in the word *prophetic*, he steers us away from a full understanding. "Such unusual talent as Strasser was ready to grant Hitler lay, however, as he saw it, in instinct rather than any ability to systematize ideas."[93] The biographer's caveat is strained because it suggests that Hitler's acknowledged political capabilities were of an inferior sort tainted by not being based on ability to systematize ideas but only on instinct. Neither messiah nor world-historical personality conforms to rule, however, and its handmaiden, systematized ideas. The word *instinct* is a synonym for genius, and Strasser wittingly, and Kershaw unwittingly, seem to be telling us that Hitler's formidable political capabilities were based simply on genius.

The fanatically inclined army lieutenant Wilhelm Scheringer would recall meeting Hitler in 1930 with this description: "Listening to him, I had the firm impression that the man believed what he said, as simple as his slogans are. He is suspended in his thinking three meters above the ground. He doesn't speak; he preaches."[94] The young Scheringer described himself in the presence of a preacher who believed what he was saying and who stood in front of him mystically levitated. In such a picture we can see the young lieutenant confronted by a German messiah but critical of his apparent lack of day-to-day political competence, as noted in further words to the effect that Hitler was incapable of clear political analysis, however powerful his talent as an agitator. Just like so many others from Eckart to Strasser, the lieutenant had observed the visionary, otherworldly quality in Hitler illustrated so well in so many photographs in which he seemed to look through the photographer and into some distant universe.

We have two Hitlers here; one is the creature of the propaganda-like treatment of hostile biographers, and the other one is a hero as seen through the eyes of contemporary followers. Each is rendered in extreme terms, and it is tempting to suggest a middle ground for some more balanced interpretation. But Hitler was one of the most determined personalities in mankind's history, and to labor to find some middle ground is to labor to find something that is not there. We are left with a cruel interpretive choice between either a bad man who did some good or a good man who did some bad. Hegel may come to our rescue here by pointing out that moral considerations of good and bad are irrelevant to a world-historical personality because he is in the process of taking an existing world and replacing it with a new one. In such a case, the irrelevance is that an old morality would be replaced by a new one and the world-historical personality would write the history of the era. Whoever Hitler was —good, bad, or a man above such consideration—his followers accepted him as savior. Axiomatically, he would become that savior when he and his followers seized political power in Germany in 1933 and 1934.

Chapter 5

OLD FIGHTERS, NEW CONVERTS, DECISIVE SUCCESS 1929–1932

I n 1929 the Nazis would achieve numerous modest successes in elections to city councils and state *Landtage* (parliaments) and national exposure on the international issue of the finalization of German World War I reparation. As a German agricultural depression set in with the collapse of the prices of farm products, the Nazis reacted more flexibly and decisively than any other party to seize the rural vote. When the great international depression struck as signaled by the fall of stock prices in August on the New York Stock Exchange, Germany was affected more rapidly and deeply than any other state. It is difficult to exaggerate the resulting social and economic despair in the various industrialized nations; the United States, for example, has claimed to have experienced the greatest social misery in its entire history during the Great Depression. Germany, with its added burden of the loss of World War I, would suffer relatively greater trauma. Under these conditions, the multiparty system of German parliamentary democracy collapsed in the middle of 1930. The Center Party chancellor, Heinrich Bruening, an experienced parliamentarian, had been unable to put together a budget agreeable to both the Social Democrats and the bourgeois parties and threatened to pass it by constitutional emergency decree. Part of the conventional wisdom has castigated Bruening too generously by claiming that he had begun to pave the road to dictatorship, presidential or otherwise, by his impatience. Another part of the wisdom, however, has suggested that the parties were to blame through their fundamental urges to protect their own interests. In the actual event, Bruening would get a budget enacted by presidential emergency decree and would attempt to get a more functional Reichstag by calling a new election.

During that election battle and following ones, Hitler would exhibit a persona that was also messianic to a degree that he not only looked and acted as one but was also able to transform himself in front of mass audiences. Impressions from the period by persons so diverse as to be almost incredible drive us in the same direction. The great biographers agree, for example, that Hitler could be characterized as utterly consistent in his world outlook from the time he departed Vienna in 1913 and stood frozen in that emotional state. The great biographers in agreeing upon this rigidity take it as a negative factor that illustrated Hitler's rejection of seeking further knowledge beyond that discovered early in life and which had resulted in his fixation on the Germans as under attack by an international enemy. The biographers trivialize Hitler's rigidity as based on late adolescent bias frozen in place and fed by the environment of the German loss of World War I. But to attribute Hitler's rigid consistency and world-altering achievements to bias, prejudice, and hatred from the Vienna period strains our credulity from the viewpoint of cause and effect. Hitler seems to have been more a product of a single coherent revelation and a resulting fixed and unalterable mission.

We can get no better insight into Hitler than his consistency in pursuing the mission of the destruction of Marxism. The consistency, however, is not based on some alleged incapacity to "grow" beyond late adolescent frustration and hate but rather on the revelation of a timeless enemy and the mission of its destruction. So do we interpret Hitler as a kind of historical fit of pique or a granite-hard, dark, avenging messiah? His relentless consistency in the attack on Marxists and November Criminals is in accord with the unalterable messages of the great Christian messiah or Islamic Prophet. The attribution of evil in Hitler's consistency because of excessive hatred of an enemy must be handled with care also. If Hitler is interpreted as messiah, or at least a man characterized most fundamentally as having the qualities of a messiah, then it was his mission to save the Germans from some enemy—presumably a considerable one. Given the dimensions of the enemy suggested by the size of Germany and its misfortune, it is difficult to imagine Hitler either as messiah or otherwise and not hating the enemy. Did Jesus the Christ or Mohammed the Prophet hate Satan or merely disapprove of him? We do not have to answer this question to get further into Hitler, but we do have to point out that Hitler could be considered to be a messianic figure notwithstanding the presence of either hate or outrage in his presentation of the Marxist enemy.

In 1929 and 1930, Hitler and his indefatigable Nazi core activists secured gains in local elections, achieved national prominence in the attempt to defeat the Owen D. Young Plan to secure long-term reparation from Germany, and then won breakthrough gains in the Reichstag election of September 1930. Hitler was forced to conduct a delicate balancing act between the rougher and more revolutionary *Sturmabteilung* (SA) personnel and the mass of his followers who adhered to his policy of the legal takeover of Germany. Hitler based his policy of legality on the winning of Reichstag and *Landtage* elections and those to more important city councils. Success in these elections would translate into government positions and the capability to effect a nationalist awakening. Out of such a picture we can see that the two most important government positions in the republic were those of president and chancellor, the former elected every seven years by direct vote and the latter arranged among several compatible parties that together had received a majority of the votes to the Reichstag. The last nonemergency Reichstag cabinet, for example, consisted of eleven cabinet ministers, namely, four Social Democrats, two Democrats, one Center, one Bavarian People's, two People's, and two nonpartisan. This cabinet was the government of Germany and reflected the fact that the parties above had received more than 50 percent of the votes in the last nonemergency election of May 1928 and therefore controlled more than half of the Reichstag deputies. And it is not surprising that the chancellor, Hermann Mueller, was a deputy from the party that had won a plurality of deputies, the Social Democratic Party.

After the successful Reichstag election of September 1930, Hitler can be generalized as driving to obtain the chancellorship during the period 1930–1933. This generalization is more complex than it may seem because the German president had been forced to pass legislation at the request of the chancellor by presidential emergency decree, in effect becoming the chancellor instead of being the titular head of state. Hindenburg did not do this willingly but was forced by the circumstances of the depression, the failure of the political parties to effect a majority coalition, and the failure of the government to win ground externally on questions of tariff treaties, armaments, and reparations because "above all, France—alarmed by the results of the September elections—refused all concessions and cultivated her hysterias."[1] Hitler could have achieved power legally most directly by obtaining over 50 percent of the votes in a Reichstag election and thereby necessarily being appointed chancellor by the president. Under the constitution, executive authority in the state was vested in the chancellor and his cabinet, and although he was appointed by the president, he would be responsible to the Reichstag. Since the Reichstag had the power of initiating bills, Hitler would have had both the legislative and executive authority to synchronize Germany with the Nazi movement. And under the circumstances of a functioning Reichstag, the president would have had no necessity to invoke his emergency powers.

No single party would receive 50 percent of the Reichstag vote in the entire period from 1919 through March 1933, and Hitler would be forced to seize the chancellorship with a near or full plurality of the votes in a system described as proportional representation or *scrutin de liste*. Under proportional representation, voters scrutinized lists of candidates presented by the parties and voted for the favored list. A mere sixty thousand votes in a Reichstag voting district would be sufficient for a party to take the first candidate on its list and place him as a deputy in the legislature. Under a system in which voters chose diffuse lists of candidates and not the candidates individually the Nazis were fortunate, because the voters would tend to be voting for their electrifying leader rather than an inherently bland and faceless list.

Hitler's single-minded drive for the chancellorship through the legal means of voting campaigns under proportional representation began with the special Reichstag election of September. The results have been described accurately as a "landslide" for the Nazis, yet they netted only 18.3 percent of the German vote. But with 18 percent, however, in a deepening super-depression internally and intransigent, near-hysterical French imposition of the Versailles treaty externally, Hitler now faced the near-term opportunity to seize the chancellorship.

The above situation is well-established, but the interpretive question remains: Who was the Hitler who confronted decisive opportunity, the banal creature of the great biographers or the messiah sometimes flickering in and out of view as a Wagnerian hero? In the former case, the biographers paint Hitler as a personal mediocrity and egomaniac who left himself no options toward the end of 1932 and was forced "as usual" to gamble on all or nothing—the chancellorship or obscurity. Under the conditions of Article 48 having been invoked by the president from mid-1930 through early 1933, Hitler also had the reasonable possibility to achieve power legally through election to the presidency. Although the possibility was there, the probabilities were remote, and in the actual events of the two presidential elections of 1932, Hitler would do extremely well with almost 37 percent of the vote in the deciding second election but considerably fewer than the absolute majority amassed by Hindenburg. To achieve power over Germany in the aftermath of the presidential elections, Hitler faced the original and now only remaining legal possibility, which was the Reichstag elections and the "seizure" of the chancellorship. Within Hitler's vision of a secure Reich with adequate space eastward, however, the chancellorship was only a way station toward completion of his mission. From such a perspective, Hitler not only had to have the chancellorship but also had to have it virtually immediately in historical-opportunity savings time.

There was not enough time when we contrast the magnitude of Hitler's remaining tasks with any reasonable expectation of his life span. In an unguarded moment of exhaustion during the second presidential voting campaign of 1932, he would harangue his *Gauleiter*, Albert Krebs in Hamburg, about fears over what he had diagnosed as approaching fatal cancer that left him only a few years to complete his mission. "I do not have time to wait.... If I had time, I wouldn't have become a candidate. The Old Gentleman... won't last much longer. But I cannot lose even a year. I must come to power quickly in order to solve the gigantic problems in the little time remaining to me. I must! I must!"[2] Hitler required the chancellorship immediately. In contrast, there was too much time for the Nazis, who were a volatile mix of disparate followers of Hitler, to evaporate into their various former incarnations. There was not enough time after the seizure of internal power to set aside the Versailles and Saint Germain treaties, rearm, and advance east. Against such a background, the play of chance in the form of the calling of a special Reichstag election for July 1932 would intervene to present the decisive opportunity for Hitler to become chancellor.

Under the system of proportional representation and in the presence of fifteen political parties that managed to get deputies in the Reichstag, the Nazis would win just over 37 percent of the total. With so overwhelming a plurality, Hitler could have expected reasonably to have been appointed as a presidential chancellor. He would have required, for example, only a tactically manageable alliance involving an additional 13 percent of the deputies for majority votes for the passage of legislation. The overwhelming probability is, however, that he would have demanded a new election and, with the prestige of the backing of the president and the enormous possibilities to influence the election through the authority of the chancellorship, have gone for an outright majority in the Reichstag. We can make this generalization with confidence because six months later, when he was appointed chancellor, he acted thus.

*   *   *

During this period, the great biographers would portray Hitler as an egomaniac and a gambler dedicated to achieving everything or nothing—literally the chancellorship or death—against the background of a shattered movement. On the issue of death, they seem to be on to something because as the options narrowed in early December 1932, Hitler's powerful, trusted lieutenant Gregor Strasser would resign over the issue of Strasser accepting the post of vice chancellor in order to salvage at least something from all of the partial successes in national and local voting campaigns, especially from September 1930 onward. In the ensuing apparent disintegration of the movement, Hitler would threaten: "If the party should ever break up, I will make an end of things in three minutes with a pistol."[3] And later in the month, Hitler would write to his revered Winifred Wagner: "As soon as I am sure everything is lost you know what I'll do. I was always determined to do it. I cannot accept defeat. I will stick to my word and end my life with a bullet."[4] Hitler had been shocked to the core by this presence of an apparent eleventh-hour Judas, but such was Hitler's uncanny hold over even a towering associate like Strasser that the latter could have remarked not long before that "I fought as one of Hitler's men and as one of Hitler's men I want someday to go to my grave."[5]

Hitler would characterize the seizure of power a month later as a "triumph of the will," but the biographers would resist so extravagant a claim by their biographical *bête noir* and suggest that back stairs intrigue by a camarilla associated with the president levered him into power. The biographers are correct in pointing out that for Hitler the position of chancellor remained the only option for the seizure of power in early December 1932 and that he would need something akin to a miracle to achieve it. Out of this they pull together the generalization that Hitler ineptly, with a gambler's mentality, had narrowed his options as in a game of poker to the draw of a final card for complete success or utter ruin. But Hitler in 1925 had already limited his options to a legal path and never varied from it. When from September 1930 through early 1933 the Nazis became the legal voting force to be reckoned with, Hitler also never varied in his invariable demand for the chancellorship. In early 1932 he told a high-level follower, Hans Frank: "I see myself as Chancellor and I will be Chancellor. I do not see myself as President, and I know I will never be President."[6] As a messianic figure dedicated to the necessarily complete success of his mission, Hitler had only one option during the entire period, and it is inaccurate to claim that he had narrowed his options through some gambler's instinct to risk all on a stubborn demand for the chancellorship in late 1932. It is closer to reality to say that Hitler's unbending demand for the chancellorship had reduced the options of the president and the intriguers to an eleventh-hour choice between Hitler and civil war.

Hitler would succeed in his flexible strategy of a legal takeover of the German government, and Nazi propaganda would characterize the event of January 30, 1933, as the seizure of power. The word *seizure* implies the manly, revolutionary takeover of the government, but no such action took place on that date. The biographers would fasten on the situation to denigrate Hitler's accomplishment by generalizing that the wicked, violent Nazis were in reality ignominiously placed in power by a government clique. The generalization is a non sequitur, however, because Hitler intended that the wicked, violent Nazis take the chancellorship ignominiously, that is, legally, and they did so notwithstanding the throwing about of words with a potentially illegal cast such as seizure, national rising, and the like. No man in Germany advised Hitler to take these courses of action, and we are compelled to ask: What manner of man could have acted so alone, so relentlessly, and on so grand a scale?

The answer to this question cannot be found in the masterfully written but propagandistically tainted great biographies. Those works, especially the ones of Alan Bullock and Ian Kershaw, must be seen as containing elements of biographical hubris—arrogant passion in the pursuit of an interpretation of Hitler as banal and evil, egomania and megalomania. Even though the latest great biographer, Ian Kershaw, would state unequivocally that world history would have been different without Hitler, he nevertheless levers him into power through the machinations of a camarilla and does not give enough credit to Hitler's inhuman consistency in his demands for the chancellorship. Hitler's claim to a triumph of the will is an accurate one strategically, although it has to be modified by acknowledging the play of chance in the form of a tactical miracle.

The conventional wisdom, nevertheless, has acknowledged Hitler's overriding consistency in driving for the chancellorship after late 1925 and qualified that consistency as a messianic characteristic. Biographer Joachim Fest could note, for example, that Hitler would react to Alfred Hugenberg's painstakingly gathered national united front of October 1931 at Harzburg by breaking it apart. "With his own peculiar consistency, Hitler realized that any community of action could mean only subordination. At best, it would imply that henceforth Germany would have to be looking up to two 'saviors'— an absurdity from Hitler's point of view."[7] Although Kershaw identified Hitler as a messiah, he undermined his insight by claiming that Hitler viewed the practical destruction of the Harzburg Front as a clever tactical move in a game among parliamentary parties. And finally, to destroy the near insight of savior, he placed the word in italics as if to suggest flippantly some egomaniacal delusion on Hitler's part as having a holy mission. The biographers commonly suggest that Hitler saw himself as a German savior, but they do so derisively, often using the words *messianic complex* to describe his condition. Hitler drove with consistency, and his own inimitable finality against the Marxists claiming that it was fated not just to defeat them in an electoral campaign but to annihilate them. He would state in a speech in Hamburg in early 1926 in a tone both apodictic (i.e., absolutely certain) and apocalyptic (i.e., prophetically revealed) that "we recognize quite clearly that if Marxism wins, we will be annihilated. Nor would we expect anything else. But if we win, Marxism will be annihilated.... We too know no tolerance.... We shall not rest until the...last Marxist [is] converted or exterminated. There is no middle course."[8] For virtually any man in the world to have spoken these words he would have had to have been presenting donations-gathering and vote-getting rhetoric. For virtually any man in a friendly audience to have heard them, he would have experienced the rhetorical violence that he yearned for but would scarcely have imagined that the speaker had presented literal truth. Faced by a man characterized by so much of the apodictic and apocalyptic, and with a third of the voters behind him in a system of proportional representation, Hindenburg and the intriguers around him had no realistic options to oppose Hitler.

And for the entire period from 1919 through 1933, no evidence of corruptibility on Hitler's part has been produced, although the search for it has lasted for close to one-half century. The search has been for evidence of corrupt promises to favor big business and wealthy individuals in ways that would undermine the purity of Nazi doctrine. In frustration, biographer Fest would note that "the National Socialists themselves lent encouragement to the most fantastic theories by practicing a psychotic form of secrecy concerning their financial resources."[9] The gratuitous selection of the word *psychotic* to characterize the Nazis and Hitler is not a good sign for an accurate interpretation of either. Fest continued to wrestle with this fundamental issue of Hitler's character in the following, more realistic, appreciation. In late 1923, "Max Amann, the party's business manager...insisted, not without pride that Hitler had given his backers 'only the party platform' in return for their contributions. This may seem hard to credit; nevertheless, there is reason to believe that the only agreements he made were on tactical lines."[10] And as a monument to interpretive schizophrenia in the minds of the biographers, their battle to deny the presence of Lohengrin in Hitler and instead to highlight a prince of darkness, one stated that "the concept of corruption seems strangely alien to this man; it does not accord with his rigidity, his mounting self confidence and the force of his delusions."[11]

*　　*　　*

Hitler subjected his audiences to late, dramatic, sudden entrances and then almost invariably would begin his speech with historical background and reminiscence, "usually lingering on the legend of his rise." With a notable dearth of either comprehension or interest, the biographers chalk off such beginnings as monotonous and trivial. But that which is repeated need not be monotonous, and that which is trivial to a hostile biographer today need not have been so to an audience of Germans in the outrageous surroundings of the early 1920s and early 1930s. For Hitler to have begun almost every mass address with historical context, especially the contrasting glories and misfortunes of the recent past, suggests the consistency of a messiah. For Hitler to have placed himself similarly within that context— "When in 1918 as a nameless soldier at the front..."—was to announce the presence of an armed savior.[12] And with virtually every mass address during the rise to power a contemporary could observe that "after about fifteen minutes... there takes place what can only be described in the primitive old figure of speech: the spirit enters into him."[13] Hitler himself could observe that in the midst of the mass meeting, he became another person.

The great biographers would come close to an effective characterization when dealing with him in his acknowledged element. After tepid praise of his capabilities as tactician, organizer, and psychologist, Fest would strike the mark with the comment: "his invincible genius came to him only in the course of mass meetings, when he exalted platitudes into the resounding words of a prophet and seemed to transform himself into the leader."[14] Fest would present a heady description of Hitler but degrade the effect with the use of the words *platitudes* and *seemed*. Platitudes—commonplace remarks, popular bombast—are associated with parliamentary politicians on the reelection trail. But as messiah and prophet of his own coming, Hitler could only speak "the resounding words of a prophet," and what would be platitudes for all others were for him words of salvation and destruction. And Hitler did not seem to transform himself into the leader; he awakened the audience to the fact that the savior was in front of it. During the second presidential election in early 1932, Hitler would declare "that he thought he was an instrument of God, chosen to liberate Germany."[15] Elizabeth Foerster-Nietzsche, the philosopher's sister, evidently agreed because she could note after a visit by Hitler at Weimar that he struck her as a religious rather than a political leader.[16] Rudolf Hess would compare his leadership personality with the founder of a religion: "He must communicate to his listeners an apodictic faith."[17] And Goebbels, the master cynic of the Nazi movement who would nevertheless die faithful to the last to Hitler, could "describe his Leader as the 'fulfillment of a mysterious longing,' bringing faith in deepest despair."[18]

Kershaw would attempt to interpret the words above as linked to the conscious manufacture of "Hitler idolatry" and "the establishment of the Fuehrer cult" because such things were necessary for the development of a movement torn by factionalism. But to see Nazism as a kind of exercise in how to hold together a movement, and Hitler as a necessarily strained creature of a Fuehrer cult, simply does not hold together. Hess, at the very inception of the movement—before his fawning period as a Hitler sycophant, as interpreted by Kershaw—would broadcast the presence of a world-historical personality. It is one thing to be seduced by a propaganda apparatus into the sway of a cult, and it is another to be converted into a disciple. Kershaw, who personifies the conventional wisdom, could note that "a war veteran dated his Fuehrer worship to Hitler's speeches during his trial in 1924. 'From that time on I had no thought for anyone but Hitler. His behavior moved me to give him my whole faith without reserve.'"[19] We see here a faith-driven conversion to Hitler that cannot reasonably be described as Fuehrer worship in early 1924 and thus cannot be associated with a contrived propaganda image. Another German who heard him speak in 1926 could claim "from that day on I could never violate my allegiance to Hitler. I saw his unlimited faith in his people and the desire to set them free."[20]

But the biographers have as a tenet of Hitler interpretation that his innumerable speeches to mass German audiences could be seen as an exchange of pathologies between him and a significant part of the German masses: "he could not have bewitched the masses if he had not incorporated all their psychoses into his own psyche...an exchange of pathologies took place, the union of individual and collective crises in heady festivals of released repression."[21] The biographer Fest indicts Germans as pathological neurotics, which was doubtful and misleadingly Germano-centric—only Germans were neurotics—and we have no historical context to aid us in a more realistic understanding of Hitler and more rational interpretation of the coming of World War II. If we accept that Hitler and "the Germans" exchanged pathologies in the fateful period 1919–1933, we must accept that "the French" and Raymond Poincaré, for example, exchanged similarly dimensioned pathologies during the French invasion of the Rhineland and associated adventures of 1923 and 1924. The biographers scatter about the words *neuroses, pathologies,* and the like, but would have been better served to have generalized that the most intense human being of the twentieth century developed a compulsion to save the Germans while simultaneously representative converts to Nazism accepted him as an object of sacred allegiance.

Hitler, of course, had a more immediate enemy than the French in the period of the rise to power, and that enemy was the Marxists —Communists and Social Democrats—and associated November Criminals. It can be stated categorically that, for Hitler, power was not an end in itself but the means by which the Marxists could be either converted or destroyed. The biographers know this; for example, Fest would state that "he had never wanted to be cast as one politician among many others. His idea was always to come on the scene as savior from the deadly embrace of communism, surrounded by his rescuing hosts, and thus take power. This role coincided with . . . his sense of being always engaged in a global struggle with the powers of darkness."[22] Since, however, Hitler had determined by 1925 to seize power legally, he would be forced in the actual event of 1933 to seize it with the permission of the president and then, with his rescuing hosts, use it to destroy the Marxists.

There is both subtlety and complexity in this interpretive image of Hitler because, as the biographers themselves agree, his role as savior "coincided with both his dramatic and eschatological temperament."[23] If eschatology can be seen as the doctrine of last or final things—for example, the end of an age, the second advent of Christ, immortality, judgment, and so on—then Hitler filled the bill as having had such a temperament. Hitler saw himself and his Nazi hosts as locked in a final struggle between the forces of good and evil in which the losing side would be annihilated—it could expect nothing less. Messiahs do not compromise, and Hitler had a vision of faith in Germany and a darker vision of faith in the destruction of its enemies, neither one of which was subject to compromise or capable of being interpreted in terms of political ideology. The eschatological road leads us to a man with the characteristics and temperament of a messiah.

Hitler committed numerous crimes in his early period, including acts of treason against the republic that should have resulted in deportation or lengthy prison terms. The biographers rail against the Weimar, Berlin, and Munich governments for not ridding themselves of Hitler for numerous unlawful acts and breaches of the constitution, implying that the latter were particularly heinous. We see both biographers and historians treat Hitler as an arrogant breaker of the laws of the republic, but not one makes the point that the legally sacrosanct republic had been brought into existence by the noteworthy, illegal machinations of the Marxist parties and splinters in October and November 1918. The situation was a perverse one indeed in which an illegally and violently constituted republic replaced more than one thousand years of princely rule and then sheltered behind the legality of its own self-serving constitution. This is a harsh judgment and should probably be tempered by the comment that illegal revolution is difficult to justify legally, particularly in its immediate aftermath. Notwithstanding his violent instincts, Hitler never attacked the constitution on the basis of its legal authority, but rather he attacked the republic on the basis of its derivation from the November Criminals. The constitution was irretrievably tainted, in Nazi eyes, through association with the November Criminals, but once Hitler embraced a strategy of legal takeover of power in 1925, the Nazis could scarcely attack the constitution of the republic on a legal basis afterwards. But perhaps most important for the characterization of Hitler as messiah, he could not remotely become involved in the details of an attack on a boring bourgeois document when he had pulled together Germans through his compelling Romantic vision of their salvation in a perfect Germany.

In piecing together the Hitler who had seized the chancellorship in January 1933, we cannot miss the religiously styled fervor described by a liberal young journalist in terms that seem to lead nowhere else: "His audience was breathlessly under his spell. This man expressed their thoughts, their feelings, their hopes; a new prophet had arisen—many saw in him already another Christ who predicted the end of their sufferings and had the power to lead them into the promised land if they were only prepared to follow him."[24] And a very different schoolteacher could corroborate with the words: "How many look to him in touching faith as the helper, savior, the redeemer from overgreat distress. To him, who rescues the Prussian prince, the scholar, the clergyman, the peasant, the worker, the unemployed."[25] This judgment of early 1932 can barely have been influenced by the apparatus of a propaganda ministry created one year later. Hitler would extend his image as savior in a movement anchored in faith in a man who would replace an entire system of talkative parliamentary parties with a very talkative solitary hero.

But in this compelling picture of a messiah and his alter ego, Hitler confounds us in his emotional breadth with yet another personality facet. The fifteen-year-old of Linz who raced for the best standing room at the base of the columns holding the imperial box in the municipal opera house already stood enthralled by the themes, settings, and personages of Wagner's heroic masterpieces. Hitler had an astonishing talent and affinity for architecture, and Ludwig Troost, the superbly educated, classically inclined architect who was a rare teacher figure for Hitler, could comment, "Yes, it's extraordinary the scope of what he knows. I've found, for example, that his theoretical knowledge of architecture exceeds mine. He has a remarkable sense for effects."[26] For both Wagner and Hitler, staging and effect were vital parts of the Wagnerian epics, and, along with the opera house itself, these elements could be considered as the architecture of heavy opera. Within his second alter ego as part of a German political opera from 1919 through 1933, Hitler must be interpreted as more than the would-be Wagnerian hero, derided by the biographers as such. But if ever there were a grand opera played out in world history, it would be Germany from the end of the First to the end of the Second World Wars. Hitler was not a would-be anything in it but rather Lohengrin writ both large and modern. But he was not only the lead voice and main actor but also the composer, librettist, stage setting director, and architect of the opera house itself. Wagner had a compulsion to have his operas set as effectively as possible, actually building an opera house in Bayreuth for that purpose and conceptualizing on a scale beyond any conventional structure the setting of his operas on a close off-shore island on a Bavarian mountain lake with audience ranged along the shore. In such architectural settings, Hitler, with his talents and interests in architectural effects and human psychology, would exceed the Master of Bayreuth.

Since Hitler expressed himself continuously in terms of these themes—messiah, world spirit, and Wagnerian hero—it would be difficult to believe in 1932, when he was offered the vice chancellorship, that party members would not understand how he could refuse and persevere in the quest for full power. Yet many did not comprehend how Hitler could refuse the success embodied in the title "vice chancellor," and began to suspect self destructive obstinacy, dark personal motive, and the like. But how could a man who comprehended himself as noted above and faced with fleeting time have settled for the position of vice chancellor? Yet a man as high in the movement as any except for Hitler himself could present the great opportunity but also potential for disaster as follows: "Along comes Hindenburg... a man of honor, who honestly and decently offers him a place in the government, and there stands the '*wahnfriedische*' Lohengrin-Hitler with his darkly menacing boys... Goering... Goebbels... Roehm.[27] In these words, Gregor Strasser would characterize Hitler's opportunity, succinctly interpret his top lieutenants, and, as his main point, suggest that Hitler should have taken the offer of a place in the government.

Yet Strasser knew the words that Hitler addressed to Germany in his final speech at the end of his nationally covered trial in 1924. Charged that he committed treason to become a minister in a new government, Hitler would explode: "I aimed from the first at something a thousand times higher than a minister. I wanted to become the destroyer of Marxism. I am going to achieve this task."[28] Since Nazis and their sympathizers looked upon Hitler as a savior, they could not be expected to be saved by anyone so incredible as a vice savior, especially one who would be disguised as a vice chancellor in a discredited political system. In retrospect, against such a situation of expectancy in the rank and file of the movement, a man who knew Hitler well enough to identify him as Lohengrin would advise him to accept the vice chancellorship or allow another Nazi to slip into such a position. Strasser got close enough to Hitler to see him acting as Lohengrin but not close enough to see him as *being* Lohengrin.

Hitler made it clear in writing that he "always came out in favor of taking a position in important questions of principle against all public opinion when it assumed a false attitude.... The NSDAP [Nationalsozialistische Deutsche Arbeiterpartei] should not become a constable of public opinion, but must dominate it."[29] But Hitler could also say that "the brilliant popular orator" will "always let himself be borne by the great masses in such a way that instinctively the very words come to his lips that he needs to speak to the hearts of his audience."[30] The conventional wisdom sees Hitler thus as a human tuning fork, sensing especially the baser emotions among the members of his audiences and being led by them to respond to applause. Hitler, however, makes it clear that he was always enforcing arguments on his audience. Only when he sensed that his audience had understood his arguments and had become convinced by them would he become elevated through passionate instinct to hammer on the accepted argument to continuous rounds of thunderous applause. We can have confidence in this generalization because he corroborates it by observing that "the speaker can tell at any moment if his audience can understand what he is saying, if it can follow the speech as a whole, and if he has convinced it of the soundness of what he has said."[31] If the speaker suspects that the audience does "not seem convinced of the soundness of his argument repeat it over and over in constantly new examples. He himself will utter their objections, which he senses although unspoken, and go on...exploding them until at length even the last group of an opposition, by its very bearing and facial expression, enables him to recognize its capitulation to his arguments."[32]

These words and numerous similar ones in *Mein Kampf* show Hitler wrestling presumably with every audience to impose his arguments on it, but scarcely as a shallow demagogue. A demagogue tells his audience what it wants to hear. A messiah tells his audience what he wants it to hear. And if there is a subtlety in this that links the old conventional wisdom with revision, it is that both the demagogue and the messianic world-historical personality are attuned to the hopes and fears of the era, but the messiah dominates them while the demagogue goes along for a short, self-serving ride. And curiously enough, the confusion between Hitler rendered as demagogue or as messiah may arise from the same thunderous applause by audiences to the accumulating spoken words of either one. But the path to the applause would be so different that to interpret him as "a mere demagogue" would miss the point of the phenomenon.

*   *   *

In the period particularly from 1925 through 1933, Hitler conspired to make his big and then his fatefully great decisions in unique seclusion. By 1925 no party committee, no party congress or parliament, no inner group of bona fide advisors, no individual advisor, no gray eminence, and no woman existed to temper or exaggerate Hitler's decisions in the drive for control over Germany. When pressed, Hitler could say to inquisitive newspaper reporters after the breakthrough election of 1930 that, if they wanted to know about his thoughts on National Socialism, to ask Rudolf Hess. But we must acknowledge that the essence of what Hess knew about Hitler was that he was the leadership personality who would save Germany. Hess, as the adjutant and secretary of Hitler, cannot be imagined to have influenced Hitler in his decision making except in terms of being a sounding board for his conceptualizations. The handful of others in the movement who could be likened to either great political *Feldherren* and general staff advisors—Strasser in the north, Goebbels in Berlin, Goering after 1928 in various guises, and Roehm all over Germany—cannot be seen to have had a decisive influence over Hitler's decision making. The conventional wisdom acknowledges this extraordinary situation by agreeing that the Nazi movement was both conceptualized and led by Hitler—unlike, for example, Marxian socialism in Russia, where Marx had conceptualized it, Lenin had successfully led it, and Stalin had inherited it.

In his first great decision of the epic year 1932, Hitler would perform as distinctive, enduring Hitler. We are fortunate to have the diary of his follower most responsible for carrying out the decision and, of course, we have the interpretive comments of the hostile biographers. The government had set the seven-year presidential election for early March, and Bruening had coerced Hindenburg to stand for reelection after being unable to craft the alternative of a second term without an election process. Hitler would face a situation that could be described in today's jargon as lose–lose, for if he ran against Hindenburg he would almost certainly lose, and if he did not run he would almost certainly lose the offensive spirit of the entire movement. Hitler faced a perilous decision, and his biographers have been at a loss to interpret his style and timing in making it. He would reply evasively to Bruening's request for a constitutional amendment that would have made Hindenburg, at age eighty-four, president for life; it became evident in the first days of January 1932 that an election would take place as scheduled on March 13.

Against this background, Hitler would not announce his candidacy for the presidency for an astounding period of approximately six weeks. Faced with this incomprehensively long period, the biographers have been forced to use words similar to the following to interpret him: "he remained impassive while Goebbels and others hammered at him to announce his candidature.... Here was still another instance of Hitler's curious indecisiveness. He had a fatalistic streak and liked to let things take their course, postponing action until the last moment.... Goebbels's diary reveals... Hitler's tortuous [sic], almost bizarre vacillations."[33] And finally, Kershaw notes "the doubts that had assailed Goebbels during the preceding weeks in the face of Hitler's weak leadership."[34] The choice of words such as remained impassive, curious indecisiveness, postponing action until the last moment, fatalistic streak, torturous almost bizarre vacillation, and weeks of weak leadership, shows Kershaw largely unable to understand Hitler's personality at all. Yet the latter had determined by 1925 never again to be pressed into decisions such as those that had led to the near-extinction of the movement in the earlier Munich fiasco. Hitler demanded that his leadership be accepted unconditionally and that each party member see in himself the supporter of the common idea—Hitler's overarching and marvelously hazy faith in Germany. Hitler would lead based on his representation of the common idea, his personification of the idea, and his infallibility in making decisions to create the perfect German state inherent in the idea.

Goebbels would indeed agonize over Hitler's failure to allow him to announce his candidacy during the period of January 9 through late February 1932. On February 22, Goebbels went to the *Kaiserhof*, Hitler's Berlin hotel headquarters, to brief him on the contents of his speech for that evening to the general membership of the west, east, and north regions of the party in Germany. When Goebbels brought up yet again the candidacy, Hitler unexpectedly and almost casually gave him permission to announce it then, only twenty-two days from the election. Until that point, as noted, the biographers saw curious indecision, wavering, postponing of things to the last moment, and weak leadership. To all intents and purposes, and to use the words of Kershaw himself, "Hitler dithered for more than a month before deciding to run for the presidency."[35]

Rather than showing weak leadership and dithering, however, Hitler can be seen more realistically as maintaining undisputed authority over a volatile movement while deciding *when* to run, not *whether* to run. He would not only make the 1932 decision in splendid isolation, but also reserve to himself the timing of its public announcement; Goebbels himself could comment at the beginning of the whole business: "Much guessing about what the Fuehrer will do." *Much guessing* would turn out to be about when he would make the decision, and it is tempting to make an analogy with Hitler's characteristic dramatic entries into his mass public meetings. He would commonly demand observations of the mood, excitement, anticipation of the audience, and, at the special moment that he sensed the audience's anticipation to be peaking but soon to dissipate, Hitler would sweep onto the scene and advance directly to the podium. In the first presidential election of 1932, before an audience of every German and many Nazis, he seemed to have consciously gauged the anticipation and timed his entry for his greatest audience and biggest speech as pulled together in the election.

* * *

During almost the entire period of the drive for power, biographers and historians alike have darkened the party's "army" partly through preconceived bias and resulting assumption that the *Sturmabteilung* (SA) was an evil organization that could be criticized without the reasonable constraints of history as nonfiction. The conventional wisdom uses words such as *terror, beer swilling bullies, criminals, sadists,* and the ever present noun *thug,* to characterize the organization and its men. It is apparently easy to ignore the fastening of the formal title *Sturmabteilung* as a result of the great *Saalschlacht* (meeting room battle) of November 1921 in the *Hofbraeuhaus* in Munich in which approximately 450 Social Democratic meeting breakers attempted to prevent Hitler from finishing a speech and were repelled by forty-six Nazi defenders. At its inception, Hitler employed the SA as an indispensable political combat detachment to protect Nazi meetings and to post and distribute propaganda and meeting announcements. To accomplish the latter, the SA had to establish the street presence necessary to carry out activity that was so dangerously provocative to the Reds who had naturally assumed domination of the public thoroughfares and plazas since the revolution.

Hitler would struggle with the concept of what the SA of October–November 1921 should become and, with his characteristically compact and compelling logic, decided was as follows: To survive as a political movement and to defeat the Marxists, he and his Nazis required force in meeting hall and street in order to shield and project a mass movement. He reasoned that to serve the political mission of a mass movement, "the SA could be neither a military combat organization nor a secret league."[36] As concerns its physical training, for example, "the emphasis must be laid not on military drilling, but on athletic activity. Boxing and jiu-jitsu have always seemed to me to be more important than any inferior, because incomplete, training in marksmanship."[37] To prevent the SA at its inception from assuming any secret character, he would insist on an "immediately recognizable" uniform and enlist the largest numbers of wearers practicable. And as concerns comprehending Hitler in terms of his elevated conception of what he and the Nazis were about, he would insist that the SA had to "be completely initiated into the great idea of the movement... and that the individual man saw his mission, not in the elimination of any greater or lesser scoundrel, but in fighting for the erection of a new National Socialist ... state."[38]

In his conceptualization of the SA as a uniformed mass organization that would march beneath the open sky, he would pull things together in words that "thereby the struggle against the present day state was removed from the atmosphere of petty actions of revenge and conspiracy, to the greatness of a philosophical war of annihilation against Marxism."[39] To emphasize the political function and expediency of the SA, Hitler would elaborate that the organization, uniform, and equipment of the political storm detachments could not reasonably be expected to emulate the models of the old army. Presented with words such as those above, dictated in 1925, and published in 1927, the chiefs of staff of the SA from 1927 through 1934, Franz Pfeffer von Salomon and Ernst Roehm, nevertheless looked upon the SA as a potentially armed military force incidentally engaged in street and meeting hall brawls. The biographers would claim that few men ever read *Mein Kampf*, and the apparent oversight in the cases of Salomon and Roehm would cost the former his job and the latter his life.

But the great biographers themselves seem to have taken liberties with *Mein Kampf* that suggest that they have selectively ignored passages in it that interfere with their preconceived necessity to disparage Hitler and the SA. Some of the disparagement supports a view that even though Hitler's autobiography and stunningly idealistic political testament had been available for them since the beginning of the era of the great biographers, they seem not to have read the two volumes or not to have understood the arguments in them. Since, however, with such superior biographies, they must have, in fact, both read the book and understood the arguments, we may assume that, clad in the invincible armor of their preconception of Hitler and his political fighters as evil, they have ignored reality.

*   *   *

In the second most important political action involving Hitler and the SA between 1922 and 1933—the political raid on Coburg—the great biographers do not use the event to characterize Hitler and give a clearer picture of the SA. Werner Maser, who could be considered as one of the great biographers, would generalize about "the ruthlessness...with which he and his 800 SA men had smashed popular opposition in the streets of Coburg in 1922."[40] Maser uses the word *ruthless* when the words *unshakeable resolve* would capture the spirit of the moment better, and he goes on to present the Nazis as smashing popular opposition. The biographer thereby presents them as crushing the opposition of the general body of the people of Coburg while leaving us to wonder why the arch-proponent of a German mass movement would want to alienate a popular body of potential supporters and to wonder about the nature of the opposition.

Fest presents Coburg in more detail but also spins us away from comprehension of Hitler and the times by presenting only half the picture of the great event. Fest would note that Hitler made his first bold stroke out of Munich and would interpret it as "the first of those challenges to the political authorities that were to dominate the following years."[41] We cannot doubt that the foray was a bold stroke and a challenge to the authorities. Hitler, however, meant to ensure that nationalist demonstrations could take place in Germany without disruption or destruction by Socialist and Communist Reds, as was the rule in most of Germany (e.g., Prussia and Saxony). He would note that "the experience of Coburg had the significance that we now began systematically, in all places where for many years the Red terror had prevented any meeting of people with different ideas, to break this terror and restore freedom of assembly."[42]

If we were to caricaturize this situation, we would generalize that the conventional wisdom presents Hitler as an evil and brutal power seeker who would terrorize the whole population of Coburg with a "private army" of strong-arm bullies. In the opposite caricature, Hitler could be imagined to see himself entering in resplendent armor with accompanying hosts of German political warriors dedicated to the salvation of the people of Coburg. The historical facts permit us to describe the event, sort out the bias, and perhaps even get a superior interpretation of the whole period based on so representative an example of Hitler in action. In early October 1922, the organizers of a nationalist German Day gathering in Coburg had invited Hitler to participate and advised him to bring an escort. Sensing opportunity to propagandize the movement outside the environs of Munich and to ensure that the Reds who dominated Coburg politically would not break up the affair, Hitler "appointed" eight hundred SA men as escort. When Hitler arrived, a nationalist deputation and a city police captain informed him that the Marxist-controlled Coburg trade unions had demanded, and the nationalists and civil authority had been forced to agree, not to allow the Nazis to parade through the streets to their overnight quarters, notwithstanding the festive, patriotic event.

The Marxists claimed that a nationalist parade would be a provocation of the proletariat and the cause of worse things—proletarian fists would be forced to break up the offending demonstration. Hitler defied everyone and marched his men away from the train in a festive parade column while accepting police guards to take him to quarters in a shooting gallery at city's edge. The police, however, led him to the presumably closer and safer *Hofbraeuhauskeller* in town center but unwittingly through growing abusive crowds orchestrated by the Marxists. The police attempted to lock the Nazis into the cellar grounds and the Red crowds out of them, but Hitler insisted on reforming his parade column and marching to the agreed Nazi quarters. The disciplined column marched out to the dark cadence of drums only, and shortly thereafter came under physical attack by

Reds throwing rocks and assaulting individual members of the column. The Nazis broke ranks and won a memorable daylight street battle, scattering the Red crowd and winning the follow-on street skirmishes that were equally furious and continued through the evening. The next morning, October 15, the Coburg Marxists called for ten thousand workers to gather in the main city square at one thirty in the afternoon to throw out the Nazis. Hitler ordered his parade column, which was scheduled to march as part of the nationalist festivities to the Coburg Fortress, to proceed by way of the square, "firmly resolved to dispose of the Red terror for good."[43] The only notable resistance offered to the Nazis was from outside newcomers who were not acquainted with the new situation in the city. As the Nazis later marched to the train station Sunday evening, the local population "broke into spontaneous cheering in many places" presumably in support of the wicked Nazis.

Prior to the tactical battles of the precedent-setting action above, Hitler had accurately suspected that a nationalist meeting of any consequence would force the Reds to disrupt it. With the example of fascist flying columns retaking several major Italian cities from internationally styled Communist control earlier in 1922, and Hitler's sense that many German cities outside Munich were similarly influenced by Marxists, he decided to make his insolent junket. After the earlier November 1921 meeting hall battle in the Munich *Hofbraeuhaus*, the SA had attracted more members and by September 1922 had formed eight "hundreds" in Munich, Tolz, and Rosenheim, well-organized and disciplined, as evidenced by their fast call-up for the passage to Coburg and their combat in the city. We see Hitler as will to action, artistic imagination, force, and wild fearlessness. The German Day committee had invited Hitler to come to witness some tame street festivities and to make a few domesticated patriotic remarks at a boring round of droning speeches. If ever a messianic personality descended upon an unsuspecting flock, it would have been Hitler and his band of recent fanatic converts on the people and the streets of Coburg.

Hitler earlier had made the decision to attend the congress based on some characteristic inspiration influenced by no other man in the immediate event: "This [invitation], which I received at eleven o'clock in the morning came very opportunely. An hour later the arrangements for attending this 'German Day' had been issued."[44] As concerns his artistically styled imagination, Hitler would personally conceptualize the hiring of a Reich train with third-class coaches to carry the entire party together to Coburg, and he would arrive with the most gripping political symbol of the twentieth century, which would be seen on armbands of his SA men and flags carried by them, and which he had personally designed earlier in the summer of 1921. And when the railway workers refused to run the hired train back to Munich, Hitler personally and convincingly warned them that he would seize all of the Red leaders he could hunt down, carry them along on the train now run by his own people, and leave to the workers' imagination what he would do with the leaders if anything happened to the train along the way. Hitler's audacity, lack of sense of proportion, and success in all of this must leave us interpretively speechless.

The biographers claim that in Coburg Hitler terrorized the workers, smashed popular opposition,[45] had as his objective a propaganda victory,[46] and carried out the first of those challenges to the authorities that would dominate the following years.[47] To support the general interpretation of Hitler as will to domination and the SA as inhabited by men who could be freely characterized as "thugs," the biographers take liberties with the facts. They claim that Hitler defied the city authorities by marching into the city in a parade column and thereby caused a street riot. The leaders of the Marxist-dominated Coburg trade unions had demanded of the celebration organizers and of the police that the Nazis not be allowed to march into the city because such an act would be a provocation and result in violence by presumably enraged workers. Both the organizing committee and the police agreed to the demand, the former through some measures of fear and cowardice and the latter through concern over the threat of violence by the Marxists. As the actual event unfolded, we see that the authorities acted on a demand of the Marxists and must acknowledge that Hitler defied an initiative of the Marxists and not of the political authorities of Coburg. The police faced the challenge of keeping a dangerous mob of Marxist-incited sympathizers and toughs away from an equally dangerous, although disciplined, marching column of Nazis.

In this action, Hitler faced several inanities that tended to give him a moral edge over his opposition. The organizing committee had invited Hitler to a patriotic event typified by marching columns, bands, and flags. But as he and the SA arrived and debarked from the train, he was directed to straggle through the city, bandsmen silent and flags hidden—not a particularly effective or appropriate patriotic demonstration by Germans on German Day. And if provocation ever existed in a situation, it would have been Germans being told (in Germany, on German Day) that no parade would be allowed because such was offensive to internationalist proponents of class war. During the rise to power, Nazi leaders of the political organization and fighters in the political army or storm section of the party advanced into cities in southern Germany, whose streets were dominated similarly to Coburg by the street-fighting apparatus of the Social Democratic and Communist Parties, with their mass followings and often tough and dangerous followers. And as Hitler necessarily expanded the movement into western and northern Germany, the SA began to break into the great Marxist enclaves such as the Ruhr, Hamburg, Berlin, and Saxony. In such a situation, it is difficult to distinguish among the terrorizers and those Germans who were being terrorized.

Within their frameworks of Hitler biography, authors have painted a picture of the SA as one filled with thugs and bullies, but the Coburg quintessential SA action does not support so one-sided a view. The Coburg authorities, for example, blamed the Marxist-dominated workers for provoking the violence. It is difficult to refute this interpretation, which also puts doubt in our minds about the SA men as bare rowdies, at least at Coburg. Kershaw is relentless, however, and notes that the police reported that even though the Marxists provoked the riot, things would have gone peacefully if the "Hitler people" had not come to Coburg. The peace, however, would have been the peace of a dead German Day celebration passing hardly noticed in its timid inoffensiveness, and the Marxists being hardly disturbed in their continued intimidating control of a German city.

As described above Hitler cannot be seen as an evil man engaged in an evil deed at Coburg, and the SA men cannot be characterized as brawl-provoking bullies and thugs. This generalization does not mean that Hitler was not engaged in evil during the rise to power. It does mean that in one of the more significant actions launched by him personally, accompanied by his early entourage and leading most of the SA men in the movement at the time, he and the Nazis came under physical attack by an inflamed and dangerous crowd of Marxist workers. We can perhaps summarize that those who were used to being the terrorizers in Coburg discovered themselves out-terrorized, and those who were used to being terrorized found themselves saved. And since the police referred to the new force in Bavarian politics not as "the Nazis" but as the "Hitler people," the Coburg populace must have sensed, at least dimly, the presence of a savior.

With its outlandish audacity, the Coburg action would remain unique. The Nazis, however, would advance similarly, although more slowly and less spectacularly, everywhere in Germany from 1922 onward. The pattern would be one of the development or insertion of leaders and political organizations in the cities and larger urban agglomerates of Germany with the purpose of conducting propaganda and attracting converts. The men of the storm section of the party were indispensable for the survival of the Nazis because of the strength and violence of the Social Democrats and Communists in the urban areas. On the offensive, the SA men had the mission to dominate the streets in support of the political organization and, in Hitler's words, to provide a free path for the advance of the idea. The free path could be looked upon physically as a street in a German city where Nazis could distribute leaflets, affix posters, solicit contributions, sell and advertise party newspapers, and present a superior German alternative to the revolutionary energy and appeal of the Marxists.

Hitler would comment that, "in Coburg itself, at least a part of the Marxist working class, which incidentally could be regarded only as misled, had learned a lesson from the fists of National Socialist labor."[48] With his extraordinary sensitivities as both mass and individual psychologist, Hitler intended the SA man to be an instrument to impress and overawe Germans but scarcely to terrorize them more or less promiscuously in the streets. Seen as such, Hitler's SA man of the rise to power represented a kind of visual propaganda—the likeness of the new German man. He projected, in turn, an image of the party as one of unparalleled vitality, drive, and youthful vigor. And in the words of a woman in a Marxist dominated town of Lower Saxony, "there was a feeling of restless energy about the Nazis."[49]

*   *   *

The conventional wisdom nevertheless has presented the SA as a band of brutal, thick-necked street fighters dedicated to violence almost as an end in itself. The picture is only partly true, largely false, and dangerously misleading. Given the importance of Berlin and the fame of its new *Gaulieter* of 1926, the biographers commonly use the Berlin SA to generalize about the entire SA. As noted by Fest, "One SA 'storm' in Wedding [a northern Berlin Communist-dominated district] called itself the Robber Storm, while many troopers assumed various desperado names—Potshot Mueller or Pistol Packer."[50] Fest writes that the SA had stores of the classic weapons of criminals: blackjacks, brass knuckles, and rubber truncheons. "In tight situations, they had their molls carry their hand guns."[51] But the biographer does not give us the context in which Berlin and the larger Prussian cities were dominated by outright majorities or strong pluralities of Marxists, who utterly dominated the streets and the political propaganda of the capital.

When Goebbels took leadership of the newly designated *Gau* Berlin-Brandenburg in early November 1926, Nazi party membership was below one thousand and split into two warring parts—the political organization and the storm section of the political organization. Goebbels faced the imposing mission of taking over a city with a population of approximately 4.2 million with a storm section of only several hundred men. After Goebbels had been in Berlin for a year and one-half and Reichstag elections took place in May 1928, approximately 39,000 Berliners voted for the Nazis in contrast to 640,000 for the Communists and 855,000 for the Social Democrats.[52] Faced with the odds against them in Berlin as reflected in these numbers, the Berlin SA and that of numerous other Marxist-dominated German cities—Hamburg, Leipzig, Dresden, Essen, Dortmund, Duesseldorf, Wuppertal, and so on—might be interpreted as beer-swilling rowdies but scarcely as bullies in the face of the numerical odds against them in the streets of the great cities of Germany. The Nazis had bottomed out in the May 1928 Reichstag elections, but even in the greatest triumph of the rise to power in the July 1932 elections they found themselves outnumbered two to one by the Marxists in Berlin. Even in the election of the latter time in Munich, the half-mystical geographical origin of Nazism, the Marxists outnumbered the Nazis in followers with 37.6 percent of the vote compared with 28.9 percent for Hitler's supporters.

These numbers demand a reevaluation of the balance of political intimidation—"terror"—in German city streets, especially in the period of Hitler's enforcement of a strategy of legal takeover from 1925 through 1933. The biographers have continued to paint the SA man as a dark and brutal street fighter while neglecting to provide the quite amazing context such as that found in early Berlin, where the Nazis found themselves outnumbered in 1928, thirty-eight to one in terms of supporters. Under such circumstances, Goebbels showed monumental audacity in provoking brawls with the street-fighting apparatuses of the Marxists, the SA man exhibited extraordinary pugnacity and bravery, and the "hundreds" into which he was organized possessed a remarkable spirit. This does not mean that the Berlin SA man was not a brutal street brawler and thug, but that if he were, he would have been a noteworthily courageous street brawler and thug. If we cast aside the exaggerated propaganda-tinged characterization of the SA man as thug and agree on his descriptor as a man capable of street brawling, we come up with a man willing to risk death or wounding in the tough street encounters that culminated in the year 1932. The antithesis of the biographers' thug can be found in SA standard leader Willi Veller, who wrote the following lines in a letter of August 1930 to Gregor Strasser:

> In my work for the NSDAP I have faced a court more than thirty times and have been convicted eight times for assault and battery, resistance to a police officer, and other such misdemeanors that are natural for a Nazi. To this day I am still paying installments on my fines, and in addition have other trials coming up. I have been more or less severely wounded at least twenty times. I have knife scars on the back of my head, on my left shoulder, on my lower lip, on my right cheek, on the left side of my upper lip, and on my right arm. Furthermore, I have never claimed or received a penny of party money, but have sacrificed my time to our movement at the expense of the good business I inherited from my father. Today I am facing financial ruin.[53]

The word *thug*, with its synonyms of criminal, crook, hoodlum, outlaw, and sociopath, somehow does not fit Willi Veller and probably not the overwhelming majority of SA men, even in the difficult days of 1925 through 1933. So how do we interpret the half of the NSDAP intended by Hitler to exert force in order to protect and project the movement of the other half? As early as February 1920, Hitler had sensed the necessity for "a house guard in the form of a *monitor service*" to keep order in the early mass meetings of the German Worker's Party.[54] He had previously employed comrades from the infantry regiment barracks in which he had lived during the first seven months of his entry into the party to evict disruptive leftist hecklers. He formed an *Ordnertruppe*, or stewards troop, to act as bodyguards for speakers and as ushers and athletic types to evict meeting disrupters. Part of this *Ordnertruppe*, which was first headed by the apprentice watchmaker, war veteran, *Freikorps* member, and Hitler bodyguard Emil Maurice, would evolve into an initially small, ultraelite bodyguard force for Hitler known as the *Schutzstaffel* (SS or protective detachment), commonly known as the SS. Most of the *Ordnertruppen* of the party would evolve through the Athletics and Sport Detachment of the spring of 1921 and into the SA in August of the same year. By this time, Hitler had perceived through historical example of the Marxists and his own unique instincts that he would need some instrument of unarmed force to protect the spread of the idea. In any case, Hitler understood force as indispensable to create the perfect German community and envisioned the SA man as a paragon of the fighter for such a community:

> How many a time the eyes of my lads glittered when I explained to them the necessity of their mission and assured them over and over again that all the wisdom on this earth remains without success if force does not enter into its service, guarding it and protecting it.[55]

For the SA man, Hitler demanded a will to succeed in an expressed heroic German mission, against greater odds, if necessary, than ordinary men would consider facing, odds that would paralyze action. In this context and with his historical style of thought, Hitler would note that "without suspecting it, a German general succeeded in finding the classic formula for this miserable spinelessness: 'I act only if I can count on fifty-one percent likelihood of success.'"[56] Hitler would elaborate that in this 51 percent lay the tragedy of the German misfortune because anyone who demanded of fate a guarantee of success would automatically renounce any idea of a heroic deed. He would demand iron will and offensive élan, and would link it with physical prowess. It remains difficult to generalize about what he actually got in the real SA men, but we must be impressed by Hitler and his forty-six in the *Festsaal* of the *Hofbraeuhaus* in 1921, Hitler and his eight hundred in Coburg in 1922, and Goebbels and his handful in Berlin from 1926 through 1932. Given the similarly organized Marxist street-fighting formations and the similar toughness of their members, and if we accept the interpretation of SA men as beer-swilling bullies and thugs, we could generalize that a smaller number of beer-swilling Nazi thugs stood opposed to a greater number of beer-swilling Marxist thugs in the meeting halls and streets of Germany throughout the Nazi rise to power. But Hitler maintained that "the young movement, from the first day, espoused the standpoint that its idea must be put forward [as inspired by a holy mission], but that the defense of this spiritual platform must if necessary be secured by strong-arm means."[57] Hitler seems to have been looking for true believers with athletic builds and an urge to battle, and photographs of the period show a surfeit of young men who, at least visually, fit the bill.

*   *   *

The great biographers have claimed that Hitler personified contempt for the masses and used his propaganda mastery over them to increase his own personal power and to feed his urge to dominate. In an undisguised flight of outlandish bias, one would compare Hitler with Richard Wagner by claiming that "they were masters of the art of brilliant fraudulence, of inspired swindling."[58] And with Hitler described thus as a charlatan, the biographers tell us that his brilliant propaganda was fraudulent, based as it was on contempt for the masses rather than admiration for them and with the purpose to pull them together into a single community. In passages in *Mein Kampf* on the subject of propaganda, Hitler would postulate that "the receptivity of the great masses is very limited, their intelligence is small, but their power of forgetting is enormous."[59] And Hitler would elaborate that "the masses are slow-moving... and only after the simplest ideas are repeated thousands of times will the masses finally remember them."[60] Writers use such statements by Hitler to support a view that he felt the masses to be mean, vile, and worthless— contemptuous. The interpretation and its intent to devalue Hitler falters in the face of the context in which it was offered. Hitler made these characteristically bold generalizations as realistic principles of mass psychology that had to be addressed in order to conduct effective propaganda. Hitler was not opining contemptuously that the individuals in his audiences were vile and mean but that these individuals, when presented in masses or crowds, represented a different mass psychology. It is one thing to despise the broad masses and a different thing to point out, as Hitler did, their fundamental characteristics around which the psychologist had to work in order to spread revealed truth as opposed to political doctrine. When Hitler said, for example, that the masses have an infinite capacity to forget important truths that therefore have to be addressed repeatedly, this does not translate into contempt for them but rather into knowledge of mass psychology and the necessity to take account of it.

*   *   *

Most biographers and historians agonize over the period of 1919 through 1933 in terms of the question: How was it possible for a man so base, common, and evil as Hitler to have come to dictatorial political power in a nation so cultured as Germany? Since this generalization about Hitler has been taken as unarguable fact, the writers proceed, in varying detail, that although the Germans were notably cultured, they were naïve about parliamentary politics. There is room to challenge the notion of the naïveté of Germans in politics given the development and accomplishments of the Social Democratic, Center, Conservative, and other parties of the Second Reich from 1871 through 1918. The Social Democratic Party, for example, had become the largest, best organized, and strongest Marxist political party on the face of the earth during that period, and the model for all others. Bismarck and following chancellors had managed to work with the German parliamentary parties by the mid-1890s to bring into play in Wilhelmine Germany the most advanced and humane social programs of any major power of the world, including the usual model democracies of France and Britain. And even the pièce de résistance offered by historians to illustrate the horrors of German political naïveté—Ludendorff as military dictator during the later part of the war—is comfortably balanced by the significantly dictatorial powers by 1917 of Clemenceau, joined later by Marshal Ferdinand Foch in France, and the largely uninhibited powers of a war cabinet in Britain in 1916 headed by Lloyd George, the erstwhile munitions minister and master propagandist of World War I. The conventional wisdom leaves us with the picture of a wicked, despicable man brought to power significantly through the political naïveté of the German public.

The accepted wisdom has elaborated that the more democratically experienced French and British survived the war's aftermath without falling prey to a Hitler-like figure. As that wisdom brings the word *democratic* into play, it accompanies it with the spectral words *German militarism*, suggesting that a population associated with such words and without an adequate grounding in real democracy would more easily succumb to Hitler. The reading public, however, is not presented with the necessary context of modern Europe in which the palm in "militarism" must go the French and Imperial Russians as exemplified by two Napoleons and various and assorted Alexanders and Nicholases. And lest the British disappear from any balanced consideration, they must take the palm in "navalism"—policies of aggressive naval preponderance identical in spirit to that of "militarism"— and be rebuked for their contribution to wars large and small across the entire earth beginning in the mid-eighteenth century. Whereas Hitler has been accused universally, although not necessarily accurately, as desiring the elusive quantity described as world domination, the British had come close to actually achieving world domination with the vaunted Pax Britannica as it existed at the turn of the century. These factors of militarism and experience in democratic politics are overused in explaining Hitler's popularity with Germans.

The single most important factor that separated the French, British, and American peoples from the Germans of the period of Hitler's rise to power was the defeat of the latter and the victory of the former in World War I. This vast historical circumstance need not have led to either a World War II or a Hitler. The Allied governments and peoples, however, would assign the entire blame to Germany for its alleged planning, starting, and inhumane conduct of the war—this assignment remains recorded in two grand historical documents to the present day, specifically the allied ultimatum to sign the Versailles treaty and the treaty itself. These documents highlight the vindictive spirit of the era that, along with the French enforcement of the treaty, pointed the way to Hitler as ethereal savior figure.

At the end of the drive to power, the twelve-year-old Egon Hanfstaengl, during a vacation stay with Hitler at *Haus Wachenfeld* in the Bavarian Alps, could recall enticing him outside with the words: "Herr Hitler, a devoted multitude is eagerly awaiting your appearance at the gateway." After Hitler went out to greet his admirers, Egon could recall that "they nearly swooned...and one hysterical lady picked up some pebbles on which [Hitler] had stepped and put them in a little vial which she crushed to her breast."[61] And inside the house, Egon would describe that during the numerous meal times "Hitler was rather gracious, for his standards. I mean he didn't make you remember all the time that he was the Fuehrer. As a rule, Hitler never converses, he either listens, or—more commonly—preaches, making his utterances as though they were endowed with the authority of revealed religion."[62]

During the period of his rise to power, biographers recounting it after the fact and contemporaries describing it during the fact present wildly different views of Hitler. In a brief but appalling lapse of credibility, Fest offers the words: "And yet we hesitate to call Hitler great. Perhaps what give us pause is not so much the criminal features in this man's psychopathic face."[63] The great biographers all debunk Nazi theories of racial differences, which they characterize as pseudoscientific and based on unredeemed prejudice, yet one of them could claim confidently, without hint of countervailing possibility, that the subject of his biography had criminal features set in a psychopathic face. If anything should give pause, it would be the combination of the prejudice and irrelevance of the claim in any attempt to interpret Hitler. In a different vein, Hubert R. Knickerbocker would comment, based on close personal observation, that "the outstanding characteristic of his physiognomy [peculiar configuration or characteristic expression of the face] is his dreamy look …there was in his eyes the look of a seer."[64] In photographs from 1914 through 1933, Hitler often presented a dreamy, distant gaze in which characteristically he stared through the lens and the photographer toward something beyond. The effect is exclusively associated with his right eye—the left eye from the perspective of the viewer of any photograph. The great biography by Werner Maser has two full-page photographs side by side in which the September 1914 winner of the Iron Cross, Second Class (ribbon, third coat button down) is juxtaposed alongside the 1925 author of *Mein Kampf.*[65] The look on the western front is distant, the eyes half asleep, the effect that of the presence of an imperious seer. The look, the eyes, the effect in the carefully posed indoor political piece with the ghostly presence of the Iron Chancellor hovering over Hitler's left shoulder, are unmistakably similar. In the visual counterparts, the right eye is somnolent and hypnotic and the left wider-open and more ordinary.

Since we cannot accuse Hitler in 1914 of striking a Fuehrer pose in the absence of a Nazi movement, and yet the same moody, trancelike qualities are obvious in both pictures, we must suspect that some of what the biographers interpret as contrived was Hitler being Hitler. We have ample evidence to show Hitler striking heroic poses for the serious purpose of placing the image of the Leader in front of Germans. The biographers also present a picture of Hitler by

1922 developing as a drummer or prophet of the coming of a great one who would save Germany. But on the verge of linking the canny political simplifier with the man consumed by a messianic revelation of German destiny, as it were, linking the left eye in the Hitler portrait with the right one, the biographers falter. They drop the reader in 1933 with an unsavory, contemptuous propagandist quite unbelievable as a man who could make new Germans, relieve Germany of the misfortune of 1918, and march it to victory over everybody and everything by August 1941.

*   *   *

After the seizure of power, Hitler would look back on the years 1919–1933 and reveal much of himself in commenting that "Other generations—they learn of sagas of heroes, the expeditions of heroes: we have lived this saga, we have marched together on this expedition."[66] He would reveal the great spiritual landing place of the expedition in characteristically historical terms: "When yesterday [November 7, 1935] a new war-flag for the Reich was hoisted. ...For the first time since Germans appeared in the world there is a single Reich, dominated by a single view of the world, protected by a single army [in World War I there were four "German" armies, namely those of Prussia, Bavaria, Saxony, and Wuerttemberg] and all that united under a single flag."[67] We see a German national movement based on faith and will and applicable singularly to Germans. And viewed as such, Nazism would bear a striking resemblance to Judaism with its absolute exclusivity. There would be so-called fascist movements throughout Europe, but only ethnic Germans or closely related peoples could practice Nazism as only ethnic Jews could genuinely practice Judaism. What greater irony could there be historically than the collision of two self-adjudicated chosen peoples?

Hitler as anti-Semite has continued to present a code unbroken for the period of his rise to power and, hence, unbroken for his entire life.

The great biographers have maintained that Hitler has remained an undeciphered code but have done so because they have underestimated the wrong man. The conventional wisdom has accurately generalized that Hitler was affected by Romantic, heroically rendered histories of Aryans and Germans and the similarly rendered epic operas of Wagner. Here we see Hitler as hero. The same wisdom has generalized that Hitler had only talentless pretension as painter and architect. Here the conventional wisdom is inaccurate and instead we must see Hitler as artist. What flashes of insight came to the young aspiring Hero and developing artist that led to the anti-Semitic storm beginning in late 1919? First, and more or less unarguably, we see him recognizing the Jews not as a conventionally recognized religious body but realizing them to be an enduring nationality—a cohesive ethnic grouping that incidentally discovered an elitist religion that served to cement the nation. Second, and also more or less unarguably, he received the inspired insight that this dispersed political nation had created Marxism, which had become its political combat arm. The biographers have underestimated the historical sweep and astounding coherence in Hitler's anti-Semitism. They have also undervalued Hitler by preferring to present him as a dilettante with a garbled anti-Semitism characterized by intense, emotionally conditioned hatred of Jews.

In the young years from 1919 through early 1922, Hitler gave ample evidence of hatred of Jews, and the view of him as raging, emotional anti-Semite seems to exist from the beginning of Nazism and dominate to the end. But curiously undigested by the conventional wisdom is his quite amazing letter as a common lance corporal to Captain Mayr on the subject of the Jews, presenting a coldly reasoned, historically coherent foundation for a rational philosophy of anti-Semitism and not the ordinary superficially rendered diatribe of others. How is it possible for the arch emotional enemy of the Jews to have produced such a document in 1919 and claimed later, in 1924, in his dictation of *Mein Kampf*, that he wrestled mightily and objectively with the question of anti-Semitism and came to quite objective conclusions about the menace from world Jewry?

The biographers present the familiar Hitler created for their reading public as the hate-filled, raging, emotionally charged personal enemy of the Jews. Hitler seems to explain the picture of the virulent, noisy street and written tract anti-Semitism of the Nazis to set the stage for the later physical destruction of the European Jews. This Hitler interpretation ever-so-subtly, however, may slip by reality because of the personal nature it claims for his anti-Semitism and the probable explanation in terms of personal frustration in his life as aspiring artist. This interpretation cannot credibly explain his April 1924 final trial vow to become the destroyer of Marxism and his early 1930s concentration on the destruction of the parliamentary political system of the November Criminals. There are too few Jews in the picture of Hitler's anti-Semitism of 1922 through 1933 to explain Hitler in terms of visceral, emotional, all-consuming yet peculiarly noisy hatred of Jews. And Hitler's totally functional interaction with Jews on an immediate personal level, in Linz, Vienna, pre-war Munich, and during World War I, does not support a view of Hitler as a personal or emotional anti-Semite. Hitler would dictate the words in *Mein Kampf* that "on grounds of human tolerance, I maintained my rejection of religious attacks in this case as in others. Consequently, the tone, particularly that of the Viennese anti-Semitic press, seemed to me to be unworthy of the cultural tradition of a great nation."[68]

Because of his intellectual predilection and thoughtfulness, Hitler cannot be seen as a religiously oriented and fantasy-bound anti-Semite, and we are driven to suspect that his anti-Semitism was incredibly distant and idealized. The Jews, in effect, were a detached historical force and not a group of human beings in any ordinary sense for Hitler. Seen as such, the Jews could scarcely have been an object of unrestrained, thoughtless hate but rather as the ideal personification of evil. Through reading of ancient myth and modern newspaper and tract, study of history, and passionate thoughtfulness, Hitler educated himself on the "Jewish question." In doing so he claimed objectivity, noting for example that the anti-Semitic newspapers he read "did not enjoy an outstanding reputation," and that he "regarded them more as the products of anger and envy than the results of a principled, though perhaps mistaken, point of view."[69]

As Hitler carried on his studies, especially between 1908 and 1910, he linked the Jews with the editors and writers of the great Viennese "world newspapers" and discovered the Zionist movement, with its developing mission to establish a Jewish political state in a large part of the Sanjaq of Jerusalem and Vilayet of Bairut (Beirut) in the Ottoman Turkish Empire—present day Israel–Palestine. Hitler would dictate the ominous objective reality in *Mein Kampf* that there could be no such thing as a German Jew (i.e., a German who happened to profess Judaism as a religion), because every Jew in Germany had to be a political Jew with primary allegiance to a great dispersed political nation that incidentally, by 1924, was in the early stage of establishing a Jewish political state in the British League of Nations Mandate of Palestine.

Hitler, however, also witnessed in Vienna the propaganda and street presence of Marxist socialism and became outraged by the stealing away of German workers in the great metropolis from their German national identity and their conversion into part of an inter- national class of "workers." The thoughtful, brooding, explosive, ide- alistic, heroically inclined, very young Hitler must have sensed the impending destruction of the Germans by Jews, Marxists, parlia- mentarians, and Slavs. Sometime in the middle of the Vienna period, probably no later than the turn of 1911 and in the midst of objec- tively styled self-study, Hitler would experience an inspired revela- tion that the Jews and the Marxists were one and the same and the mortal enemy of the German Aryans. This Hitler would carry this revelation out of Vienna, into prewar Munich, away to Flanders, and back to postwar Munich, where war, revolution, and chance con- spired to deliver him to the *Sterneckerbraeu* in September 1919.

Hitler's anti-Semitism must be fit into so vast a picture, and one in which the entire pre-history and history of the German Aryans was pitted against the same situation ·with the Hebrew Semites.

Against this context of Hitler's anti-Semitism, the best the biographers and historians have been able to produce is an image of a superficial young man who had become seized by a crude, brutal, and lethal anti-Semitism. With such an image, the conventional wisdom guides us into an interpretation of his anti-Semitism as a morally defunct focus on a single propaganda enemy. The conventional wisdom would have us believe that the moral defunctness—the evil—in his anti-Semitism resided in the singling out for attack of an innocent, unoffending, and helpless people. The evil demanded in such a case for Hitler, however, would be far worse if it could be shown that he attacked the Jews in order to bring himself to power as a German tyrant because of the criminal psychological necessity to possess power. But Hitler would combine convincing historical argument, unconvincing contemporary observation, and near-incontrovertible claim of Jewish and Marxist internationalism into a fearsome picture of an idealized enemy. Hitler discovered Jews and Marxists who were so vast and idealized that they could not credibly be considered as tactical creatures designed to increase the effect of propaganda or to advance toward the goal of seizing political power for their own sakes. Faced with the vastness of Hitler's anti-Semitism and anti-Marxism, the conventional wisdom has acknowledged that he was a convinced ideologue, that he actually believed his own propaganda. But interpreting Hitler as a political ideologue misses him as badly as interpreting him to have been a demagogic propaganda adept.

*   *   *

The full measure of Hitler's anti-Semitism can be seen in the contrast between his vision of a heroic Germany and that of a demonic enemy. Hitler's ideal Greater Germany was so antipodal to his ideal enemy that the whole business must be understood as one in which Hitler seized followers based on their faith in his vision of a resurrected people. Hitler had faith in an impending German resurrection and was its voice, eyes, and messenger. As early as October 1923, in a conference concerning a march on Berlin, a right wing military man recalled that "Hitler now had definite Napoleonic and Messianic ideas.... He declared that he felt the call within himself to save Germany and that this would fall to him, if not now then later. He then drew a number of parallels with Napoleon, especially with the return of Napoleon from Elba to Paris."[70] But Napoleon would slip out of Elba and march on Paris to save his dynasty and reconstitute an imperial France. Hitler would contemplate a march on Berlin more simply and heroically to save Germany. Hitler would recoup the low of April 1924 by vowing to become the destroyer of Marxism, and as such, axiomatically, to become the savior of Germany. In 1925 he would even dash off a visual representation of German salvation in his extraordinary sketch of a vast, domed structure seemingly suspended in space and apparently pulling together out of his inner mind a vision of Germany united and saved.[71]

By 1933, too many Germans saw Hitler as a messiah to support the propagandistically styled conventional view of Hitler as tyrant over Germany. If, for example, Hitler could be conceptualized and accepted by a plurality of Germans as a messiah, it becomes difficult to accept an interpretation of him as a tyrant, for messiahs can hardly be seen to tyrannize over consenting disciples, followers, and sympathizers. How can a messiah tyrannize—rule with unjust and oppressive severity—when his followers and sympathizers accept his revelation and work toward it? The religious prophet of the Arabs, Muhammad the Praised, cannot be seen to have tyrannized over them, notwithstanding his absolute control over converts to Islam. By March 1933, when 43.9 percent of voters in the Reichstag election voted essentially for him and his vision, Hitler cannot be seen as having to tyrannize over those who voted for the Nazi list of candidates. The remaining 55.1 percent of Germans voting presents a different picture, but all were German citizens, some were nationalists, many were patriotic bourgeois, and many were Social Democrats, themselves patriotic in a conventional manner. And since Hitler had come to power legally, these Germans would be forced to acknowledge the play of legal parliamentary events in early 1933 which had been shielded by the authority of the president and the power of the army. Only the Communists fall out of the historical equation above as disciplined Soviet Russian–styled internationalists. They were a mortal danger to all German political parties, and if they could not be converted back to Germans by the Nazis, they would be "tyrannized."

In such a picture we cannot see Hitler as a study in tyranny but rather as a study in the conversion of the Germans to faith in Germany: "It was my aim to make new Germans" are the words that reoccur out of *Mein Kampf* to illustrate the whole period from 1919 through 1933 as the dawning of an intended German age. Yet even though the conventional wisdom since Bullock would unfailingly present Hitler as driven by the historical notion of the superiority of the earlier culture-bearing Aryans and the mission to save the contemporary German Aryans, it has interpreted the same period as one in which Hitler drove to power in order to tyrannize over the people who he would save.

Chapter 6

TRIUMPH OF A MESSIAH WITHIN GERMANY
1933–1934

Hitler would prove to be a study in extraordinary tempo in his foreign policy of the 1930s. He would also be a study in similar tempo in his nationalization of the Germans. If German history were to be seen as grand opera unfolding in the 1930s, Hitler, in his second alter ego as Wagnerian hero, could be understood not only as lead voice but also as conductor in a piece interpreted entirely in *tempo prestissimo*. France would be a study in France being France, and Britain would be a study in Britain being Britain. The biographers would be studies in their disembodiment of the period 1933 through 1939 from the context of the times—namely, *1919* through 1939. The historians and biographers would present a homogeneous interpretation of the period as one in which a vile and depraved man broke international law and violated the sanctity of treaties. The same scholars would present the same vile and depraved man as one who terrorized selected parts of the German population. Scholars would be forced to consider that Hitler nevertheless effected a spiritual and material resurrection of the Germans so great that the interpretation of him as a bad man who did some good might actually be *possible*, even though it is so unthinkable. In all of the above, however, the conventional wisdom has handled Hitler as if he were a personal nonentity and extraordinary propagandist writ inexplicably large as a villain. There can be no more flagrant misunderstanding than to consider Hitler as being personally ordinary, conducting propaganda as popularly construed, and acting merely villainously.

The biographers have given us a rich, descriptive account of Hitler during the period, but none has presented an overarching interpretation that credibly and realistically accounts for the astounding tempo of the alleged international criminality and similar pace of the domestic synchronization of Germany with the Nazi movement. The biographers have presented a tired theme of international aggression in the 1930s and domestic totalitarianism. The theme is exhausted because it has been repeated by every great biographer and presents Hitler as an international criminal and domestic terrorizer of the leaders of Marxism and the entire, although diminutive, body of Jews in Germany. The interpretation is exaggerated in the case of the international picture, accurate in the case of the internal violence, but leaves us with an understated picture of Hitler pulling the remaining approximate 99.5 percent of the population out of the economic depression. Hitler, for example, would personally turn the first spadeful of earth that symbolized the beginning of the construction of the *Autobahnen* on September 23, 1933 on a bank of the Main River near Frankfurt. These architecturally styled engineering masterpieces centered on great ribbons of concrete road surfaces and inclusive bridges. They would employ an average of one hundred thousand workers yearly, stimulate the motorization of Germany, and further German national unity. Earlier, on February 11, 1933, only twelve days after having become chancellor, Hitler gave the opening address at the International Automobile and Motorcycle Exhibition on the *Kaiserdamm* in Berlin. In the speech, he would elevate the automobile industry to be the most important of the future and link it with a vast program of road construction. He would simultaneously advance the idea of a people's car for Germans—a *Volksauto* —and link it with the *Autobahnen*.

The most recent great biographer, Professor Ian Kershaw, would trivialize Hitler's role in this conceptualization and implementation of the motorization and superhighway-altering of Germany. He would maintain derisively that Hitler, "lacking as he did even the rudiments of economic theory,"[1] could hardly have been called an economic innovator, and that his "propaganda instinct, not his economic know-how led him toward an initiative that both assisted the recovery of the economy (which was beginning to take place anyway) and caught the public imagination."[2] The great biographer thus would denigrate Hitler as being an economics cipher and operating largely with instinct for propaganda effect. But Hitler, alone and with remarkable vision, took advantage of the chance event of the Berlin international exhibition to deliver a psychological masterpiece that projected a motorized Germany complete with more and better roads. We see a distinctive Hitler, complete with lack of sense of proportion, unerring instinct, its alter ego, genius, and constant companion, luck. He would project the idea in February, push aside bureaucratic argument of the transport ministry and *Reichsbahn* (German Railways system), and create a German Motorways Enterprise headed by Dr. Fritz Todt answerable by the end of November 1933 only to himself.

In what was an outsized undertaking, we have an opportunity to test the conventional wisdom's interpretation of Hitler. It is difficult to assign depravity and evil to Hitler for his conceptualization and implementation of the building of a Reich motorways system. He saw the advertising of such a system so early as the second month of 1933 as a psychological tour de force to restore morale in Germany and boost his own popularity. It is difficult to the point of impossibility, however, to assign popularity and implied power as the primary motives for the Reich motorways. Since we are attempting to place Hitler within the context of his actual life rather than within a preconception of meanness, it is easy to discover his adolescent project of the underground rail system through Linz. The presence of transportation systems in both projects is eye-catching but largely incidental. Once our eye has been caught, however, we see two identically functioning Hitlers. In the younger one, we detect an inspired vision of an architecturally perfect Linz with everything else subordinated to the vision—cost, international rail line, workers' flats, and so on. In the adult Hitler, we detect an inspired vision of a civil engi-

neering architectural masterpiece intended not only to be the psychological basis for the social motorization of Germany but also a
visual movement to its glory.

Hitler would claim, for example, to have already determined
before he came to power "that immediately [after] the government
fell into our hands I would begin the preliminary work for the production of a car whose price would enable it to become a real means
of transport for the great mass of the people. By this means the
motor-car would at last cease to be an instrument of class division."[3]
And in utterly vintage Hitler, echoing his stress on heroic proportion
as necessary for heroic action, he would exclaim in a speech that "in
[the] case of the German people there is a demand not for two to
three hundred thousand, but for six to seven million motor-cars!"[4]
This social motorization and these autos would be possible only with
an enlarged road system, which in turn would be centered on the
new superhighways. Hitler would point out later, as the Reich
motorways project had developed by the end of 1937, that "the
system of *Autobahnen* is the largest building undertaking in the world
and already, with a displacement of 240 million cubic meters of
earth by far exceeds the building achievement of the Panama
Canal."[5] We see little evil in the project, although Kershaw would
interpret him as exploiting the transitory psychological effects of
announced motorization and super highway construction and then,
by some dark miracle, as sending the right signs to a gloomy automobile industry. We thereby miss the more substantial Hitler who
would not only retain his propaganda instincts but would also be
driven to accumulate another mighty achievement.

And the automobiles and *Autobahnen* cannot even be connected
with the potential for evil in rearmament. Even though some lesser
biographers and greater historians would link automobiles and
superhighways with military purpose, the German Army would
advance against France so late as 1940 with only fourteen motorized
divisions out of a total in the attack of 120, that is, it would remain
largely horse drawn and foot marching. And the same army would

transport itself about Europe by railway, in moves of any significant distance, for the entire war. For Hitler, automobiles and superhighways represented a grand project of social change and heroic architectural dimension that would add up to inspired achievement. None of this proves that Hitler was a nice person, but all of this warns us that he moved from inspiration to inspiration at the outer edge of reality for all others. And as concerns how he fit his architectural masterwork into his artistic vision of the world, he would comment in an unguarded moment that the *Autobahnen* would become his Parthenon.

In the face of the above visualization and action by Hitler, the biographers' title of dictator similarly does not convey the measure of the man. We can recall Hitler today as having been German chancellor but we cannot characterize him as such for posterity. He was more than that. In the second case, we are told today that Hitler would fasten dictatorship on Germany and as the dictator wreak havoc in Europe, but we cannot adequately characterize him as having been a dictator. He was more than that as well. With greater comprehension, we can see him by August 1934 not as a political dictator who had come to full power in Germany but as the private individual, Adolf Hitler, who had crushed the Marxists and had begun to build new Germans. From such a perspective we can more adequately see Hitler as a messianic furnace—the dark destructor of the Communists and the savior of the Germans. As the destructor of 1933, he would move on to become the leader of the march of a synchronized Germany toward its revealed eastern destiny. We have neither chancellor, politics, nor dictator here, but rather messiah, destructor, and destiny.

Favored by circumstance, chance, and his own personality, Hitler would subdue German domestic opposition in the astonishingly brief period of the year 1933. And well before the end of the following year he would accomplish a final reckoning with the unmanageable leadership of the *Sturmabteilung* (SA). Germany stood exhausted by the divisive and dysfunctional style of parliamentary democracy under pressure and its latest incapacity to master the depression. Germany stood disadvantaged and outraged by the continuing disabilities enforced under the Versailles treaty by vindictive French governments. And if this were not enough, Germans remained intimidated by the Communist armed uprisings of the 1920s, street violence of the early 1930s, and incessant bloody verbiage—shortly before the Reichstag fire, the official Communist news organ, *Red Sailor* "openly called for violence: Workers to the barricades! Forward to victory! Fresh bullets in your guns! Draw the pins of the hand grenades!"[6] The same Communists in the immediately preceding Reichstag election had managed to attract six million voters, who accounted for 17 percent of the votes cast. We are presented with the fact of six million Germans being exhorted to pull the pins on six million hand grenades, presumably to be thrown in the direction of other Germans. The Communists, with their internationalist revolutionary intentions, cries of havoc, and proven capacity for violence, would be seen by most Germans as a clear and present danger to the security of the republic. The Communists characteristically painted themselves into inane corners and escaped damage due to lethargic and fearful hesitation on the part of republican authorities to take action against them for incitation to armed rebellion.

On February 24, however, the new Prussian minister of the Interior, Hermann Goering, apparently took the incitation at face value, ordered the police to raid the Karl Liebknecht House in Berlin, and claimed to have seized large quantities of incriminating documents. Earlier in the month, on February 4, the government had brought out the decree for the protection of the German people, prepared a year earlier to combat Communist violence associated with the Berlin transport strike. Hitler, Franz von Papen as vice chancellor, the cabinet, and Goering (particularly in his role as head of the Prussian state police) were genuinely concerned about Communist violence, particularly in terms of a general strike. Within this framework, Goering would order the Prussian police to combat organizations hostile to the state. The Kommunistische Partei Deutschlands

(KPD or Communist Party of Germany) was the organization more hostile than any other to the existence of a German nationalist state and any other kind of German state and bore the brunt of the attack. And since Hitler equated the seizure of power with the annihilation of the Marxist internationalists, it can be no surprise that Goering curtailed Communist newspapers, street demonstrations, meetings, and any attempts to interfere with nationalist activity.

Within two months, based largely on the destruction of the Communists and other opponents through the use of emergency decrees, Hitler had subdued the Reichstag and manipulated the passage of the Law to Remove the Distress of the People and the State, passed on March 23 and promulgated the next day. This law altered the constitution by enabling the national cabinet to enact laws prepared by the chancellor.[7] Within four months, Hitler produced a propaganda triumph in the skillfully orchestrated Day of National Labor on May 1, followed almost immediately by the dismantling of "the largest democratic trade union movement in the world"—the German Social Democratic Party—and the establishment of the German Labor Front.[8] Within six months, Hitler had suppressed, or convinced to self-liquidate, every political party in Germany. Within twelve months, Hitler and his darkly menacing boys Goering and Roehm, joined by tens of thousands of lesser disciples, who worked toward him with or without immediate direction from above, had created a state in which Germans began to sense that they were becoming bound together for some greater purpose than simply escaping the depression.

The situation above has become well-known, but through incompleteness and bias, the biographers have not used it to give us a better comprehension of Hitler. For the Reichstag election agreed to by President Paul von Hindenburg for March 5, Hitler personally provided the slogan for both the Nazis and the government as "Attack on Marxism." For a chancellor expected reasonably by most Germans to pull them out of the Great Depression, they could more reasonably have expected a slogan like "Attack on Unemployment."

With consistently not associated with ordinary politics, Hitler would continue to illuminate the Marxists as the chief enemies of Germany and to present every National Socialist with a target for attack during the Reichstag election. Goering, for example, as Prussian Interior minister, would order the state police to cooperate with the SA, the *Schutzstaffel* (SS), and the *Stahlhelm*, and then, on February 22, to incorporate them as auxiliary police to support national propaganda and to combat organizations hostile to the state. In the immediately following days, an overwhelming combination of police, SA, SS, and *Stahlhelm* operatives paralyzed Communist political action. The Communist Party had played to perfection the role of an organization hostile to the state, and the Prussian police were able, on February 24, to raid and search its Berlin headquarters building and, not too surprisingly, find subversive literature. Goering would embellish the report of this finding into Communist plans for a murderous uprising and isolate them from support or sympathy of the German population.

No evidence exists to show that Hitler and his initiative-filled followers at any level had intentions other than to maintain effective levels of violence and intimidation through the Reichstag election scheduled for March 5. It is a monument, therefore, to the play of chance in the lives of world-historical personalities that chance presented Hitler with the surprise danger and opportunity of the Reichstag arson. Hitler and Goering were obviously surprised by the event, and notwithstanding the sarcastic and confident claims of authorities so disparate as the *Manchester Guardian* and German Communists that the Nazis had set the fire, we cannot seriously accept such views.[9] At an improvised meeting the same evening in the Prussian Ministry of the Interior, for example, they remained in so ineffectual a state that it took National State Secretary Ludwig Grauert to keep his head and suggest an emergency decree for Prussia aimed to control acts of terror in that state. By the next morning, however, the Reich minister of the Interior came up with a draft decree for the protection of people and state that would apply to the entire republic—the target of the supposed terrorist conspiracy, after all, had been a German one in the form of the Reichstag and not the Prussian *Landtag*. The decree as put into effect later in the day placed emergency power over the entire Reich in the hands of the Reich government. In the words of Kershaw, "the hastily constructed emergency decree amounted to the charter of the Third Reich."[10] There was not a factual hint of conspiracy on the part of Hitler and the Nazis in the event. And in the rush of historians to present them in an unfavorable light, none has commented on the presumption of a Communist-inspired citizen of a foreign country to enter Germany and burn to the ground its national parliament building for the purpose of precipitating successful internationalist revolution in that country. Accused and convicted as an arsonist, Marinus van der Lubbe, handled by all writers as a lumpish, deranged pawn, would in fact accomplish his mission of accelerating events in Germany toward the destruction of the republic. He would do so, however, through the irony of Hitler and the Nazis affecting its destruction and even quicker obliteration of the KPD.

Although enabled legally to dismantle the KPD, Hitler would permit the Communists to continue in the election campaign, win close to five million votes, and seat the impressive number of eighty-one deputies in the Reichstag. He would press immediately for legislation by the new Reichstag that would enable the National Cabinet to pass laws that might deviate from the constitution. The piece of legislation would "alter" the constitution and require Hitler to get a two-thirds majority for the passage of the act, thus making the eighty-one Communist votes critical in any calculation of success. Hitler allowed the Communists to seat deputies in the Reichstag and then legally, under the emergency decree of February 28, arrested them—a strategy that comprised an odd mixture of ruthless, lawful, bloodless elements. He nevertheless still faced daunting prospects in the mathematics of March 1933. The two Marxist political parties—Social Democratic and Communist—controlled almost 31 percent of the seats in the Reichstag, only a hairbreadth from the magical 33 percent required to defeat the bill. It is not so much, therefore, that Hitler cleverly removed the Communists from the voting but that he had to remove them, cleverly or not. Even so, the Social Democrats alone would retain a percentage of votes in opposition so large that Hitler would require the support of the difficult, independent Catholic Center Party to pass the bill. And the whole business was so closely run that the Center Party would decide only at the end of the recess preceding the vote (i.e., only minutes before) to cast a positive bloc vote, notwithstanding various objections.

Hitler had mastered challenges almost beyond comprehension to present himself shortly after two o'clock in the afternoon of March 23, 1933, as German chancellor before the first business session of a newly elected Reichstag. It has remained literally true that Hitler, who fewer than fourteen years earlier had been an unknown soldier still living in a Munich army barracks, had, through some fateful combination of blind chance and conscious intent, projected himself into the Knoll Opera House. In his first appearance before the German parliament, he would read off a speech that was remarkable for its prudence and moderation.[11] In a second, unplanned appearance later in the day, he would reveal himself as in few other moments in his life, and no biographer can do better than to show how and why this was so.

As the voting unfolded after six o'clock in the evening for acceptance or rejection of the Enabling Act, Otto Wels, chairman of the Social Democratic Party, moved to the speaking platform and delivered the refusal of his ninety-four remaining deputies to vote in favor of the act—twenty-six additional deputies were missing due to arrest, flight, and so on. The great biographers comment variously that his refusal was courageous, moderate, dignified, low-key, and—although poorly delivered—ended movingly by upholding principles of humanity, justice, freedom, and socialism held dear by Social Democrats.[12] But Hitler would advance on the speaker's podium in immediate, instinctive fury ignited probably by outrage over Wels's presumption as a Marxist to claim that the Social Democrats were capable of having actual German policies. Hitler had been observed taking notes during Wels's discourse; and, impromptu, Hitler would deliver a masterpiece of spontaneous invective that characterized himself as vengeful savior and that has furnished us with a salutary, revisionist picture of Social Democracy as seen through the eyes of a notable contemporary critic.

Hitler, the human cultural wilderness of the great biographers, would point his finger at Wels and utter a quote from a work by Germany's greatest dramatist, Johann C. F. von Schiller: "You come late, but still you come." In this spontaneous quote, Hitler told the Social Democratic leader that his democratized Marxists had had fourteen years to put in effect their "pretty theories" and had achieved no more than ruination and division in Germany. And now, late in the game, indeed, at the end of the game, they would have the raging temerity as a parting shot to lecture Germans on the principles that had supported their misfortune. Hitler would make telling points that comprise the ultimate revisionist interpretation of the incident. In Prussia, the dominating German state, the Social Democratic Party with only a modest plurality, had run the government holding the positions of minister-president, interior minister, Berlin police commissioner, and so on, during the entire period 1919–1933. Wels would argue that criticism of the present government was salutary or healthfully conducive to a superior political situation and to persecute it would accomplish nothing. Hitler would argue that when the Social Democrats governed Prussia, Nazi criticism of the Marxist government was not seen as salutary, and Hitler's followers were vigorously persecuted. As counterbalance to the conventional wisdom's attribution of moderate, enlightened social democracy to the Social Democrats, Hitler would present the following picture from experience as one of their opponents:

> You talk about persecution. I think that there are only a few of us here who did not have to suffer persecution from your side in prison.... You seem to have forgotten completely that for years

our shirts were ripped off our backs because you did not like the color.... We have [progressed beyond] your persecutions.

You say furthermore that criticism is salutary. Certainly, those who love Germany may criticize us, but those who worship an Internationale cannot.... Here too insight comes to you very late indeed, Mr. Deputy. You should have recognized the salutariness of criticisms during the time we were in opposition.... In those days our press was forbidden and forbidden and again forbidden, our meetings were forbidden and we were forbidden to speak and I was forbidden to speak for years on end. And now you say criticism is salutary!

You also say that not even we can abolish Social Democracy because it was first to open these seats here to the common people, to the working men and women and not just the barons and counts. In all that, Mr. Deputy, you have come too late. Why didn't you, while there was still time, make your principles known to your friend Grzesinski, or your other friends Braun and Severing [all Social Democrats and, respectively, Berlin police commissioner, Prussian minister-president, and Prussian Interior minister] who for years kept saying that I was after all only a house painter! For years you asserted that on your posters.... And finally you threatened to drive me out of Germany with a dog whip.

From now on we National Socialists will make it possible for the German worker to attain what he is able to demand and insist on. We National Socialists will be his intercessors. You, gentlemen are no longer needed!... And don't confound us with the bourgeois world.[13]

And to summarize his outrage and scorn, he would put together the following words—distinctively Hitler, with their characteristic jarring combination of cerebral analogies, prophetic vision, and passion: "My feeling is that you are not voting for this bill because by the very nature of your mentality you cannot comprehend the intentions that animate us in asking for it... and I can only tell you that I do not want you to vote for it. Germany will be free but not through you!"[14]

Kershaw transforms the words above into "the most savage of

German peasant husband and wife—essence of the *Volk* of the countryside in the early 1900s. *(Painting by Albin Egger-Lienz.* Husband and Wife, *Study for Life Cycles, 1910. Private collection.)*

Hitler as Fuehrer, President, and Reichskanzler, comforting a woman overcome by private grief, November 9, 1935. *(Image courtesy of the Arthur S. Alter collection, Hoover Institution Archives.)*

Hitler with a mother and child in a modest German home. Hitler is relaxed yet visibly fatigued. *(Image courtesy of the Arthur S. Alter collection, Hoover Institution Archives.)*

German architectural pavilion, Paris Exhibition of 1937, designed by Albert Speer and approved by Hitler. Theme "Will to Culture." *(Image courtesy of the Library of Congress.)*

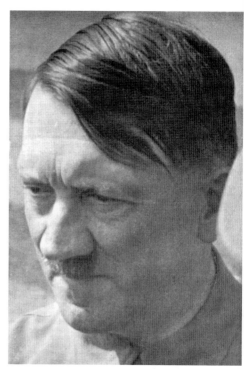

Hitler, profile view *(left)* and full-face view *(right)*, wearing party-style shirt, September 24, 1938. *(Stolfi private collection.)*

German dispatch courier in World War I. Hitler was a courier in a frontline infantry regiment for more than four years—this could easily have been a sketch of Hitler. Survival: miraculous. *(Sketch by Elk Eber. Dispatch Courier, 1938–1939. Private collection.)*

Hitler on his fiftieth birthday being congratulated by a helmeted bodyguard. *(Image used with permission from the Associated Press from New York.)*

Hitler stylishly attired at a diplomatic social affair with Italian foreign minister Count Galeazzo Ciano *(far left)*, May 22, 1939, in Berlin. Note the omnipresent Iron Cross First Class and wound badge on Hitler's tunic. *(Image used with permission from the Associated Press from New York.)*

Hitler with a distant, messianic stare, the right eye in particular unfocused. Polish foreign minister Jósef Beck, in contrast, looks as an ordinary human being on camera. *(Image courtesy of the Arthur S. Alter collection, Hoover Institution Archives.)*

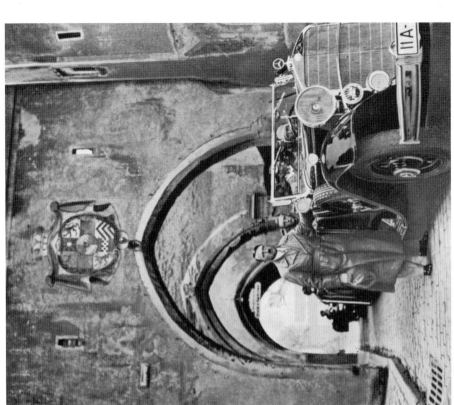

Hitler at Landsberg City Gate ten years after his release from fortress detention. Note the beautifully tailored clothes and accompanying motorized security force at the rear. *(Image courtesy of the Arthur S. Alter collection, Hoover Institution Archives.)*

This poster art presents an image, intended or otherwise, of Hitler as a seer, prophet, or mystic. But there are two Hitlers here, as seen in the eyes—in his right eye that of an otherworldly mystic, unfocused, dreamy, trancelike; in his left eye that of a fierce political orator demanding thunderous applause.

Hitler about to be introduced by Himmler for an address at the Nuremberg Party Day rally, about September 1937. The recently completed, great, neoclassical façade and stadium faces an area capable of holding approximately 500,000 listeners. Hitler firmly grasps his left arm, and the conventional wisdom has consistently interpreted the pose as one in which a hysterical Hitler fights to control nervousness. Revision suggests that Hitler is controlling the physical damage from the severe wounding of that arm in the firefight with police in Munich in late 1923. Hitler's prison physician had forecast that Hitler would go to his grave with a damaged, prone-to-trembling left arm. (*Image used with permission from Getty Images.*)

Spirit of the early Nazi movement—Hitler orating in a dingy, windowless cellar room with a stalwart meeting protector under the flag behind him. (*Image courtesy of the US Army Art Collection, Washington, DC.*)

War in the west. "The single episode depicted in this image is of no importance. Nor will anyone mistake the soldiers' heads for portraits. The viewer is influenced by the mystical content rather than the episode of portraits."—Robert Scholz. *(Painting by Paul Mathis, Padua, 1941. Private collection.)*

Hitler visits Luftwaffe Flak Unit in the Ukraine, midsummer 1942. He is immaculately uniformed and looks exceptionally relaxed for that time in the war. *(Image courtesy of the Arthur S. Alter collection, Hoover Institution Archives.)*

replies,"[15] and Joachim Fest saw them as characterized by "bravura crudity and zest for crushing an opponent."[16] We can just as well see, however, Hitler tearing into shreds Wels's protestations of the moral superiority of the Social Democratic position, and doing so based on the artistically imaginative application of a quote from a notable dramatist and iron consistency in sticking to the theme of the past fourteen years of Social Democratic rule of injustice, persecution, false accusation, and threat of violence. At a representative juncture in which the Marxists could be considered to have been destroyed, namely, the successful vote in favor of the altering of the constitution, Hitler ignited as spontaneous passion. Kershaw would characterize the rejoinder as one in which "departing now from the relative moderation of his earlier prepared speech, Hitler showed more of his true colors."[17] As concerns true colors, the biographer would note bullying tactics. But Hitler had had no intent to bully anyone in his Reichstag speech and had delivered a moderate, statesmanlike address intended to convince the deputies to master the German crisis decisively. Only when stung by Wels's pretension of concern for German national honor and a German foreign policy and protestations of support for justice, democracy, socialism, and so on, did Hitler explode as a fiery, avenging messiah. Perhaps, though, Wels drove Hitler over the edge of the functional persuasion in his prepared remarks by final, ill-advised greetings "to his friends and victims of persecution."[18] In any event, the biographers see Hitler as consciously adding to a maturing Fuehrer cult and being an immoral, criminal historical figure, even though he had acted spontaneously in delivering his attack against the Social Democratic Wels, who he did not consider to be a personal enemy but rather a personification of Germany's misfortune.

*   *   *

The great biographers point out *ad infinitum* that Hitler was harsh and cruel as a dictator and support this contention with his rough handling of the Marxists and Jews in Germany from 1933 onward. They do not effectively present the harshness and cruelty—as it were, the evil—in terms of the numbers of people affected and in a way that gives us a superior comprehension of Hitler. Hitler's *raison d'être* from 1919 through 1933 can be seen retrospectively to have been the destruction of Marxism and the making of new Germans after the internal poisoners of the people had been destroyed. Such cannot be understood in terms of either politics or personal pique but rather as mission inspired by revelation. Hitler looked upon Marxism as neither a political nor a personal enemy but as an opposing historical philosophy marked necessarily for destruction if National Socialism were to succeed in making new Germans. The sheer physical dimension of Marxist socialism in Germany, as reflected in the March Reichstag elections in which 7.18 million Germans voted as Social Democrats and 4.85 million as Communists, presented Hitler with yet another insuperable task as characteristically courted by the man. Just how did Hitler proceed in order to "destroy" the 31 percent of Germans reflected in the voting numbers above? He evidently divided the Marxists into those who could be "destroyed" as Marxists by being converted into Germans and those who could not. Given his messianic qualities, Hitler evidently felt capable of saving the vast Marxist rank and file by converting it into a vast German Host. After all, in Hitler's mind, the Social Democratic and Communist workers were Germans misled by a fanatic leadership elite incapable of conversion and marked for extinction.

The Marxist leadership elite would present a special proposition to destroy, and Hitler would sanction the arrest and internment of the Marxist leaders in aptly named concentration camps. Goering, as Interior minister of Prussia, established the first concentration camp in March 1933, and Himmler, as a lesser figure at the moment with his office as police president of Munich, would set up an official camp during the same month only a few miles from that city at Dachau. During the remainder of the year, several additional camps were set up and the Marxist leadership was "destroyed" by being deposited in political internment camps. Prior to the National Socialists coming to power in Germany, the Social Democratic–controlled government of the state of Prussia had established a secret state political police as organized under a Berlin Police Bureau and with a mission to protect the government against both right and left wing subversive elements. Since the Social Democratic Party controlled the Prussian government during the entire period of 1919 through mid-1932 by means of a plurality of seats in the Prussian *Landtag*, it is a supreme irony of the interwar period that the Social Democratic leaders themselves began to be concentrated as subversive elements into internment camps by their own secret state police organization, now packed with Nazis and redirected in mission.

The conventional wisdom has presented Germany thereby as a police state exemplified by the concentration camps that came into existence in March 1933 and matured during the period 1933–1939. The wisdom has presented the situation in terms such as "the ferocious repression of the Left" and has necessarily left the impression of a Germany carpeted with such camps.[19] Given Goering's energy and Himmler's persistence, the camps for Marxist functionaries would seem to have accomplished their purpose by 1935. In the summer of that year, with Himmler now in control of a unified German police, the great biographers give the number of internees as a minuscule 3,500. At that time, as the concentration camp system seemed to have become dormant, Himmler would exploit the concept of "protective custody" to include additional categories of Germans that could menace state security and dilute the qualities of a heroic National Socialist Germany. Himmler and his first lieutenant Reinhard Heydrich, leader of the Reich Security Service, the premier political counterintelligence service in Germany by 1935, would begin to expand beyond Marxists, Jews, and Freemasons as those who could menace internal security. New categories would include undesirables such as "gypsies, homosexuals, beggars, antisocial, work-shy, and habitual criminals."[20] As a result, the number of persons detained in concentration camps would rise from 3,500 in

summer 1935 to 25,000 in 1939. Most would have been arrested with
the order: "Based on Article I of the Decree of the Reich President
for the Protection of the People and the State of 28 February, 1933,
you are taken into protective custody in the interest of public security and order. Reason: suspicion of activities inimical to the State."[21]

In 1935, therefore, Hitler's "destruction" of the Marxists could be
equated with the 3,500 concentration camp internees—mostly
former Marxist functionaries and the reorganization of the several
millions of Marxist-influenced workers into the German Labor
Front. It is a remarkable circumstance that Hitler and Himmler, his
determined proponent of an Aryanized National Socialist Germany,
could have considered that so tiny a number of Marxist leaders
detained would assure German internal security. The population of
Germany in 1935 was approximately sixty-eight million, and the
presence of 3,500 inmates in concentration camps cannot support
any view of a pervasive concentration camp system. By 1939, however, Himmler had increased the number to 25,000 "dangerous undesirables" in concentration camps. But the population of Germany had
risen to approximately eighty million through acquisition of Austria
and Sudetenland and through the effects of a rising birthrate. This
number of internees in ten camps within the Germany of September
1939 also does not support a view that there was a system so pervasive
that Germans and foreign visitors would sense its physical presence.
On the other hand, Hitler uncannily appointed Himmler as *Reichsfuehrer SS*, the perfect inquisitor, who established control over all
police in Germany and established a single, central Reich Security
Service Office with a single Secret State Police Office, all of which
"provided everything necessary for the spiriting away of active opponents and the ruthless policing of every corner of the Reich."[22] The
realistic generalization can be made that through the independent
zeal of a faithful, deep, and abiding follower, Hitler set in place
during the 1930s a body of men that was capable of maintaining the
internal security of the Reich. For all his alleged slavishness to Hitler,
Himmler showed remarkable initiative, boldness, and tenacity in

piecing together the body of men into an SS that had the primary and foremost duty to attend to the protection of the Fuehrer "but also the widened duty... to secure the interior of the Reich."[23] And to understand the pervasiveness of the somewhat underpopulated concentration camp system of the 1930s, we must understand that it was characterized more by Hitler's will and Himmler's zeal and less by numbers of opponents and undesirables interned during those years.

As concerns evil, Hitler is painted as illegally undermining the constitution, interning the Marxist leadership, and beginning a more lengthy process of depriving the Jews of citizenship. These accusations are made to apply to Hitler interpreted as emerging dictator, and within such an interpretation, they are largely valid. The constitution, however, had been made possible by Marxist revolution and had been created by bourgeois politicians and lawyers. And as the underpinning of divisive, parliamentary governments, it could not be seen by Hitler as German. Hindenburg nevertheless, as the ultimate representative of all things German and supported by the army, adhered to the document and thereby forced Hitler to do likewise—to stick to a policy of legal takeover of Germany. In the role assigned to him by the conventional wisdom as power-hungry, demagogic dictator, Hitler can be seen as having evil and illegal intent in his erosion of the constitution. As savior of the Germans and their messianic, infallible leader, however, he could not have seen himself as engaged in evil by the incremental erosion of such a document— nor could most Germans by mid-1933.

On the other hand, and seen as self-anointed man of destiny, Hitler exuded an urge to violence in the defense of the Germans. As such, he could hardly shy away from the application of force in the internment of the Marxist leadership. Hitler saw himself as locked in a prodigious struggle between the forces of good and evil in which the loser would face annihilation. Neither he nor his followers nor many other Germans could have seen much evil in the relatively mild internment, especially of the Communist leaders in the period of 1933 through 1935. The Communists had led numerous armed uprisings and conducted threatening and intimidating propaganda and street violence. Yet the great biographers would present the Communists during the great election campaigns of the early 1930s as no danger any longer to the Germans. Under such an interpretation, the Communists would take on the cast of a body of Germans attacked exaggeratedly by Hitler in speeches and then persecuted by his government in 1933. Reality would seem to be that the Communists had been and would continue to be a threat to the Germans who, in turn, would be relieved to see Communist leaders interred. After 1935, however, Himmler, with his command over both the German police and the SS, converted the internment camps into collection centers for undesirables. The relatively mild evil of the internment camps evolved into the greater evil of the collection centers.

As concerns "the Jews," Hitler took action largely in reaction to events. With his accession to the German chancellorship, party activists pressed violence from below on "opponents, Jews, and anyone else getting in the way of the Nazi revolution."[24] And "Without any orders from above, and without any coordination, assaults on Jewish businesses and the beating up of Jews by Nazi thugs became commonplace."[25] Kershaw's powerfully insightful thesis that Hitler's power lay in the initiative-filled action of his followers working toward him came into play and would be reflected in a kind of noisy, street anti-Semitism, undirected by either Hitler or Himmler. Well-organized Jews in America in late March 1933 would attempt to put in place a worldwide boycott of Germans goods and, somewhat ignominiously, Hitler would be forced to react to the Jewish action with one of his own, namely the imposition of a one-day "counter-boycott" of Jewish businesses in Germany on April 1.[26] The situation was bizarre: Hitler, impelled by the American Jewish Congress, to take action against the German Jews. It gives us insight into Hitler because, as Kershaw would claim, "as usual, when pushed into a corner Hitler had no half-measures."[27] In important challenges, Hitler indeed had no half-measures. But to imply that when pushed into a corner he would gamble on all-or-nothing actions in the manner of a petulant, power-accruing political dictator, does not fit Hitler.

Faced with the challenge in 1919 to do something about Germany's national agony and not forced into any corner to do so, Hitler would set himself the mission to take power in Germany and create an ideal German Reich—mission: impossible. Faced with the problem of the international Jewish initiative of late March 1933 and forced to take some action to solve it, Hitler would react with his peculiar finality. He would frame a boycott that would affect every Jewish business and professional office in all of Germany and be of indefinite duration. His intended action was the beginning of official government anti-Semitism and could be seen as the beginning of the march toward his decision in 1942 to exterminate the Jews of Europe. Based on complex circumstances, Hitler would execute the boycott for only one day, and the concept of "tackling" the Jews with a single massive economic blow would be replaced by the incremental disenfranchisement of the Jews as German citizens.

With discernment and a wish to comprehend Hitler, we can capture him in this moment. Kershaw, ironically because of his lack of intent to do so, would snare Hitler in the words: "Goebbels would be summoned to the Obersalzberg. In the loneliness of the mountains, he wrote, the Fuehrer had reached the conclusion that the authors, or at least the beneficiaries of the foreign agitation—Germany's Jews—had to be tackled. "[28] How can we fail to see a messiah? In the snowy wilderness of early spring in the German Alps, with no man advising him and believing himself to be in communion with Providence, Hitler would make the decision. We do not see Hitler closeted with cabinet ministers of his new government and we do not see him in chambers with the highest-level figures of the party. We see Hitler solicit advice from no one, ponder the problem with astonishing intensity, and act according to solitary inspiration. Isolated, yes, but the messiah does not get world-historical inspiration—breathe in the will of Providence, destiny, or fate—by discussing action to be taken with either bureaucrats or acolytes. This man would seem to be a more plausible Hitler than the shabby power seeker and crude ideologue of the great biographers.

* * *

As concerns the year 1933 and Hitler, in his initial foray into foreign policy, he would remove the German representatives from both the world disarmament conference, which was meeting at Geneva, and the League of Nations, under whose auspices it was being held. Hitler would begin the most successful and rapid string of diplomatic victories in modern European history with these two related actions. It follows that they should provide decisive clues to the personality of the man, the international situation in Europe in 1933, and the approach of the nearly Europe-wide war in 1939. The great biographers and modern European historians, however, do not present the year 1933 as part of an already existing continuous march toward the 1939 war. The Allies as exemplified by France, and France as personified by Clemenceau and Poincaré, had perpetuated the accusation that the German government and the entire German people were solely responsible for war in 1914. The judgment was vindictive, cruel, unjust, and baseless, but it underlay every paragraph of importance in the treaty and had given the Allied governments license to disarm Germany when the treaty came into effect. The Allied action was unprecedented in modern European history; for example, Bismarck's government after its victory over France in 1871 had done nothing to restrict the size of France's army through means of the treaty of Frankfurt.

The Allies, however, were aware of the radical and unjust reduction of the numbers of the German army to one hundred thousand and wrote into the Versailles treaty that the action was to be the first step toward world disarmament. After the League of Nations took over the task of administering the Versailles treaty, it established a committee to organize a world disarmament conference that, after five years of preparation, first met in February 1932 in Geneva.

During that year, the negotiation took on the appearance of a battle between the French and the other fifty-nine delegations over the disarmament of France downward to some level equal to a revised level upward for Germany. But the League faced imposing obstacles to change because, in the view of numerous historians and experts "above all, the League was manifestly an organization managed by the victors for the preservation of the *status quo*."[29] And Lloyd George could add in speaking of Poincaré that, "under his influence … the League became not an instrument of peace … it was converted into an organization for establishing on a permanent footing the military and thereby the diplomatic supremacy of France."[30] Franz von Papen, German chancellor of mid-1932, would instruct his foreign minister, Konstantin, baron von Neurath, to demand equality in armaments, with the main point being for the other powers to reduce theirs to the German level. Neurath would end his statement of the German position of early September 1932 by noting that "no one can expect Germany to tolerate further discrimination that affects our honor and threatens our security."[31] The German position was so strong and timely that the League of Nations issued a communiqué on December 11, 1932, that "the Governments of the United Kingdom, France, and Italy have declared that one of the principles that should guide the Conference on Disarmament should be the grant to Germany … of equality of rights in a system which would provide security for all nations."[32]

Fewer than two months later, Hitler would arrive as German chancellor and project himself on the international scene as if from some distant galaxy. He would agree with Papen and Neurath on the necessity for German equality of treatment. And he would be in tune with Germans for relief from a treaty that was characterized by hatred and arrogant disregard for historical fact. When the negotiations began again in February 1933, Hitler faced the dangerous international situation of being forced to negotiate some new level of armaments for Germany because of the combined strictures of the Versailles treaty and membership in the League. As concerns foreign policy, therefore, Hitler arrived as chancellor in the midst of a world disarmament exercise in which the possibilities for German armaments ranged from continuation of a disarmed Germany through a Germany with a 300,000-man army with France armed likewise. It is difficult to imagine Hitler and the Germans armed thus attacking anyone, and we are left to wonder how he would extricate himself from so impossible a situation.

Only the following supreme irony of the interwar period would allow him to make his first great foreign policy move. Faced with French intransigence toward any change in existing armaments and German demands for equality, British Prime Minister Ramsay Mac-Donald presented a draft convention in early 1933 that the French and US governments accepted and, on May 17, Hitler did likewise. The accepted draft convention called for France and Germany to have equal armies of 200,000 men in five years. The French government, however, during the adjournment of the conference from June through October 4, prevailed on the governments of Britain and the United States to accept an "amendment." The proposed French amendment to the accepted draft convention: no change in armaments for four years while the world could observe if Germany were ready to return to a peaceful community of nations, and only after eight years the beginning of some measure of rearmament. The French government thereby reattached moral approbation to the German people and delayed the beginning of German rearmament for an additional eight years. The French government expected that the Germans would accept the controls and the moral condemnation as probationers but succeeded in driving them out of both the disarmament conference and the League.

The above scene represents the first international action that led toward World War II in which Hitler was involved as the statesman representing Germany. He had had nothing to do with the preparation of the conference and any of its meetings prior to February 1932. He directed the acceptance of the MacDonald draft conventions and had every expectation that he would be ensnared by the accepted convention in drastically limited rearmament for several years. But in a scene similar to the Paris Peace Conference, the French government would impose its will on the British and American governments to accept modified conventions. The erstwhile Allied governments had apparently forgotten nothing and learned nothing, and Hitler could proclaim justifiably, on October 14, that:

> After the German Government, on the basis of the express recognition of German equality of rights, had recently declared itself willing to resume its participation in the deliberations of the Disarmament Conference, it was late communicated to the Foreign Minister of the Reich and to our delegates... that this equality of rights could no longer be granted.
>
> Since the German Government regards this action as a discrimination against the German people which is as unjust as it is degrading, under such conditions... it feels itself no longer able to take any further part in deliberations which could lead only to further "Diktats!"[33]

With these words, and others similar, Hitler led Germany out of the League disarmament talks. We know also from his speech of February 1933 to the senior officers of the treaty *Reichsheer* that swift rearmament would be indispensable for the regaining of German influence internationally. Although Hitler had a case morally superior to that of the French in the immediate events of September and October, he stands indicted as intending eventually to advance east, including the possibility of armed action and the outbreak of World War II. Various French governments, however, dismantled all attempts at reasonable and timely disarmament. For so deplorable a policy, the French government and most specifically Édouard Herriot, must be indicted in 1933 for steering France toward a likely armed confrontation with Germany and the same result of World War II. We can generalize that Hitler's towering vision of a future Third Reich was counterbalanced by various French governments' visions of the continuation of French military domination of western Europe. In the face of the above situation, biographer Fest has suggested that if Hitler had been challenged on his action to depart from the disarmament conference, the world might have been spared much. He might have added that if the French governments of 1919 through 1933 had replaced their vindictive intransigence with policies more functional, the world may have been spared Hitler.

We know why Hitler made his decision, but we remain less certain about whether he made it as dictator or, less despicable although still quite terrifying, as messiah. Papen, as chancellor in 1932 and vice chancellor in 1933 and 1934, had innumerable close dealings with Hitler and has left valuable impressions. Papen was an intelligent, conservative, Christian gentleman of considerable cultural attainments and was neither admirer nor fanatic enemy of Hitler. He would note that the power of Hitler's personality was difficult to describe. "There was little hint of either domination or genius in his manner or appearance, but he had immense powers of persuasion and an extraordinary and indefinable capacity for bending individuals and . . . the masses to his. Even people who differed from him fundamentally became convinced of his sincerity."[34] And as Hitler wrestled with the decision of how to react to the Geneva negotiations, Papen gave the following insight into Hitler's decision making.

It had become known to both Papen and Neurath with the reopening of the disarmament talks on October 4 that Hitler intended shortly to pull out of both the talks and the League. Papen and Neurath agreed with the decision to abandon the talks, but Papen "opposed with utmost vehemence" the decision to withdraw from the League. As events began to unfold quickly, Papen attempted to contact Hitler in the developing crisis. Quite remarkably, Hitler had left for Munich where he could conduct no serious government business and would seem to have been out of touch with the whole situation. Papen followed him there the same Friday night "and the next morning spent several hours with him in the bourgeois surroundings of his flat." We witness therefore the vice chancellor of Germany discussing with the chancellor the most momentous foreign policy decision of 1933—not in Berlin, but in Munich, in the middle of Hitler's weekend getaway. Hitler slept on the matter Saturday night, and Papen described the next day's scene: "He walked into my room [at the Hotel Vier Jahreszeiten] in a state approaching exaltation. 'It is all quite clear to me now.... There is only one solution and that is to withdraw from the League. We must make a clean break. All other considerations are completely irrelevant.'"[35] We suspect that Papen presented himself as one who attempted to restrain the wicked Nazis from leaving the League with all of its possibilities for resolving international crises peacefully. But in the seemingly incidental detail of the encounter, we get invaluable insight into how Hitler functioned.

As inveterate Bohemian and susceptible to no bureaucratic restraints—"get the car, Schreck, we're going for a drive"—Hitler had fled to the relaxed, familiar, and silent surroundings of his Munich apartment. As messiah, necessarily infallible and permanently on duty as concerns his mission, he gravitated into isolated situations in which he could ponder challenges. Papen unwittingly presented a realistic Hitler, although only as background detail to his own heroic efforts to preserve and fortify peace. Hitler, "in a state approaching exhalation," had evidently received an infallible inspiration. Hitler showed imposing pragmatic skills in politics and was in the advanced state of establishing political control over Germany by 1933. Yet the words Hitler used to describe his first great foreign policy decision cannot be seen as comprehensible in terms of political dictatorship. His words have a ring of prophetic surety and finality as opposed to that of foreign policy maneuvering, and he seems to have communed with destiny to reach an unalterable decision. We know what Goethe said when he conceptualized Napoleon as the World Spirit clattering by on horseback in the street of a German city, but what would he have said if he had seen Hitler drive by in a three-axle Mercedes® touring car? Over and above his astonishment at the advanced technology, he could hardly have been heard to exclaim: There goes an unsavory, power-driven dictator.

*   *   *

Hitler had founded the *Deutsche Arbeiterpartei* (DAP or German Workers' Party) in 1919, founded the *Nationalsozialistische Deutsche Arbeiterpartei* (NSDAP or National Socialist German Workers' Party) in 1920, and had pieced the latter together as a political organization and a political street-fighting detachment. He had made it clear as early as 1925 in writing that the party storm detachment would exist to brawl with Marxist toughs in streets and to overawe German onlookers on sidewalks. The two most prominent leaders of the *Sturmabteilung* (SA), Franz Pfeffer von Salomon and Ernst Roehm, however, preferred to see it as a thinly disguised, potentially armed force that would be capable of seizing political power and replacing the treaty army. As one great biographer would succinctly generalize: "The disagreement on the purpose of the SA was old and Hitler continued to hold that the brown formations should carry out a political, not a military function. They were to be an enormous 'Hitler shock troop,' not the cadres of a revolutionary army."[36] There cannot be much doubt that Roehm saw the SA as the basis for a new and truly revolutionary German army. In a far more radical way, however, he seems to have envisioned converting Germany into an SA state with SA men having special claims to positions in the government and private sectors. By the turn of 1934, Hitler faced the great, immediate, and perilous destabilization of Germany by Roehm and his permanent revolutionaries who would also be an army. But Germany already had an army, and one so good that Sir Basil Liddell Hart would describe its generals in a war soon to come as "the best-finished product of their profession—anywhere."[37] Roehm decried these generals as spiritless experts and fulminated that Hitler would take the heart and soul out of the movement if he chose to inherit a ready army rather than continue the revolution with an SA militia. We must be impressed by Roehm's revolutionary *élan* exemplified by his words that the SA represented the chance to do something really new and great, something that would lift the world off its hinges. We must be even more impressed by Hitler's glance into a future that would be made by him and would coalesce into panzers on the move in the dust clouds of the summer of 1941 in the east. A militia does not fit into this glance.

In all of this, at the turn of 1934, Hitler faced the deepening twilight of Hindenburg's life and the necessity to secure the presidency for himself. We can generalize that the "seizure" of the office would in fact signal the real and final achievement of power. We can also generalize that he would be capable of seizing the presidency both legally and practically, only with the support of the army. We can generalize finally that this army, whose support would secure Germany domestically, would be the same army that would secure the European space necessary to create a Third Reich. It was as if Hitler were putting together a new Germany in the manner of assembling pieces of a puzzle, and by the middle of 1934 only two pieces remained—a Nazi president and a German army susceptible to his control. Roehm would desperately misread the situation of 1933 and suffer its culmination in 1934. On the surface it seemed to have been one in which Hitler had opted for the rearmament and expansion of the army rather than the ornament of a mass revolutionary militia. Under the surface, however, the following new condition had arrived in Germany:

By the turn of 1934 Hitler had become the near-political master of Germany and had done so less as a politician and a dictator and more as a "chosen one." The results of the plebiscite he called on the question of approval for his removing of Germany from the League of Nations cannot be explained in terms of politics. For his bold defiance of the executors of the Versailles treaty, Germans rewarded him with 95.1 percent of the vote in favor of his policy, a remarkable result in which they gave Hitler overwhelming support—but also a believable one in which more than two million held out against his powers of persuasion. Roehm does not seem to have realized that Hitler had elevated himself above the revolution itself. He was no longer the protégé of 1920, and in the world of 1934 could no longer be the personal friend or equal of any German.

Divorced from the reality of Hitler's deeds and elevated image, Roehm would argue with and disobey this man. "Adolf is and always will be a civilian, an 'artist,' a dreamer...all he wants to do is sit up in the mountains and play God." In these words, Roehm gives an effective appraisal of Hitler, although it would have been more accurate for him to have said that Hitler "communed with Providence" rather than "played God." In using the word *Adolf* in the presence of his subordinates, Roehm exhibited a lack of respect for Hitler and a badly mistaken sense of being an equal with him in some kind of conventional revolution in which many voices would discuss strategy and many more men enjoy the fruits of victory. But Hitler was running no mere political revolution and could hardly have made more clear what he required of party and movement. In February, in a Berlin address to his assembled *Gauleiters*, he would demand that "the party must act as a kind of monastic order, assuring the necessary stability for the entire future of Germany.... The first Leader had been chosen by destiny; the second must from the start have a loyal, sworn community behind him. No one may be selected who has a private power base: Only one man can be the Leader."[38] Roehm, through his refractoriness, had become a unique menace to Hitler. And Roehm's senior associates, in their grab for luxury, could not count as members of a monastic order. Hitler would attempt to "cleanse the SA of the incalculability and wildness of the years of struggle and give [the SA men] the hardness and sobriety which are needed in a ruling class."[39]

On June 4, 1934, Hitler made a final attempt in face-to-face discussion to dissuade Roehm from his dysfunctional demands for a second revolution and failed after five hours of argument. We are treated to the spectacle of the Leader of German millions arguing over principle with a recalcitrant subordinate who considered himself to be his friend. But a messiah can have no friends. There can be little doubt that the timing of the Roehm affair was dependent entirely on the impending death of the president. But the form that the affair took was dependent almost entirely on the relationship— the "friendship"—between Hitler and Roehm during the preceding fifteen years. Roehm, for example, had had a bookplate prepared for presentation to Hitler that showed *Mein Kampf* with a sword on it and two clasped hands above the book and the sword.[40] Can we imagine in wildest imagination a Hess, or even a Gregor Strasser, claiming the relationship suggested by the illustration? The Roehm affair, as it culminated in the Blood Purge, signaled the end of a friendship in which "one of the two friends refused to recognize the elevation of the other to a godlike status."[41] Earlier in 1934, Hess had sworn-in the entire party simultaneously through means of radio and microphone and presaged the oath by the words that through it; Germans would bind their lives to a man through whom superior forces act in the fulfillment of destiny.[42] But Roehm would characterize his chief as a civilian, artist, and dreamer, and through some obtuse death wish continue action that would require Hitler to destroy him.

Hitler as both creator and recreator of National Socialism could never be in error about National Socialist doctrine. Even an unerring prophet, however, may face mutiny within the ranks of the faithful; and how does a prophet destroy a disloyal follower as opposed to a common enemy? Hitler had the option of putting Roehm on trial for treason against the German state, but it would have left any result out of Hitler's hands and put it into those of an array of judges, jurors, bureaucrats, and newspaper editors. And the real issue was not treason against the state but revolt against the savior of the Germans. In such a situation, Roehm would have to be indicted on a charge of interfering with God's messenger, an accurate charge (in Hitler's mind) but one not susceptible to treatment by any conventional legal system. Hitler also had the option to depose Roehm from his position as chief of staff of the SA but could use it only with the danger of open civil war within the party.

Papen, in his ghost-written Marburg address of June 17, would characterize the offending SA as comprising "the elements of selfishness, lack of character, mendacity, beastliness and arrogance that are spreading under the guise of the German Revolution."[43] A key in all of this for a superior comprehension of Hitler is that he was forced to tolerate the peculiar mixture of discipline and indiscipline associated with parts of the SA and the homosexual cliquishness of its higher leaders. During the period of 1930 through 1934, when Hitler imposed his will on every associate in Germany, one man alone resisted successfully his powers of persuasion. Roehm was a difficult friend, who was now out of his league and standing in the way of destiny. By June 1934, Hitler stood poised to pass beyond friendship with any man and into the realm of the lonely, distant Leader. But Hitler could never pass into that realm with Roehm alive and serving as a reminder of Hitler's own historical mortality. Roehm had to die, and Hitler had to kill him.

The biographers, both great and lesser, nevertheless assign the word *murder* to describe the eventual killing, but the word is more contemptuously pejorative than useful in discussing what took place. First and foremost, the killing of a human being to be classified as murder demands the presence of malice aforethought—the killing must be willful, premeditated, and deliberate. With murder seen as such, Roehm cannot be seen to have been murdered by Hitler, although that would have been scant solace to him, for death is death. Hitler had shown enormous forbearance with Roehm, and no actions that suggest malice aforethought could be seen on Hitler's part through mid-June. Toward the end of June, however a late-coalescing quadrumvirate of Goering, Himmler, Heydrich, and Goebbels fed Hitler report, document, and rumor of an impending SA putsch. During the same period and specifically in his meeting of June 21 with President Hindenburg and Werner von Blomberg, Hitler would receive an ultimatum to the effect that "internal peace was the first priority. If Hitler could not remove the present intolerable tension . . . the president would declare martial law and turn the job over to the army."[44] At this moment, Hitler would have faced the necessity for decisive action, including the possible killing of Roehm, to halt the impending disaster of army intervention.

So late as June 21, however, Hitler still had no plan of action to head off disaster and the options would have continued to be legion. Roehm's refractoriness to Hitler's pleas and arguments from January

1933 onward, however, would be joined by evidence of plans for outright uprising. Hitler informed Blomberg on June 25 that he intended personally to arrest Roehm and the higher SA leaders the following Saturday morning at Bad Wiessee, where they would be concentrated in a scheduled conference. At this point the army, backed by the president, put its authority and resources (e.g., motor vehicles, weapons, etc.) behind Hitler and his gathering police and SS arresting *Kommandos* (detachments). Hitler as chancellor and arresting authority, however, would require charges against Roehm. As the situation stood on June 25, Hitler had little more than Roehm as nuisance to state and army and challenge to Hitler's authority over the party. But Roehm had become a big nuisance, and the president himself and Blomberg, "stiff and Prussian" and not his usual malleable self, had demanded decisive action against him.[45]

For most men and even the greater ones, real power must usually destroy them through the corruptive temptations of pleasure. Hitler was impenetrable to such temptation and was characterized by the legend of his monastic frugality with its quality of the pitiful, saintly, and awe-inspiring.[46] For the greatest men in history who continue the climb to the colder regions of power, there is no longer any tangible enjoyment, and only the pride of the heights can compensate them for the icy burden of responsibility and the constant fear of downfall.[47] To ascend to the final coldest height, Hitler could have no friends but only followers sworn in loyalty to fate's messenger. With Hitler interpreted as aspiring political dictator, however, we cannot see the events of June as capable of satisfactory interpretation to the present day. Alan Bullock, as the first great biographer, would postulate that "it is impossible to penetrate Hitler's state of mind in the last week of June." And Kershaw, as the most recent, would note: "What Hitler had in mind at this stage [the last week in June] is unclear."

It is easy to believe that a power-hungry dictator would have moved through an organized conspiracy to murder Roehm. The great biographers have agreed that Hitler was such a tyrant, but none has been able to show or has even attempted to show that Hitler was part of a murderous conspiracy. This does not mean that Hitler can be absolved from killing Roehm and other high-level SA leaders, but that he marched to a drumbeat different from all others. He should have led a conspiracy demanded by the situation of that June and triggered by the president's demand for action. Quite astonishingly, however, he ascended the mountains above Salzburg to ponder the historical juncture, isolated from all others from mid-Friday to Monday. We see no advisers and we sense the presence of a destiny whisperer. The whispering ended on Monday, when Hitler informed Blomberg that Roehm would be arrested the following Saturday. This strategic decision could be seen as etched in stone, but even here Hitler confounds us with his tactical pragmatism. Rudolf Hess's Monday evening radio address, which could have been written by Hitler, warned Roehm against the second revolution and specifically invited him back into the fold. But for whatever reason, Roehm did not reply to Hess's peace offer, and Roehm's enemies would continue to disseminate evidence, both real and bogus, of an imminent SA uprising.

At this point, the great biographers center our attention on the momentarily innocent stance of Roehm and the SA higher leadership from Wednesday through Saturday morning of the last week of June. But by that time, Roehm had already doomed himself. Hitler had been presented evidence that claimed that Roehm was involved in an unlikely but potentially deadly conspiracy that involved Kurt von Schleicher, Gregor Strasser, and the French ambassador André François-Poncet. The reports of an impending SA putsch were believable to Hitler, notwithstanding whether they were bogus or real. And the entire business could be summed up in terms of the situation in the Silesian Army Corps Area. Its commanding general personally visited the German Army commander-in-chief and his chief of staff in Berlin on Friday to report that the local SA claimed to be reacting to army alerts against it. Werner von Fritsch summoned the head of the Army Office in the War Ministry, *Generalmajor* Walther von Reichenau, who commented laconically and with a sense of the inexorability of fate: "That may be true, but it's too late now."[49]

In the final three days—Wednesday, Thursday, and Friday—of the period of Hitler's decision to "arrest" Roehm, Hitler most likely had committed himself to deposing him. The deposition would have included also the homosexually dominated higher leadership of the SA by some decisive but probably nonlethal means. But Goering, Himmler, and Heydrich plied Hitler with evidence of impending bloody SA rebellion, and he reacted with increasing rage over evidence of mutiny and disloyalty. By late Friday afternoon, Hitler would have committed himself to the arrest and probable shooting of people. As afternoon moved into evening, Hitler began to get more threatening news of rebellion. Around midnight, he received a telephone call from Himmler that an SA uprising was planned for Saturday afternoon in Berlin and then a second call from Munich that disturbances were already developing there. At that moment, Hitler was located in Bad Godesberg on the Middle Rhine, about three hundred air miles from Berlin and 275 from Munich, and unable to see for himself either the Berlin evidence or the Munich disturbance. The two phone calls became the chance event that triggered the action exemplifying the Roehm affair to the present day—Hitler's spontaneous, bold, early morning raid on Roehm's hotel on the Tegernsee. Hitler's ignition into a dangerous raid and his utterly consistent accusations of disloyalty demand that we qualify Hitler's action as a crime of passion against the infidelity of those sworn to loyalty. Confusion exists in the interpretation of the event because Goering and Himmler acted in a manner of premeditated murder, and the great biographers untidily lump Hitler together with the others. But Hitler, still in a fit of homicidal passion only hours after Roehm's seizure, would make his personal position clear. In a brief address to party leaders hastily gathered at the Brown House around noon, he would agonize over the "worst treachery in world history."[50]

The Marburg conservatives had intended their earlier speech as a lever to induce the president either to force Hitler to curb the SA or to dismiss him and turn over the job to the army.[51] The impressive irony was that Papen had said publicly what Hitler already knew to be the truth: the SA was out of control. As irony followed irony, the conservatives, not Hitler, opened the final phase of the battle for the succession to the presidency by forcing him to take decisive action against Roehm and the SA.[52] In the culminating, grand irony, Hitler would take action so immediate and decisive that the Marburg conservatives, the president, and the war minister would all have their demands fulfilled. The conservatives thereby, through their own initiative, would have rendered themselves superfluous to the further course of German events. The great biographers would interpret the Roehm affair as one in which "once again Hitler had acted wholly in terms of the ends of power."[53] But there can be neither sublimity nor finality in an act committed for the sake of power: Did Hitler proclaim in 1924 in public trial that he would be known as the destroyer of Marxism? In February and March of 1933, did he destroy the Marxists for the sake of more "power"? Or did he destroy the Marxists for the purpose of becoming historically great as the savior of the Germans from them? It would seem more likely that with the destruction of the Marxists and the killing of Roehm, Hitler arrived at a higher level of historical drama rather than a higher political–scientific score for personal power.

The words of a contemporary associate of Hitler sum up the meaning of the Roehm Affair more perceptively than those of latter day interpreters: "the mass character of the horrors silenced the question of good and evil, justice and injustice, in men's souls, leaving [Germans] with the feeling that a hideous necessity had worked itself out. By this gruesome deed of June 30, 1934, Hitler, in the eyes of the German people, definitely assumed the dimensions of a historical, superhuman being, whose rights and reasons could no longer be questioned."[54] Hitler had already saved the Germans from the Marxists in the events of 1933. In the later events of mid-1934, he would save them yet again—this time from the permanent revolutionaries of his own movement. Hitler thereby ran out of domestic enemies from whom to save the Germans. And although he continued to be revered by millions as savior, Hitler would be cast as German destiny itself after August 1934.

Chapter 7

ARRIVAL OF A WORLD-HISTORICAL PERSONALITY IN EUROPE 1935–1936

With his domestic consolidation of power, Hitler would not only continue to make new Germans internally but also begin to regain freedom of maneuver internationally through repudiation of German disarmament. This generalization is well known. Biographers and historians, almost without exception, have indicted Hitler as totally responsible for the outbreak of World War II as it developed out of this process. This indictment is also well known. What remains less well-known is how a single man could be saddled with the blame for, or alternatively the feat of, starting World War II. To accomplish this, he first had to take possession of Germany; given the circumstances of the time, he then had to rearm it. Ideological *élan* and messianic fervor could take a movement only so far, and then the young men possessing such *élan* would have to be seriously armed— no more brass knuckles, knives, walking sticks, and pistols. This does not mean that Hitler would renounce his unique emphasis on the creation of new Germans but that the new men among them would have to be effectively equipped for war. It is easy to anticipate, therefore, that Hitler would take his next major foreign policy action as one that would free up German rearmament.

By the time that Hitler would announce the fact of already-existing rearmament and the reimposition of conscription in March 1935, he had effectively removed himself from domestic politics. By that time, Hitler can be seen to have transformed such politics into propaganda and indoctrination—the nationalization of the German masses to support the impending wars for living space. Domestic politics would exist to create a "strong, impregnable 'national community.'"[1] During the entire period 1935–1939, Hitler engaged in domestic politics through broad directives exemplified by his speeches at the yearly Party Day rallies at Nuremberg in the month of September. During the same period he would face a challenging situation in the German economy in which he would have to balance the production of armaments against consumer goods and food. Being able to see only evil in the regime, the biographers present the period domestically as one dominated in Germany by the oppression of Marxist leaders, Jews, and "undesirables," presenting the latter as victims of social prejudice. Unable to resist at least mild exaggeration in the matter of oppression, Professor Ian Kershaw, the most recent great biographer, notes that "victims of social prejudice ... were readily to hand: prostitutes [legally constituted as such in Germany], homosexuals, Gypsies, habitual criminals, and others seen as sullying the image of the new society by begging, refusing work, or any sort of 'antisocial' behavior."[2] We are presented thereby with habitual criminals as victims of social prejudice and deflected from the relatively successful action of Hitler to create a new society that would be a genuine community of heroically magnetized Germans. With these Germans figuratively magnetized, of course, Hitler can be seen in March 1935 to have completed the transition to foreign policy and to have begun his notorious series of marches into World War II—March 1935: conscription; March 1936: Rhineland; March 1938: Austria; March 1939: the Czech heartland.

But things are not always as they seem to be in Hitler biography and European history of this period. Kershaw's biography, for example, is one of stunning detail, acerbic wit, profound insight, and complete self-assuredness—but nevertheless it slips by both Hitler and the period. In the case of the announcement of German rearmament on March 16, 1935, as exemplified by the imposition of conscription, Kershaw speaks as the complete spokesman of the conventional wisdom and pictures Hitler as dictator and gambler. The man is presented as disturber of peace and breaker of international law—specifically the peace of Europe of the 1930s and the international law that had proceeded out of the Paris Peace Conference. But the peace of January 1935 continued to be for Germans a reminder of fifteen years of imposed international servitude. On January 13, shortly before the armaments imbroglio of March, the League of Nations would conduct a plebiscite in the territory of the Saar Basin lying in the southeastern German Rhineland, contiguous with French Lorraine. The basin was an industrial entity built around the coal field lying under it, which was one of the three largest in continental Europe. From the partition of Merzen in 870 until 1919, the area had been German under various petty princes and bishops and finally the kings of Prussia and Bavaria for more than one thousand years, with only two brief interruptions. By the 1910 Prussian census, of the 571,690 inhabitants of the Prussian part of the Basin, 568,096 gave German as their "mother tongue," and 342 gave French.[3] In the face of this historical and demographic situation, French prime minister Georges Clemenceau, in March 1919, nevertheless had demanded "as a minimum that the whole Saar Basin" be annexed by France.[4] Wilson and Lloyd George resisted the French demands for outright annexation but in April agreed to suspension of German sovereignty, administration of the Saar territory by a League of Nations commission, and French ownership of every coal mine for a period of fifteen years—at the end of which a plebiscite would be held on the choice of the inhabitants between French or German sovereignty.

The conventional wisdom as represented by Kershaw would interpret the situation as one in which "it was always likely that the majority of the largely German-speaking population where resentment at the treatment meted out in 1919 still smoldered fiercely, would want to return to Germany."[5] This statement is notably economical with the objective reality of this way station to World War II. The French government, in the form of Clemenceau and André Tardieu, in their near-successful attempt to annex the Saar Basin would create a situation in 1919, independent of Hitler, which would encourage a war of perceived injustice on the part of later Germans. The conventional wisdom neither connects the action with the near-future outbreak of World War II nor connects any Frenchman with the action. And to refer to the population of the Saar Basin as "largely German speaking" when German speakers outnumbered French almost 1,700 to 1 doesn't give an accurate sense of the enormity of the situation. For purposes of Hitler biography, we are left with the picture of an opportunistic propaganda victory on the part of a wicked German dictator. For purposes of understanding the outbreak of World War II and the contribution to it by other men and other governments, we could just as readily picture the joyous end to the work of a wicked French prime minister dedicated to dismemberment of 1919 Germany. On March 28 of that year, for example, Clemenceau had advanced the statement to US president Woodrow Wilson that there were 150,000 Frenchmen in the Saar whose rights should be respected.[6] This claim would underlie any moral justification for the near-annexation of the rich, coal-bearing area. But fifteen years later in a newspaper interview, Hitler would be able to point out that "this territory was torn from Germany on the basis of the assertion that in it were living 150,000 French people. After fifteen years of government by the League of Nations...it is now established that there are but 2,000 French... settled in this territory.... Can one then wonder that a treaty built up of arguments so false as this failed to bring any happiness or blessing to mankind?"[7]

Hitler's contention was a factual one, for the results of the plebiscite showed 2,124 voters, probably French, opting for annexation by France. Hitler's accurate contention that Clemenceau, the French, and the Versailles treaty were wicked entities as concerns the exploitation of the Saar Basin does not mean that Hitler was good. It suggests, however, that the French government was bad and that the French passion for the subjugation of Germany and parallel necessary domination of the continent qualified as such. Historians and Hitler biographers nevertheless have indicted Hitler as totally responsible for the outbreak of a Europe-wide war in late 1939 through his actions and intent from 1933 onward. Yet French governments had held the rancorous likes of Clemenceau, Tardieu, and Poincaré, relieved only by the more gentle image of Aristide Briand, whose favorite maxim was "life is made of rubber."[8] But the harder types would predominate to channel Europe toward war. And as concerns the spirit of French leadership, a wit of the day would remark that "Briand knows nothing and understands everything; Poincaré knows everything and understands nothing."[9]

Similar to the situation above in which Hitler's internal enemies tend to become invisible in terms of being interpreted realistically, his external competitors disappear as realistic entities in the great biographies. From 1933 through 1935, Hitler began his foreign policy march with concern about German armaments and the struggle for more realistic balance among the armaments of the major European states. Hitler had remarked in writing so early as 1925 that German rearmament would first be a moral struggle to create Germans willing to fight and second a struggle for numbers of armed men and production of the latest weapons. Hitler would face a great international battle to get these Germans armed and to begin the brief but hugely dramatic period in European history described as the "age of *faits accomplis.*"[10] If a *fait accompli* is a thing accomplished and presumably irrevocable, then Hitler's earlier removal of Germany from the disarmament conference and the League at Geneva fit the bill and marked the beginning of the age. The expression suggests that Hitler flared up and, with evil intent and dangerous potential consequence, presented the innocent and unoffending diplomatic world with an immoral and illegal accomplished fact. But the disarmament conference had been based on the Versailles treaty, and the article in it that had directed the disarmament of Germany *pursuant to* the rest of the world similarly being disarmed. But of all the *faits accomplis* of the interwar period, the Versailles treaty itself must qualify as the first and the greatest—the mother of all in the interwar period.

As concerns the approach of World War II and responsibility for its outbreak, Hitler would have appeared to many contemporaries as a brash, young German patriot dedicated to overturning the unfair parts of the Versailles treaty. Neither the French nor Hitler could have been seen as already leading their countries into World War II. But if such a thing were possible to conceive in 1933, Hitler would have appeared to many as willing to fight in order to set aside an inordinately enduring, unfair treaty. The French, notwithstanding the motives of any of their allies, would have appeared as willing to fight a war in order to maintain an outmoded but advantageous evil. The great biographers, however, gripped by other evils seen when looking back through 1945, would have been unable to resist the temptation to interpret Hitler as prime mover in a surprise action intended as part of a march to World War II.

Hitler would tell us much about himself in the early 1935 rearmament crisis. As concerns his incarnation as German statesman, he would astound his opponents with his boldness and defend his actions with superior argument by critical examination of logical consequences. He would note that "Germany, in demanding equality of rights [that] can only be achieved by the disarmament of other nations, has a moral right to do so since she herself has carried out the provisions of the treaties."[11] Of course, the 1933 disarmament crisis was prologue to Hitler's following major international *faits accomplis* of the decade. But the Geneva confrontation set the pattern for every crisis that followed through Munich to the Polish summer of 1939. In every case, witness lingering Allied iniquity from the Paris Peace Conference, bold Hitlerian challenge, Allied disarray, and near-miraculous Hitler triumph. The revisionist part of this pattern lies in the point that every international crisis that involved Hitler in the 1930s stemmed from an iniquity on the part of the Allies in the Paris Peace Conference of 1919. But we are searching for Hitler and not the Allies, so how does this revision help us find him? The dictator must be seen as more than a dictator and the Allies seen as less than nice. And to agonize that they would become ineffectual appeasers—if only Winston Churchill had been British prime minister in the later 1930s rather than Neville Chamberlain—misses the point that a world-historical personality had marched, outraged, out of the desert of shattered Flanders fields, and the former Allies had not even superior morality to shield themselves from him.

As Hitler wrestled with the necessity to announce German rearmament, he would nevertheless conclude a ten-year nonaggression pact with Poland in January 1934. Hitler timed the pact well because it came shortly after he had shaken the former Allies by withdrawing Germany from the World Disarmament Conference. The pact counterbalanced many of the ill effects of the withdrawal because it reinforced his propagandized image as the man of peace in Europe —the unlikely German statesman who had begun the unlikely labor of normalizing relations in so emotional a situation. Not even Gustav Stresemann, Germany's great statesman of the 1920s, had been inclined to risk political suicide by attempting an accommodation with the Poland that had been created by the Paris Peace Conference and the Poles of history. But Hitler, as German destiny walking, required weapons and armed men, which in turn demanded relaxed international tension. Hitler's nonaggression pact with Marshal Jósef Piłsudski's Poland was a masterpiece of apparent peaceful intentions that increased acceptance of German rearmament and began to break up the French continental alliance system that was so dependent on keeping Germany encircled in the east. But we know such things as part of the diplomatic history of the period. We are less certain of how either the National Socialist ideologue of the great biographers or the messenger of destiny could be so accommodating with so fundamental an enemy. But mere ideologues pale in comparison with what Hitler represented in terms of German and Polish destiny.

Later in 1934, Hitler would face a serious international setback with the attempted coup of the Austrian Nazis in Vienna in late July. After Hitler had become chancellor, the Austrian Nazis had been emboldened to attempt to seize political power in Austria and carry out union with Germany. But they ran into two formidable obstacles: internally, the Christian Socialist Engelbert Dollfuss had become chancellor in 1932, proclaimed a dictatorship in March 1933, and dissolved all political parties in February 1934. Externally, the Italian and Yugoslav governments increased their support for Dollfuss's government and particularly for his policy of Austrian independence. And if all this were not bad enough for Hitler, the French, British, and Italian governments jointly declared on February 17 a common view of the necessity to maintain Austria's "independence and integrity" in accordance with relevant treaties.[12] Things looked bad for Hitler when Austrian Nazis broke into the chancellery and, in the ensuing scuffle, wounded Engelbert and allowed him to die through lack of adequate medical help. Things looked worse for Hitler though the bizarre historical chance that Dollfuss's wife and children were in Rome as house guests of Mussolini, the chief international guarantor of Austrian independence at the moment of the killing. Hitler came across as international accessory to rebellion and murder in a neighboring state. He was seen as a menace to Austria's independence and a threat to the "relevant treaties" that established it.

But things are not always as they seem to be in Hitler biography. Dollfuss, after all, was a tough dictator whose Fatherland Front may not have represented the wishes of Austrians as concerns independence. And the former Allies sought to enforce it based on dictated treaties that did not reflect the wishes of the Austrians from the viewpoint of national self-determination. But the Austrians of 1918 and 1919 had voted overwhelmingly for union with Germany, and it is tempting to generalize that most in 1934 would have voted in favor notwithstanding an intervening fifteen years of burgeoning particular interests in an unwanted republic. The generalization is particularly enticing because, in 1938, the Austrian people approved union by public acclaim so ecstatic that they pulled Hitler himself along into the almost immediate assimilation of Austria into a Greater Germany. Within such a situation, Hitler appears less as an accessory to bloody uprising in 1934 and more as an accessory to the impending arrival of a German messiah in 1938—the man who would save the Austrians from Saint-Germain and make them into new Germans.

*   *   *

When the French government in May 1934 rejected the second British disarmament plan, it signaled that it had given up on the League of Nations as a mechanism to effect satisfactory armaments levels between France and Germany. The French foreign office, referred to as the *Quai d' Orsay* because of its location within Paris, turned to a policy of independent action. The policy had been worked out by the top career official at the Quai d' Orsay, its secretary general Alexis Saint-Léger Léger, who attempted to box in Hitler's Germany with a continental alliance system that would include the Soviet Union and Italy.[13] For purposes of Hitler biography, the French policy shows France not honoring its legal obligation to disarm under the Versailles treaty. It also shows France obstructing League efforts to enforce disarmament. Neither Léger nor the most aggressive foreign minister he advised, Jean Louis Barthou, had the slightest intention of disarming France to the German level. From the viewpoints of both action and aggressive intent—to maintain the unilateral German disarmament and collateral French domination of the continent—the French government contributed to an unfair and outmoded situation significantly responsible for the outbreak of war. This French connection with the outbreak of World War II has vanished within Hitler's shadow, and perhaps understandably so. With feigned astonishment that any man could believe differently, Léger would claim that he intended from the beginning to make a shambles of the Versailles treaty. Hitler would do so over the next several years, and in a grand historical perversity, set aside a vindictive, cruel treaty and replace it with a vindictive, cruel war.

As it became apparent by mid-1934 that French disarmament would not take place and German rearmament probably would, the various governments, especially French, British, and German, began to adjust to the new reality. Hitler would issue an order in October raising the size of the German Versailles army to the Geneva-discussed level of 300,000 men. Since, however, it would take approximately two years to train the conscripts, Hitler would have the larger army only by October 1936. The French government of Pierre Flandin would extend the term of service for the conscripts in its large peacetime army to account for the dip in the birth rate from late 1914 through 1918 and the coincidental suspected increase in German armaments. In a word, Flandin would expand the size of the French army. The British government was more concerned with the sizes of air and naval forces. Based on its assumption that the Germans were beginning to rearm, the British government announced the beginning of air rearmament on March 4, 1935. Based, therefore, on the refusal of the French to disarm and the declared increase in armaments by both France and Britain, Hitler would announce on March 16, 1935, that Germany would begin to expand its army to 550,000 personnel.

And during this second installment of the disarmament crisis, in which he would announce conscription, Hitler would present the situation in words difficult to match for sarcasm, innuendo, and outrage. The words are Hitler's; he had no speech writer. He could summarize roughly verbatim within his May 1935 Reichstag speech:

> I cannot avoid expressing my astonishment at a statement which was publicly made by the British prime minister, Mr. MacDonald, who said with regard to the restoration of a German defense force that the other states had been right after all in being cautious about disarmament. For according to this view the Allies and Germany conclude a treaty. Germany fulfils its obligation and the Allies fail to fulfill theirs. After years of warning, Germany also finally states that the treaty is no longer valid for it, whereupon Mr. MacDonald is entitled to declare that thereby the Allies' previous breach of the treaty has now received subsequent moral justification in that Germany has now also abandoned the treaty.[14]

With dry British wit, MacDonald had disparaged Germany in a phrase in his statement that was virtually impossible to counter. His comment could be vernacularized as: wasn't that just like the Germans, and weren't we fortunate not to have fallen for it? His words, vernacularized or otherwise, were difficult to defend because they summed up a complex issue in only a few words, yet with self-assured, unmistakable criticism of the Germans. Hitler was incensed by this one-sided rendering of world disarmament from 1919 through 1935 and would fly to the attack with the ice-cold yet sarcastic simplification noted above.

If we were to put faces into this picture of armaments from 1933 through 1935 and relate it with the Versailles treaty, we could generalize that Jean Louis Barthou determined illegally not to disarm France but to increase its armaments, and that Adolf Hitler determined (less) illegally to rearm Germany. Prime Minister J. Ramsay MacDonald, after prodigious and courageous efforts to bring France around to honor its treaty obligations and faced with evidence of impending German rearmament, illegally began to increase British air armaments in early March 1935. Multiple illegalities characterized the armaments picture in the spring, but the most astonishing and final irregularity would be the Anglo-German naval agreement of early summer. The British government was moderately concerned about ground armaments, more deeply concerned about air armaments, and terminally concerned about naval armaments. The British government had entered World War I based significantly on its perception of a threat to its naval supremacy from the rapidly industrializing turn-of-the-century Germany. Hitler, as both a self-adjudged and undeniable "student of history," subtly exploited the situation. The exploitation was subtle because instead of menacing the British with excessive demands like equality in naval armaments, Hitler would menace them with a ratio so seductive that the British government could not refuse it. The ratio—one hundred major British warships versus thirty-five German—must have been seen as epochal by the British foreign minister, Sir John Simon, in light of the prewar Imperial German construction of a more threatening Navy. Simon would sign the Anglo-German naval agreement on June 18, 1935, and thereby condone Hitler's illegal "open breach of treaty" and necessarily become a party to it.

Quite astonishingly, earlier in April, MacDonald and Simon had met in Stresa on Lago di Maggiore in Italy with their opposite numbers from France and Italy and issued a formal three-power protest against the German action. The opportunistic British adherence to a naval pact with the Germans in June condoned breach of treaty, undermined French security, and demolished the Stresa Front. This remarkable British action does not make Hitler a nicer person. He was, after all, not just interested in destroying a dysfunctional treaty but also dedicated to the formation of a German empire on the European continent, notwithstanding its imposition on several European peoples. The British action, however, does give pause for thought about British motivation for the outbreak of World War II. The British government, after all, was not just interested in reducing the damage from an unruly German dictator on the continent but also dedicated to the continuation of a world empire, notwithstanding its imposition on numerous world peoples.

As 1935 turned into 1936, Hitler would face further mortal danger to the creation of the vision that he carried in his mind of a celestial German city. And, as usual, the danger would come from the Versailles treaty and less usually, but just as decisively, from an off-shoot known as Locarno—a group of treaties designed primarily to reassure France and her various allies of their security against Germany. Notwithstanding the restrictions and burdens imposed upon Germany by the Versailles treaty, the French government had continued to obsessively fear for its security. France, for example, would receive most of the German economic reparation and could use the issue to dominate Germany politically. The French government would argue with unsympathetic logic that the reparation was not excessive and the Germans were not paying on time, in various cases, because they did not want to.

At the turn of 1925, the French-influenced Allies declared that because of German failure to fulfill the Versailles treaty provisions of disarmament, occupation forces would not be removed from the Cologne Zone of the Rhineland on January 10 even though it was required by treaty. Gustav Stresemann, as German foreign minister, would connect the recent Ruhr invasion with the nightmare possibility of permanent French occupation of the Rhineland stemming from exaggerated French security fears. The work exaggerated is applicable to the contemporary situation in which a French army of over 700,000 men was linked with a defense pact–allied armies in Poland, Czechoslovakia, and Belgium that totaled approximately 600,000 more along borders contiguous with Germany. They stood opposed to the one-hundred-thousand-man German Army. This horror story for Germany of being outnumbered approximately 13:1 in men under arms was aggravated by the fact that the Versailles treaty forbid the German army to have weapons effective for serious ground war. Through fear of lengthy and capricious French occupation of the Rhineland, Stresemann proposed in a February 9, 1925, memorandum to the French government a mutual guarantee of the existing border between France and Germany. Stresemann intended the guarantee to be an act of conciliation great enough to relax France and ease the burden of the Versailles treaty on Germany.

For his own reasons, the French foreign minister Briand welcomed conciliation, and the British and Italian governments agreed to participate in discussions that led to a conference at Locarno in October. The conference was the most important of the 1920s in Europe and resulted in the signing of seven treaties in December 1925. The most important was the Rhineland Mutual Guarantee Pact among France, Germany, and Belgium, with Britain and Italy as guarantors. This was the treaty that faced Hitler and the Germans ten years later, and it had a dark edge in it for both. Notwithstanding Stresemann's statesmanlike press for conciliation, the treaty had been coerced out of him by the French violence of 1923 and the threat of indefinite military occupation of the Rhineland at the turn of 1925. The dark edge for Stresemann in an otherwise shining treaty of conciliation was that he had been forced to accept the permanent prohibition of German troops and military installations in a significant part of German territory. The dark edge for Hitler, ten years later, was that the Locarno-enforced German military vacuum in the Rhineland would freeze him in any attempt to move east.

Stresemann can be seen as one of the two great statesmen of Europe in the 1920s and one who combined the qualities of European breadth with those of a German patriot. But he was still only a great statesman. He had been constrained both by French power and his acceptance of the diplomatic rules of the game to move slowly. Stresemann would score high marks for enlightened attempts at conciliation with an irreconcilable France and low marks for the advantages presented to France by Locarno and The Hague. But he would affect a remarkable reversed conciliation. In it, a defeated Germany would conciliate a victorious France rather than the more reasonable situation in which a victor would conciliate a loser through the prudence of removing cause for revenge. And in accomplishing this reversed conciliation he would move at a pace so slow and with statesmanlike goals so limited that more than one-half century would pass before Germany might be free. In contrast, Hitler was a historical force in a hurry.

Years later, Hitler still had a long way to go on March 4, 1936, when the French National Assembly ratified a Franco-Russian mutual defense pact that had been signed a year earlier under a Flandin government. But he could go no place in the presence of a German military vacuum in the Rhineland, an adjacent French Army, and a Rhineland Mutual Guarantee Treaty that mandated such a situation. Hitler had to set aside the treaty, and he could not operate in the relaxed mode of a great statesman but would require instead the impatience and sense of fleeting time of the world-historical personality. As previously noted, Hitler could state as applicable to his opponents that "they had better realize that we see things in terms of a historical vision."[15] Hitler glimpsed a Reich that would regenerate itself with each new generation, as it were, passed on in the blood of the nation. But such a passage in time could be possible only through the vision and achievement of the first generation—the messiah and his first disciples. Hitler and the first generation had to succeed. Otherwise, by no rational account could the following generation and ensuing ones have heroes exemplar enough to guide them for one thousand years. Hitler alone conceptualized and ordered an armed march into the Rhineland, and the great biographers have interpreted him significantly as a gambler who would take any risk to further his own power. But we must distinguish between the necessity to achieve and the compulsion to gamble, as it were, between the necessity to take risks and the compulsion to take them. To succeed, Hitler had to do things, and to do things, he had to take risks. In his Rhineland move, Hitler would face his greatest international danger of 1933–1936. It was one thing to walk out of the world disarmament talks in 1933 and another to march, armed, into the Rhineland in 1936.

In the months before the march, Hitler had shown his characteristic political dexterity. It would be easy to mistake him for a politician at this time, but the practice of politics does not necessarily demand a politician. During the whole period from March 1935 through 1936, Hitler would flicker in and out as two personalities—not in the sense of some sort of clinical schizophrenia but in the sense of being two different men in international diplomacy. Hitler, for example, would call in the French ambassador, André François-Poncet, on the afternoon of March 16, announce German rearmament, and claim that his intentions were defensive. Although the ambassador was an intelligent, polished diplomat, Hitler would convince him that German rearmament had resulted from concern over Soviet Russian Communism and was directed against it. We see two Hitlers here: The first was a devious German dictator but a consummate political tactician; he would deflect French action just enough by devious argument to prevent a career-ending French counterstroke. The other Hitler was the voice of German destiny. It spoke the unswerving truth that Russian Communism was the world's international enemy and revealed a sacred intention to destroy it. In such a picture, France was merely an honorable ancient competitor of the Germans and not an enemy to be destroyed. But France was caught at the wrong time and the wrong place in history as bystander in the greater drama of the approaching eastern cataclysm. Hitler had no quarrel with France—no interest in war for its own sake—but France was in the way, caught up in its ancient enmity. In the case of France, Hitler would find it necessary to protect a devious account of intent with a bodyguard of truth.

*   *   *

Later, in March 1935, Hitler met in Berlin for two days with the British foreign minister Sir John Simon and discussed peace in Europe and the question of armaments. The circumstances were moderately bizarre because only days before Hitler had announced the reinstitution of German conscription in defiance of the Versailles treaty, and only a month later the British government would meet at Stresa in Italy with French and Italian governments to condemn the action and form a diplomatic front against Germany. Within such a context, Sir John would actually invite the Germans to discussions in London on the subject of naval armaments, which would lead to the Anglo-German naval pact of June. The Berlin conference was important; Hitler would personally conduct its meetings. According to Anthony Eden, Hitler conducted the discussions "without hesitation and without notes, as befitted a man who knew exactly where he wanted to go."[16] Hitler would argue calmly and politely, having made the leap to polished international negotiator in no less refined company than statesmen of the British Empire. Here was the Hitler who was exceptionally well-read in subjects of interest to him, and they included history both ancient and modern—from Dorian tribes pressing in from the north to populate the Grecian peninsulas with Western man to more modern

European scenes populated by Frederick the Great and Otto von Bismarck. The man had historical sweep, as reflected in his suggestion "as a student of history" that Britain and Germany combine in an alliance that would dominate Europe and have world-wide implications. But when negotiations turned to the subject of an Eastern Locarno—a guarantee of the borders among Germany, Poland, Czechoslovakia, and Lithuania with Soviet Russian involvement—the diplomatic Hitler became the *other* Hitler.

The Lithuanian government had recently put on trial a number of Germans in the seaport of Memel for alleged treasonable correspondence with Germany. With the word *Lithuania*, the other Hitler would abruptly appear as "his eyes blazed, his voice became hoarse, and he rolled his *r*s. In a moment the storm subsided and once more he was the polished negotiator."[17] The ostensibly minor issue of Memel suggests a revised picture of Hitler. Interpreted as the devious dictatorial leader of a volatile German political movement and collector of power, he should not have been particularly concerned with Memel, especially during far-reaching negotiations with the British government over balances of sea power and stability for all of Europe. But Hitler had become outraged enough on both days of the conference to become a different man and not a devious one.

The Memel affair was deeper than it might have seemed to the British negotiators contemporaneously and great Hitler biographers more recently. It reflected the entire German condition, and Hitler, interpreted as a fiery messiah, would be particularly unhappy with it. Memel had been founded by the fabled Teutonic Order of knights in 1252 and was first called New Dortmund—perhaps not unlike New York and New Jersey several hundred years later in a New World. The seaport on a sandy stretch of Baltic seacoast would remain populated almost entirely by Germans and under various German governments during the intervening 667 years until it encountered the Versailles treaty. The Allies, under the treaty, forced Germany to cede Memel to the "Allied and Associated Powers" and to accept

whatever disposal they made of it. The port was a natural one for a
newly constituted Lithuania, and the Allies suggested that the
Lithuanians accept a free city status under controls shared with the
League of Nations. The Lithuanians refused and instead seized
Memel in a surprise attack in January 1923 with armed troops strong
enough to force the French garrison to surrender and evacuate. To
add insult to injury, the Lithuanian government insisted that the
Memel citizenry, approximately 90 percent of whom were German,
had risen spontaneously to become part of Lithuania.

The Germans had a moral superiority in the Memel issue based
on the Wilsonian principle of free determination of peoples. To
make the situation more outrageous, the Allies had brought modern
Lithuania into existence based on the same principle, and the
Lithuanian government had violated it through the irony of seizing
a German city for reason of economic convenience. If Hitler had
been a mere dictator colored as ideologue, it is unlikely that the
jailing of Germans for treason against Lithuania would have disturbed him. But it did disturb him. And it disturbed the flow of
discussion at the conference. Hitler, as one party to discussions that
led to an Anglo-German naval pact in June, would seemingly
become possessed by a demon at the mention of the word *Lithuania.*
It is unlikely that Hitler employed the incident for some transitory
tactical advantage and it is unlikely that he had become possessed by
a demon. It *is* likely that Hitler combined the intensity in one person
of a German messiah and a darker prophet—one to whom destiny
had revealed the path to German salvation. As such, he was supposed
to be outraged. And momentarily, he was more outraged by the
Lithuanian injustice than he was capable of concentrating on naval
armaments, military parity, and general political settlements.

*   *   *

At the end of 1935, France was still the strongest military power in
western Europe. In spite of its economic depression and associated

financial problems, France maintained a defense establishment—army, navy, and air force—of about 620,000 personnel. The German defense establishment, on the other hand, including the expansion of the air force and the navy and the inclusion of the rural police elements of the Prussian and other state police, stood at just under 400,000. And in the period from 1933 through 1935, French governments had spent more money on their armed forces in terms of comparable currency—specifically 10.1 billion French francs of 1913 value compared with 9.2 billion French francs for Germany.[18] Thanks to the realities of Franco-German strategic geography, the French army and air force could be concentrated along a common border with Germany and would be faced by a Rhineland devoid of German fortification, military installation, and soldiers. And, in the event of any defensively construed French counter-thrust into the Rhineland, Hitler would be faced with the danger of Belgian, Czech, and Polish armed intervention in support of France. Such were the vagaries of international relations, however, that the Stresa diplomatic front had disintegrated with the Italian invasion of Ethiopia in October. The disintegration of accord over the containment of Germany did not give Hitler an argument to present in support of German reoccupation of the Rhineland, but it did present fleeting opportunity. Both argument and opportunity would come on March 4, 1936, when the French Chamber of Deputies ratified a military alliance with Soviet Russia that gave Hitler reasonable cause to set aside the Rhineland Mutual Guarantee Pact.

Ten months earlier, at the end of May 1935, the German government had circulated a memorandum to the Locarno Pact signatories that the French government's signed alliance with Soviet Russia was not compatible with the pact. Hitler, therefore, did not pull the Franco-Russian Alliance as a rabbit out of a hat to support a sudden *fait accompli*, but had argued through diplomatic channels for ten months against it. Hitler argued persuasively and validly that France had unbalanced the Locarno system by introducing Soviet Russia into central Europe. He would present as undisputed facts that the Franco-Soviet pact was directed against Germany and that in the event of a conflict between Germany and Soviet Russia, France had obligations that would compel it to take military action against Germany. He would point out that France alone had the right to decide on its own judgment if Germany were the aggressor in the event of a Russo-German conflict and suggest in a sarcastic double negative that any judgment would be a foregone conclusion —"France has not concluded this treaty with a European Power of no special significance"—he would argue that Soviet Russia would be an extraordinary danger to both Germany and Europe because it was not only a great power but also "the exponent of a [world] revolutionary political and philosophical system organized in the form of a state."[19] And with additional sarcasm, he would state that the French government had attempted to brush aside Germany's apprehensions by referring to the unwieldy and unfit nature of Russia as an ally in a European conflict.

The president of the French Chamber of Deputies, Édouard Herriot, however, would simultaneously attempt to convince the Chamber of the strength of a Soviet Russia as a military alliance partner. Hitler was able to note, thanks to Herriot and the information presented to the Chamber, that the Russian army had a peace strength of 1,350,000 men, war strength and reserves of 17,500,000 men, and the largest tank and air forces in the world. These numbers and adjectives qualify as possibly unwieldy but impossibly dangerous. And in the event of a war between Russia and Germany, the French army could aid Russia only through an advance into a demilitarized German Rhineland, an act incompatible with Locarno. The French-imposed situation was a recipe for disaster for Germany, mitigated only by the geographical incidental that Soviet Russia and Germany had no contiguous border because they had been separated in 1919 by the creation of Poland and Czechoslovakia at the Paris Peace Conference. But France had military pacts with both Poland and Czechoslovakia, and Soviet Russia had signed a military pact with the Czechs at the end of May 1935. This situation has been characterized by one distinguished authority as a "policy of independent French action to keep Germany hemmed in by a ring of bayonets."[20]

Hitler faced the above situation, in which Germany looked suspiciously like the aggrieved party, during the impending ratification of the Franco-Russian military pact in February and early March 1936. This view does not change the demonstrable fact that Hitler intended soonest to seize territories by armed force in the east. He saw the morally defensible advance west into the Rhineland as the indispensable first move demanded by an amoral vision of an advance east. The word *vision* is important, for we cannot comprehend Hitler by claiming that he functioned in 1936 in terms of any commonly understood plan. Hitler advanced against a vast French alliance system that could be characterized as a French diplomatic empire underpinned by the evil assumption of German guilt for the outbreak of World War I and kept in place by French army power. It could be understood as the continuation of war against Germany by other means. This French-oriented picture of Europe at the turn of 1936 is harsh, revisionist, and authoritative. Hitler would present it in two foreign policy speeches of May 21, 1935, and March 7, 1936, and skillfully direct his attacks not against France but against a situation in which World War I had perpetuated itself into peacetime. Hitler's arguments, although jarring to today's ears, were largely valid then and remain largely valid today.

The great biographers take the position that Hitler used the Franco-Russian pact as a pretext to denounce Locarno and reoccupy the demilitarized zone of the Rhineland.[21] This self-assured claim by the biographers supports a view of Hitler as an aggressive statesman who used the Franco-Russian pact to cloak his real intention for remilitarizing the Rhineland. But the pact can be seen as dangerous actuality as much as convenient pretense. It was true that the pact was directed at Germany, as were the military pacts that France had with Poland, Czechoslovakia, and Belgium. These pacts, when added to the one-sided demilitarization of the German border area with France, must be seen as a potential mortal danger to Germany. The following is a question of importance for a realistic revision of Hitler: Did he comprehend the French-inspired pact as pretense, actuality, or perhaps something else that has continued to elude us?

Hitler himself provided powerful clues to his intentions in almost incredibly candid public speeches and party pronouncements year after year. In May 1935, shortly after the signing of the Franco-Russian military pact, he would state in his most important foreign policy speech of the year that "in so far as Bolshevism can be considered a purely Russian affair we have no interest in it whatever. Every nation must seek its salvation in its own way. So far as Bolshevism draws Germany within its range, however, we are its deadliest and most fanatical enemies."[22] France had always been, in Hitler's eyes, a culturally advanced and respected nation-state. It was, however, the architect and enforcer of the Versailles treaty and had become the state that would attempt to introduce Soviet Russia into the Western diplomatic mix. We cannot doubt that Hitler by the end of 1935 recognized the opportunity to reoccupy the Rhineland and cannot doubt that from a military point of view he saw the action as an "absolute necessity."[23] About one week before the French Chamber of Deputies was due to vote on the Franco-Russian pact, however, Hitler granted an interview with the French journalist Bertrand de Jouvenel of *Paris Midi*. In this interview, Hitler would argue in his incarnation as man of European destiny that the time had arrived for the reconciliation of the French and German peoples—the Latins and the Germans. With due regard for the politics of plebiscites, he would inform Jouvenel that 90 percent of Germans, as embodied in the single individual Adolf Hitler sitting in front of him, desired reconciliation. He would pronounce with the solemnity that so often characterized him: "I beg you to take heed of this: in the lives of peoples there are decisive occasions. Today France can, if she wishes it, put an end forever and ever to this German peril!"[24] Taking the interview as a whole and as punctuated by comments such as this, we see Hitler argue that the historical moment had arrived for France to depart from the politics of

German peril as embodied in the military pact with Soviet Russia and embrace the politics of mutual recognition of two great, culturally dominant peoples. But how is it possible for Hitler to have argued so decisively against approval of the Franco-Russian pact at the critical time of the final debates in the Chamber? The conventional wisdom has demanded that Hitler used the pact as a pretext for the remilitarization of the Rhineland and that final approval by the French was a consummation devoutly to be desired.

But Hitler, from the mid-1920s onward, had repeated that "rivers of blood" had been spilled for no other purpose than minor rectifications of borders in a Europe filled with peoples set within long-existing, distinct areas. Yet Germans were Germans and French were French, inconvertible one to the other and set within well-defined boundaries. Hitler was willing to give up a lot in support of his theme of the purposelessness of war in western Europe; in January 1935, on the occasion of the Saar plebiscite, he had announced in words beyond misunderstanding that Germany had no further territorial demands on France. Hitler was being peculiarly diplomatic because the reincorporation of the purely German Saarland into Germany could not be seen as having been a territorial demand against France. And with the same words he would renounce German claim to Alsace-Lorraine. The picture above supports a view that Hitler, with his characteristic historical sweep, had embraced a design of peaceful accommodation with France that amounted to a near-impossible attempt to secure a free hand in the east.

With the Soviet military pact, however, the French government would continue its outmoded formula to keep Germany encircled by a ring of bayonets with its axiomatic danger of fruitless and bloody national war. Hitler would face the stern reality of an unbending France, an unfortified border, an impending Soviet Russia, and a more dangerous Czechoslovakia. He would also face an enormous but premature opportunity to regain sovereignty over the Rhineland. The opportunity was premature because Hitler seems to have been thinking of remilitarization as not likely before 1937, and then with safer conventional negotiations to convince the Locarno signatories to grant Germany the equal right to have troops and fortifications on its borders with Belgium and France. In either case Hitler had a striking argument—the Franco-Russian military pact was incompatible with Locarno, and the Versailles–Locarno demilitarization of the Rhineland was based on the immoral proposition that Germany alone had been responsible for the outbreak of World War I. Hitler nevertheless has been interpreted as a treaty breaker, even though Versailles was an evil treaty and the part of Locarno that he repudiated was inequitable. In early 1936, we have a marvelous complexity: a bad man would break a bad treaty and leave us to ponder the question of the greater evil.

The French government faced new fears with German guns within range of Strasbourg. But France stood with a divided population, a neglected army, and an outmoded foreign policy that could not be supported by either. "When a country hasn't an army that fits its policies, it must have policies that fit its army"; and France did not have an army that matched its foreign policy of 1936.[25] When the weak interim coalition government headed by the radical Albert Sarraut called on the chief of the French general staff, Maurice Gamelin, for the possibilities of armed action, the latter replied that the choices were total mobilization of the republic or no action at all. Neither Sarraut nor British prime minister Stanley Baldwin were craven opponents but rather politicians forced to operate internationally in 1936 within hopelessly outmoded parameters set in place in 1919. Hitler's foreign policy would be a study in the repudiation of the Versailles treaty and Saint-Germain, and his real opponents of the period may have been the formidable ghosts of the Clemenceau, Poincaré, and Lloyd George of 1919 Paris.

Hitler, of course, calculated the possibilities of French, Italian, and British counter-action, and did so with political scientific aplomb. He also engaged in the art of forecasting the future. But we can hardly claim that he based his action on either science or art, even though little basis remains for action after the application of knowledge (science) and skill in doing (art). But Hitler was Hitler and had become a historical force by 1936, inspired from his adolescence by ideal solutions. In February 1936, the boundary stakes between Germany and France were still placed thirty miles north of the Rhine River. The ideal solution to this cruel reality would be simply to carry them to the French border one dark night without negotiation, announcement, or realistic chance of success. What looks today as if it were assured—"The risk in fact had been only a moderate one"—was on March 7 a risk of momentous proportion.[26]

And Hitler showed more than just boldness in advancing into the mouth of unrealistic chance of success; he showed a stunning sense of the heroic. Returning from Cologne by train with Hans Frank, he would have records played of Wagner's *Parsifal* prelude and the funeral march from *Goetterdaemmerung*, themes that involved, in his own words, the "glorious mystery of the dying hero."[27] We can understand the Rhineland reoccupation more perceptively for purposes of comprehending Hitler as an ideal solution, a great simplification disguised as a *fait accompli* and carried out by a hero. The conventional wisdom, however, has presented Hitler as a gambler, although consummate psychologist, who outwitted his international opponents. And the same wisdom would say that this success gave "his boundless egomania another massive boost" and miss the truth of Hitler yet again.[28]

Hitler dwelt in a world of grand historical simplifications and did not shrink from the logical necessities of his own thought. He offered the French a twenty-five-year nonaggression pact that he probably hoped would lead to an ideal *modus vivendi* with France. In such an arrangement, France would be assured of its Alsace-Lorraine boundaries, and Germany would be permitted to expand east to reduce its population density. And to suggest that Hitler would have turned on France after exhausting the advantages of such a modus would be a misreading of Hitler. We cannot claim that he intended to make colonial peoples out of less cultured Slavs and simultaneously claim that he intended to subjugate French and

British peoples of culture equivalent to German. Hitler sought ideal but unrealistic accommodations with the French and British, but urgency in time—a distant goal and a single lifetime—forced the pace. Hitler would say that "we have made the world the most generous offer ever expressed in history" and would claim to hope that the offer be accepted because it would not be made again.[29] In final analysis, Hitler would have had the ideal situation for advance east if he could have succeeded in a nonaggression pact among diplomatic equals in the west. But to have achieved this ideal settling of traditional antipathies, he would have had to have made new Frenchmen.

*   *   *

During the whole period 1933–1939 within Germany, Hitler commissioned cultural projects associated with the fine arts. These projects and the significance that he attached to the fine arts give us insights into the man that rival any we are likely to get from his foreign and domestic political actions of the same time. During that mysterious period of childhood and adolescence in which every man becomes set in final character, Hitler came out of the genetic and environmental cauldron as an artist. And Providence would spare this artist in four years of combat on the western front in order to deliver its message. The things above translate into a terrifying combination of artist and combat soldier, imagination and intensity. This interpretation is obvious and difficult, if not impossible, to refute.

We glimpse a child painter in 1904 who would become a towering architectural planner by 1933 and who, through significantly chance circumstance, became the savior of the Germans. The child artist became the adult painter and architect, but his potential artistic career would be ruined by his calling to become the German redeemer. Curiously enough, we have a unique piece of firsthand evidence that links the artist and the hero in the formative period of Hitler's life. His young friend August Kubizek would relate, decades after a performance of *Rienzi* around 1906 in Linz, that Hitler would drag him to the top of a nearby hill and, bathed in midnight starlight, announce that he was experiencing a vision in which he would be the savior of his people. We see the artist and the hero linked already in Linz prior to Vienna, the war, and 1919 Munich. After 1919, the hero would dominate. But Hitler as historical rarity would be driven to integrate both painting and architecture into politics. This integration has become well known. The great biographers present it, however, as the work of a half-educated painter and megalomaniacal amateur architect.

Kershaw would make the case that "outside politics Hitler's life was largely a void" and that "he was, as has been frequently said, tantamount to an 'unperson.'"[30] He claims that "Hitler's non-political life is not a pretty one. We are faced with a vulgar [common, plebian, coarse] uneducated upstart lacking a rounded personality, the outsider with half-baked opinions on everything under the sun, the uncultured self-appointed adjudicator on culture."[31] This somewhat insensitive view of Hitler as private person is not only based on shaky foundations, but once placed on them, also magnifies misperception in the usual direction of underestimation. Hitler, for example, in the period of 1910 through 1914 earned a living in Vienna and Munich by painting in watercolors and oils, and during the entire period of 1904 (when he was fifteen years old) through 1945 has been estimated to have produced between two thousand and three thousand drawings, sketches, and paintings.[32] Hitler produced much of this work early in the period, and "most historians have underrated the early years of activity and have buried Hitler's theories about art and his role as artist in fleeting references."[33] The quality of Hitler's paintings was in most cases excellent, especially from the viewpoints of both drawing skill and the rendering of color.

Private buyers could be impressed, and Dr. August Priesack, an NSDAP archivist responsible for authenticating all discovered Hitler art, could relate experiences such as the following: "While searching for Hitler's watercolors in Munich, I visited the chemist Dr. Max Schnell.... He received me in ... an amazing room ... com-

pletely paneled in wood...hung with lovely rococo carvings he had
acquired from one of Ludwig II's artisans. In the midst of these...
royal surroundings hung six watercolors by Hitler which Dr.
Schnell's father had ordered and purchased directly from him in
1913 and 1914 for twenty gold marks apiece."[34] Hitler would match
his competence in painting with studied reading of art and architectural history. He would retain an intense, informed interest in
painting throughout the period of struggle as evidenced by his reaction to the 1931 fire in Munich's great art gallery, in which its collection of German Romantic art was destroyed. Hitler rushed to the
fire with his friend Heinrich Hoffmann and futilely watched its
destruction. He would declare to his architectural mentor Paul
Ludwig Troost that "his first project," presumably among many
others, would be the construction of a new gallery.

Hitler had conceptualized by the early 1930s a German art to be
painted by German artists and to have its purpose to pull Germans
together into a homogeneous community. He would characterize
international art as a descent into chaotic experimentation and
divorcement from the community around it. In contrast, German art
would have to be comprehensible and subject to eternal artistic standards of beauty, pathos, and technical skill. Hitler would argue persuasively that the concept of "modern art" was to reduce art to the
level of contemporary fashion in dress with the motto "every year
something fresh"—Impressionism, Futurism, Cubism, Dadaism. He
would suggest that "there was a conspiracy of incapacity and mediocrity against better work of any age."[35] Hitler would note with his
characteristic knack for biting sarcasm that rather than a detraction,
"it was only an attraction that these works of art were difficult to
understand and on that account very costly: no one wished to admit
lack of comprehension or insufficient means."[36]

In his opening of a new House of German Art in Munich in July
1937, Hitler would reminisce about the road to the completed structure in apolitical, prophetic terms. He would reveal himself as an
idealistic dreamer who valued a cultural renaissance for Germans to

be as important as political and economic reform: "There is no prouder proof of the highest rights of a people to its own life than immortal cultural achievements. I was therefore always determined that if fate would one day give us power that I would discuss these matters with no one but would form my own decisions, for it is not given to all to have an understanding for tasks as great as these."[37] Hitler's words indicate that he was in deadly earnest about immortal cultural achievements as the basis of a people's right to existence.

He would pose the question: "Is not the satisfaction of the material needs of life for the time being of greater moment than the erection of monumental buildings?"[38] He would answer the question with the analysis that "in [its great cultural achievements] is incorporated the deepest, the essential force of a people. But never is it more necessary to lead a people to this unending force of its eternal character and being than at the time when political or economic cares might only too easily weaken its faith in its higher values and thus in its mission."[39] Hitler drew a quasi-mystical, cloud-soaring image of a goal for new Germans that lay beyond politics and economics. Hitler would present these hopelessly idealistic words to a mass audience at the Nuremberg Party Day rally in late 1935, and it cannot be claimed that he was telling his Versailles-trammeled, economically straitened mass audience what it wanted to hear. Rather than a political propagandist exploiting the baser instincts of an audience, Hitler comes across as a passionate savior enlightening his people about what he was saving them for—superior cultural achievement.

Hitler hoped that the new Germany would produce a few new Germans capable of being recognized as great masters who would "echo in music the emotions of our soul...immortalize then in stone."[40] Hitler would emphasize painting and architecture in this cultural renaissance and attack the chaotic and fashionably changing schools of modern painting as "the art of the decline."[41] As part of such characterization of modern art, Hitler in 1936 would forbid conventional art criticism and replace it with art reporting. In such a system, "the critic" would describe works of art and "the people" would make its own judgment on beauty, harmony, reality, and so on. For diverse reasons political, esthetic, and philosophical, Hitler rejected modern painting as neither art nor skillfully done.

For different reasons, the erudite historical philosopher Oswald Spengler would agree. He would postulate a supremely imaginative theory of the development of Western civilization in terms of its spring, summer, autumn, winter, and inexorable extinction. Within such a theory, art was possible in Western civilization only in its springtime followed by a brief autumn renaissance. For Spengler, Western civilization had entered its winter by the turn of the twentieth century, and the time for great art had passed irretrievably. He would opine: "We are civilized not [cultured] people; we have to reckon with the hard cold facts of a *late* life, to which the parallel is to be found not in Pericles's Athens but in Caesar's Rome. Of great painting or great music there can no longer be, for Western people, any question."[42] He would elaborate that "we cannot help it if we are born as men of the early winter of full Civilization, instead of on the golden summit of a ripe culture, in a Phidias or a Mozart time."[43] By noteworthily different roads, Hitler and Spengler had come to similar conclusions about so-called modern art. Spengler would assert that it could not be considered "modern" and could never be great. Hitler would assert that art could not be equated to changing fashion: He would demand an "eternal art" conditioned by the unchanging character of the people that creates and sustains it—Nordic Aryan through Greece, Rome, and the European Renaissance. Hitler cannot be considered to have been the amateur adjudicator of art suggested by his biographers. He was not only an artist but also a knowledgeable art historian and a prophetic visionary who would make new Germans linked especially by eternal values in painting. We are left with the uneasy feeling that an inscrutable destiny chose to write its will across the sky through the medium of an artist.

Chapter 8

REDEEMER OF THE GERMANS
1937–1939

By 1937, in foreign policy, Hitler seems to have given up on Britain as the unique alliance partner that might have made possible a German free hand in the east. For various reasons, he had already made a fateful swing toward fascist Italy as appropriate for the circumstances of 1937. Hitler had developed out of the early 1920s a natural and obvious affinity for Mussolini the man and fascism, Mussolini's political achievement in Italy. The affinity would not bear any practical result from 1922 through 1933 because Hitler was not in power in Germany. And for several years after Hitler came to power, the two leaders would face seemingly insuperable difficulties over the lingering World War I issues of Austria and South Tyrol. The latter was inhabited largely by Germans who had voted in a provincial government plebiscite held on April 24, 1921, with 145,302 votes in favor to 1,805 against.[1] The Allies would ignore this expression of self-determination, and Mussolini would inherit a problem. He would have the military strength to prevent any union of South Tyrol with Austria, but he would face the nightmare possibility of a revived Germany achieving a union with Austria and endangering South Tyrol. After many foreign policy adventures, however, between 1933 and 1937, Germany and Italy had drawn together. During Mussolini's state visit to Germany in late September 1937, Hitler and Mussolini agreed in general terms that Italy would have a free hand in the Mediterranean and Germany would have a free hand in Austria. It is difficult to overestimate this distancing of Mussolini from Austria. For Hitler, secure control over Aus-

tria would be the indispensable first step in the drive east, and he would
be willing to pay the price of abandoning the Germans of South Tyrol.

Only a month after Mussolini's tour through Germany—
although with no necessary cause and effect—Hitler would reveal
the most astonishing intentions of any man in the twentieth century
who had the power to carry them out. At a meeting to include the
war minister, the heads of the three armed forces, and the foreign
minister, Hitler would unveil some sensational ideas. The conventional wisdom has characterized these ideas presented in a two-hour
nonstop speech as his plan for conquest.[2] But the characterization of
the ideas as that of ordinary political calculation writ extraordinarily
large in terms of evil intent does not fit the ideas or Hitler. As savior
of the Germans, he actually intended to save them. In line with his
much earlier comments of the mid-1920s to the effect that "our enemies had better realize that we see things in terms of an historical
vision," he would present the vision. The great biographers would
present the Reich Chancellery meeting in terms that "Hitler
launched into a familiar theme" and that it was "the same old concept from which he had never strayed, which had become the fixed
point of all his steps and maneuvers."[3] The great biographers would
denigrate Hitler's vision by choices of words such as "the same old
concept" that suggest he was mired in dogmatically held ideas that
had gone out of fashion by late 1937. But Hitler was possessed by the
single dogmatically held idea that he had a single holy mission. To
denigrate him for inflexible lack of fashionably fresh ideas is to miss
the point that messiahs are inspired not by *fresh* ideas but by *one* idea.

Hitler would first swear his miniscule, elite audience to secrecy.
He would then declare that in the event of his death, his exposition
should be regarded as his final will and testament. Hitler would
expostulate that his mission was to secure the existence of the racial
community of Aryan, Nordic Germans into the unforeseeable
future. With uncompromising logic, he would argue that the existence of the Germans as a great people could be guaranteed only by
enough space in Europe. Every word counted in this generalization

because every bit of space was already occupied and could be mastered only by force. And force—Clausewitzian armed violence—was always attended with risk. No man at the conference, including Hermann Goering, had had an inkling of what was coming. As if arriving from some distant mountaintop inhabited by himself alone, Hitler had entered the room to announce German destiny. The great biographer Joachim Fest would mirror the conventional wisdom's view of destiny as "sweeping plans, which required steady nerves, a readiness to take risks, and a kind of brigand's courage."[4]

But to refer to Hitler's exposition as sweeping plans is to make the understatement of the millennium. Hitler had embarked Germany on a Nordic saga that would be inhabited by heroes facing risky odds against tough peoples who already occupied the rolling plains and vast forests of the North European Plain. The army commander, Werner von Fritsch, must have sensed the onset of such a saga when he remarked fatalistically not long afterward that "this man is Germany's fate and this fate will go its way to the end."[5] Fritsch gets high marks for prescience in making this comment twice in 1938. Hitler gets high marks in favor of being interpreted as a world-historical personality: inspired by the circumstances of late 1937, acting entirely alone, driven by some passion for absolute historical finality, he would present the onset of the armed German saga. The type of man with whom the world was dealing and the attendant anxiety of the times stand out in the following words, written earlier in 1920 by Albert Speer:

> Perhaps there are really uncomprehended "super" heroes all around us who because of their towering aims and abilities may rightly smile at even the greatest of horrors seeing them as merely incidental. Perhaps, before handicraft and the small town can flourish again, there must first come something like a hail of brimstone. Perhaps nations which have passed through infernos will then be ready for their next age of flowering.[6]

Speer, the distinguished German architect, wrote these words seventeen years before Hitler's somber November revelations, and they capture the man and the times as well as any. When Hitler walked through the door of the conference room, he would do so with "towering aims and abilities." He would announce the "greatest of horrors" in the indispensable application of "force" in the east, but he would see them as only incidental to change in the course of history. On the other hand, both Goering and Werner von Blomberg would suggest to an unbelieving Erich Raeder that Hitler had presented theater with the purpose to accelerate Fritsch's rearmament of the army. But if Hitler had presented theater, then theater had become reality. The words of November 1937 would become the triumphant reality of 1938, continuing successes, and bitter end. But Hitler had presented the saga since the second volume of *Mein Kampf,* and it remains difficult to this day to comprehend how men so disparate as Goering, Blomberg, and Konstantin, baron von Neurath could have been either so stunned by or so uncomprehending of the November speech.

The biographer Fest came close to reality with the incidental observation that the German conservatives, and especially the military leaders, "found to their astonishment that Hitler meant what he had said. He was, as it were, actually being Hitler."[7] And to confound the conventional wisdom of the great biographers, this man, who would actually be Hitler at the conference, cannot simply be seen as an oddly constructed, banal-yet-terrible dictator. His words reflect the presence of a kind of super-Lohengrin determined not just to save the medieval western Europeans from the Hungarians for a generation but to save the Germans permanently.

Germany would soon have the strongest armed forces in Europe, and if through some means they could neutralize the British, defeat the French, and seize the Russian heartland, they would decisively influence world history. This generalization follows axiomatically from the fact that the British, French, and Russian Europeans had seized so much of the world's land surface and heavily influenced what remained. It cannot be said convincingly that Hitler intended world domination in 1937 or at any other time. But it can be said that Germany would have vastly increased its world influence through the effects of military "victory" in Europe. The conventional wisdom's indispensable and never-failing comment that Hitler desired world domination must be taken in the spirit of the self-confident moral censure offered. The same wisdom has presented the words of November as Hitler's plan for conquest, but the "plan" did not contain a hint of world dominion. The words of November as scribbled so fiercely by Colonel Hossbach for posterity say it all— Austria, Czechoslovakia, Poland, the rendering harmless of the British threat, the defeat of France, the conquest and occupation of western Russia. Hitler's vision was not trivial, and it allows us to characterize him as a world-historical personality but not as possessed by some chimerical drive to enslave the world.

At this point we see a subtle circumstance that surrounded Hitler, and it was his probability-defying luck—his providentially successful affair with chance. Instead of being doomed by an ill-fated chance event in either his personal life or the historical actions associated with him from 1914 through 1940, he flourished. What seems to be an obscure point of passing interest may define the man himself. It would be difficult to define luck as a fundamental characteristic of most power-accruing, evil dictators who have abounded historically. But the impossibly rare world-historical personality must tempt fortune and triumph over chance event to be such a phenomenon. Neither shell fragment nor sniper's bullet nor war gas either killed or maimed Hitler during his almost four and one-half years at the front in the west. No bullet got him in a Munich street in November 1923.

In politics, Hitler would be similarly favored by chance circumstance. He would repeatedly face unforeseen happenings that sometimes portended disaster and other times represented providential opportunity. Examples are legion. He would survive the chance disaster of November 1923 and turn it into the providential opportunity of the trial and fortress detention of 1924. And when the legal takeover of Germany and the leadership principle balanced on a razor's edge a decade later with the effective defection of Gregor Strasser, this redoubtable leader would suddenly crumble and leave Germany for a vacation in Italy. It must be less of a surprise, therefore, when Hitler faced the indecisive conservatism and lack of comprehension of his 1937 vision on the part of the war minister and the army commander, and chance materialized to banish them.

What is the probability that the war minister would marry a registered prostitute with an arrest record, Hitler and Goering would be witnesses to the wedding, and the ceremony would take place only two months after Hitler's November testament? And what is the probability that at virtually the same time, a police file would be produced that showed that an army officer named Fritsch had once been charged with homosexuality? The Blomberg affair had stemmed from his own bad judgment in choice of wife. The Fritsch affair had resulted from inept police work on Reinhard Heydrich's part in failing to realize that the Fritsch of the police dossier was not the army commander. In both cases, Hitler stood desperately embarrassed. He had to distance himself from Blomberg and conceal a prestige-damaging situation. Although Fritsch would prove to be innocent, such are the evil vagaries of false accusation that Hitler would be forced to part with him and similarly hide the actual circumstances. Blomberg and Fritsch were officially said to have retired on health grounds.[8] Hitler would explain to his cabinet in what would prove to be its last meeting the need to stick to the official version of events. Quite by chance, therefore, Hitler would reshuffle men and positions in such a way that the words of November 1937 would translate into the deeds of 1938 in Austria and Czechoslovakia.

*   *   *

On the eve of Hitler's foreign policy breakout of March 1938 in Austria, therefore, he would no longer have the potential backing of Blomberg and Fritisch, who exemplified the old army, and Neurath, who exemplified the old diplomatic corps. We know this. We also know that Hitler had arrived at this propitious juncture through the support of the army for conventionally styled rearmament, the foreign office for conventionally styled hegemony on the continent, and the leading German industrial firms for conventionally styled economic supremacy. But there was nothing conventionally restrained about Hitler's sense of historical mission and the hats that he wore—unknown soldier, armed Bohemian, Rienzi, messiah, Lohengrin, Fuehrer, chosen one—all, perhaps, fusing into the impossibly rare world-historical personality. The great biographers, particularly Professor Ian Kershaw, give us sometimes brilliant detail of the gathering storm but in accounts that amount to a history of the period rather than a cracking of the Hitler code. Particularly at the time of what would prove to be the beginning of the German saga, we must understand Hitler or remain burdened with the underestimated man of the present historical interpretation for the years 1938 and 1939.

Opportunity struck for Hitler in February 1938 as the Austrian government, headed by the Christian Socialist chancellor Kurt von Schuschnigg, struggled with accumulated unresolved frictions from the breakup of the Austro-Hungarian Empire in 1919. The Allies had set up an awkward, ineffectual Austria that consisted almost entirely of Germans but did not include the eastern rimland of Czechoslovakia that was inhabited initially by a solid bloc of 4.1 million Germans. The state was awkward because it was a tiny country dominated by the outsized capital city of a former empire. The capital was also the industrial center of the state and held a dominating percentage of "workers" organized in a Socialist Party strong enough to give it the *soubriquet* of "Red Vienna." But the Christian Socialist Party challenged the Marxist Socialists in Vienna and, along with Agrarians and Nationalists, would control the provinces and the other larger cities under an overall republican parliamentary system of government. The Christian Socialists, Marxist Socialists, Agrarians, and Nationalists all looked with favor upon the union of German Austria with Germany. The Allies, and particularly the

French government, however, had forced the infant republic under the 1919 Treaty of Saint-Germain to renounce union with Germany and had forbidden the appellation of German Austria as the name of the state. After the treaty signing, the Republic of Austria stood politically isolated and economically crippled, and it was threatened by Socialist uprising internally and Hungarian and Yugoslav encroachment externally.

Particularly in the southern provinces of Carinthia and Styria on the Yugoslav and Hungarian borders, *Heimwehren* (home defense units) sprang up and could be characterized as anti-Socialist, anti-Communist, and nationalist. They would engage in irregular warfare with armed bands of Hungarians and Yugoslavs until plebiscites and Allied pressure settled the border frictions by 1922 largely in favor of Austria. The *Heimwehr* formations would continue to flourish locally throughout Austria and be characterized everywhere as anti-Socialist. In 1927 the Socialists would orchestrate massive rioting in Vienna followed by a general strike throughout the republic, but the *Heimwehr* would defeat them everywhere and become a national political force. As such, the loosely organized movement became antiparliamentarian and aimed at the establishment of an authoritarian state on the Italian fascist model. By 1931, however, the Austrian National Socialists had gained ground enough to absorb various *Heimwehr* units and grow into a movement dedicated to synchronization with Hitler's Nazis. The Austrian situation would become a complex one that involved a struggle among the Christian Socialists of Chancellor Engelbert Dollfuss, dedicated to an authoritarian state modeled on Mussolini's Italy, the Marxists, and the Austrian Nazis. Internationally, the struggle involved the French government enforcing the Versailles and Saint-Germain treaties, the Mussolini government safeguarding Italian-held South Tyrol, and Hitler, who would redeem the Austrian Germans. The Austrian "people" tend to become lost in all of this. They can be generalized, however, based on the overwhelming vote of their representatives in 1919 to become part of Germany, as still dedicated to redemption.

By the turn of 1934, Dollfuss and the Christian Socialists, with the indispensable support of the fascist-styled *Heimwehr*, and under pressure from Mussolini to create a fascist Austria, would take measures against the Socialists. The latter, with ill-advised militancy, would revolt in Vienna in February, but the Austrian army, state police, and *Heimwehr* would defeat them in bloody street combat. Dollfuss would dismantle the Socialist Party, and on May 1 he promulgated a new constitution that would abolish parliamentary government in favor of authoritarian rule. Dollfuss would become dictator of Austria. He would rule through an authoritarian constitution with a single political party, designated the Fatherland Front, and dissolve not only the Socialist but also all other political parties. Dollfuss would be forced into internal policies intended to form a fascist-styled state and external policies that would demand an independent Austria. In such a situation, Dollfuss would run into resistance by the powerful young Austrian Nazi movement and be slain in an outlandish, abortive coup in late July 1934. The Fatherland Front would prevail and Dollfuss's close collaborator, Kurt von Schuschnigg, would become the new dictator of Austria and struggle along with the same policies through the fateful February of 1938. By that time Hitler, through considerable diplomatic skill and luck, had detached Mussolini from his policy of support for Austrian independence. Through the chance occurrence of the Blomberg and Fritsch affairs, Hitler had gained freedom of maneuver internally to begin the German saga, still disguised in historical interpretation as Hitler's foreign policy. And in a chance event within the Blomberg and Fritsch affairs, Franz von Papen would be dismissed from his four-year posting as ambassador on special mission to Austria. Immediately after learning of his dismissal, although sensing that he had served his purpose, Papen nevertheless decided to drop in on Hitler in Berchtesgaden "to obtain some picture of what was going on."[9]

There, Papen found Hitler exhausted and "distrait"—inattentive because of anxiety—and offered the observation that "his eyes seemed unable to focus on anything."[10] Part of Hitler's anxiety was based on the disastrous situation in Austria. The Austrian Nazis and the milder, traditional Pan-Germans stood locked in incident after incident in 1937 with the tough *Heimwehr* formations of Schuschnigg's fascist Fatherland Front. On May 1, in Pinkafeld—a small town in the Burgenland—a young Austrian army lieutenant would order his men to take down a legally displayed German flag on a private residence. This small local affair would escalate almost instantly into an international incident and illustrate much about Hitler. On May 2, he would order Papen to report to him personally in Berlin, but on May 3 apparently forgot that he had summoned his special ambassador. Only on May 4, after being reminded, would Hitler receive Papen and the following scene unfold: "I found him red in the face pacing up and down the main reception room in Bismarck's old palace. 'This is outrageous,' he shouted. 'These people cannot go on treating Germany in this cavalier fashion. This business of dragging our flag through the mud is too much.' With these words he would begin a tirade of abuse against Austria."[11] Papen would continue with the quite astonishing observation—not opinion, apologia, or self-justification—that "in accordance with my usual practice, I let him work off this outburst of rage, and for about half an hour made no attempt to say a word."[12] Papen would then proceed with mild self-adulation to show how he would bring Hitler to reason and defuse the situation. The point is to recognize the precious observation and innumerable similar ones and not to take the opportunity to defame Papen for self-praise. Hitler continuously made rational calculations in accordance with the diplomatic situation in Europe relative to Austria and made similar diplomatically shaded calculations relative to internal affairs in Austria. But as virtually all firsthand observers have verified, he was characterized utterly by monologues of dark outrage on the one hand and shining images of a crowning German unity on the other. Hitler was a messianic tirade waiting to happen and then constantly exploding during the accumulating crises of 1937 through the dénouement of August 1939. And if the messianic tirades were genuinely inspired, we cannot consider Hitler to have been either a European statesman or a political dictator.

As we have seen in the diplomacy of the period 1933 through 1936, Hitler held a tangible moral advantage in every major international crisis involving Germany. Similarly in February and March 1938 during the Austrian crisis he would have a moral advantage over Schuschnigg and the Fatherland Front as well as the former Allies. And later, in 1938, during the broader international crisis over Czechoslovakia, he would have an advantage over the essentially Czech government and those of the former Allies. Perhaps during the whole period the essence of the matter may have been that Hitler had a moral advantage over everyone, and perhaps the way to get at him was to show why and how this was so. We have to accept the premise that Hitler was not a moral man but he nevertheless held a moral advantage. Hitler, however, was not immoral but rather amoral, and to so great a degree that he rose above or fell below any conventional context of good and evil. In effect, we cannot apply any conventional standard of criticism to such a man, and we are not suggesting a simplistic concept for Hitler that he personified the formulation that the end justifies the means. He would reiterate that any end for Germany short of the finality of an unassailably defensible state was not worth the effort. An end is an end, but such logical finality stands aside from any conventionally understood end. This man, this bundle of outrage and logical finality, entered the Austrian crisis, and we may have to admit that his outrage was deserved.

When Papen, in February 1938, suggested a meeting between Hitler and Schuschnigg, the situation between the two states had deteriorated to such an extent that such a meeting was necessary to replace failed diplomacy, ineffective internal Austrian policies, and the shadows of the Versailles and Saint-Germain treaties. We know this. The great biographers, however, present the situation as one in which a wicked Hitler had caused diplomacy to fail and the Austrian Nazis influenced by him had been the major contributors to political instability. The same biographers almost entirely ignore the foundation of the crisis comprised of the French imposition of an independent Austrian republic on bitterly disappointed Austrian Germans. Ironies again abound because Hitler had been forced by the French and Italian shadows of the Saint-Germain treaty to conduct a remarkably restrained foreign policy vis-à-vis Austria. One irony: the man who in late 1937 alerted the army and the foreign office to near-future armed advance eastward had embraced and adhered to a policy of evolutionary change to bring Austria and Germany closer together. Hitler and Schuschnigg would meet in the notorious drama at Berchtesgaden on February 12, and Hitler would pressure him into concessions to be applied almost immediately. But the concessions were evolutionary ones that included specifically the coordination of foreign policy, the appointment of the Pan-German Dr. Arthur von Seyss-Inquart as interior minister, and a sweeping amnesty that would allow the Austrian Nazis to participate legally in Austrian politics. If there were a bottom line to the Austro-German political imbroglio of the entire Hitler period from 1933 through early 1938, it could be seen as the entrenchment of a dictatorship of the Christian Socialist Party and *Heimwehr* over an artificial state created earlier by the Allies. Dollfuss as parliamentary federal Chancellor would suspend parliamentary government in March 1933, dissolve the Austrian Nazi Party in June, dissolve all political parties in early 1934, demolish the Austrian Socialist movement in February, and soon after, in April, push through the national assembly a new constitution that would set up a Christian Socialist, Fatherland Front dictatorship. After Dollfuss's assassination, Schuschnigg would become his successor as dictator for the next three and one-half years and not permit any national election.

Schuschnigg would make the Berchtesgaden changes shortly after the meeting, and Hitler, in a restrained Reichstag speech on February 20, would praise them. Schuschnigg would reply four days later with an ill-advised speech, in which he would demand support for Austrian independence rather than emphasize the more relaxed possibilities of evolutionary change. His speech would re-fuse the situation. Clashes would escalate between the Austrian nationalists of the Fatherland Front on one hand and the Austrian Nazis and Pan-Germans on the other. Schuschnigg was unable to gain the support of the Socialists internally and could no longer count on the external support from Mussolini, who advised him to make peace with the Nazis. But the French government, more than any other including the Italians, had been responsible for the creation of an Austrian republic in 1919. France was committed to the continued existence of an isolated, ineffectual Austria, but the French government could not expect its citizens to fight a war in support of an unpopular dictatorship. Schuschnigg faced internal violence, lack of external support, and suspicion that he did not have the support of a majority of Austrians for his strident policy of independence. In this situation he made the decision to panic—to act in the desperation of an ill-considered idea—and announce on March 9, 1938, the holding of a national plebiscite the following Sunday.

In announcing the plebiscite, Schuschnigg would annul the Berchtesgaden agreement with Hitler and stabilize the Austrian situation in favor of his Fatherland Front if the Austrian people voted favorably on the question. The conventional wisdom has taken Schuschnigg's action to have been a courageous one in the face of Hitler's earlier bullying tactics, and a decisive one that would have made a union of Austria and Germany improbable. But Schuschnigg's courage, if we grant him such, would have resulted in the permanent division of the German peoples and the entrenchment of a single-party dictatorship in Austria. Schuschnigg would frame the question, "Are you in favor of a free and German, independent and social, a Christian and united Austria?" It was a heavily propagandized jumble of words that invited a yes answer. And the result of a yes-vote for the plebiscite would have been the almost diabolical outcome that an artificial state created by an Allied force of arms would have been transformed by a self-serving Austrian political dictatorship into a stable artificial state.

And Schuschnigg scores high marks for manipulation of the

plebiscite. Only three days were available for its organization within Austria, and the same, apparently impossibly short, time period for Hitler to prevent it by outside pressure. Because the Austrian dictatorship had not allowed elections for the preceding four years, the electoral register had not been kept up to date. There would not be enough time to organize the ballot, particularly in the remote rural areas where the Nazis were strongly represented, and it would be impossible to register in three days the younger voters who had come of age since 1934.[13]

In summary, a somewhat common political dictator in Austria would attempt to keep in power a Fatherland Front through a desperate, shady plebiscite in the face of a neighboring dictator. The descriptor *shady* is a strong one for serious historical interpretation of Schuschnigg's action, but it is borne out by the following outlandish detail: a voter who wished to vote yes on the plebiscite question would be provided a ballot at polling stations. A voter who wished to vote no would have to present his own ballot of specified form and validated only with a stamp purchased from the government. It is difficult to separate good from evil in all of this. The great biographers must present Hitler as an uneducated, banal man immersed in wicked purpose and Schuschnigg as a calmer, nicer intellectual struggling to shield Austria from Hitler. But the Austrian Empire had vanished, and to conjure up its German fragment as a bona fide independent state was to proceed from false premise. With the empire gone, its German fragment had become what it had always been as the *Ostmark*—the eastern march or frontier area of the Germans in a half-enveloping sea of Slavs and Magyars. For various reasons, some wicked and some not-so-wicked, Hitler had determined to save the Germans of the *Ostmark* from their political defenselessness and economic isolation. And for various reasons, some wicked and others not-so-wicked, Schuschnigg had determined to enforce the division of the Germans in the southeast.

It is one thing to seize an opportunity and another to be forced to take action. Schuschnigg would spend Thursday resolutely adhering to his decision to abrogate the Berchtesgaden agreement.

Hitler spent the same day alerting the German army to a probable advance into Austria on Saturday morning. Schuschnigg would go to bed Thursday evening fully satisfied that the Nazi threat to the plebiscite had been scotched.[14] At two o'clock Friday morning, however, the German army general staff issued a completely improvised written invasion plan designated Operation Otto. The plan assigned the Sixteenth Army Corps as the spearhead of the entire operation on an axis from Passau (east of Munich on the Danube River) through Linz (Hitler's "home town") and Saint Poelten to Vienna, a distance of 170 miles. The corps held the only panzer divisions of the German army in existence at that moment, and only the Second Panzer Division, stationed around Wuerzburg 250 miles from Passau, could get to the Austrian border in time to lead the advance on Vienna. By midnight on Thursday, the corps commander had already issued orders by spoken word for the Second Panzer Division and its single motorized reinforcing unit, the Berlin-stationed *Leibstandarte SS Adolf Hitler* (Hitler Bodyguard Regiment) "to move off at once with destination Passau."[15] The two military units would be located 250 miles and 428 miles, respectively, from the border very early on Friday morning and ordered to move across it at eight o'clock in the morning on Saturday.

In a unique analysis of the possibilities of armed advance into Austria, it could be noted that ordinary nonmotorized divisions would have taken approximately seven days to march to Vienna at an optimistic rate of twenty-four miles a day. In the actual event, *Generalleutnant* Heinz Guderian's Second Panzer Division moved across the border one hour later, at nine o'clock, but its powerful advanced detachment of two panzer reconnaissance battalions and one motorcycle rifle battalion accompanied by Guderian reached Linz at noon. As he was leaving the town in the direction of Saint Poelten and Vienna, Guderian met *Reichsfuehrer SS* Heinrich Himmler and the Austrian federal chancellor Seyss-Inquart, who requested him to secure the city for the arrival of Hitler later in the afternoon. Guderian would accomplish the task with the main body of the panzer division while ordering the advanced detachment to move out toward Vienna but halt at Saint Poelten. Hitler would arrive at dark, and Guderian, as eye witness to the scene, would comment: "Neither before nor since have I ever seen such tremendous enthusiasm as was shown during those few hours." At nine o'clock at night, Guderian would move off to join his previously halted advanced guard at Saint Poelten and would reach the town around midnight. He would then personally lead the motorized formation, initially through a blinding spring snowstorm, into downtown Vienna by approximately one o'clock Sunday morning. His formations had motored all the way from Berlin and Wuerzburg through the early morning darkness of Friday, and then the evening hours of the same day and into Saturday. In doing so, they would execute a completely improvised military move indispensable for the success of the political *fait accompli.*

The man who had ordered this move had already exclaimed to Schuschnigg at Berchtesgaden: "I am telling you once more that things cannot go on this way. I have a historic mission; and this mission I will fulfill because Providence has destined me to do so. I thoroughly believe in this mission; it is my life."[16] Hitler was deadly, apolitically earnest in his outrage over any man who would divide people identifiable as Germans. In one of the most violent incidents during his rise to power, Hitler, in late 1921, would personally disrupt a meeting of the Bavarian separatist Otto Ballerstedt. Hitler probably personally beat Ballerstedt during the ensuing disruption, and enough evidence of a breach of peace accumulated to send Hitler to jail for one of two times in his life.[17] Hitler took Ballerstedt and his advocacy of the division of the German peoples seriously enough to have him killed during the Roehm affair thirteen years later.[18] Faced thus with Schuschnigg and the immediately impending threat of a permanently independent Austria, Hitler— the man who probably hit Ballerstedt with a chair and stick—was forced by Romantic barbaric inclination and immediate political danger to pummel Schuschnigg with more substantial instruments of violence. It remains difficult to believe that the Austrian federal chancellor would take action that would force Hitler's hand. Only days before, on March 7, Schuschnigg would dispatch an appeal to Mussolini, who would warn him colorfully that with a plebiscite he was preparing a bomb that would go off in his hand.[19] And on the day of the advance, the British Foreign Office would instruct its ambassador to Germany, Sir Nevile Henderson, to protest to Goering about the invasion. Henderson would deliver the protest but agree with Goering "that Doctor Schuschnigg had acted with precipitate folly."[20] Friday in the *Reichskanzlei* would be the scene of precipitate action taken by Hitler and Goering in the face of the danger and opportunity offered by Schuschnigg's precipitate folly.

Goering would get much credit for the exploitation of the opportunities of Friday into the Sunday union of the Germans. He would bombard Schuschnigg and his cabinet with demands for the plebiscite's postponement and Schuschnigg's resignation. He would do this by messenger from Berlin and the sympathetic Austrian interior minister, both directed by telephone from Berlin. At two o'clock in the afternoon, in an attempt at compromise, Schuschnigg agreed to postpone the plebiscite but not to resign. At three o'clock, Goering would demand in the form of an ultimatum that in addition to the postponement of the plebiscite, Schuschnigg and his cabinet would have to resign, Seyss-Inquart would become chancellor, and a telegram would be sent to Berlin requesting German help. At around four o'clock, Schuschnigg tendered his resignation in accordance with Goering's ultimatum, but sixty-six-year-old President Wilhelm Miklas would refuse to appoint Seyss-Inquart as chancellor. Schuschnigg would have to insist, however, and at 7:50 p.m. announced by radio to the Austrian people that his government had put itself out of business. Only minutes later, Goering would have this information and pass it on to Hitler, urging him to go ahead with the invasion. Under enormous stress from the international ramifications of an invasion, Hitler would sign the order at quarter to nine for the march of the German Eighth Army into Austria the following morning. The most important and immediate ramification remained the lingering nightmare possibility of an armed confrontation with the Italian Army moving in from the contiguous border between the two states. At 10:25 p.m., however, Hitler's special emissary in Rome, Prince Philip von Hessen, phoned to tell him that "Il duce took the news [of the planned invasion] very well indeed. He sends his very best regards to you."[21]

The great biographers paint a picture of Hitler as wracked by bouts of hysteria and indecision during the period of the announcement of the plebiscite through the pronouncement of the union. They emphasize Goering's astonishing self-confidence and energy in crafting the ultimatum, pressing for the invasion, and recognizing the fleeting opportunity for an immediate final solution in the union of the two states. In an imaginative transformation, we can almost see Goering becoming Hitler on Friday and then again on Sunday. Perhaps this transformation is not so imaginative as it may seem because the fundamental thesis of Kershaw is that Hitler derived his power from innumerable followers who worked toward the Fuehrer on their own initiative. It would be a mistake, however, to assume that Hitler drifted hysterically through the Austrian crisis to be saved by Goering's initiative. Papen, as eye witness to the Friday events, would contribute unwittingly to a picture of an ineffectual Fuehrer with the words that he "was ushered in to Hitler, who was in a state bordering on hysteria."[22] But Papen would add, "I let him have his say [hysterical outburst], as usual." and then say that it would still be possible to postpone the plebiscite if Hitler were to point out that it would not only be unconstitutional but also quite impossible to organize a free and fair vote in only three days.[23]

But Hitler would issue in the first hours of Friday morning the initial directive for the invasion. It was a formidable document that cannot be attributed either to a politician or a statesman. It opens: "If other measures do not succeed, I intend to march into Austria with armed forces in order to restore constitutional conditions there and to prevent further outrages against the nationalistic German population."[24]

Although the sentence is not short, it is simple declarative. There may be a danger of arguing too much from too little in it, but we can nevertheless use the sentence to interpret both Hitler and the crisis. Above everything else, Hitler ordered the army early Friday morning to be prepared to cross the Austrian border early Saturday morning. There would be no bluff associated with the activity of the army on the border, although it would advance only if "other measures" had not succeeded. But other measures had not succeeded on Thursday, and with time fleeting on Friday, they had been reduced to the final measure of an ultimatum. Goering presented this ultimatum as a series of nonnegotiable demands by messenger and telephone from about ten o'clock in the morning through shortly after eight o'clock at night. And when the new provisional Austrian government under Seyss-Inquart requested German assistance, he seems to take the palm for having overcome Hitler's fears and hesitations.

But Goering's boldness was based on Hitler's earlier express determination to march into Austria with armed forces to prevent further outrages against the nationalists. And as concerns Papen's observation that Hitler was in a state bordering on hysteria, and if we take the word to mean an outbreak of wild emotionalism, then we must agree that he probably was. The wrinkle of comprehension for getting at Hitler is that he was wild emotionalism incarnate; it was his characteristic style. Papen would even say in the *Reichskanzlei* that "as usual" he let Hitler have his hysterical outburst and then brought him around to calmer reflection. In all of this, particularly with Hitler's never-failing expressions of his holy mission, we see a fiery messiah. His wildly emotional outbursts during the Austrian crisis reflect outrage about the possible division of the Germans rather than fits of pique about Schuschnigg's tough, clever action to abrogate Berchtesgaden. Hitler was especially outraged by the fact that, in an Austria that had had no national election for four years, a plebiscite would be conducted by a government that could call on the support of only a "numerically small minority."[25] Hitler would estimate that Schuschnigg had the support of only 10 to 15 percent of Austrians and calculated the chances of success for an armed but bloodless occupation of Austria as extremely high.[26]

When Hitler followed the Second Panzer Division into Austria along the road from Passau to Vienna, therefore, he did so with a popular cause. As Hitler's motor column moved along the road toward the first night's objective of Linz, it was slowed in villages by demonstrations of spontaneous, delirious enthusiasm, some people touching his big Mercedes® as if it were a sacred relic. Demonstrations would escalate in Linz and Vienna to proportions inexplicable in terms of politics and deliberate propaganda. In the early darkness of Saturday evening, Hitler would address a throng in Linz in a brief speech that would include the following mystically cast passage:

> If Providence once called me forth from this town to be the leader of the Reich, it must in doing so, have charged me with a mission, and that mission could only be to restore my [beloved] homeland to the German Reich. I have believed in this mission. I have lived and fought for it, and I believe I have now fulfilled it. You are all witnesses and sureties for that. I know not on what day you will be summoned; I hope it will not be far distant. Then you must make good your pledge with your own confession of faith.[27]

Hitler would claim that when he "went forth" from Linz years before, he bore within himself the same profession of faith in a Greater Germany that filled his heart in front of the spontaneously emerged, delirious multitude of that bitterly cold Saturday evening. We cannot accept his claim as literal truth. We can accept it as invaluable retrospect, a contemplation of past events. Hitler would tell us today, and the citizens of Lower Austria earlier, that Providence had charged him with a mission to link a German Austria with a German Reich. He did not claim that he received a directive, written or otherwise, from Providence, God, or fate in 1908 when he departed Linz for Vienna. He did claim retrospectively that it was fated he would save the Austrian Germans. He had already saved the Germans themselves from the Marxists, and on Saturday evening in

Linz he had begun the ingathering of the contiguous Germans of Austria, Czechoslovakia, Poland, and Danzig indispensable for the eastern saga. We seem to see Hitler engaged in an act of naked political aggression, a conspiracy, to seize Austria by force of arms. But as Hitler would exclaim in a Sunday interview with a British newspaper correspondent: "I assure you in all sincerity that four days ago I had no idea at all that I would be [in Vienna] today or that Austria would have been embodied, as she is of tonight, with the rest of Germany."[28] This does not mean that Hitler did not covet a closer conventional political tie with Austria but that he saw the whole business as a mystical fusion of the Germans.

*   *   *

Hitler would turn almost immediately toward action designed to redeem the remaining several million Austrian Germans who, at war's end, had been forcibly prevented by the Allies to be included either in Austria or Germany. Instead, they had been pressed into a new state called Czechoslovakia where they had become an unhappy, oppressed minority. As messiah, Hitler stood outraged by the enforced division of the Germans. As a more conventional international aggressor, Hitler had an unsurpassed appreciation of the strategic geographic dangers from a Czechoslovakian state allied with France and Soviet Russia. And as the Czech crisis unfolded in late spring of 1938, even Goering, described by Hitler as "brutal and ice-cold in crises...ruthless and hard as iron" during the Austrian affair, would wither in the face of Hitler's outrage and brinksmanship over the situation in Czechoslovakia.[29]

The situation at the turn of 1938 was an enormity described succinctly, accurately, but grudgingly, by Fest as one of the "inherent contradictions of the Versailles system.... Czechoslovakia was one grand negation of the principle on which it was supposedly based. Its creation had been far less connected with the right of self-determination than with France's strategic interests. For Czechoslovakia was a small multinational state in which one minority was pitted against the majority of all the other minorities.... Chamberlain had once denigrated it as not a state but 'scraps and patches.'"[30] A solid bloc of Austrian Germans in the Sudeten upland region comprised the most numerous minority outside of the Czechs themselves. The Germans were so numerous that they outnumbered the Slovaks; if numbers had been a basis for the name assigned the state it would have been Czechogermania. Hitler would address himself to this situation with consistency and intensity. The consistency in his spoken word was so great that the English scholar who gathered and edited his speeches and interviews would repeatedly edit out Hitler's never-failing words describing the melancholy historical picture in Europe with the editorial comment that "the picture followed familiar lines, and it is unnecessary to reproduce it here."[31] Comprehension of Hitler, however, lies in the "familiar lines" which, in the case of Czechoslovakia, would comprise fury, intensity, and outrage over the melancholy picture of the Germans there. He would point out in a frightening and little-known statistic that 600,000 Germans had fled the Sudetenland after the war based on evil economic conditions associated with heavy-handed food allocations favoring Czechs over the minorities.

As the Austrian crisis ended and the first Czech crisis began, Hitler would reveal himself as a towering mystic. He could argue in his final speech before the April vote for or against the incorporation of the Austrian republic into Germany that "I want to speak as a man who is himself completely guiltless of all that which Germany has suffered in the past."[32] Such was simple fact. He would then proceed to the historical situation in which he had done his duty as a soldier; he had never delivered speeches; he had only obeyed orders.[33] Such also was simple fact. But he would follow with the half truth and soaring fiction of myth:

> And then after the war when I found my native land again divided, defenseless, deserted by all then I, as the nameless soldier formed

the decision: after I had obeyed all these years—I would speak. I would tell [what] alone could lead to a resurrection in Germany ...for that there is a condition: the people must come together into one closely united body....I believe that it was God's will to send a boy from here into the Reich, to let him grow up, to raise him to be the leader of the nation so as...to lead back his homeland to the Reich. There is a higher ordering and we are all nothing else but its agents. When on 9 March Herr Schuschnigg broke his agreement then in that second I felt that now the call of Providence had come to me.[34]

These words help us to get at Hitler and indicate that neither political science nor an emotional search for the evil resident in him can help us much. Surely these words were intended to foster the myth of a heroically driven leader. But that was the point of Hitler; he was a heroically driven leader.

It is so unlikely that he made up such a quasi-mystical scene that we are left with the sculpture of a man who made a resolution and felt the call of Providence. We see Hitler functioning on a plane higher than that of political scientific "aggressive warfare" and different from that of "evil." And as concerns the lingering possibility that he nevertheless conveniently made up ingredients of myth in 1938, Albert Forster would read a letter in April that refutes such a possibility. Much earlier, during fortress detention in Landsberg in October 1924, Hitler would agonize in writing that he had "but one longing—that the day might come when my former homeland might be included within the garland of the German states of a common [Greater] Germany."[35] The longing would end with Hitler's overwhelming success in the great poll of April 10, 1938, on the question of the unification of the Austrian republic with the Reich. In the poll, 99.09 percent of combined German and Austrian German voters would opt for unification. The result was even more astonishing than may seem at first glance because, somehow, former Social Democrats, Christian Socialists, Agrarians, Bavarian People's adherents, and so on. had become Germans on the issue of a single greater Reich.

*   *   *

After the success of April 10, Hitler had become one of the most significant statesmen in the history of the Germans and without a single further advance would have achieved historical greatness. But within weeks of his success, he would lead Greater Germany through the so-called first Czech crisis. It would develop in April and peak in the Czech mobilization of May 20 and the parallel occupation of the German districts of the Sudetenland by Czech armed forces. If any point were difficult to interpret at this juncture, it would be the almost incredibly short time period for the development of the Czech weekend crisis of May 20–22. It was as if the "previous" Austrian crisis did not end but simply become part of a single Austro-Czechoslovakian crisis of the year 1938. Hitler had already postulated in speech and interview, beginning with his eight-point European pacification suggestions of January 1937, that changes would have to take place in the conditions "among those nationalities who are forced to live as a minority within other nations."[36] And beginning in the late Springtime of 1938, the time had come to save the Sudeten Germans.

The issue, in both the first and second Czech crises of 1938, of whether or not the Czechs had mistreated a solid bloc of more than 3.5 million Germans, could be replaced by the issue of how these people got themselves into a position to be mistreated. Hitler was notably outraged by both issues—Allied inclusion of Germans in a Czech state and their mistreatment in it. In his own words, he would note that "it was a short-sighted arrangement which the statesmen of Versailles devised for themselves when they called into being that monstrous formation—Czechoslovakia. Its commission—to do violence to the masses of other nationalities, to ill-treat these millions."[37] With bitter sarcasm, Hitler would develop a picture that Czechoslovakia "is a democracy, that is to say it was founded on democratic principles, since the overwhelming majority of the inhabitants...without being asked their opinion, were compelled one day...to accept and to adapt themselves to the construction which was manufactured at Versailles. As a genuine democracy this [Czechoslovakian] State forthwith began to oppress, to ill-treat, and to deprive of its vital rights the majority of its inhabitants." Hitler would continue with the same sarcasm but on a higher plane that "the Almighty did not create [the Sudeten Germans] in order that by means of a state construction designed at Versailles they should be handed over to a hated alien power. And He did not create the seven million Czechs...to watch over and take under their care— much less that they should outrage and torture these three and a half million [Germans]."[38]

As the first Czech crisis peaked in late May, we detect the presence of a man who could say with dizzying mysticism that "however weak the individual may be in the last resort in his whole being and action when compared with the omnipotence and will of Providence, yet at the moment when he acts as this Providence would have him act he becomes immeasurably strong. Then there streams down upon him that force which has marked all greatness in the world's history."[39] Hitler would be relentless in both his mythologizing and mysticism: "My motive as an unknown soldier in taking up the struggle for the regeneration of Germany had as its deepest ground my belief in the German people—not belief in [Germany's] public institutions, her social order and social classes, her parties, her state and political power, but belief in the eternal values inherent in our people."[40] But more privately he could state with little regard for Providence that Germany's future depended on acquiring sufficient living space in Europe and postulate that Germany's first objective must be to secure its eastern and southern flanks by securing Czechoslovakia and Austria.

We seem to have two Hitlers functioning as the first Czech crisis broke in May, each dedicated to radical change. And if such were the case, the interpretive historical question for the twentieth century would be: Which of the Hitlers dominated as Europe edged toward war in 1938? By mid-May, Hitler had brought pressure to bear on the

Czech government, most specifically on its president, the tough, unbending Edvard Beneš. Czech Prime Minister Milan Hodža had been forced to announce a forthcoming nationality statute and to allow communal elections in the Sudetenland. Hitler would apply pressure through the Sudeten German Party, whose leader, Konrad Henlein, would present the demands of the German community in the form of an eight-point program for change announced on April 24 at Carlsbad, a predominately German city of Bohemia located about twenty miles south of the Reich border. The points included overdue, just demands for improvement in the status of Germans, but also less reasonable ones for the synchronization of Czech and German foreign policies and for autonomy for the German bloc. Beneš would inflexibly reject the entire program, Hitler would inflexibly insist on it, and Henlein would inflexibly orchestrate resistance to inflexible Czech political authorities. Within such a context, tensions remained high and peaked on May 19, when the British and French ambassadors in Berlin heard "rumors" of German troop concentrations on the Czech frontier and passed on such rumor to London and Paris.

On May 20, Beneš, allegedly fearful of imminent German invasion, partially mobilized the Czech army "to reinforce the garrisons in the Sudetenland."[41] On May 21, based on unverified rumor, the British government through Edward Lord Halifax as foreign secretary warned the German government that Britain would probably fight if the French intervened in the Czech situation. On May 22, however, Sir Nevile Henderson as British ambassador would verify that the rumors of German troop concentrations that he had passed on to London—the basis for the British threat of war—were unfounded. Neither the British military attachés surveying Silesia and Saxony nor the French attachés to the areas around Dresden and Leipzig were able to detect any signs of significant German military activity. Captain Paul Stehlin, the French assistant air attaché, would remark that "our Czech friends...had deceived themselves to the extent of describing a military situation which existed only in their imagination."[42]

It was unlikely that the excellent Czech military intelligence service would mistake relaxed German military activity for anything else, and the question begs, therefore, why did the Czechs actually mobilize? The conventional wisdom suggests that Beneš ordered mobilization because of prudent concern over what nevertheless proved to be exaggerated and distorted reports. The timing of the mobilization suggests otherwise. The first of a series of long-overdue "communal" elections had been scheduled for May 22, and Beneš was concerned over both the outcome and the potential for incidents in the Sudetenland. The massive reinforcement of the Czech army already concentrated in the Sudeten borderlands would serve to influence the election and maintain Czech control. At least one authority on the situation, although a notably biased one, would agree with this analysis. Hitler would comment that "in the present year in Czechoslovakia after a succession of innumerable postponements of any popular vote, there were to be held elections at least in the communes."[43] He would then claim that "even in Prague [people] were afraid of common action on the part of the German and other nationalities...and that resort must be had to special measures...to be able to influence the results of the voting."[44] Hitler would reason that for the Czechs to produce the required level of intimidation, they would need the massive demonstration of force associated with army mobilization. And as vintage Hitler, he would rage that "in order...to give plausibility to this [mobilization] in the eyes of the world the Czech Government, Mr. Beneš, invented the lie that Germany had mobilized her troops and was on the point of marching into Czechoslovakia."[45]

Hitler's comments comprise a plausible explanation for Beneš's act of mobilization, its timing, and the necessity to explain it in terms of alleged although bogus German concentration for an invasion. And Hitler would expand his argument to note that the Czech government "in its complete lack of scruple...did not hesitate to cast suspicion on a great State and to throw all of Europe into a state of alarm, and was even prepared to take the risk of driving Europe into a bloody war."[46] For whatever the reasons, however, and for whatever the potential consequences, Beneš's "infamous deception" would ignite Hitler into an enraged and unbending passion for the destruction of the Czech state.[47] The Western press had spread the story that Beneš's gallant action and British and French support of it had forced Hitler to call off his invasion. Ernst von Weizsaecker, the secretary of State in the revamped foreign office under Joachim von Ribbentrop, would present the deadly inanity of the hostile press situation in the fewest words: "Hitler had embarked on no military enterprise... and could not therefore withdraw from one."[48]

Beneš produced an error of terrifying proportion similar to that of Schuschnigg a scant two months earlier in the spring of 1938. In both cases, Hitler had had no intention of taking military action in the immediate future until each opponent took ill-advised precipitous action. And in both cases, as well as an earlier one of similar importance to him, he would treat his opponents as if they were anti-Christs, great antagonists who would fill the world with wickedness. In the earlier case in 1922, Hitler, as previously noted, would break up a mass meeting of his "most dangerous opponent" Otto Ballerstedt the Bavarian Separatist. He was the one who would divide the Germans into ineffectual tribal groups and would consign them all to historical oblivion. Hitler and his followers would incidentally shove Ballerstedt off his own stage, and Hitler, in a portent of bigger things yet to come, would be accused of "disturbing the peace." Sixteen years later, Hitler would face Schuschnigg and Beneš, both linked as men who would keep the Germans divided—although for different reasons and on bigger historical stages. In the case of Schuschnigg, Hitler would be forced to take immediate armed action to prevent the Austrians and Germans from remaining divided during his foreseeable lifetime. In the case of Beneš, Hitler would be outraged by his mobilization deception, and as a result hyperbolically radicalize the purpose and timing of German action against Czechoslovakia. And, of course, Hitler's contemporary antagonists and postwar biographers would see him as disturbing a peace greater than that of the Ballerstedt affair.

The great biographers have spun the Hitler of both the Austrian and Czechoslovakian crises toward being an aggressive dictator. And although the biographers have acknowledged his sense of mission, none has given it precedence over all other things as the explanation for the man and his actions. From 1919 through 1938, this rough and somewhat uneasy balance had existed between the evil of the dictator and the potential for good in the morally superior messiah. It could be shown, however, that in every Hitler crisis from minor domestic to major foreign, both Hitlers had to have been present. By 1922, for example, Hitler had come to dominate in the no-account National-sozialistische Deutsche Arbeiterpartei (NSDAP) of the day and was seen by his opponents as an outrageous demagogue. By the same time, however, he had attracted followers so disparate as Dietrich Eckart, Rudolf Hess, Hermann Goering, and Ernst Hanfstaengl, who would sense the presence of a personality capable of rising above politics and saving Germany. And, much later and internationally, Hitler would be seen by the sophisticated although somewhat biased French government as an international criminal—the man who would violate both the Versailles and Saint-Germain treaties that forbade the union of the Austrian republic with Germany. Simultaneously, however, 48,799, 269 German voters would approve of Hitler's action and would raise him onto a dais above both politics and wickedness.

After May 20, however, Hitler exhibited behavior and took actions that have remained largely inexplicable in terms of conventional international relations and conspiracy to commit aggressive war. His actions in the penultimate month of September suggest some inexplicable urge to self destruction and general catastrophe. Earlier, after a hastily called conference on May 22 to reconsider the Czech situation, Hitler would remain hidden, sequestered in the mountains for several days. Only after three days alone would he come down for a conference in Berlin with his military and foreign policy leaders on May 28, having made the unalterable decision to smash the Czech state by military means no later than October 1, 1938. In his decision, he would combine daring political–military calculation with pas-

sionate disregard for potential consequences. But strong men dominated by passion rarely calculate. Hitler, however, both calculated and
utterly disregarded the results of calculation. He would analyze that if
the German Army could give proof of immediate, decisive advances
into Czechoslovakia and defeat the Czech army within four days of
the beginning of the attack, as reflected in the seizure of Prague and
Pilsen, there would be no Europe-wide war. In the event that his calculation failed, he seemed to have accepted the resulting struggle as a
heroic, holy war for German freedom.

To comprehend Hitler, however, the most important factor may
not be what he concluded but rather where he made his decision.
What other political leader in twentieth century Europe would
ascend into mountain fastness to make his decisions? And Hitler
would make the great decision in solitude—no Goering, Walther
von Brauchitsch, Franz Halder, Ribbentrop, or German ambassador
to Czechoslovakia. Hitler would brood over maps sent from Berlin to
calculate the probabilities of a motorized breakthrough force finishing off Czechoslovakia so quickly that no British, French, Soviet,
or Polish government—alone or in whatever combination—would
make the decision to fight. At a higher level, he would commune
with Providence over the timing necessary to achieve Germany's
destiny. Such timing would not be so much the almost insanely dangerous and precise October 1, 1938, but the time he perceived as
soon enough to create his envisioned Reich in his lifetime. By whatever means and entirely alone, he would transport himself to the
level of an "unalterable" decision. Hitler would not get his war on
October 1, but he would achieve the armed occupation of the Sudetenland and the disarming of the Czech army formations in it.

After signing the fourth version of Plan Green, the directive for
an invasion of Czechoslovakia, Hitler would proceed with intensity,
outrage, and intransigence so great during the summer that it would
lead to behavior in September inexplicable to numerous contemporaries except in terms of insanity. In that month, British prime min-
ster Neville Chamberlain, in a private letter, would refer to Hitler as

a "lunatic" and give other evidence that at the least he had come to believe that the Fuehrer was "half mad."[49] "In the view of the British Ambassador Nevile Henderson, Hitler 'had become quite mad' and …had crossed the borderline of insanity!"[50] One great biographer would query: "Was Hitler actually on the edge of madness, or a sort of Dr. Jekyll and Mr. Hyde?"[51] As concerns Édouard Daladier late in the game at Munich, he was impressed by the hard, strange look in Hitler's eyes.[52] Sigmund Freud, now in London and world-renowned, would comment that "you cannot tell what a madman will do. You know he is an Austrian," and when he took over that country it seemed to go to his head.[53] Carl Jung, as noted, would characterize Hitler as being in the category of the truly mystic medicine man, and even his immediate entourage of chauffeurs, body guards, and personal adjutants would refer to him as "the manitou" —a mysterious power or spirit. Considered as such, Hitler could hardly have been considered as normal by a wide variety of people around him. As concerns the accusation of lunacy, however, we have blatant lack of comprehension of Hitler by the accusers.

Yet as the crisis peaked in September, Hitler would present the historical rectification required by Germany and the action necessary to set it in place with unmistakable clarity. Dictators are able to present things more clearly than statesmen in democratic parliamentary states, and a thousand-year messiah more clearly than any dictator. On September 12, in his closing Party Day speech at Nuremberg, Hitler would say:

> What the Germans demand is the right of self-determination…not mere phrases. But if the democracies should be of the conviction that…they must support…the oppression of the Germans then the decision will have serious consequences! I believe that I shall serve peace best if I leave no doubt on this point…I have not put forward the demand that Germany may oppress three and a half million Frenchmen…my demand is that the oppression of three and a half million Germans in Czechoslovakia shall cease and that its place shall be taken by the free right of self-determination.[54]

Tensions would rise in the Sudetenland over the next twenty-four hours, Czech state police would "shoot down" twenty-one German demonstrators, and Prague would declare martial law in the border districts. German invasion seemed imminent.

Against such a foreground, the British prime minister would telegraph Hitler late on September 13 to suggest a face-to-face meeting to work out a settlement. Hitler would accept the suggestion on the afternoon of September 14 and describe his feelings "with a colorful idiom that would have perplexed Milton: 'I fell from Heaven!'"[55] From wherever Hitler fell, he would invite Chamberlain to the great villa on the Obersalzberg for the first of a unique set of meetings. Chamberlain's action shows a bold and tough negotiator on the issue of self-determination for the Sudeten Germans. Hitler's action, and the earlier words of the Party Day rally, show an outraged messianic figure dedicated to the redemption of his people held by force and circumstance within an alien state. And in this confrontation Chamberlain was dedicated to redressing German grievances in the cause of peace. He was armed with Hitler's earlier demands for self-determination and in possession of Lord Runciman's findings that the Czechs had, in fact, mistreated the German minority during the entire period of the Allied assignment of it to a new Czech state. Armed with dedication and knowledge, Chamberlain would address German grievances and the cause of peace by reaffirming with his own cabinet the necessity for German self-determination. He coordinated with the French and labored with the Czech government to accomplish it. Chamberlain would succeed in this no mean feat between September 15 and 22, but it would be too little, too late. It remains mildly bizarre that an Englishman would intervene literally in Germany and more figuratively in Paris and Prague to decide the fate of Czechs and Sudeten Germans in the name of an empire centered on India and a commonwealth inhabited by states so distant and disinterested as Canada, Australia, New Zealand, and South Africa.

Bizarrely or not, Chamberlain would achieve agreement on a

plebiscite in the Sudetenland and begin to earn the *soubriquet* of "appeaser"—one who accedes to demands in return for peace. Specifically, Chamberlain agreed to demands for Sudeten German self-determination in return for the halting of a potential German invasion. Chamberlain's action has come to be seen as the pusillanimous caving in to wicked demands in return for peace. But the ostensible issue in the Czech crisis was German self-determination, and Hitler's demand for redress of so legitimate a grievance could not be seen as wicked. In revisionist retrospect, we could see Chamberlain as not redressing German grievance quickly and decisively enough. After all, he faced a deadly combination of twenty-year mistreatment of Germans, and by his own estimate Hitler was a "lunatic" statesman, although one with morally superior demands and fearsome power to back them. In immediate crisis time in September, Chamberlain had acted with remarkable speed and decision. But from 1918 through 1938, previous British governments had failed to redress epic German grievances and victimizations. In the presence of those inequities that had been created and accumulated during the longer period, Chamberlain and his advisors seem strangely out of touch with the human condition of the Germans— now Hitler's Germans, thanks to that lack of touch. Chamberlain, for example, had arrived in Berchtesgaden not empowered through consultation with his cabinet to come to an agreement with Hitler on the issue of self-determination. And he had arrived knowing that Lord Runciman, as a result of his August mission to Czechoslovakia, had determined that the Sudeten Germans had bona fide, long-term grievances. Over the following seven days, Chamberlain and Daladier would agree on self-determination for the Germans and force their decision on Beneš. When Chamberlain met with Hitler again, this time at Bad Godesberg on the Middle Rhine, he would present him with the near-impossible victory of self-determination for the outliers of the German flock.

The conventional wisdom has interpreted Chamberlain's achievement as the beginning of the "dismemberment" of Czechoslovakia.

Perhaps more realistically, it could be seen as the ending of injustice to the Sudeten Germans. Either way—dismemberment for the Czechs or justice for the Germans—Hitler would steer Europe into the culminating final seven days of the Czech crisis. Those days remain astonishing for Hitler's intensity in the pursuit of his written intent to smash the Czech state and his outrage over the misfortune of the Germans in it. With the accomplishment of self-determination for the Germans in his hands on the late afternoon of September 22, Hitler would present Chamberlain with the "softly and almost regretfully"-spoken words: "I am exceedingly sorry, Mr. Chamberlain, but I can no longer discuss these matters. This solution, after the developments of the last few days is no longer [capable of being put into effect]."[56] The following late evening of September 23, Hitler would present Chamberlain with the fresh, near-impossible demand for the immediate evacuation—to be completed by September 28—of Sudeten territory determined to be German according to earlier census data. Around midnight, Hitler would make a concession to delay Czech evacuation until October 1, and Chamberlain would depart later in the morning to reveal the ultimatum to the British cabinet and the French and Czech governments. Both the French and Czechs would reject outright seizure of the predominately German part of the Sudetenland. And, although faced with the clear and present reluctance of the Commonwealth states to support a war over the Sudetenland, Chamberlain would warn Hitler of probable British support for the Czechs and French in the event of war. By the evening of September 26, 1938, war loomed in Europe.

The great biographers present Hitler as one who would smash the Czech state and continue on to smash a notable variety of larger states as part of a conspiracy to commit aggressive war. Kershaw would even reject the notion that the Germans had any moral case at all during the Czech affair with the remarkable words that "during the Sudeten crisis, some sympathy for demands to incorporate the German-speaking areas into the Reich—for another Anschluss of sorts—still existed among those ready to swallow Goebbels's propaganda about the maltreatment of the Sudeten Germans by the Czechs, or at any rate prepared to accept that a further nationality problem was in need of resolution."[57] These words are remarkably spare with the reality of the Allied assignment of over four million Germans to a Czech state in 1918 and the violence of their unsuccessful resistance. Most importantly, however, the words spin us away from the Hitler who could not have seen himself as part of any conspiracy to commit aggressive war from 1918 through November 1937. In that period, Hitler would portray himself as a nameless soldier who had come out of the war to orate nonnegotiable demands for internal German unity.[58] By August 1934, he had achieved a half-mystical unity in Germany, and by September 1938 would be on the verge of completing the ingathering of ten million Austrian Germans. This Hitler did not get to November 1937 by leading a conspiracy to commit aggressive war but arrived at that juncture from the heights inhabited by a handful of world-historical personalities, this one clothed as savior. This savior, this messiah, this complex Wagnerian hero, Thomas Mann's artist, and Troost's architectural genius, stood poised to initiate war in Europe in the last week of September 1938. The great biographers would have Hitler concretely conspiring to commit aggressive war more or less suddenly in late 1937 when for the previous twenty years he had been conspiring to commit the final, millennial salvation of the Germans. Either way, a war is a war. But the premise for each would be entirely different, and it would seem that a messiah was about to commit Germany to a war of salvation, rather than a power-hungry dictator to a commonly construed war of aggression.

Two things nevertheless stood out in the last week of September that show both Hitlers functioning. As aggressive dictator, Hitler would unveil that incalculably bold strategic idea that the year 1938 presented fleeting opportunity for Germany to defeat the west and gain freedom of maneuver in the east. This hair-raising idea was the partial rationale for the fourth iteration of Plan Green. If executed on October 1, the plan would have resulted in the certainty of war with Czechoslovakia, the probability of war with France, and the possibility of war with Britain. The army high command and various high-ranking officers viewed the plan as insanely reckless, believed that it would lead to certain German defeat, and conspired to remove Hitler by force in the event of the order to execute it. But Hitler went ahead with his invasion plans, come what might, and in retrospect they combined elements of "shrewd calculation, intuition and an irresistible impulse."[59] Hitler shrewdly calculated on the one hand and sensed on the other that literally with every minute that passed from 1938 onward, potential enemies—especially France, Britain, and Soviet Russia—would grow relatively stronger than Germany. Here we have a rare world-historical personality psychologically crossing a Rubicon that, in the final flow of events, would not have to be crossed physically. So much for the shrewdly calculating dictator in this personality's makeup. But the intuitive Hitler, the passionate one, the man of irresistible, furious impulse, would seem to have been the one who dominated after Beneš's terrible error in invoking the baseless claim of impending German invasion earlier in the year. It is too easy to see Hitler as dominated by personal pique over that incident. It is more likely that Beneš ignited in Hitler that apolitical sense of mission that dominated him as a "lonely wanderer out of nothingness" and converted him during the Czech crisis into a dark, remorseless redeemer of the Germans.[60]

At the peak of the crisis, on September 26, Hitler would pull together his view of it and place it within his invariably crafted historical context. He would do so in a speech at the twenty-thousand-spectator, indoor Berlin *Sportspalast*. The great biographers would characterize the speech as one of rare abandon and venom and therefore useless excess for understanding both crisis and Hitler. But Hitler *was* abandon, excess, and a kind of walking crisis, and his speech presented a compelling German view of the imbroglio and an insightful self portrait. The historical situation could be seen to have been so outrageous that its description invited abandon and venom. With effective psychology, Hitler would personify the misfortune of the Sudeten Germans in the person of Beneš: "In this name is concentrated all that which moves millions, which causes them to despair or fills them with fanatical resolution."[61] And near the end of the speech, he would emphasize that "the decision now lies in his hands: Peace or War," and present as his last sentence: "Now let Mr. Beneš make his choice."[62] With superior propaganda technique, Hitler focused on a single enemy. But Hitler was more than propaganda, even though his technique was unparalleled in history. Hitler would portray Beneš not as the president of Czechoslovakia but as a Satan-esque figure who embodied the misfortune of the Sudeten Germans. Hitler was not doing propaganda; he was locked in battle with the forces of evil. Calculation, propaganda, and lust for power can take men only so far. Then a handful rise above or fall below all others through belief in mission and destiny.

For an outraged messiah, Hitler would express his case with a peculiar emphasis on numbers. He would fulminate over his data that 600,000 Sudeten Germans had been forced to leave Czechoslovakia because of the ravages of starvation due to food allocations in the aftermath of the war. He would note that the Sudeten Germans had the highest death rate, lowest birthrate, and highest unemployment rate of all the "German tribes."[63] He would present cumulative numbers of German fugitives after the Czech imposition of martial law in the Sudetenland on September 13 as totaling 214,000 by the time of his speech and claim that they were the result of German fear of violence from Czech security forces.[64] This mathematics of cruelty was probably accurate, supported Hitler's moral outrage, and presented propaganda opportunity. We are presented with a rare animal who was capable of shifting easily from concrete numbers to the mystical union between him and all Germans. He would argue that, through Beneš, the Czechs annexed Slovakia and "since this State did not seem fitted to live [took] three and a half million Germans... in violation of their right to self-determination. Since even that did not suffice, over a million Magyars had to be added, then some Carpathian Russians, and at last several hundred thousand Poles... I am naturally spokesman only for the fate of my Germans."[65]

He would make a historical analogy between the 1919 French requirement for a 1935 plebiscite in the Saarland to assure a fair voice for a miniscule French population and a 1938 plebiscite in the Sudetenland to assure a similar voice for a huge bloc of indigenous Germans. He would quote the sometime French air minister, Pierre Cot, as saying, "We need [Czechoslovakia] because from this State German business life and German industry can be most readily destroyed by bombs."[66] In his earlier September 12 closing address at Nuremberg, Hitler had made this same point with the addition of an exceedingly complex and sarcastic comparison between the dropping of bombs and the advance of civilization. Hitler would suggest that bombs carried on aircraft launched from Czechoslovakia and dropped on Germany could be seen by Cot as having a civilizing effect on barbaric Germans.[67]

By September 26 we can see Hitler and Chamberlain as crossers of the same abyss—war between Germany on the one hand and the usual allies and Czechoslovakia on the other. But through special emissary and resident ambassador, Chamberlain would point out to Hitler that he had already been granted self-determination for the Sudeten Germans, a fact that amounted to the seizure of the Sudetenland in the brief time required to complete a plebiscite. War, therefore, could be seen as an inordinately high price for Hitler to pay for quicker completion of the already-agreed seizure. Chamberlain, however, would be paying the same price for not allowing Hitler to seize the Sudetenland more quickly. We are in the presence of two apparent dysfunctional inanities. Both statesmen had agreed upon the transfer of the Sudetenland to Germany, but Hitler would go to war to get it immediately, and Chamberlain would go to war to prevent him from doing so. But Hitler's apparent foolishness was none at all, because he was set on war in 1938. Chamberlain's parallel apparent foolishness seems to have been based on the notion that he had done everything he could do to "appease" Hitler but now had been forced to stop at the immediate transfer of the Sudetenland.

But Hitler was setting the clock of historical evolution in Europe to its correct German-saga time. More or less incidentally, he was also demanding an immediate halt to twenty years of injustice to Germans in Czechoslovakia. Either way, Chamberlain was giving up too little, too late. Chamberlain could not have known that he was dealing with a historical phenomenon. But even if he believed that he were dealing with an aggressive German statesman, he had distanced himself from the realities of the European historical condition. When Chamberlain returned from Munich to London on September 30 and exclaimed with honest fervor that there would be peace in our time, his condition was not one of naïveté in trusting the written signature of a criminal statesman. Chamberlain can be seen retrospectively to have trivialized the historical condition of continental Europe as one in which the righting of a single injustice to Germany—only one in a long string of similar injustices—could have been equated to the pacification of Europe. Hitler, in contrast, viewed the Czech crisis as another step toward setting a mighty clock of historical evolution to its correct time.

Hitler would neither smash the Czech state in 1938 nor have his war with France. But his determination to do so consciously, as another step toward the securing of German destiny, places him in a rare historical category. Even Julius Caesar, when he took over the governorship of Transalpine Gaul—modern southeastern France— would not consciously envision that it was his destiny to string together seasonal campaigns into the conquest of "Gaul." And when Napoleon initiated his international career as French revolutionary commander of the army of Italy, he did not remotely aspire to the conquest of Europe. Yet Hitler, who can be compared with these two in his effect on the course of history, can be contrasted as having had a superior sense of his own destiny. He would see himself as a German messiah as early as 1922. And as world-historical personality, he would dictate in fortress prison only two years later that a reckoning with France "can and will achieve meaning only if it offers the rear cover for an enlargement of our people's living space in Europe."[68] Then this man in September 1938, already embarked on a mission during the preceding sixteen years, would demand the immediate salvation of the Sudetenlanders. Chamberlain, however, as honest peace broker, would treat the situation as if it were a one-time Czech crisis rather than part of an all-time rectification of the European historical condition.

As the month of September continued to unfold, it would be dominated by the first eight words of Plan Green, the single one, which was so strange, so hard, so peculiar to Hitler: that the situation was "unalterable." The word seems to hover several inches above the innumerable pages on which it has been reproduced and to catch the eye as dramatic, mystical but extraneous—do we really care that the decision was unalterable? A decision is a decision. But an unalterable decision in the matter of an impending great historical event gets us into the realm of historical inevitability, a foggy area in which nothing is inevitable except the play of chance.

When Hitler made his unalterable decision, he rose above the play of chance in history. In such a situation he could be comprehended more realistically as one who would impose his will on history and not as a lucky tyrant, the "gambler" depicted by his great biographers. In the final outcome of his unalterable decision, he would neither smash Czechoslovakia nor have his war with France. It would take the last-minute miracle of the end of September, however, to prevent Hitler from having his war in 1938. And on the verge of completing that epic month, we should know more about Hitler personally and artistically.

*   *   *

No less a critic than the intellectually well-armed French ambassador François-Poncet would reflect on Hitler, after six years on the *Pariserplatz* in Berlin, in this way:

> [Hitler] is changeable, dissembling, full of contradictions, uncertain...the same man with the debonair aspect, with a real fondness for the beauties of nature who discussed reasonable ideas of European politics around the tea table is also capable of the worst frenzies, the wildest exaltations and the most delirious ambitions. There are days when, standing before the globe of the world, he will overthrow nations, continents, geography and history like a demiurge stricken with madness. At other moments he dreams of being the hero of an everlasting peace, in which he would devote himself to the erection of the most magnificent monuments.[69]

François-Poncet has presented several Hitlers in the word picture above, and they include a stunning mixture: a capable European statesman, a man of justice and peace, a demiurge creative god stricken with madness who would overthrow nations, and yet a hero of an everlasting peace dedicated to the erection of the most magnificent monuments. To comprehend Hitler toward the end of the 1930s, we cannot just proceed from the first part of François-Poncet's description, which roughly explains the destruction of Marxists, democrats, and particularists in Germany, the harassment of Jews, and the great international offensive against the Versailles and Saint-Germain treaties. And François-Poncet, with the use of the descriptor *demiurge* comes close to presenting Hitler as the world-historical personality of Hegel. But in his perceptive characterization of Hitler as the hero of an everlasting German architectural saga, Poncet forces us into a fresh comprehension of Hitler as architectural genius and as the stage designer of political grand opera.

And Albert Speer could remark in 1938, upon receiving the two earlier Hitler sketches as part of his architectural assignment to rebuild Berlin, that "what is startling is less the grandiosity of the project than the obsessiveness with which he had been planning triumphant monumental buildings when there was not a shred of hope that they would ever be built."[70] And Speer would note that when Hitler handed him the two sketches drawn on small cards he would add that "I made these drawings ten years ago. I've always saved them, because I never doubted that someday I would build these edifices. And this is how we will carry it out now."[71] In all of this, Speer's word *obsessiveness* somehow slips by Hitler. With so pejorative a word, Speer seems to be presenting him as compelled by the devil to accomplish something wicked rather than as a man preoccupied with an idea. But Hitler could be qualified more accurately as visionary intensity.

In 1925, the year of his two building sketches, Hitler put together a fantastic political creature of his imagination. It would be the reconstituted Nazi party of that year and could be likened to the chimera of Greek mythology, although not in the sense of a fire-vomiting hybrid monster. It would be tempting to present so unattractive an image as representative of Hitler and the Nazi movement, and it is surprising that the great biographers have not. If we look, however, upon a chimera as the ultimate example of fanciful imagination and relate it with Hitler, we see a man with a chimerical style of addressing life. A British dramatist of the early nineteenth century related man, genius, radically inventive ideas, and chimeras in a brief line as "persons of genius in their wildest chimeras."[72] We could see Hitler as a man of genius who existed in his own world of chimerically proportioned political and architectural expectations. We know that a single man in 1925 would go on to become the vessel of a Greater Germany in 1939. Less well known is that the entire other half of the single man lay in his vision of a new Germany in stone. After all the hue and cry of the political saga that Hitler had in mind for Germany, he had seen that by the end of a millennium, all that would remain of the great saga would be the ruins of the monumental architecture that he would create in his lifetime.

By 1938, Hitler had given Germany four capitals—if we define capitals as architectural expanses—from which Hitler determined German destiny. He would lease, purchase, and use the small country house Wachenfeld as his center for solitary inspiration through one crisis after another and then begin to convert it into the Berghof super-villa from which he would be capable of running the

Reich. And Hitler did not just order the Berghof to be built. He borrowed a drawing board and other implements from Speer to sketch the overall plan, renderings, and cross sections of his building to scale, refusing any help. Hitler also led Germany from Berlin, the formal capital. Munich was the psychological and administrative center of the Nazi movement, and Hitler spent much time there running the movement from the Barlow Palace (later called the Brown House) and from various hotels in Berlin from 1929 through 1933. With the seizure of the chancellorship, Hitler would continue to spend significant time in Munich, not only relaxing in its congenial atmosphere but also conducting serious party and state business through the facilities of the Brown House. With the 1935 completion of the Fuehrer Building and its twin administrative building on the opposite side of Munich's impressive *Koenigsplatz*, Hitler would be able to do more than just relax in Bavaria. It is easy to forget that Hitler erected the Fuehrer Building in Munich and felt comfortable enough to host in it the Great Power conference of September 1938.

From 1929 onward, Nuremberg became the site of the vast Party Day rallies and could be considered one of the four "Nazi cities." Various masses of people would assemble as spectators and participants in presentations, demonstrations, speeches, and the like, during both day and night. Hitler intended that the brilliantly staged assemblies would pull Germans together into a sense of belonging to a single body mystically bound by a sense of common destiny. The rallies were dominated by demonstrations on two great cleared and leveled areas of the *Zeppelinwiese* (Zeppelin meadow) and *Luitpoldhain* (Luitpold glade). The city, with its massive medieval buildings, resembled a stage setting and would remind rally participants and spectators of a somber, common German past.

This other Hitler can also be seen in the explosion of similar collaborations with Fritz Todt, Speer, Hermann Giesler, Paul Bonatz (*Autobahn* bridges), Ludwig Ruff (Nuremburg party congress hall), Werner March (Olympic stadium), and numerous other architects. We do not know if the enduring adolescent of Linz and Vienna and the sketchbook dreamer of the mid 1920s gives us a more realistic picture of Hitler than messiah or power-hungry tyrant. Was Hitler a political messiah with an irresistible artistic passion for architecture or an impassioned architect consumed by a sense of historical mission? The answer would seem to be that he was a messiah with a passion for the arts. We cannot even be certain that he was dominated by the politics of his mission to save Germany; however, he dictated in 1937 that for National Socialists every building associated with the German saga had to be a monument:

> These works of ours shall...be eternal...that is to say not only in the greatness of their conception but [also] in the clarity of plan, in the harmony of their proportions they shall satisfy the requirements of eternity...magnificent evidence of civilization in granite and marble...these buildings of ours should not be conceived for the year 1942 nor for the year 2000, but like the cathedrals of our past, they shall stretch into the millennia of the future.[73]

Hitler would commission Paul Ludwig Troost earlier, in 1933, to design and build two temples of honor, each centered on eight iron coffins that would frame the east end of the main avenue of the eventual Munich forum. Hitler and the entire Nazi movement would stand out in a kind of resplendent mysticism with the consecration of the structures and a roll call of the martyrs at midnight on November 8, 1935. The assembled tens of thousands would answer together, "present," with each call for the dead. Troost would be chosen to design the Fuehrer Building and the Party Building facing each other across a transverse north–south axis. They would be completed in 1936 and, along with Leo von Klenze's 1860 Doric propylaeum or colonnaded entry structure to the *Koenigsplatz*, would define the first Nazi forum.

We see Hitler as dedicated to heroic imagery and open a door of comprehension rather than denigration. We sense his interest in the following scene:

"The Professor told me that the stairwell in the Fuehrer House is being paneled today. I can hardly wait to see it. Brueckner send for the car—we'll drive right over."...He would hurry straight from the car to the stairwell...inspect it from downstairs, from the gallery, from the stairs, then go upstairs again, full of enthusiasm. Finally he would look over the entire building. He would once again demonstrate his familiarity with every detail of the plans and sufficiently astonish everyone.... Satisfied with the progress, satisfied with himself because he was the cause and prime mover of these buildings, he went to his next destination.[74]

Several years later, after the completion of the Munich forum, Hitler would tersely assign the young Speer the mission to center Berlin on a super forum. His patience exhausted by the Berlin city government, Hitler remarked literally with the force of law: "From now on you make the plans. Take this drawing along. When you have something ready, show it to me. As you know, I always have time for such things."[75] He envisioned a north–south avenue roughly four hundred feet wide and three miles long, which would connect an enormous assembly hall for the German people with a monumental triumphal arch inscribed with the names of the 1.8 million German soldiers fallen in World War I. The avenue itself could be used to assemble approximately one million Germans on festive occasions in addition to the 150,000 inside the domed *Volkshalle* at the avenue's north end.

The great biographers have interpreted this immense forum as evidence of architectural megalomania on the part of both Hitler and Speer. The use of such a word suggests criticism motivated by hostility and leaves us with both Hitler and Speer as megalomaniacs. We can hardly doubt that Hitler had a passion for architectural display on a grand scale. In similarly scaled architectural works, however, other builders have not been singled out as megalomaniacs.

The Ulm Cathedral begun in the 1300s has the tallest spire in Christendom, for example, and no historian has disapproved of it as stemming from megalomania among the tiny numbers of *Buerger* who constructed it. And Hitler would analyze it as a place of assembly capable of holding the entire fourteen-thousand-person population of Ulm in the 1400s. He would specifically point out to Speer that by medieval standards, the great Berlin *Volkshalle* was scarcely over-whelming. Philip II of Spain, after his victory over the French at Saint Quentin in 1557, swore that he would erect a suitable monument to God's help. The result would be his construction of the Escorial, a gigantic, integrated monastery, cathedral, and library similar in dimension to the *Volkshalle* although located in a barren, lonely high-land northwest of Madrid. No historian, however, has hastily cited either the cathedral or the monastery as examples of megalomania on the part of the people of Ulm and the King of Spain. In the 1600s, with the construction of the Palace of Versailles by Louis XIV, histo-rians have noted fiscal recklessness and love of pomp and display on the part of the Sun King, but never megalomania. All of the structures of the middle ages and the early modern period are distinguished by their sheer size. Yet every one was linked with a grand purpose, which, for its realization, demanded notable size and monumental style.

With Hitler we see a man driven to relate art and architecture with the historical existence of Germany. And with that solemn, annunciatory mysticism that would often come over him, he could present himself to the world as follows:

> What our people during the history of two thousand years has achieved in heroic greatness is numbered among the mightiest experiences of mankind. There were centuries during which Ger-many, as in the rest of Europe, the works of art corresponded with this greatness of the human soul. The lonely sublimity of our cathedrals gives us an incomparable standard by which to judge of the truly monumental cultural outlook of those ages. They compel us to pass from admiration of their work to pay our tribute of profound respect to the generations which were capable of planning and of realizing such great conceptions.[76]

In all of this architectural tumult, we may extract a significant part of the actual Hitler. We may find an architect who climbed some mountain of singular precipitousness seeking artistic fame only to emerge partway along the ascent from the underground shelters of a gunfire hell to become something else. Whichever Hitler, he was capable of expressing the scene:

> During the long years in which I planned the formation of a new Reich I gave much thought to the cultural cleansing of the people's life...was convinced that peoples which have been trodden underfoot...have all the greater duty consciously to assert their own value...and there is no prouder proof of the highest rights of a people to its own life than immortal cultural achievements. I was therefore determined that if fate should one day give us power I would discuss these matters with no one but would form my own decisions, for it is not given to all to have an understanding for tasks as great as these. Amongst the plans which floated before me in my mind both during the war and after the collapse was the idea of building a great new exhibition palace in Munich.[77]

Munich would acquire the mission to be the capital of German art and "to be the home of the sublime and of the beautiful."[78] Hitler spoke these words at various events associated with the buildings that would house collections of German painting and sculpture and embody state architecture. Hitler would conceptualize that art was art, created by the gifted men of various peoples and conditioned by the unchanging character of the peoples who produced the artists. Hitler would fulminate that art was not subject to changing fashion invented by artists and critics who had become hopelessly distanced from the people. Art was the eternal companion of an entire people and the ultimate measure of its culture. And it would be displayed in suitably dimensioned structures—large, gigantic, megalomaniacal, heroically bold—depending upon the bias of the observer. As concerns the size and the splendid ruin value in terms of marble and other natural stone, the Munich House of German Art seems to have been representative of the artist–architect Hitler. We can go farther and generalize that Hitler was the House of German Art. In his incarnation as artist–architect, he marches by us as a neoclassical monumental temple.

The sheer size of the forums, associated structures, and assembly areas, however, has driven hostile biographers, historians, and Speer himself to accusation of architectural megalomania. The writers, however, fail to correlate the magnitude of the political victories anticipated by Hitler with the magnitude of the monumental architecture required to celebrate them. The French would commission their great engineering son, Alexandre-Gustave Eiffel, to erect a structure so gargantuan as the iron tower associated with his name merely to mark the center of their international commercial exposition of 1889. Hitler and Speer could be seen in retrospect to have been less than megalomaniacal in dimensioning their German people's assembly hall as a monument to the setting of the clock of cultural evolution to its "correct" time in Europe.

*   *   *

In the twenty-year period prior to his assumption of the special burdens of war fighting, Hitler showed behavior appropriate to the circumstances of his life. He made it clear that he could never marry because of the image necessary for a man who would save the Germans and not just affect a program of improvements to last his lifetime. He would make the point that no great leader in history had a son who had proven capable of continuing the achievements of his father. Rome, for example, had been favored uniquely with the two succeeding world-historical Caesars, Julius and Augustus—the latter a great-nephew of Julius and named in his will as successor. And Hitler on no account, for the safeguarding of his superhuman image, could risk consummated sex with virtually any woman. He was a remarkable ascetic who stood out as self-contained. Yet this man had an overwhelming inclination toward pretty young women. He was relaxed and charming in their presence and delighted in sitting next to and among them in social situations. He would commonly invite selected ones back to his quarters of the moment for brief continued social interaction. It is difficult to escape the suggestion that he engaged in touching, fondling, hand holding, kissing, and the like, actions short of consummated sex but safe physically and innocent enough socially to avoid political repercussion. This interpretation of casual and innocent interaction with casual female acquaintances such as showgirls, singers, actresses, and other entertainers is buttressed by his similar behavior with closer acquaintances. Hitler would ask the twelve-year-old Henriette Hoffmann in 1924 if he might kiss her, and when she answered no, he strictly desisted.[79] In autumn 1926 he would be attracted by the sixteen-year-old Maria Reiter and go so far as kissing in a forest glade on the Obersalzberg.

The first affair, and one which probably involved Hitler's first dependence on a woman, developed slowly with his half-niece Angela "Geli" Raubal, whom he first met briefly in 1926 when she was only eighteen years old. It ended five years later with her suicide in September 1931 at age twenty-three. The second affair developed much more slowly and overlapped his relationship with Angela, and it was the second affair that would develop out of Hitler's chance encounter with Eva Braun. She was only seventeen years old when he first met her in October 1929 in Hoffmann's photographic shop on the same street as the Brown House. There were numerous other women in Hitler's life with potential for romantic engagement or emotional attachment. Jenny Haug, for example, the young sister of Hitler's first chauffer and early bodyguard of 1920, Hans Haug, would have been such a candidate. She would accompany him home in the back seat of his automobile as a volunteer, pistol-armed bodyguard, and probably the petting and hand holding affected by Hitler occurred. But his first of only two unmistakable attachments to a woman blossomed when his half-niece Geli moved into his recently leased, expansive second-story flat at 16 *Prinzregentenplatz* in February 1930. His bodyguard and chauffer Emil Maurice averred that "He loved her but it was a strange affection that did not dare to show itself, for he was too proud to admit to the weakness of an infatuation."[80] With broader insight, we could observe that in his chosen role as the holder of German destiny he could scarcely descend to the level of an affair with his half-niece.

The great biographers uniformly march toward a relationship between Hitler and his young niece as one of lovers. They know that his father married Franziske Matzelberger, who was twenty-four years his junior, and Hitler's mother, Klara Poelzl, who was twenty-three years younger than his father. But Hitler's father, Alois, in his first marriage, would wed a woman who was fourteen years his senior. It is difficult to generalize about Hitler's sexual preferences from the behavior of his father, even though the younger Hitler delighted in the company of young actresses and dancers at dinners associated with artistic entertainment. On the other hand, he declared his undying love for the more mature Helene Hanfstaengl in a somewhat embarrassing scene in her own home. Later in the decade of the 1920s, when he decided to move his niece into his quarters on *Prinzregentenplatz*, we are left with the picture of Geli as an object of both sexual infatuation and powerful protective instinct on the part of Hitler. Geli was interested in various young men in both Germany and Austria. It is doubtful that she was physically attracted to Hitler or had sexual relations with him: "He was too reserved to openly court any woman and too cautious to ruin his political career by taking a mistress into his own apartment particularly the daughter of a half sister."[81]

Although the great biographers have seen Geli as Hitler's single true love, we must see another young woman as his only real one. Geli cannot be said to have loved Hitler, even though he had become inspired with a foolish and extravagant passion for her. Hitler's "love" for Geli was not only unrequited but also tempered by his perceived duties as her uncle and protector and the necessity to shield his image as Germany's destiny. In late 1929, however, only months before Geli would move in with him on *Prinzregentenplatz*, Hitler would meet and become attracted to the very young, seventeen-year-old Eva Braun. Unlike Geli, who never loved her repressive and not particularly fun-loving uncle, Eva had fallen desperately in love with Hitler after two years of various encounters. Then, in November 1932, she would attempt suicide by pistol shot, "allegedly aiming at the heart," apparently distraught by unrequited love from Hitler.[82] Unlike Geli, who would die through strikingly similar means (although for quite different reasons), Eva would survive through the fateful vagaries of pistol bullet trajectories. Hitler would take greater notice of her, she would remain his only mistress, and the years from 1932 through 1935 would be ones of tortured uncertainty for Eva as concerned Hitler's love for her.

In late May 1935, Eva would attempt suicide for the second time and would be miraculously saved as she had been in the first attempt. Hitler would be moved to acknowledge her devotion, and she would become discretely but ever so decisively his premier and only mistress. She seemed to suit him physically, with her trim and athletic fairness. He had become used to her and genuinely fond of her, and she must be seen as a special influence in his life. From the end of 1935 onward, Eva could also be seen as Hitler's ultradiscrete de facto wife, and a man's wife must tell us much about the man. Eva revealed in her diary that she had been in love with Hitler since at least 1932, and we know that the relationship between them tightened and matured to the end in 1945. To know Eva, then, is to know a significant amount about Hitler.

Heinrich Hoffman, who originally introduced Hitler to Eva, has taken the position that she was decent, nice, pretty, but even by her nineteenth year gripped by "a somewhat childish and naïve air."[83] And she may have been lighthearted and perhaps even "feather-brained" at this young age. But she would pursue Hitler even so young with a mature determination and consistency. Hoffmann would also relent about his early impressions and in perhaps the most succinct, comprehending picture of Eva, write: "Later under the influence of the tremendous events through which she lived…Eva's mental stature grew, her character broadened and deepened; and by her final gesture and decision to remain at the side of her protector to the end, she attained heights which more than atoned for the vanities and frivolities of the past."[84] A very different man, Albert Speer, would make a visit to the underground bunker adjacent to the *Reichskanzlei* in Berlin in the last days of April 1945 to bid Hitler a final good-bye. Eva would invite him to her small room and talk honestly during a time when Hitler had withdrawn. Speer could remark that "she was the only prominent candidate for death in this bunker who displayed an admirable and superior composure."[85] She would say that Hitler wanted to send her back to Munich but that she had refused, adding the words "I've come to end it here."[86]

How is it possible that the biographical *bête noire* of the twentieth century would have attracted so innocent, decent, and perceptive a child who would have become his wife in shadowed waiting in 1935? During the time that she had actively pursued him before the turn of 1935, he was in his attractive forties and not yet frozen into the forbidding figure of late 1939. He wore superbly tailored suits and uniforms and was fastidious in his personal hygiene, a trait identified by Kubizek much earlier with a nineteen-year-old Hitler. Several of his more important acquaintances would remark about his intense personal modesty and similar personal shyness. Men so disparate as Hoffmann, Hanfstaengl, and Speer would independently remark about these traits so astonishing in light of his ferocious public image. The young Eva would fall in love with an attractive middle-aged man. This man would soon be revealed to her as one of the important men in Germany after September 1930, the most important young man after 1933, and the leading man of the entire state from August 1934 onward. Eva's tortured diary entries and suicide attempts in the face of Hitler's early neglect show that she loved him. Her enduring of the necessary secretiveness of their relationship points to a loyalty almost beyond comprehension.

Eva Braun shows how much care we have to take in pulling together a picture of Hitler. Thomas Mann flickers in, ghostlike, with his earlier admonition that although it is our duty to hate him, in our better moments we must acknowledge the fascination of the man. How many bad men in history have attracted so much fresh-faced attractiveness and sterling loyalty into their personal lives? We must add to Hitler's capability to extract fidelity from the leadership and rank and file of the movement an ability to attract loyalty in his personal life. Love and loyalty in the personal lives of a man and woman are necessarily reciprocal, and we are driven to believe that Hitler not only loved her but would also be steadfast in his loyalty. Hitler would continue to delight in the presence of pretty young women at table and reception. He would navigate his way with political acumen through the looming, adoring presence of the beautiful young Englishwoman Unity Valkyrie Mitford. From 1935 onward, however, not a shred of evidence exists to suggest that Eva and Hitler strayed from their politically constrained love affair. To comprehend Hitler better, we must see an athletic, decent, pretty one who dedicated her entire life to him and ask, how is this possible for the power-hungry creature of the great biographers? We can never know how much Eva saw in Hitler as an object of power to be exploited by her in terms of personal vanities and the increase of her own power over others. Unbeknownst to either, she would inexorably become his wife in waiting and finally wife herself. Hitler comes off as loyal and decent in the relationship—the latter word being one that has no pejorative uses.

*   *   *

There are more pejorative words that can be used in the description of Hitler and "the Jews." Hitler would be forced of practical necessity to deal with Jews as human individuals in personal encounters, especially in numerous business transactions in his intercourse with them as a skilled professional painter. Hitler would encounter these individual Jews largely in the years 1909 through 1914 in Vienna and Munich. He would be calm, modest, polite, and functional in these dealings. No exceptions to this generalization exist in the literature on Hitler. He had these dealings in the period before he went into politics in late 1919, and his behavior would probably have been different in the 1920s. On the other hand, Hitler had these calm, functional encounters with the Jews of Vienna and Munich after "the scales fell from [his] eyes" in mid-1909, revealing the Jew as the underlying force behind Marxism and the drive to internationalize the world. We are left to wonder how history's arch enemy of "the Jews" interacted so easily with individual Jews under such circumstances. The conventional wisdom has assigned to Hitler a visceral —deep, organic, emotional—hatred of them. But his interactions with individuals suggests an entirely different kind of anti-Semitism based less on emotion and more on hard, emotionless logic. He would remark in a more general context that he would be known as the hardest man in history, not the most hate-filled.

Hitler can be seen as indifferent to the existence and presence of the individual Jews of a dispersed but cohesive international tribe. His behavior suggests an indifference that demands a counterintuitive reevaluation of the visceral hatred of Jews assigned to him by the conventional wisdom. The easily assigned concept of such behavior spins us into a Hitler seen as the personal enemy of every individual Jew and a man driven by some form of personal vengeance. But Hitler would claim that his 1909 studies in Vienna and his 1924 studies and dictation during Landsberg fortress detention would coalesce into an impersonal world-historical outlook. In this outlook, Hitler would proclaim the Jews—the extended tribe in its entirety—to be the supreme enemy of the Germans. He would proclaim this outlook as immutable Nazi doctrine and drive the doctrine to its logical finality in 1942. In such an outlook there could be no room for either personal vengeance or personal hatred. Anti-Semitism was a holy duty necessary to protect Germans from an international force. Hitler was peculiarly detached from hatred of the individual Jew and only lukewarm in support of tactical harassment that aimed to exclude them from Germany. These tendencies point to a Hitler viewing the Jews of Europe as an abstraction of pure evil and necessary to be eliminated if the National Socialist idea were to make any sense.

Hitler would emerge as a thoughtful anti-Semite at the imme-diate beginning of his political career with his written exposition of the "Jewish menace" directed by his commanding officer, Captain Karl Mayr. Hitler would make it clear that the final aim of what would become Nazi anti-Semitism "must unquestionably be the irrevocable [expulsion] of the Jews" from Germany.[87] Rarely has a portent of things to come been so clearly drawn. He would never-theless maintain personal detachment from the German Jews and cannot be seen to have hated them in the sense of gutter, religious, anti-Semitism. As thousand-year messiah, however, he would refashion the Jews into a nonhuman body of evil marked necessarily for attack in seizing political power in Germany. As the same mes-siah and with an associated penchant for logical finality, he would see the salvation of the Germans as requiring their destruction.

Given these general truths, Hitler nevertheless would pursue tough courses of political action throughout the 1920s that would involve little and often no anti-Semitism after a noisy beginning in 1920. But even in that year, in the turning point, successful defense of the Munich *Hofbraeuhaus* mass meeting, the potentially fatal menace was from Marxist factory workers and not from some unlikely bands of Jewish toughs. And in 1923, the year of the near-destruction of Germany, Hitler would see the enemy as Marxists, November Criminals, provincial Separatists, and the French—but hardly German Jews. In early 1924, in his final words at his treason trial, he would sum up the achievement for which he would be known historically, and it would be as destructor of Marxism in Ger-many. Later, in the 1920s, he would focus his action against the Marxists and bourgeois November Criminals (the latter especially) in his 1929 attacks on acceptance of the Young Plan for finalization of German reparation payments. And a year earlier he would fly in the face of overwhelming German public opinion in favor of the return of the Germans of South Tyrol to Austria. He would actually complete an unpublished second book that argued that the enemy of the Germans was not the Italian government but rather the

November Criminals who, by their lack of support for the field
armies, had delivered South Tyrol to the Italians and were now
exploiting a latter-day, opportunistic patriotism. We see relatively
little anti-Semitism in the face of these issues and the reorganization
of the party from 1925 through 1928.

In the early 1930s we see the same dearth of anti-Semitism on
Hitler's part as compared with stronger concentration on other
issues. In the 1930 Reichstag election he would attack a corrupt
republican parliamentary system that put party interests above those
of the nation. He would attack the Marxists—Social Democrats and
Communists—for their internationalism and ineffectual efforts as
parliamentary parties in helping Germans. More than three million
German workers and lower middle-class breadwinners would be
without work and incapable of supporting their additional millions
of wives, children, and parents. The situation would intensify in
1931 and double in numbers of unemployed by 1932, the year of the
five great elections. In such a situation, anti-Semitic propaganda
could not have had much effect on Hitler's goal of seizing power.
Germans needed work, especially from 1930 through 1935, not the-
oretically tinged propaganda alleging a Jewish plot to take over the
world and laced with gutter images of this enemy. In the years 1933
and 1934, Hitler would face Marxism, economic recovery, Versailles,
Roehm, and the opportunity offered by the death of the president.
This litany of concerns for Hitler suggests that anti-Semitism could
not have been either an effective propaganda theme or high priority
for Hitler from 1930 through 1935. The situation becomes bizarre
when we also consider that fewer than one percent of the people
living in Germany in 1933 were Jews.

Most of the Jews lived in a few larger cities—notably Berlin,
Frankfurt, Breslau, Hamburg, Cologne, Leipzig, and Munich—
where they were vastly outnumbered by Germans. The remaining
40 percent of Jews lived in smaller cities, towns, villages, and countryside in insignificant numbers and largely indistinguishable from
Germans in dress and appearance. We are left to wonder in this sit-

uation of insignificant numbers of invisible German Jews why Hitler could consider them as towering menace and how he had come to see them as such.

Several factors stand out. He had first identified a Jewish presence in German Austria, an eastern frontier area with a significantly larger percentage of Jews that included large numbers of Middle Eastern–styled Jews. Hitler would claim accurately that the Western-styled Jews were present in the fields of law, medicine, university education, entertainment, and newspaper publishing in disproportionate numbers compared with Germans. He would simultaneously be inspired to discover that these Austrian Jewish intellectuals and others in Germany were the creators of Marxism. Hitler's studies that led to the discovery of the linkage were dispassionate, and "the Jew" for Hitler would become and remain an ice-cold logical abstraction. In contrast, Hitler would pursue the destruction of this logical abstraction with intensity and passion. He would also be concerned with the Jew as alien but ordinarily human intruder in Germany. Hitler would place this less theoretical Jew in the forefront of his popular speeches that had anti-Semitic content. We can generalize that Hitler was consumed by anti-Semitism, especially with our knowledge of the 1942 decision to begin genocide. Knowing this oncoming genocide, we are almost forced to claim Hitler's total preoccupation with anti-Semitism from 1919 through 1942.

Yet this tendency to do history backward can readily lead to an interpretation of Hitler that may be easily digestible but not necessarily real—Hitler emerges as a raging, visceral anti-Semite. It must nag at the reader that Norman H. Baynes, in his two-volume, 1,980-page collection of Hitler's speeches, could annotate: "It is surprising to observe how little the Fuehrer has said on the treatment of the Jews by the National Socialist state. It would seem that the following brief collection of abstracts exhausts the material on the subject so far as the printed reports of Hitler's speeches."[88] And Speer could comment that it had repeatedly surprised him, in later years, that "scarcely any anti-Semitic remarks of Hitler have remained in my memory."[89] The great biographers have noted *ad infinitum* Hitler's prewar years of never-ending monologues at supper. In them, they note the recurring themes of history, art, Hitler's experiences of war, and the development and success of National Socialism. Neither the great biographers as researchers nor Speer as eye witness have noted anti-Semitic subjects in his prewar supper monologues. In contrast, in his collected wartime monologues Hitler spent more time discussing the Jews, but still only a miniscule amount compared with other subjects.

Perhaps the above picture is not surprising. Hitler faced numerous enemies and challenges early from 1923 through late 1934 in which the Jew disappeared into the background as concerns his success and survival. During this extended gap in anything approaching a dominating anti-Semitism, Hitler was able to maintain in his mind the Jew as the *Weltanschauung* enemy of the Germans and pull up his granite foundation anti-Semitism penned for Captain Mayr in 1919: "Jewry is unequivocally a race and not a religious community...by thousands of years of inbreeding the Jew in general has preserved his race...more keenly than many of the peoples among whom he lives. And thus...the fact that among us a non-German, alien race lives, not willing and also not able to sacrifice its racial peculiarities...and which nevertheless possesses the same political rights we do."[90] Hitler thus, rationally and calmly, pictured the German Jew—Hitler's German Jew. With this Jew in place, he would go on to describe his necessary future: "[Ordinary] anti-Semitism [based] on emotional grounds will find its expression in the form of pogroms. The anti-Semitism of reason, however, must lead to the planned judicial opposition to and elimination of the privileges of the Jews...its ultimate goal, however, must be the removal of the Jews altogether."[91] These succinct, prophetic words of September 8, 1919, lead unerringly to the Nuremberg Laws of 1935 and the decision in 1942 for the physical destruction of the European Jews. The Nuremberg Laws deprived Jews of the rights of German citizenship, thus eliminating their privileges as expressed by Hitler sixteen years earlier. And by early 1939, Reinhard Heydrich as head of the SS Reich Security Service had been given the task to solve the Jewish problem through emigration and evacuation. By that time the effective deportation of the Jews had begun, thus advancing the removal of the Jews as expressed by Hitler two decades earlier. The question for Hitler biography as opposed to general historical account is: Who was the man who put all of this into motion in 1919?

It is difficult to escape a feeling that the young man who began in 1919 to create the anti-Semitic possibilities of 1935 and who personally created a Nazism characterized by gutter anti-Semitism stood aside from a large part of his own anti-Semitism. Hitler, however, could stand aside only if he did not see it as an end in itself. It is doubtful that he saw anti-Semitism as such but rather as a means to the end of a distantly secure Reich. With so distant a goal, Hitler could not countenance a 1,600-year-old, religion-oriented, spluttering persecution of Jews. As German messiah and world-historical personality he could hardly see mere harassment of Jews as resulting in the salvation of the Germans. Instead, we see Hitler implementing the Nuremberg Laws of September 1935 in a direct line from the epic, succinct, rational 1919 exposition of the Jewish problem. The conventional wisdom would see the laws as brutally stripping the Jews of their citizenship rights in a spirit not much different from that of the emotional, gutter anti-Semitism associated with the Nazis, and particularly high-level ones like Julius Streicher. But Hitler stood aside from the emotive anti-Jewish aspects and would state that "it is true that we have made discriminatory laws, but they are directed not so much against the Jews as for the German people to give economic opportunity to the majority.[92] He would dilate that "the Jews who formed [fewer] than one percent of the population tried to monopolize the cultural leadership of the people and flooded the intellectual professions."[93] Here we see Hitler making the argument that the Nuremberg Laws were intended to protect the rights of a crushing 99.4 percent majority of native Germans in 1935 against the intrusions of an alien race.

*   *   *

Thanks to a superb German civil service that ran the day-to-day affairs of Greater Germany and the phenomenon of National Socialists in party organizations and the civil service working toward the Fuehrer, a country of eighty million functioned with modest demands on Hitler's time. As the perfect Bohemian, Hitler had created this reality and reveled in it. As a Bohemian, Hitler did those things that personally interested him, including innumerable road trips, descents upon road and building construction sites, opera performances, art exhibitions, automobile manufacturers, the Nuremberg extravaganzas, and the great southern mountains of Germany. Hitler's daily schedules in fixed locations were also monuments to indifference to common convention. In Berlin from 1933 to 1939, he would appear around noon for government and party reports and discussion, lasting a brief hour or two, and then proceed to a lengthy mid-afternoon lunch often "until half past four in the afternoon."[94] After lunch, which normally included higher ranking members of the government, Hitler would have informal, impromptu discussion with favored guests lasting until around six o'clock in the evening. Then he would retire to his apartments above the dining area and reappear for supper around nine o'clock at night with an entirely different group that could be likened to a family and included adjutants, doctors, photographers, personal pilots, and personal business managers. At the finish of supper at about ten o'clock, Hitler would have movies shown until roughly one o'clock the next morning and then hold forth on the performances and any other subject of interest to him until about two o'clock. Once in the sleep part of this twenty-four-hour cycle, Hitler apparently got along with seven to eight hours when not affected by any medical condition that would keep him awake.

Hitler affected the above sequence when largely in control of a great modern state during peacetime in the period from 1933 through 1939. The sequence qualifies as Bohemian to so extreme a degree that it is doubtful that we are dealing with an eccentric tyrant. For one man uniquely close in fellowship with Hitler as his most esteemed architect, "Hitler's lax scheduling could be regarded as a life style characteristic of the artistic temperament."[95] Speer was baffled at the way Hitler squandered his working time and would often ask himself: When does he really work? According to Speer's observations, Hitler would often allow a problem to mature during the weeks when he seemed entirely taken up with trivial matters and then arrive at a sudden insight into its solution.[96] Similar to this Berlin style of apparent triviality and torpor, Hitler would spend the weeks before the great Nuremberg rallies on "the mountain" on the Obersalzberg, successfully avoiding the bureaucracy of a major power and putting off the dictation of his sometimes vast pronouncements on Reich policy. More commonly than for Nuremberg preparations, however, Hitler would ascend the mountain to conduct his life in the Bohemian manner of the artist who would not submit to regular work. Under the conditions of both Nuremberg preparation and the rejection of bureaucratic process, however, Hitler seemed to have been "tinkering" with projected political actions. Those actions would have been of interest to him and known to him alone. We can generalize that Hitler did mostly what he felt like doing in the period, and only sometimes did what he had to.

*   *   *

In September 1938, this artist-messiah confronted Chamberlain, Daladier, and Beneš, who had inherited ugly and outmoded historical situations out of the past. Although Chamberlain and Hitler had agreed upon a plebiscite in the German districts at their Berchtesgaden meeting, the Czech authorities immediately began to use Czech army and police forces to frighten the German residents out of the country. Under the existing military occupation and with the institution of martial law the Czech authorities accelerated beatings of Germans and burnings of offending homes. Between the meetings at Berchtesgaden and Godesberg, therefore, the Czechs daily engaged in acts of abuse associated with military occupation and martial law applied to a bitter foreign population. Hitler's dramatic and seemingly bizarre capriciousness is explained significantly by the consideration that every day in which the already-agreed-upon plebiscite was delayed the German population would suffer more casualties and damage. Chamberlain was unsympathetic to the immediate occupation of the German Sudetenland even though "to be sure, the new boundary proposed by Hitler corresponded very closely to the line we have been considering."[97] And Ivone Kirkpatrick, a member of the party that received Hitler's repeated demand of "the need of immediate steps to rescue the Sudeten Germans from 'Czech Tyranny'" was uneasy about the prime minister's reluctance to agree to the immediate entry of German forces.[98] Kirkpatrick would think that "if we were prepared to agree to the cession of the territory, it seemed illogical to object to its [timely] military occupation."[99]

Hitler's revised memorandum of September 23 set forth his proposals for the redeeming of the rimland Germans as tersely as such a thing could be done with a view toward urgency and finality. But Chamberlain would characterize the document as an ultimatum and his accompanying ambassador to Germany would refer to it in a notable historical irony as "*ein Diktat.*" Hitler would reply with a kind of sardonic innocence that it was entitled, "Memorandum." Then, in a brief scene in which Chamberlain encapsulated the pique of a mighty overseas empire and Hitler the frustration of a powerful, more straightforward ground power, the following words flew: Chamberlain would observe that Hitler "was behaving like a conqueror," and Hitler would retort, "No, like an owner of his property."[100] Hitler would propose that since incidents involving violence to Sudeten Germans were increasing, it was essential that the separation agreed to by the Czechs "be affected without any further delay." Chamberlain would consider Hitler's time table initially to begin September 26 and then altered to October 1 as so presumptuous that war was the necessary alternative to the beginning of Czech evacuation of Sudeten German territory. In London, the

South African high commissioner delivered a message to Chamberlain from Prime Minister General James B. M. Hertzog which stated "that he and his colleagues feel that the Berlin proposals should be accepted" and reiterated "that South Africa cannot be expected to take part in a war over Czechoslovakia."[101] And later, on the morning of September 27, Hertzog would sum up the entire moral balance in the crisis in a message to London that "if after this a European war is still to take place, the responsibility for that will not be placed upon the shoulders of Germany."[102]

But war would not take place because, through the last-minute miracle of the September 30 Munich conference, Hitler would insert the Sudeten Germans into a Greater Germany. As the Czech crisis subsided and the Polish crisis dawned, the British and the French, as "the Allies" of 1918, would continue to bear fearful burdens for every important international crisis that had involved Germany from 1918 through 1939. But how could Hitler, as a world-historical personality, be hemmed in by such a scene? Perhaps it could be generalized that the Franco-British times had created a German messiah who, by the turn of 1939, would complete the transition to a full-blown world-historical personality. No member of any British or French government could have known of the very existence of Corporal Hitler in 1919, and none would know his intentions twenty years later. Seen as such, those governments cannot be absolved of their decision to fight a preventive war by claim of clairvoyance about Hitler. Fueled by their own earlier perfidies and injustices and according to an agenda of the continuation of hegemony over the continent, they advanced into a war forced on themselves by themselves. But Hitler, literally as a single man—although speaking for unwitting Germans in the matter of a European war—would advance into it as a war forced on himself by himself.

We face a historical phenomenon of two bodies of blame occupying the same place at the same time. Such a situation can end only in an unsatisfactory interpretation of shared blame for the war and suggests the following reality: two wars broke out in 1939. The

British and the French governments would open a war against Germany at a time and a place of their own choosing over the ostensible issue of Polish territorial integrity, in contrast to the actual issue of maintaining their political and military control of the continent. The French and British governments would intend a Europe-wide preventive war against Germany. Hitler would open a war against Poland at a time and place of his choosing over the ostensible issue of German territorial integrity in contrast to the actual issue of seizing a land empire in the east. Hitler would intend a war exclusively between Germany and Poland. Neither side had a particular moral advantage on the ostensible issues: Hitler had a reasonable case for adjustments in the Polish Corridor and German Danzig but had degraded his case by the military occupation of the Czech part of the new Czechoslovakia earlier in the year; the Allies thus had a reasonable case to intervene politically because of Hitler's earlier action. But in the actual issues embraced by the opposing sides, we see two wars beginning between September 1 and 3.

The Allies would commit themselves to a toughly conceived preventive war against an enemy hopelessly misconceived as the same old Germans disturbing the peace of Europe. Hitler, however, was not a same old German, and when unwittingly forced into a war with Britain and France in early September, would commit himself to one of breathtaking proportion. The Allies could not conceptualize that they were dealing with a man who had recently saved the Germans from the Marxists internally in 1933. And they could not know that this savior, unknown to them, had made the transition to world-historical personality by the turn of 1939. The earnest adolescent of Linz and 1908 Vienna described by Kubizek had arrived as the most intense personality of the ages. The can't-you-see, matchless personality defined by Hess, the proto-messiah agonized over by Eckart in Berlin and Munich, the golden-voiced, silver-tongued speaker rapturously described by Hanfstaengl, the some-sort-of-magnetic-gift witnessed and recorded by Prince Otto von Habsburg, the thousand-year genius granted by Franz Pfeffer von

Salomon, the stunning voice of guttural thunder artfully analyzed by Konrad Heiden: "Inside this unlikely creature there resided a miracle." All these guises must be factored in to measure the man in 1939. This unwilling foe of the British and the French—brother nations of highest culture—was characterized by infinite seriousness and an unmatched artistic will to create the stone monuments merited by an immortal Reich. This *wahnfriedische*–Lohengrin–Hitler was also armed with the unmatched political will to subdue the eastern Slavs and the iron logic to pull together the whole business as a cataclysmic struggle between the German nation and the forces of Jewish Marxist internationalism.

This above historical handful—this Adolf Hitler—would enter 1939 with the military occupation of the Czech part of Czechoslovakia in a bitterly cold March. With this entry, Hitler would face the immense consequences of no longer having a moral advantage over his diplomatic adversaries. Although Hitler linked the occupation of Bohemia and Moravia with support for a powerful Slovakian independence movement, he had nevertheless set aside the Munich Agreement. Within three weeks, a severely piqued Chamberlain would unilaterally guarantee the territorial integrity of Poland, the Polish government accept, and the French government accede. If Hitler blundered in 1939, it was probably at this moment. But he was already on the move toward smashing the Polish state and could not accept the presence of a Czech war front in any realistic calculation of success. If Chamberlain blundered in 1939, it would have been to have continued to trifle with German power, particularly in combination with the moral strength of Hitler's Polish challenge to the Paris Peace Conference and notwithstanding his morally indefensible occupation of Bohemia and Moravia. But Chamberlain continued to be divorced from the lingering inequities of Paris. And with breathtaking ruthlessness in the pursuit of British interests, he would guarantee Poland's territorial integrity without the remotest military capability to do so, even allied with France.

On the other hand, later, between June and August, the British,

French, and Soviet governments would conduct negotiations for a diplomatic front with the realistic potential to constrain Germany. At the beginning of August, Hitler faced the impossible prospect of a war simultaneously with Poland, Britain, France, and Soviet Russia if he were to order an advance to smash the Polish state. Chamberlain and Daladier faced the unenviable prospect of a war with Germany and the towering, although apparently invisible, moral dilemma of being incapable of securing Poland. Józef Beck, the intrepid but overconfident Polish foreign minister, proceeded with reckless disregard for the realities of revived German power, Soviet Russian claim to territory lying to its west, and Anglo-French distance and lack of dedication to the immediate defense of Poland. And in early August, to compound Hitler's difficulties, Josef Stalin would allow the conduct of dilatory but dangerous negotiations with the British and French governments for some agreement over the Polish situation. Earlier in 1939, however, he had replaced the perennial Western-oriented foreign minister Maksim Litvinov with a new man, Vyacheslav Molotov, capable of conducting a supremely pragmatic foreign policy to include serious negotiations with Hitler's foreign minister.

By mid-August all things were in place for change on the continent of Europe. The British and French were prepared to fight a preventive war over the Polish issue under conditions that they had come to assume would be more auspicious than at any future time. The Polish government, with infinite disregard for reality, was not necessarily prepared for war but entirely prepared to fight one. During the first half of the month the Italian government in the Ciano negotiations had given Hitler additional freedom of maneuver by agreeing to fight if Germany went to war. Within this picture of danger and opportunity Hitler stood immobilized by the forbidding potential of a four-front war—naval fronts in the North Sea and Baltic and land fronts with France and a Poland reinforced, in some way or other, by Soviet Russia. But on August 19 in Moscow, Molotov would hand to the German negotiator, Ambassador Count Friedrich Werner von der

Schulenburg, a draft of a nonaggression pact to go along with a completed and about-to-be signed economic agreement. The economic agreement would be signed on August 20, and the diplomatic coup for the ages—the German-Soviet Nonaggression Pact—three days later. For Hitler, the timing of this supreme coup was exquisite. It allowed for an autumn ground campaign against Poland under weather conditions favorable for German ground and air forces on the offensive. And at the highest level of political–military calculation, Hitler had come to believe that any further delay in the near-inevitable war in the west must result in Britain and France growing relatively stronger than Germany.

During 1939, Hitler would still have preferred a vast strategic accommodation with Britain specifically to recognize its overseas empire and parallel control of the ocean seas. In return, he would have required a free hand in the east. The position of France in such a situation illuminates Hitler particularly well. No evidence exists in terms of specific word or general argument on Hitler's part to show that he "hated" the French or France. With a kind of calm detachment, Hitler, at worst, would manage to say that in any diplomatic crisis in Europe, France would always be ranged with Germany's enemies. He would acknowledge the similar superiorities of the French, British, and German peoples in culture and civilization, and this acknowledgement would make the French proof against boundary change or colonization in the event of German victory in the east. But no Frenchman knew this, and every French government had to assume through its own hate and prudence that Hitler's Germany would turn on France at first opportunity and "destroy" it. Hitler, therefore, faced the almost insufferable dilemma and historical inanity of having to subdue a France that should not have been an enemy of Germany according to his own National Socialist *Weltanschauung*. We could generalize colorfully that Hitler would pass by us in late 1939 as the "*wahnfriedische*–Lohengrin " on his way to save the Germans from Soviet Russia, the great danger and opportunity lying to the east. Unlike Lohengrin, however he would face

equally great danger from the culturally allied peoples lying to the
west who were—momentarily, at least—more concerned about
being saved from Germans than being overrun by Russians.

Chapter 9

THE SIEGE OF GERMANY

Hitler faced a nightmarish strategic–geographic situation on September 3, 1939, in which he had cast Germany into a war on two land fronts in Europe. At the highest level of consideration, he had hoped to have a free hand from the west for a short campaign against Poland. He hoped to have the same free hand for a great, final advance into western Soviet Russia. But after his masterstroke of the nonaggression pact with the Soviets, the British government nonetheless opted for a preventive war against Germany and he found himself locked into his ultimate nightmare: not only an unintended war against Britain, but also one on two fronts. The Poles would surrender Warsaw on September 27, signaling the end of the campaign in fewer than a month. The quick German victory would support a view that the Polish campaign has little interest either militarily or politically because of the mismatch between the opposing armed forces. But on September 3, no one knew of the future German victory of September 27, and the strategic situation for Germany was hardly a mismatch with Britain, France, and Poland opposed to it. Alfred Jodl, as chief *Oberkommando der Wehrmacht* (OKW) operations staff at war's outbreak, would remark that Germany faced potential immediate defeat in the war in the event that the 110 divisions of the French Army moved against the twenty-five German divisions in the west. The essence of the matter for Hitler on September 3 was that the *Wehrmacht* had to not just defeat the Poles but defeat them immediately. Neither Hitler nor the army, with the baggage of World War I still on both of their backs, could have anticipated a campaign of fewer than several months with the attendant danger of a French advance and Soviet change in outlook. The campaign was never a mismatch from the viewpoint of the speed with which it had to be executed, and it cost the Germans significant casualties. Hitler had no serious impact as concerns the military operations and only in October, after the Polish Campaign, did he begin to function as the effective commander of the *Wehrmacht* at war.

Having been forced by chance into the wrong war, although probably at the right time, Hitler had to adjust to a new reality of Germany endangered in its very survival. He had practically no time to make this adjustment, yet by October 9 he had issued a directive for an attack in the west. In accordance with this directive, *Oberkommando des Heeres* (OKH or high command of the army) issued the operation order of October 19 for such an advance scheduled for November 12. OKH had little confidence in the success of the attack but was unable to deter Hitler in a last-ditch confrontation a week before what it considered to be an advance into planned disaster. For purposes of comprehending Hitler, we have a unique opportunity at the beginning of his conduct of World War II to understand his characteristic style and the concept that dominated his strategy.

With astonishing quickness, Hitler would direct the field armies to the west for an immediate attack against France and Belgium. Scheduled for November 12 and then rescheduled for twelve days later, the attack flew in the face of the most fundamental consideration for offensive military operations—season and associated day-to-day weather. If the attack had taken place, it would almost certainly have failed to achieve any decisive result because the German operational trumps, namely, their excellent and numerous air force and moderate-sized but tactically superior motorized ground forces, would have been negated. Hitler would persist nonetheless and give as high level strategic rationale for an immediate offensive that every day that passed the allies would grow relatively stronger than Germany. The great biographers and historians have recognized this immoderate urge to attack and linked it with seamless determination on Hitler's part to knock France out of the war in a blitz campaign. The operational plan controversy over which plan to employ for an attack in the west fails to support the conventional wisdom's view of Hitler's intent for the French campaign and, necessarily, the remainder of the war. *Generalmajor* Erich von Manstein, at the time chief of staff of Army Group A, one of only two army groups assembled for offensive operations in the west, published the most authoritative account of the whole business shortly after the war's end. In his account, he presented a crushing indictment of the Hitler and OKH attack order of October 19, 1939, which continued in effect through February 20, 1940. In his objections to the order, he noted that "the 1939 operation plan...contained no clear-cut intention of fighting the campaign to a victorious conclusion. Its object was, quite clearly, partial victory (defeat of the Allied forces in northern Belgium) and territorial gains (possession of the channel coast as a basis for future operations)."[1] In support of this view that Hitler had no intention to launch a blitzkrieg to conquer France, Manstein quoted the general intention of the entire attack in the west as: "To defeat the largest possible elements of the French and Allied Armies and simultaneously to gain as much territory as possible in Holland, Belgium, and Northern France as a basis for successful air and sea operations against Britain and as a broad protective zone for the Ruhr."[2] Based on such evidence, it must be held that Hitler had no intention of conquering France in a single, swift blow. *General der Artillerie* Franz Halder, chief of staff at OKH, would note in his war diary Hitler's concern over the situation in the west, which could be paraphrased: one dark night during the autumn fogs, the Allies will move into Belgium and take it without firing a shot.[3] The commander of Army Group B, *Generaloberst* Fedor von Bock, would note in his diary: "Once again [Hitler] justified the compelling necessity to attack soon with the need for greater security for the Ruhr region, and with the necessity for better air and U-boat bases."[4] For whatever the reasons, Hitler was determined from late September 1939 through February 20, 1940, to launch the main concentration of the German Army into an attack in the west with indecisive objective.

When Hitler personally put in effect the new and final plan of February 20—the so-called Manstein Plan—the army would receive a directive with the decisive objective to destroy the French army and occupy France. Manstein would envision nothing less. Quite amazingly, however, and independently of Manstein, Hitler had come to virtually identical conclusions about the scheme of maneuver for the great opening advance. Two powerful minds would therefore agree over the opening moves. It does not necessarily follow, however, that they both either intended or expected a blitz victory over France with the unfolding of those identical opening moves. Manstein intended such a victory, but compelling evidence exists to show that Hitler intended a more certain seizure of Belgium and had little or no expectations of the conquest of France. Months before the adoption of the Manstein Plan, Hitler had pressed for an immediate advance for late October or early November against the west. Hitler could not have made more clear its purpose and dimensions.

Bock, for example, would be directed along with others to meet with Hitler on October 25 and noted the following conclusive thinking:

> The Fuehrer…justified the need for the attack. If the enemy arrives at the Belgian–German border first, the situation for us— he said—would be untenable, for the threat to the Rhine industrial region…would paralyze the production potential in the heart of our armament industry. We cannot wait! Our situation is favorable, the situation over there is not. But in time the others will become stronger than we can. As well there is the risk that one fine day we will wake up to the news that the enemy is standing at the Belgian–German border![5]

Hitler at that moment saw the advance in the west as an immediate necessity to seize Belgium and was willing to risk an attack by the entire German army for so indecisive an objective. Hitler would later conceptualize an advance through the Ardennes virtually identical to that of Manstein, but he would intend it to seize Belgium more quickly and surely.

Two other pieces of evidence cement this view of Hitler as locked into a mentality of siege lines drawn around Germany by Britain and France. As the advance of May 10, 1940, opened according to the Manstein Plan of maneuver, Hitler would order halts to the attack of the main armored force advancing west along the French–Belgian border toward the channel. Early on May 17, *General der Panzertruppen* Heinz Guderian, leading the main armored spearhead of the entire advance in the west, would be ordered to halt only seventy miles from Sedan and less than halfway to the channel. If Hitler had enforced his own order more successfully, the result would have been incalculable and would have included the possibility of the Allies not being forced even out of Belgium. In the second, better-known order, Hitler would halt Guderian's armor near Dunkirk. Notwithstanding this order, however, Hitler would at least achieve the seizure of Belgium three days later.

These orders, the first one still virtually unknown to the great biographers, reveal Hitler as a tactically nervous new *Feldherr* concerned largely about the assured conquest of Belgium but hardly that of France. In the first order, Hitler would fear that French forces moving up from the south would interfere with the assured fall of Belgium. He was not concerned that the German "armored wedge" would get to the channel and seal the fate of France. Halder would annotate on May 17: "An unpleasant day. The Fuehrer is terribly nervous. Frightened by his own success, he is afraid to take any chance and so would pull in the reins on us."[6] And on the following day, Hitler would continue to act in a way not understandable to Halder: "The Fuehrer unaccountably keeps worrying about the south flank [the armored wedge and trailing infantry out of Sedan]. He rages and screams that we are on the best way to ruin the whole campaign and that we are leading up to a defeat. He won't have any part of continuing the operation in westward direction [to achieve the conquest of France]...and still clings to the plan of a north-western drive [to achieve the assured conquest of Belgium]."[7] It is difficult to escape the feeling that Hitler saw the French campaign as actually a Belgian exercise in the improvement of the siege lines drawn around Germany in the west.

In spite of his unanticipated blitz success in May, Hitler would continue to intervene in operations in June, now exclusively in France. He would show the same concern about German war pro-duction and the siege lines of early June around Germany. In the face of the great advance south, which began on June 5 and showed OKH pursuing the quick military defeat of France, Hitler would give the following version of the goals of the rest of the campaign. Halder would paraphrase Hitler as arguing that the June campaign was calculated to deny the enemy possession of his iron ore resources in Lorraine. Hitler argued, "With them gone, it's all over with his armament industry."[8] Here we see him within a fluid cam-paign in June, and the final part of the great blitz envisioned by Manstein arguing for the seizure of Lorraine rather than the destruction of the French army.

*   *   *

From the beginning of the October 1939 planning for the campaign in the west, the commander of the German navy, Admiral Erich Raeder, had emphasized the concept of a counter siege of Britain that would require naval bases along the Belgian and northwestern French coasts and Norway. As planning for an attack in the west pro-ceeded in 1939 and actual alerts for attack were issued, Raeder warned that in the event of a German move into the Lowlands, the British might seize a base in Norway. Independently of Raeder, Vidkun Quisling, an influential nationalist politician in Norway, would visit Hitler on several occasions in 1939 and warn him that the Norwegian government had agreed not to oppose a British invasion if Norway became involved in hostilities with Germany. Most significantly in all of this was that, "as long as the Lorraine mines stayed in French hands, the German war machine was absolutely dependent on Swedish iron ore. During the warmer months the ore could be shipped...through the Baltic; but in winter when ice closed the Baltic ports, the ore had to be loaded at Narvik on the Norwegian Atlantic coast."[9] The ore boats would then travel one thousand miles in Norwegian territorial waters and through a short, loose British naval blockade to Germany. In the event of the British seizure of Norway, Hitler would face the reality of a terminal tightening of the siege lines around Germany, exemplified by the loss of the Swedish iron ore.

On December 14, Hitler instructed OKW to investigate how the German armed forces could take Norway and stipulated strict secrecy. The secrecy was so tight that Halder would note in his diary on February 21, 1940, that "not a single word has passed between the Fuehrer and ObdH [*Generaloberst* Walther von Brauchitsch]; this must be put on record for the history of the war."[10] Hitler could be generalized as taking personal responsibility for this daring, successful campaign and put army *Generalleutnant* Nikolaus von Falkenhorst in charge of planning under control of himself and OKW. The situation was complicated by the Soviet attack on Finland in late November 1939. The danger emerged that the British and French governments would seize Narvik in order to come to the assistance of the Finns by way of that port and northern Sweden. The signing of a peace treaty between Russia and Finland on March 12 would avert this menace for Germany and remove, temporarily, the opportunity for the British and French governments to act. But after March 21, the new French premier, Paul Reynaud, committed France to more aggressive prosecution of the war, and the Allied Supreme War Council put together two operations that were intended to cut off Germany from the Swedish iron ore. Operation Wilfred involved the laying of minefields in the Norwegian territorial waters, known as the Leads, to interdict the German ore boats.

Allied Plan R4 involved an Anglo-French amphibious operation against Norway with the armed seizure of Bergen, Trondheim, and Narvik and the conquest of about half the country.

Hitler, using OKW, would put together Operation *Weseruebung* and would forestall so dangerous an Allied adventure. Hitler put together a theater-level operation of boldness and daring unmatched in World War II. He would launch an amphibious operation against an enemy who had complete control of the sea and was prepared for the contingency of German counter-action against Allied violation of Norwegian territory. On April 1, Hitler conducted a review of *Weseruebung* and commented that the days until the occupation of Norway was complete would impose on him the greatest nervous strain of his life. The Fuehrer Directive of March 1 for the Norwegian invasion had promptly brought a wave of protests from the army and Luftwaffe, and Hitler would have had substantial support only from the navy. In so lonely a situation, Hitler would later show tactical jitters during the campaign. His strategic nerves, however, would hold until the time that success in the west assured similar in Norway.

Hitler would order *Weseruebung* to begin at 0515 on April 9, 1940, and encounter the most bizarre opening of any campaign in World War II. At virtually the same time, an Allied mine-laying force operating under Operation Wilfred had begun to lay mines in two fields in Norwegian waters between Bergen and more northerly Trondheim on the morning of April 8. The British mine-laying force accordingly found itself in and among German warships laden with troops already on the move and tasked to land and seize Trondheim and Narvik on the morning of April 9. The Allies had also concentrated army units and shipping for landings in Norway in the event that the Germans showed that they intended to land there as a counteraction to the mine laying. Accordingly, it is difficult to determine whether the Allies or the Germans were the aggressors in Norway in April 1940. The generalization can probably be made that both were aggressors, and the Germans turned out to be the more effective ones.

From the German side, Hitler was the driving force in bringing the campaign into existence even though he had initially been lukewarm to Raeder's cautious 1939 entreaties. But when he faced the danger of an Allied move through northern Norway to aid the Finns at the turn of 1940—and the associated loss of the Swedish iron ore imports—Hitler recognized the strategic necessity to seize Norway before the Allies. Although Hitler would need the indispensable support of the *Kriegsmarine*, he would be the bold designer and nervous executor of the campaign. He would employ OKW to put together the pieces of the operation. He would not inform OKH and its included army general staff and instead present it with a *fait accompli* in late February. Similar to his pacing of the French campaign to the assured seizure of Belgium and resultant security for the Ruhr, he would pace the Norwegian campaign to the seizure of Narvik and the resultant security of the high-grade Swedish ore fields lying immediately to the southeast. Perhaps the surest indicator of Hitler's motive in creating and launching *Weseruebung* would be the British motive in creating and launching its own Norwegian operation. The British in particular would recognize Germany's weakness in terms of strategic natural resources and what amounted to tight siege lines drawn around Germany, especially in the west and Scandinavia. Late in November 1939, for example, the British Ministry of Economic Warfare expressed the view that, cut off from the Swedish ore supply, Germany could not continue the war for more than twelve months.[11] And earlier in September, the first lord of the admiralty had submitted a plan to force the straits into the Baltic to stop the summer Swedish ore traffic. The British operations in April 1940 can be seen almost exclusively intended to block that traffic and cause the Germans acute if not fatal embarrassment. It follows almost axiomatically that Hitler intended an entire campaign of World War II to safeguard an economic resource and, in effect, to improve the encircling lines set around Germany.

As concerns Hitler's capabilities and style as highest level military commander, he presents strategic boldness and daring difficult to exaggerate. Later in the war and far away in the Pacific, the most powerful naval forces of the war—the US Pacific Fleet—would spend months, in some cases from 1943 onward, in air attack, surface naval engagement, and shore bombardment intended to achieve aerial and surface supremacy around small island targets prior to amphibious landings. Hitler would launch his campaign into the teeth of the British navy in its own front yard of the North and Norwegian Seas, all with modest air superiority compared with the doctrinal air supremacy of the Americans in the Pacific. The Allies would be strong enough between April 14 and 19 to counter-land eight thousand troops north and south of Trondheim. Hitler's strategic boldness would stand out in the mismatch among forces in the campaign to the disadvantage of Germany. Raeder would present the almost hopeless German situation during the following crisis. The Allied threat to Trondheim threw Hitler into a tactical panic that led him, on April 22, to propose using the liners *Bremen* and *Europa* to transfer an entire division to Trondheim. Raeder would protest and put the whole campaign within its daring perspective by noting that "the entire fleet would be needed to escort the ships and that the probable outcome would be the loss of both transports and the [entire German] fleet."[12] The Germans would be forced to transport the first waves of the earlier successful landing in fast warships that boldly took advantage of varying degrees of surprise to disembark troops over Norwegian port facilities.

The German forces would ultimately be rewarded with complete success. The army would seize and hold Narvik, and the Luftwaffe would successfully resupply the ground forces at several crucial junctures and keep the British Fleet at bay. The navy, in spite of its weakness, delivered troops and supplies in the warship groups and the following sea transport echelons with initially heavy but eventually manageable losses. Similar to the case in the west, Hitler would force the pace of the planning for the operation and would interfere severely in the details of the actual battles. We are left with a picture of Hitler conducting the Scandinavian campaign similar to the way he conducted the French. This is not surprising, and it gives us valuable insights into how he conducted the early successful campaigns. Knowing how Hitler conducted, or at least participated in, the two campaigns nevertheless spins us away from *why* he conducted the two campaigns at all. After Hitler blundered into a war with the West, he had choices of strategies to pursue. By late June 1940, both the French and the Scandinavian campaigns had been completed, and we should be able to discover why he conducted each and the common factors that connected them.

The entrenched wisdom would claim that Hitler conducted the French campaign as a purposeful blitzkrieg. It would support its view partly by claiming that Hitler constructed the *Autobahnen* for military purposes and supported the motorization of the German army for anticipated future blitzkrieg-styled operations. It cannot be claimed seriously, however, that Hitler constructed the German super-highway system for military purposes. He constructed it to provide work for Germans beginning in early 1933. He also did it to encourage the relatively small German automobile industry to expand— specifically to produce as many as six million "peoples' autos" to be used on an improved road system. But on the other hand, no less an authority on blitzkrieg than Heinz Guderian recorded that, at a demonstration of motorized troops at Kummersdorf south of Berlin in early 1933, Hitler was impressed and said repeatedly: "That's what I need! That's what I want to have!"[13] It is doubtful that he anticipated a partly motorized war against serious opposition in the coming few years. It is more likely that he sensed possibilities for the bloodless *faits accomplis* that took place between 1936 and 1939. Despite the success of the motorized forces in Poland, Hitler cannot be seen as having had realistic hope of defeating quickly, or otherwise, the higher quality and larger French and British armies deployed in France.

By the end of June, Hitler faced success both in the west and north. Based on his two quick successes, the conventional wisdom as noted has seen the French campaign as a purposeful blitz intended to conquer France, and the Norwegian campaign as a parallel naval blitz intended to seize Norway. But additional evidence exists to show that Hitler did not intend a blitz to overwhelm France. In early March 1940, Hitler attended a conference in the *Reichskanzlei* in which the higher commanders in Army Group A presented their tasks and how they intended to carry them out. The army group, with its more than forty divisions, had become under the Manstein Plan the point of major effort in the offensive. Within the army group, the main point of effort lay with Panzer Group Kleist and ultimately its Sixteenth Panzer Corps under Guderian. Manstein's planned victory over France would be won or lost according to Guderian's success. Hitler's planned seizure of Belgium would be carried or miscarried according to the same success.

Guderian was last to speak and described his task as, after various adventures in the Ardennes, to cross the Meuse River on the fifth day. Notably, this conference about the course of the entire campaign, either Manstein's or Hitler's, focused almost exclusively on crossing the Meuse. From the level of the big picture, Hitler asked, "'And then what are you going to do?' He was the first person to ask this vital question."[14] Guderian replied that he intended to continue his drive westward, and Hitler would have to decide whether his objective would be Paris or Amiens. Guderian opined that the correct course would be to drive past Amiens to the channel. Hitler nodded in assent. At this point, one of three army commanders comprising Army Group A exclaimed, "I don't think you'll cross the river in the first place!" This statement in front of Hitler suggests that many in the army viewed a lightning conquest of France as hopelessly optimistic. The concern over the crossing of the Meuse and lack of attention about what to do afterward suggests that Hitler's fundamental concern about the seizure of Belgium and associated channel ports was realistic and in touch with the art of the possible prior to the attack. A problem in history, or perhaps *the* problem, was that the end result might have actually intruded on reality. Because Hitler won a blitz victory over France does not necessarily mean that he intended such.

Hitler's Luftwaffe adjutant, *Hauptmann* Nicolaus von Below, was in close proximity to Hitler from 1937 through 1945—close enough to note in late November 1939 as evidence of that closeness: "After the evening meal Hitler took me into the large situation room, where we walked the length of the room together. He wanted to speak his thoughts aloud in order to detect errors in his planning."[15] This walk took place on the same day of Hitler's meeting with the highest level commanders of the three armed forces and shows Hitler using the taciturn and laconic Below as a trusted sounding board for his own ideas. Below could recall Hitler remarking earlier in the day that the outcome of the war would depend on who held the Ruhr.[16] He would also recall Hitler remarking that it was important to have better bases from which to strike England from the air. In October and November, Hitler would also spend a great deal of time contemplating, in the OKW situation room, a relief map of the territory in Belgium and France over which the attack would take place. While tactically juggling two mobile divisions, he recognized the strategic advantages of mossing the bulk of the German armor for a daring, more decisive drive west through Sedan. As noted previously, the plans of advance of Manstein and Hitler would coincide, but the former intended the quick defeat of France while the latter intended adequate protection of the Ruhr. But success of the Manstein Plan would automatically result in the defeat of France and protection of the strategic resource. Hitler nevertheless incessantly proclaimed protection for the Ruhr as his intent for the advance in the west. This extraordinary half-measure paves the way to a more adequate interpretation of Hitler's conduct of the war on the offensive. The apparent half-measure of the Ruhr can be interpreted as a strategy to establish and maintain fortress lines around Germany adequate for eventual victory over the West.

Hitler would operate under the same rationale in the later Balkan and Russian Campaigns. Reality is obscured by his unwitting success in France and the presence of a blitz army operating alongside of a siege Fuehrer. Reality is obscured further by Hitler's unparalleled boldness in launching himself into full-fledged campaigns to secure unexciting territorial targets in order to protect even less exciting economic areas. Obscured or otherwise, this reality gives us a superior interpretation of Hitler's conduct of the winning phase of the war. His conceptualization of indispensable economic areas and the strategic imperative to hold them gives us a half-century missing interpretation of his inflexible conduct of the losing phase of the war. The revised interpretation reveals Hitler as having the same strategic imperatives at the beginning of the war as at its ending. The imperatives: seizing boldly and holding inflexibly the fortress lines necessary for German survival.

In July 1940, after the victories in France and Norway, Hitler faced the question of what to do next in the war. His military operations had exceeded expectations, having led to the defeat of one major power and caused another "to beat a retreat to his island fastness."[17] Faced with icy indifference to his peace offer to Britain, Hitler seemingly would be forced to thrash about to develop a revised grand strategy. The air battles over southern England and the channel that began in July and lasted until October had no clear or decisive military objective. As such, the air battles seem to show Hitler muddling. But for Hitler the bombing raids, particularly on London, were supported by political and psychological rationale and were intended to ease Britain into a political settlement. As the air battles developed over Britain in July, Hitler would conceive the plan to tackle Britain by invasion but would not make up his mind to execute his own plan. The plan, Operation Sealion, was bound to involve big risks and was broached by Hitler too late to take advantage of the last late-summer weather of August to make a realistic amphibious operation in southeastern England. The "Battle" of Britain would drag on to about October 31 and end with heavy losses on both sides: somewhat surprisingly, 1,172 British Hurricanes, Spitfires, Blenheims, and Defiants of the Royal Air Force (RAF) Fighter Command compared with significantly fewer, 845 German BF 109Es and BF 110Cs. The Germans had, of course, heavy additional losses in bombers, but the whole business would be summarized by a British authority as: "Neither side had been defeated, but both sides were battered and weary."[18]

From July through October, Hitler wrestled with the possibilities of either easing or knocking Britain out of the war. He could not have thought that he could end the war with long range bombardment of any enemy of the quality of the British. And as concerns an invasion of the island, he was plainly unwilling to accept the defining consequences of a defeat: "It was clear even then that Hitler did not have his heart in the operation. At all levels the preparations lacked that driving force from the top which was usually so apparent."[19] And driving force notwithstanding, Hitler faced an intact RAF and Royal Navy combined with the onset of autumn weather that alone could have prevented a landing. A compromise plan for invasion would only be put together by late August, forcing the landing itself into dreaded autumn. The plan, however, gave "the Army a landing force and a landing area it believed inadequate, and the Navy a responsibility for transport which it feared would be too great."[20] The Luftwaffe gave little consideration to the matter while indirectly supporting it with its own private war with the RAF.[21]

By this time in the war, after the Battle of France, Hitler had ceased to consult the commanders-in-chief of the three armed forces on matters of grand strategy and ultimately made decisions based on his inspirations alone. Hitler applied superior instincts, brooded over operational maps, and used strategic–geographic analysis to get at the possibilities for German victory in the war. These instincts and his characteristic intense study of problems would have led him to the more realistic option to ease Britain out of the war by aerial and naval warfare.

The conventional wisdom has taken the view that after the conquest of France, Hitler saw victory in World War II as equivalent to the defeat of Britain. The defeat could be seen as a mutually agreed, negotiated settlement as forced on Britain by German success in an aerial bombing campaign or outright invasion and conquest. Hitler had accomplished none of these by the time of the cancellation of Sealion on September 17, 1940. The great biographers accordingly have characterized Hitler's strategy as one to force Britain out of the war somehow, in spite of the above. But earlier, in July, at the beginning of the aerial battles over Britain and the inception of Sealion, Hitler had also directed *Generalfeldmarschall* Brauchitsch to submit plans for a campaign against Soviet Russia. This was a lot of activity even for a world-historical personality. And the question for a busy July 1940 is: Did Hitler embark on the defeat of Britain and incidentally throw Russia into the strategic mix, or did Hitler embark on the world epochal saga to the east?

The great biographers italicize Hitler's words recorded by the army chief of staff Franz Halder to the effect that the surest way to force Britain out of the war would be to deny her the hope of salvation by a powerful alliance partner—specifically, Soviet Russia. It is difficult to believe, indeed impossible to believe, that Hitler used these words as anything other than a softening justification for the enormity of an attack on Soviet Russia. Since the dictation of *Mein Kampf* in 1924 and 1925 and his second unpublished work in 1928, Hitler had asserted that Germany's destiny lay in the east and would be realized only through force of arms. For the great biographers to assert that Hitler attacked Soviet Russia to knock Britain out of a war in the west is historically grotesque—deformed by interpretive malnutrition. We are asked to believe that Hitler would plan and execute an attack that, if victorious, would achieve final German destiny, but that he would do so with the lesser included intent to knock Britain out of the half-war of 1940 and 1941. We see the great biographers presenting an Anglocentric view of the course of the war in those two years that flies in the face of German and Soviet Russian power.

We are better served to see Hitler directing the beginning of planning for an attack against Soviet Russia that would achieve German destiny and win World War II notwithstanding virtually any course of action that might have been taken by Britain. July was a busy month in which Hitler directed the Luftwaffe against Britain, planned a cross-channel invasion, and prepared for an attack on Soviet Russia. Even in the life of a thousand-year world-historical personality, Hitler showed impressive activity—orders to attack the greatest sea power and the largest air and ground power in the world. Such a scene presents a biographer with the opportunity to define Hitler and the course of World War II. Particularly with the army, Hitler had to be convincing in his rationale for so extreme a situation. Even for the man who had begun to make the great strategic decisions for Germany entirely alone, his decisions had to be carried out by others, particularly at the higher levels, who had to be convinced of the rationale, necessity, and desirability of his directives. But for Hitler, his premier strength both as messiah and as world-historical personality was his capability to be convincing. When Hitler was only nineteen years old, his friend August Kubizek could record in amazement Hitler's capability to convince his father to allow his son to study at the Vienna music academy rather than continue to apprentice as a furniture upholsterer. And Kubizek would put Hitler together at the same age as a bundle of the two following characteristics: essentially, intensity without equal and the ability to convince. Given the active circumstances of July, a serious Hitler would require a convincing rationale to embark almost immediately after the French campaign in an attack against an opponent with the dimensions of Soviet Russia.

In his July 31 conference at the Berghof with his military leaders Hitler would expound on the course of the war to that date and then move to a momentous conclusion obviously intended to be convincing and conclusive. After stating earlier in the conference that "Russia was the factor on which England is relying the most,"[22] he would conclude according to Halder's notes: "With Russia smashed, England's last hope would be shattered.... Russia's destruction must therefore be made a part of this struggle. Spring 1941!"[23] We do not know how Kubizek's Hitler made these remarks. But we must admit that, notwithstanding how convincingly he made them, his rationale for an attack against Russia was palatable. But things are not always as they seem to be with Hitler. He had been dictating, writing, and orating since 1924 that Germany's destiny lay in the seizure of the western half of European Russia. Ten days before the conference at a time months remote from knowledge about the outcome of potential bombing and cross-channel amphibious operations against England, he had already directed Brauchitsch to plan an attack in the east. Although Hitler was a notable authority on the German conduct of World War II his announced rationale to knock England out of a war in the west through the attack and defeat of Russia in the east must be viewed with suspicion. Although the rationale might have seemed to make sense, in fact, logic, circumstance, and Hitler himself mitigated against it as convincing for an attack against Soviet Russia. No logical argument can support the rationale of an armed invasion of the contiguously located largest state in the world with the largest army and most numerous tank and air forces in order to force England out of a half-war by sea and air. The defeat of so great a power would be a war-ending event and present us with the illogical spectacle of a campaign to knock a greater and more immediate enemy out of a war to get at a lesser and more distant one.

Such illogic does not mean that Hitler did not embrace it but warns us that probably something else was afoot. Kershaw would argue that "having advocated since the 1920s a showdown with the Soviet Union to destroy Bolshevism and win '*Lebensraum*,' Hitler had now come back to the idea of a war against Russia for strategic reasons to force his erstwhile would-be friend Britain ... to terms."[24] But Hitler had advanced against the Allies in the west determined to seize Belgium, safeguard the Ruhr, and conduct operations against Britain more effectively by sea and air. And as chance and the army would have it, the Belgium advance was so successful that like it or not for Hitler, it was able to be transformed into a following attack against France. As noted, however, Hitler held it up, insisting that the Lorraine iron ore fields be seized before further advance into the French strategic heartland. He stated on June 6 to Brauchitsch, for example, that "the present campaign is calculated to deny the enemy possession of his iron ore resources in Lorraine."[25] There is an iron consistency in Hitler's conduct of the war during this period: the Scandinavian campaign intended to secure Swedish iron ore, the French campaign intended to seize Belgium and thus safeguard the Ruhr, and the final drive into France held up by Hitler to assure the immediate seizure of the iron ore in Lorraine. In this unmistakable consistency in Hitler's war-fighting mentality, there must be clues to Hitler's behavior and intentions in July 1940. And in this consistency, there must also be some granite necessity in Hitler's mind for the direction of the war.

First of all, Hitler did not want the war that was declared against him by the British and French governments in September 1939. He would have preferred, above all things, to have had a free hand in the east and not a war in the west. A free hand would have allowed him to fight a war against Soviet Russia alone and with an acceptable probability of winning. The outlandish aim of fighting so powerful an enemy had to have a corresponding outlandish necessity, and this necessity has been garbled in the accounts of the great biographers. Kershaw, for example, has noted that "Paradoxically having advocated since the 1920s a showdown with the Soviet Union to destroy Bolshevism and win '*Lebensraum*,' Hitler had now come back to the idea of a war against Russia for strategic reasons...to force...Britain...to terms."[26] But Hitler had already destroyed Bolshevism in Germany and had said in a major speech at the height of the Rhineland crisis, as concerns the intrusion of the Soviets into central Europe, that each country has a right to choose its own way to salvation. Bolshevism in Russia was a choice for the Russian people, but if they tried to export it to Germany or countries close by, they would find Hitler as their most deadly and fanatical enemy. And as concerns *Lebensraum*, Hitler was seriously interested in a smaller number of Germans per square mile in a Reich expanded into the relatively underpopulated east. But he was terminally interested in the raw materials and food of the Ukraine, the industrial plant associated with the area around Leningrad, and the dangerous capability of the Soviets to raid the

Romanian oil fields from the Crimea. Hitler's express fundamental intent after the seizure of power internally was to secure the strategic resources indispensable to project a Third Reich beyond his lifetime and into the unforeseeable future. Germany would not be great because Bolshevism had been eliminated in Russia. Germany would not be great because it had fewer people per square mile. Germany *would* be great because it had the contiguous strategic resources to give it impregnable finality as a political power.

To argue, therefore, that in July 1940, with the great historical clock of the twentieth century ticking—the brief period of time in which the world-historical personality had to impose himself on history itself by the conquest of European Russia—that Hitler would attack Russia for purposes of knocking a badly wounded Britain out of a half-war in the west cannot fly. The defeat of Britain would remain for Hitler *a* consummation devoutly to be desired but not *the* consummation. In July, and wasting no time after the defeat of France, he would direct planning for further operations against Britain and the offensive of the twentieth century, the attack into Soviet Russia. The attack on a thousand-mile front against the largest army and biggest country in the world would demand, as noted, a satisfying rationale for the commanders of his three services. Hitler would present the palatable fiction that the purpose of the attack was to deny Britain its last hope in the half-war of 1940. In a reversal of Churchill's dictum that sometimes truth has to be protected by a bodyguard of lies, Hitler would present a lie that had to be protected by a bodyguard of truth—the desirability of forcing Britain out of the war. And Jodl, for example, in OKW at a level higher than that of the commanders of the three services, would remark to his staff after a meeting at the Berghof on July 29 that Hitler was planning a preventive war against Soviet Russia.[27] Hitler also faced limitations to complete his eastern mission in both historical and biological time. He was concerned that every passing day would see the Soviets become relatively stronger with the accompanying probability that they might become too strong for him to attack at all. He was concerned that his life expectancy might be too short to see through an attack. And he suspected that Stalin may already have begun to plan an attack of his own.

In the actual events of the months following July, the aerial battles over England would peter out to the advantage of the British and Hitler, who did not have his heart in an autumn cross-channel attack, would call it off in September. But for the entire time from July 1940 through June 1941, the army in particular would plan, train, build up and concentrate for an attack in the east. Hitler would never falter in his determination to attack. The words of the 1920s, the actions of the 1930s, and the inexorable preparations for an attack in the east in 1940 and 1941 support an interpretation that Hitler both planned and launched the attack in the east as an end in itself.

It would be even more accurate to say that Hitler saw a successful attack against Soviet Russia as the end point for the securing of the Germans in history. The attack that would eventually take place under Operation Barbarossa would be the culmination of all things that Hitler had worked for and the final messianic necessity in his life—the unalterable securing of a place in the sun for the Germans. To arrive at this momentous juncture, he had accomplished the political trek of the twentieth century from decorated foot soldier to Fuehrer. By July 1940, Hitler's string of impossible achievements continued with the defeat of France and the driving of Britain from the continent. Each complex achievement, impressive as it was individually, led necessarily to the next, and all to the final result of a strategically impregnable German community, free of Marxism internally and freed from the aging concept of the boundaries of 1914 externally and with open access to the resources of Scandinavia, France, and the Balkans. Hitler's Germany stood poised to attain strategic immortality, or at least exceptional longevity, as a political state. Hitler had seen the end result of all of the above, and the seizure of the resources of western European Russia as his millennial, immortal achievement. In July, he faced the momentary embarrassment of half the West lingering in the war, although off the continent. He also faced the daunting prospect of planning and executing the epochal "showdown" with Soviet Russia.

Hitler had strategic freedom of maneuver in July 1940. No immediate circumstance forced him into any action. He could have proposed a serious peace settlement with Britain; he could have pursued an all-out, cross-channel invasion; he could have ignored Britain and pursued the final drive to the east. The only limitation on Hitler's freedom of maneuver would be time. Time, master of all things, would force Hitler to make a decision almost immediately to do something. In actual circumstance, Hitler gave himself two options: Sealion and Barbarossa. The possibility for success for both depended on the time of year that they would begin, and one depended on being executed as quickly as possible to take advantage of Germany's fleeting relative strength advantage of the last half of 1940. When preparation time for Sealion required an autumn beginning for the amphibious operation, the risks involved caused Hitler to cancel it. He would have preferred to begin Barbarossa as soon as possible, and specifically in November, but climate conditions would have made such an attack impossible. With Russia growing stronger and Stalin bringing dangerous opportunistic pressures to bear in the Balkans, Barbarossa became more attractive and necessary. The Soviets, for example, would seize in June both Bessarabia and the northern Bukovina 19,300 square miles of territory up against Romania, Germany's single source of oil.

For Hitler, time was fleeting. He had probably set Barbarossa in stone as early as the July planning. He also unrealistically hoped to execute it in November. He, finally, realistically scheduled it for May 1941. Every success of Hitler from 1919 onward led toward the armed seizure of the resources of western Russia that translated, in 1941, into the success of Barbarossa. Whether successful or unsuccessful, Barbarossa would be the hinge on which the history of the twentieth century would turn. Such is the importance of the impossibly rare world-historical personality that, either in success or failure, Hitler would superimpose himself on history itself. To know

Barbarossa is to know Hitler and the course of world history after he imposed it on Europe and the world. The importance of the outcome of the initial German drive into Soviet Russia has lain obscured because of the circumstances of the continued war by land and sea around Britain. It has lain obscured also by the circumstances of gross misinterpretation of its chances of success and the importance of its failure. The short-lived argument by Hitler that Russia had to be tackled in order to knock Britain out of a half-war over England can be explained as a bodyguard of fiction to make palatable the enormity of Barbarossa. And the failure of the greatest offensive in the history of warfare has caused the great biographers to trifle with Barbarossa as foredoomed to failure. Historians and great biographers alike have sought out reasons for the failure, virtually every one of whom was spurious and has spun us away from comprehension of Hitler and the course of World War II.

The planning for what would become Operation Barbarossa would go through several iterations associated mostly with OKH but interfered with by Hitler. He was, of course, both political and military master of Germany and the word *interfered* has to be used advisedly. But Hitler could not escape the grip of a siege mentality and would turn his Directive 21 of December 18, 1940, headed *Operation Barbarossa*, into an exercise for the assured seizure of the industrial plant associated with Leningrad and for the domination of the Baltic. The directive ordered the massive combined forces of Army Groups Center and North "to annihilate the enemy forces in the Baltic area," after which "the cities of Leningrad and Kronshadt must be captured."[28] Only then would offensive operations leading to the seizure of Moscow be continued. OKH issued its operation order in support of Hitler's Directive 21 on February 3, and it was a monument to elegant simplicity and directness: drive the fifty-one full-strength divisions of Army Group Center directly at Moscow, force the main concentration of the field armies of the Red Army to defend the capital, and destroy it. The directive and the army plan differed fundamentally, and the divergence was never rectified.

As preparations developed for Barbarossa, Hitler faced danger to the Romanian oil fields that developed into the German campaign in the Balkans in the spring of 1941. In a pattern virtually identical to the earlier campaigns in Scandinavia and France, Hitler would fly to the defense of the oil fields as the Russians seized the eastern Romanian province of Bessarabia and began to build up their troop strength along the new Romanian border in the second half of 1940. And if this were not danger enough, Mussolini's Italy would seize Albania in April 1939 and give the British government the opportunity to guarantee the independence of Greece. And when the Italian army invaded Greece at the end of October 1940, the British sent forces to Crete to back up the Greeks on the basis of the guarantee. Hitler would direct German troops into Romania in the meantime, on October 8, 1939, in order to protect the oil fields, and when he sent German troops into Bulgaria at the beginning of March 1940, the British embarked a substantial expeditionary force to land on the Greek mainland near Athens. At that time Hitler would face clear and present danger to the oil fields from the RAF, which had earlier requested permission from the Greek government to survey airfields in northern Greece. The stakes were enormous. Romania produced an impressive 9.64 million tons of oil in 1935 compared with 25.0 million for Soviet Russia. Since Germany and the remainder of Europe produced almost no oil, Hitler as military strategist would face literally the loss of the war without control over, and adequate space around, the Romanian oil fields. The Germans had synthetic fuel plants producing gasoline from coal, but they could not sustain German wartime demands. And when a political coup in Yugoslavia in late March overthrew the previous pro-German government of the regent, Prince Paul, the new situation invited a stronger British presence in Greece. Hitler immediately triggered the Balkans campaign.

OKH had not been given advanced warning of an offensive against Yugoslavia and Greece and improvised the Balkans campaign in the extraordinarily brief period from March 28 through April 6, 1941. On the morning of the latter date, the Luftwaffe would attack Belgrade and units of the Second Army advanced into the rest of Yugoslavia. A day later, German army units would cross the Greek border into a campaign that would be the perfect political–military storm of the war in Europe. Hitler would order an impossibly bold attack against two foreign states to begin in an impossibly short time. The brief time for planning and concentration and the lightning success would not allow Hitler to meddle in either the preliminaries or execution of the campaign. The German army, momentarily unconstrained, would exert unequalled command style, operational prowess, and tactical efficiencies to carry out a master blitz. The campaign provides invaluable insight into Hitler as political–military strategist in World War II.

Significantly in the French case, and almost entirely in the Scandinavian situation, Hitler would order an entire campaign based on his perceived imperative to safeguard a strategic resource or seize one. Hitler would embrace this pattern with impressive consistency. The consistency demands an interpretation of Hitler as inspired to set barrier lines around Germany effective enough to make it terminally independent of any resources outside of them.

The Yugoslav government under Peter II and his prime minister, General Dušan Simović, would capitulate on April 17 after a twelve-day campaign, and the Greek government would join them six days later. The campaign in Greece would be brief but not easy and characterized by bold moves from the Germans across inhospitable and immobilizing terrain. The German will to advance during this period of the war could be awe-inspiring, and early in the Greek campaign *SS-Sturmbannfuehrer* (Major) Kurt Meyer could write: "We hid behind the rocks not daring to move.... I yelled at Wawrzinek to press the attack but good old Emil looked at me as if he doubted my sanity.... I too was crouching in full cover and fearing for my life.... In my distress I felt the smooth roundness of an egg grenade in my hand. I yelled at the group. They all looked at me, thunderstruck when I showed the grenade, pulled the pin, and let it roll behind the last grenadier. I have never seen such a unified leap forward."[29] The

German political–military synthesis of Hitler and the army would force two potential enemy states out of the war, force a powerful sixty-thousand-man British Expeditionary Force off the continent and then off the island of Crete, and bring the entire Balkans under German control. Hitler's roaring, unrealistic political boldness was matched by the competence of the army general staff, the verve of commanders in the field armies, and the *élan* of the troops. The combination of Hitler and the army translated into a likely victory in World War II.

*   *   *

During late July 1940 through mid-June 1941, the Germans carried out uninterrupted planning and preparations for Barbarossa. Not even various crises associated with the peripheral war with Britain, for example, would interfere with Hitler's dedication to the great final adventure. The challenge of pulling off a successful beginning to the super-advance of World War II brings into focus both Hitler and the course of the war—Hitler as the master personality of the twentieth century and Barbarossa as the master military operation. Hitler's boldness in ordering such an attack was beyond almost any adjectival descriptor. And for so bold an attack to have any chance of success, it would require astounding skill and luck in achieving surprise at the opening of the campaign. It can be stated categorically that if the Germans could not have achieved surprise in the opening of the operation, it would have failed with an accompanying, much quicker German defeat. To achieve the required surprise, Hitler and the army would execute the greatest deception in the history of warfare. Hitler would be able, for example, to make a virtue out of the necessity of the continuing war with Britain. Can we imagine a deception so vast as an ongoing war against a major world power?

Hitler would require OKH to move 157 German divisions up against the Soviet border. Such a move would have been a feat in itself, but these divisions would have to be transported under conditions of darkest, unfailing secrecy. The army general staff would attempt to accomplish this next-to-impossible task in four waves beginning in early February 1941 with the issuing of the army's operational order for the attack. Most of the divisions had to be moved from all over Europe. The divisions left behind after the Polish campaign, and those redeployed there after the French, had to be moved closer to the frontier. The army and Luftwaffe high commands (OKL) gave the impression to most of their own troops that their presence was designed to cover up an impending invasion of England. Goebbels himself was directed to write and publish an article in the *Voelkischer Beobachter* entitled "Crete as a Model"—a great parachute operation reinforced by troops delivered by sea—to reinforce the deception that an invasion of Britain was imminent. In mid-March, a small German bomber force of about four hundred aircraft continued an aerial offensive at night with increasing efficiency that suggested it was a bigger effort than it actually was. The bomber offensive had in fact become "merely a diversion, part of the grand scheme intended to convince the enemy that the main German effort remained in the West."[30]

Against the background of concealment and deception similar to that above the OKH began the concentration (*Aufmarsch*) of the armies on February 4 for the attack. The general staff would have to move seventy-seven divisions from France and Germany to the east, push the forty-four divisions already in the east up against the frontier, move an additional twenty-four divisions immediately behind, and position further OKH reserve divisions behind all of the above. A formidable general staff would accomplish this task in four waves. The Germans emphasized secrecy to so great a degree that the thirty-one Panzer and motorized infantry divisions employed in the initial attack and deployed as far as 165 kilometers from the frontier in the fourth wave of the concentration were moved up only four days prior to the opening of hostilities. Thanks to the vast strategic deceptions of the war with Britain and the German-Soviet Non-aggression Pact and the innumerable deceptions and concealments of the concentration of forces, the Germans would achieve total surprise. And as B-Day (literally, "Barbarossa Day") approached, they also discovered that they were going to catch the Red Army too close to the western borders of the Soviet Union and too heavily concentrated in the Ukraine. In addition, the aircraft of the Red air force would be displayed in peacetime arrays on runways and parking areas of air installations concentrated too far to the west.

Hitler's intentions for the campaign stand out in the wording of Directive 21. They should have also stood out in the words and scheme of maneuver of the army operation order for the same advance. Hitler's Directive 21 was an unfocused document having no objective that could be seen as resulting in victory over Soviet Russia. The most decisive words in the document would be to halt Army Group Center east of Smolensk in order to assure the seizure of the Baltic region and specifically the cities of Leningrad and Kronstadt. Hitler personally crafted this eccentric maneuver away from any decisive military objective. The objective was one of the seizure of strategic resources and associated territory. The objective lay in a direct and unmistakable line of earlier objectives: the iron ore of Sweden and the Norwegian port of Narvik, the German Ruhr and nearby Belgium, the oil fields of Romania. And later in the actual campaign on August 20, 1941, with Army Group Center halted through his vacillation in contradistinction to Soviet resistance, Hitler would order Army Group Center's mobile forces into an eccentric move south, into the Ukraine. In contrast to all of this, the army plan of February 3 aimed to win the campaign without extraneous alarms and excursions. And in the political act of war, the surest way to achieve the political objective is through military victory.

Hitler and the army would go to war against Soviet Russia with divergent objectives. Hitler's was to establish more effective siege lines around Germany; the army was trying to win a war. The army accordingly would fight a double battle, one against Hitler and the other against the Red Army. Hitler would win or lose World War II based on victory or defeat within the Barbarossa operations in the summer of 1941. The German army would never be stronger, and the armed forces of the potential new allies, Britain and Russia, would never be weaker in the entire war. Whereas every other campaign or big battle of the conflict in Europe led simply to yet another in a long and drawn-out continuation of war, Barbarossa had the singular capability to result in victory or defeat. Any adequate interpretation of the course of the conflict in Europe depends on the outcome of the double battle that the German army had to fight in the near-perfect combat weather of the Russian summer of 1941. And any adequate interpretation of Hitler depends on his handling of the same events at the same time. His decisions early in the campaign, and no other time in his life, had the potential to lead to his own destruction and that of the Nazi movement and Germany. In the actual event, the German army would be proven to have had the capability to defeat the Red Army but not win the double battle against it and Hitler.

The most important operational question of the projected war was one infrequently discussed in existing literature. It was whether the Red Army would disengage from the Germans along the border and reengage at a time and place of its own choosing deep in the hinterland. The question was crucial because, had the Soviets disengaged opposite Army Group Center, dropping off powerful rear guards to slow the Germans, they would have retired intact to the great natural obstacles of the Dvina and Dnieper Rivers. The escape of the Soviet forces opposite Army Group Center was the premier fear of both Hitler and the army. The escape would have been a disaster for Hitler considering his strategic–geographic compulsion to seize the area around Leningrad immediately at war's beginning at the expense of every other move. Had Army Group Center been forced to engage Soviet field armies that had retired unscathed to the Dvina and Dnieper, it would not have been available for eccentric diversion either to Leningrad or to the Ukraine. For Army Group Center, Soviet escape would have been a strategic-level, war-losing disaster because the group would confront intact Soviet field armies behind natural defenses five hundred kilometers inside the Soviet

Union. Bock conducted a great pre-Barbarossa war game on April 9 and 10, 1941, in Army Group Center's headquarters in Posen. He, his staff, and his senior commanders agreed that a quick victory over the Soviets would be chancy if they traded space for time and made their stand around Smolensk on the upper Dnieper. In his diary entry for June 22, Bock would note that the question of whether the Russians planned to get away was still to be answered. And Halder noted darkly on June 23 that all reports indicated that an enemy attempt to disengage must be expected. But on June 24, Halder would brighten and write that the Soviets were not thinking of withdrawal. The assistant operations officer of Army Group Center would note more emphatically that he was "astonished" that the Russians fought on the border.

As the invasion of Russia began, the conventional wisdom has universally claimed as a kind of inbred truism that Hitler foredoomed himself to defeat in World War II. The same wisdom has claimed that OKH and the German field commanders underestimated the rigors of a war in the east and the strengths of the Red Army and were similarly doomed to defeat. The great biographers and historians have particularly emphasized the contemporary German estimates of the length of the campaign variously from six to ten to seventeen weeks as hopelessly divorced from reality. The conventional wisdom has worked from a known end result and has selectively looked for and chosen evidence to support a view of gross underestimation of the rigors of the theater and the strengths of the Soviet armed forces. That same wisdom, after presenting an interpretation of hopeless optimism on the part of Hitler and the army in planning and preparation for Barbarossa, has naturally handled the military operations in a similar manner. It has interpreted the opening offensive as one in which the German army was gradually slowed by an underestimated Red Army and ground to a halt before the fabled "gates of Moscow"—not surprisingly, in wintertime. This drab picture for Hitler and the German army is not supported by the facts of the German preparations and the course of the German advance. And the resulting misrepresentations have presented the reading public with a flawed view of Hitler and an interpretation of the course of World War II that is less than inspired.

As concerns Hitler, he had been more modest in his rearmament of Germany than has been generally supposed from 1933 to 1939 and had not intended to get embroiled in a war with the West in September 1939. With the fall of France in June 1940, Hitler was probably most concerned with the military balance between Germany and Soviet Russia. He had set relatively low levels of war production adequate to win battles in 1939 and 1940 and to maintain his popularity at home. He seemed acutely aware, however, that such levels would not be satisfactory if the Soviets expanded their defense production in anticipation of a war with Germany. Hitler's reasoning and timing for Barbarossa were realistic because further Soviet preparations for war in 1941 and much of 1942 would have been disastrous. The Soviets would have had at least twelve months to develop further border fortifications, expand their peacetime army, improve their tanks and aircraft and produce more of them, deploy frontier forces more effectively, and take steps to prevent a surprise attack. Hitler and OKH agreed early in the planning that the attack against the Soviet Union would not only take place in 1941 but also only "make sense" if it were finished quickly. But how does any army finish an opponent the likes of Soviet Russia quickly?

Earlier in the war the German general staff, based on a brilliant plan and the operational verve of the panzer leaders, had put the French army as a cat in a bag to win the Battle of France. Certainly European Russia was different from France, and Russians from Frenchmen, but it could be deduced that the Red Army was no more than a bigger cat in a bigger bag and subject to the same principles of war exploited by the Germans in France in 1940.

As concerns the rigors of the impending campaign, Hitler can be quoted to prove that he underestimated the Soviets, but equally decisive comments can be produced to show concern for the dangers of a Russian campaign. At a conference on January 9, 1941, Hitler was quoted in a war diary as saying, "The Russian Armed Forces are like a headless colossus with feet of clay but we cannot foresee with certainty what they might become in the future. The Russians must not be underestimated. All available resources must therefore be used in the attack."[31] The first part of the first sentence has been quoted misleadingly by writers anxious to buttress the view that the Germans underestimated the Russians. Quoted in its entirety, Hitler's estimate is a sober, realistic analysis. When Hitler discovered in the early stages of planning that the Luftwaffe intended to keep a significant number of its antiaircraft guns in a reserve pool for home defense, he ordered every cannon in the pool to be turned over to the army for use against ground and air targets in Russia, commenting that every available gun would be used against the Soviets.[32] Whether Hitler underestimated or overestimated the Soviets, it is easy to forget that he made the right decision—the only decision—that would give him a realistic opportunity to win World War II.

For Hitler to win, he was dependent almost completely on playing Germany's trump cards—his political audacity and the army's battle-winning style. The alternative was awaiting certain defeat by losing the initiative and encountering the overwhelming strength of an enemy coalition. Hitler would display correct instinct and reason in the choice of a surprise attack against the Soviets in 1941, but in doing so he decided to engage a colossus and must be suspected of having had a clear appreciation of the risk.

Writers dedicated to the proposition that the German army had little prospect of winning Barbarossa point to estimates of six to ten weeks to defeat the Soviets as the strongest evidence of the army's underestimation of the strengths of Soviet Russia. Examining the estimate of six weeks, we must be struck by the actual 195 additional weeks the war lasted beyond German estimate. But in fresh analysis, if the Soviets were so much stronger than estimated, why did it take them 195 weeks after Barbarossa, and with the notable assistance of Britain, the United States, Brazil, and so on, to master the German assault? The answer lies in the damage inflicted by the German army in the first six weeks of Barbarossa. And this damage must have been so great that, based on it, the German army stood only a hairbreadth away from victory over Soviet Russia. But the writers do not relent and have continued to develop the interpretation that the rigors of the eastern war theater and the strengths of the Red Army were too strong for Hitler and the army to have mastered.

As concerns the army, the acid test for gauging whether or not it underestimated the eastern theater is probably how it approached logistics. American and British writers face historical culture shock in this area because in World War II, Allied logistics pivoted around ships and oceans and trucks and roads. But for OKH and OKL alike, the concentration of the field armies and the air fleets centered on railways. The army general staff was largely responsible for the entire concentration and would move approximately seventeen thousand train loads, which totaled more than ten million tons of men and material. With the completion of the concentration, the army would base its logistics in the planned attack on a rail system constructed into Soviet Russia immediately behind the field armies. The army faced a unique challenge because its railway construction battalions not only had to repair Russian attempts at demolition but also narrow the track width of the entire system to conform with the rest of Europe. The railway troops could not, of course, keep up with the panzer spearheads, which quickly disappeared over the horizon. To bridge the anticipated gap, the quartermaster general of the army would provide Army Group Center with approximately forty-five thousand tons of truck freight capacity. The railway construction workers moved fast and aggressively, and the eighteen thousand men assigned, for example, to Army Group North were armed with pistols, rifles, and light machine guns. They reported eighty-four combat engagements with scattered Soviet troops and 162 combat casualties to themselves. These details of the European-gauge railway construction into the Soviet Union support a conclusion that OKH accurately forecast the indispensable logistical necessities for Barbarossa. In the great battles in June, July, and

August, the German army cannot be claimed to have been thwarted by insuperable logistical challenges in its drive toward Moscow.

As the great operational advances moved east out of the edge of darkness on June 22, Army Groups North and South routed the opposing Soviet forces and allowed Bock to push forward Army Group Center uninhibited by lesser events. In the opening encounters in the Białystok–Minsk battles, Bock, Guderian (Panzer Group Two), and *Generaloberst* Hermann Hoth (Panzer Group Three) would form the most effective command team of the war in Europe. With political boldness that was unequalled, Hitler had looked with contempt on his generals' caution in the risky advances and narrowly averted wars in the Rhineland, Austria, and Czechoslovakia. Once he found himself in war, he discovered that the politically timid generals included war fighting lions whose military daring was also unequalled. Under the army plan, OKH would give Bock the mission to destroy the massive Soviet forces opposite him by effecting an encirclement 350 kilometers into White Russia at its capital city of Minsk. Hoth, however, felt that this initial encirclement should have been set east of Smolensk, 700 kilometers into the Soviet Union, and Bock agreed after being presented with the idea. It is not clear how Hoth envisioned setting the lines of encirclement around this super pocket that could be estimated as 350 kilometers long, 120 kilometers wide and holding roughly 1.1 million Soviet troops. Voicing Hitler's battle-fighting timidity, however, Halder adhered to the first pocket, closing at Minsk around approximately one-half million Soviet troops. In the actual event, Hoth's Panzer Group Three would set the northern wing of the encirclement at 2200 on the evening of June 25, directly north of Minsk and only three days and twenty hours into the Russian campaign.

In the face of this war-winning pace at the point of major effort in Barbarossa, Hitler would brake Army Group Center. Halder would note on June 25 that OKH received "a Fuehrer order" that betrayed concern that Army Group Center was operating too far in depth and comment, "The same old refrain. But that is not going to change anything in our plans."[33] Hitler would continue to rein in Army Group Center and argue on June 30 that "mastery of the Gulf of Finland must be secured quickly. For only elimination of the Russian navy will give us free passage through the Baltic [for Swedish iron ore shipments]. After seizing the Russian seaports from the land side, we must allow three to four weeks for all enemy submarines to be...out of action. Four weeks means two million tons of iron ore."[34] Hitler was consumed by the necessity to take Leningrad and the probability that Army Group Center would have to be halted and diverted to help in its seizure.

By July 2, however, it had become evident that the two great pockets between Białystok and Minsk had burned out and that Army Group North was doing well in the Baltic. Hitler would give the green light for the panzers of Army Group Center to advance on Smolensk and Moscow. Those panzer formations were moving at a war-winning pace in distance advanced and damage inflicted: 350 kilometers, 332,000 prisoners, 3,188 tanks destroyed or captured, and 1,832 artillery pieces destroyed or captured. Soviet tank losses in this first battle were virtually identical to the entire tank strength of the Germans for Barbarossa, and all of this progress came only ten days into the campaign.

A strong case can be made for German victory over the Soviet Union in summer 1941. Directed politically by Hitler to defeat the Russians in a quick military campaign, the German army, dominant service of the German armed forces, planned to do exactly that. It is difficult to believe that with the collective experience it brought to bear in an attack against Soviet Russia that the German army could have deluded itself into one that had little chance of success. Every German war game had confirmed that the German army could quickly defeat the Red Army. But every war game was based on the assumption of an uninterrupted drive by Army Group Center directly on Moscow. Such a drive continued on July 3 in the direction of Moscow, and on July 15, Hoth's Seventh Panzer Division would interdict the unpaved Russian superhighway between Smolensk and

Moscow a scant twenty-three days into the campaign and only three hundred kilometers from the capital. Violent battles would develop around a great pocket immediately north of Smolensk and to the east where fresh Soviet forces began to mass to block the way to Moscow. The panzer divisions were forced to fight static infantry-style battles until the following horse-drawn, foot-marching infantry divisions caught up with them about seven days after the motorized units had already arrived in Smolensk and Jarcevo. On July 28, Bock would note that the relief of the panzer divisions by infantry divisions had begun. Bock and virtually every officer and man in Army Group Center both hoped and assumed that the attack on Moscow would take place after the "unprecedented" success around Smolensk— 310,000 prisoners in yet another bag.

Hitler, however, on July 13, had reiterated the idea of using Army Group Center to help to seize Leningrad. But then, toward the end of July, he decided instead that the army group swing powerful armored forces to the southeast to take the Ukraine in a gigantic encirclement of a huge Soviet force. Halted according to plan along the east bank of the Dnieper, Bock would affect the refurbishing and rest of the panzer and motorized infantry divisions by August 12 for Guderian's panzer command and August 14 for Hoth's. He had also seized the road communications center of Roslavl south of Smolensk as the second major axis of advance on Moscow. On the morning of August 14, Army Group Center stood prepared to advance on the Soviet capital through the powerful but badly battered main concentration of the Red Army. The advance that Bock visualized was one that would lead to the seizure of Moscow and attendant, concurrent destruction of the force defending it—the main concentration of the Red Army. Moscow had become, through the modernization of Russia, the hub of the Soviet rail, road, and telephone systems, and the single largest industrial complex in the new Soviet Union. Moscow had remained the psychological and governing center of the masses that still revered an older Russia. And it had become the same center for a newer Soviet Union. Moscow was the place at which the Soviets had to make their stand and face the inescapable result of total defeat in the event of its seizure by the Germans. This was especially true in Soviet Russia because the Russian peasant masses could not be expected to support an oppressive, crushing government incapable of defending its own capital.

As concerns the outcome of the campaign and the course of World War II, Hoth had correctly predicted that a Russian campaign would have to be won as a "blitz blitzkrieg," and Bock agreed as he voiced the order: "Every leader and soldier is to have hammered into him for this eastern campaign the foremost order: above everything else swiftly and ruthlessly forward!"[35] Time had run out for both sides in the east by August 1941. The Soviets had no space left to trade for time to gather themselves and survive. Had the Germans taken Moscow in August 1941, they would have won the campaign and war. Almost as surely, when Hitler delayed the final strike for Moscow until October, the Germans had little chance of winning. These generalizations lead to a fundamental reinterpretation of the war that, had the Germans taken Moscow in late summer, they would have won, and conversely their hesitation by time and strategic circumstance would lead to certain defeat in the entire war—all in the time of a single month. To make this argument, however, it must be proved that Army Group Center had the capability to defeat the main concentration of the Red Army roughly handled but continuously reinforced between the group and Moscow.

Adolf Hitler, however, intruded on history to sign the Fuehrer Directive of August 21, the single most significant political–military document of the twentieth century. The directive and no action taken by the Red Army halted Army Group Center and diverted it for two months south into the Ukraine. Hitler's decision as embodied in the brief, five-paragraph document marked Germany's irretrievable loss of World War II, literally, on August 22, the day that OKH received the directive and began to execute it. Hitler's directive demanded a revised interpretation of his conduct of the war. It also demands a revised interpretation of the course of the war. Halder would fulminate,

"I regard the situation created by the Fuehrer's interference unendurable for OKH. No other than the Fuehrer himself is to blame for the zigzag course caused by his successive orders, nor can the present OKH ... tarnish its good name with these latest orders."[36] This quotation by Halder illustrates the outrageousness of the situation and the potential for war-losing disaster as seen through the eyes of a consummate general staff officer. Halder seems to be saying that the latest zigzag defied the army plan to drive a concentrated Army Group Center directly at Moscow and carried the possibility for disaster in the campaign. Given the circumstances, we are impelled to believe that the Russians experienced a second miracle of the Marne.

As concerns a necessarily revised interpretation of Hitler as "warlord," he would conduct his war as an extraordinarily conservative set of campaigns, every one intended either to protect or to seize strategic resources necessary for German survival. There was an iron consistency in the pattern. As already noted as a repetitive theme for Hitler, the French campaign was a Belgian campaign to secure the Ruhr; the Scandinavian campaign was one to secure Swedish iron ore, the Balkans campaign was one to secure Romanian oil. These things have been discussed and parts of them are well known to the conventional wisdom. What is less well known is Hitler's conduct of the penultimate Russian campaign and how it fits in so consistently with the pattern repeated above. We cannot doubt that Hitler intended a "showdown" with Bolshevism in the Soviet Union. And we cannot doubt that he intended an improvement in German living space. These two factors are well known and unarguable. In the actual historical event, however, Hitler conducted the campaign as an immense exercise in the seizure of the strategic space and resources of European Russia. Similar to the way that Hitler viewed the "French" campaign as a Belgian one, he would view the "Russian" campaign as one described as Balto–Ukrainian. This restrictive clause does not diminish Hitler's stature as world-historical personality, because even here the diversion of part of Army Group Center into the Ukraine would result in the greatest battle of encirclement in history.[37]

Hitler's words of August 21 verify the generalizations above. He would state that the OKH proposals for concentrated attack against Moscow with intention of decisive and final military victory "do not conform to my intentions."[38] Remarkably for the man who said the campaign would make sense only if it were finished with lightning speed, he would voice the following war-losing intentions: "The principle object that must be achieved yet before the onset of winter is not the capture of Moscow, but rather in the South, the occupation of the Crimea and the industrial and coal region of the Donets [River Basin] together with the isolation of the Russian oil regions in the Caucasus and, in the North the encirclement of Leningrad."[39] With these words, Hitler can be seen as executing Barbarossa to establish improved defensible siege lines around Germany to endure a war of indefinite length. The words also anticipate the German 1942 summer campaign with its intention to seize the Caucasian oil fields based on Hitler's intent to include them within the siege lines around Germany. Other words abound to show Hitler as similarly oriented and having no intention of securing a decisive military victory over the Soviet Union, for example, in the Barbarossa directive itself: "The final objective of the operation is to erect a barrier against Asiatic Russia on the general line from which the Russian air force can no longer attack German territory." Under the general intention for the campaign, Hitler gave as its final objective to erect a barrier along a line from which a presumably still-intact Soviet air force could no longer attack German territory. And if this were not enough to show Hitler with a barrier or barrier-line mentality, he would order, in a highest level armaments conference on November 29, a shift in production toward heavier tanks and antitank weapons "to defend ourselves against all attackers."

As concerns the German army and the chances of outright military victory at the end of August, convincing arguments can be offered that it would have seized Moscow. Bock, for example, intended to attack on August 14 with the fateful objective to seize Moscow and destroy the Red Army deployed at its highest and final strategic level for its protection. Bock was the expert as concerns the striking power of his own army group and the strength of the opposition. Bock judged that he would take Moscow. This does not prove that he would have been successful, and part of the conventional wisdom has taken the view that he had been halted by furious Soviet resistance along a line about sixty kilometers east of Smolensk. Bock, however, had not been halted by Soviet resistance but by the planned refurbishing of the mobile divisions followed by Hitler's objection to the continuation of the drive to Moscow. Hitler would freeze Army Group Center in positions that it had seized so early as July 17, and Bock would not make the August attack with objective Moscow. We are therefore faced with consideration of the most elusive of all things—the *if* in history specifically to support an argument about the winning or losing of the war by the Germans in August 1941. Thankfully, two enormous historical events came to our assistance to give overwhelming argument that the Germans would have been in Moscow in late summer. Such argument also demands a fundamental revaluation of both Hitler and the course of World War II.

On August 25, Guderian would lead a modest-sized panzer army—three panzer and three motorized infantry divisions—south into the Ukraine. Exactly three weeks later, his Third Panzer Division would link up with the Ninth Panzer Division of Army Group South to close an encirclement around Marshal Semyon Budenny's combined armies, totaling approximately 1.1 million men. The Germans would complete the battle by September 25 and take out of the pocket, by that time, 665,000 prisoners. The point for comprehending the possibilities for success of an attack by Army Group Center against Moscow is that the excursion allowed the Soviets an exorbitant seventy days to mass forces from the interior, construct defenses, and rain incessant counter attacks on the fixed position of Army Group Center. In the case, for example, of the German Seventh Panzer Division, it would remain in the positions it reached on July 17 for seventy-six days before it would finally advance toward

Moscow on October 2. The Soviet High Command had been able to mass nine field armies behind field positions thirty-five kilometers deep between the army group and Moscow. Army Group Center, allegedly battered and exhausted by Soviet counterattacks, should not have made any impression on the main concentration arranged as such, and with a command that had regained its composure. Yet when Seventh Panzer Division advanced north of the immense, unpaved highway toward Moscow, it would move 115 kilometers in 106 hours to Vyasma and trap fifty-five Soviet divisions now lying behind it to the west. By October 12, Army Group Center would take a staggering total of 658,000 prisoners in two huge pockets formed during its initial attack. Only the muddy season, which began gradually about five days into the attack and lasted for five weeks, would halt the Germans and save the Soviets.

Given the actual historical result of Army Group Center's advance under the outrageous conditions recounted above in autumn, we can generalize that it would have advanced earlier in summer weather to success in the campaign and, by its timing and dimensions, victory in World War II. This generalization demands the following reevaluation of Hitler: His decision to advance against Soviet Russia was correct and necessary. Hitler could have made Germany impregnable only through seizure of the strategic resources and space of European Russia. His decision was so bold and fraught with consequence for history that it pressed him into the category of world-historical personality. His decision did not doom him to lose, rather it gave him clear and present opportunity to win. Within the ongoing campaign, Army Group Center had the striking power and physical location on August 14 to seize Moscow. There has always been a time and a place in history for everything. The time for Hitler and the Germans to have won World War II was in August, and the place was closely west of the enduring city of the vanished Dukes of Muscovy. As concerns Hitler, he made the decision unwittingly to lose the war in surrounding diversions and eccentricities—Halder's aptly described zigzags. As concerns Hitler as world-historical personality, he alone created Barbarossa, and he alone, in the face of resistance and legion objection, destroyed it. His utter loneliness in decision making from Munich 1938 onward, and the world-altering consequences of that loneliness in the inception of Barbarossa, place him in a category distant from the tyrant of the great biographers.

Barbarossa had possibilities and consequences so great that it demands a fundamental reevaluation of the course of World War II. The German army attacked Russia to win. The army had the capabilities to win. The army placed itself in geographic position to win. These are historical facts. But the German army failed to win, and this failure has obscured the reality of August 1941 and replaced it with the reality of December. Historians have seen World War II as an exercise in early German victories followed by Hitler's alleged mistake of the attack on Soviet Russia and a gradual downhill slide into defeat. No historian has made the interpretive point that Hitler's mistake was not in attacking Russia but in failing to defeat it immediately—in six to ten weeks. All historians and the great biographers, however, have ridiculed the estimated length of the campaign as almost absurdly optimistic. We are left at the highest level of interpretation of World War II as one that could never have been won by Hitler and spiraled downhill after June 1941 through the fascinating military turning points of El Alamein, Stalingrad, Kursk, and Normandy. We are left also with a picture of Hitler as a mere tyrant, who finally got in over his head in Russia, a good German army but not good enough to defeat the Red Army, and the lessons of the great war of the twentieth century as those associated with the styles of the victors. The situation is based on ignorance of the realities of Barbarossa and the necessity to reevaluate the existing thin and aging interpretations.

The concept of turning points brings into focus the course of the war. Barbarossa was *the* turning point of the war. The ordinarily assigned battles of El Alamein, Stalingrad, Kursk, Normandy, and a few more qualify as turning points only in the sense of leading to other phase within the war. Logic demands, however, that there could be only one point in World War II at which Hitler irretrievably lost any chance of German victory. After Barbarossa, even if the Germans had avoided encirclement at Stalingrad, they would not have gained victory in the east on that account. If the Germans had stopped the British attack at El Alamein they would not have won the campaign in the Mediterranean. If the Germans had won at Kursk they would have only delayed further Soviet offensives. The well-known turning point battles remain fascinating and indispensable for their battle fighting lessons, but they are incidental to the issue of overall victory or defeat in World War II. That issue had already been settled by the German inaction of August 1941. Notably, the German army had not only put itself in position to win World War II in only two years, but also with few casualties and little damage compared with the ponderous, almost four-year allied aftermath of Barbarossa—approximately two million dead versus seventeen million.[40]

In late 1941, Hitler, the hardest man in history—or at least the most obdurate—would witness probably the hardest army group in history, Army Group Center, falter in its delayed, unrealistic push toward Moscow. Virtually unknown to almost every writer, the Red Army was favored on the defense by the coldest winter in the climate history of the European world, one dating back to 1715 and based on records kept in the Netherlands. Moscow, for example, would experience its coldest winter of the entire time weather records had been kept in the capital. The ubiquitous Seventh Panzer Division, which had set encirclements from the north at Minsk, Smolensk, and Vyasma, would experience record low temperatures of -40°F on November 27 near Moscow at the Yakhroma rail bridge, which it had just crossed over the Moscow Canal thirty-five miles directly north of the Soviet capital. Only a similar climate improbability might have given Hitler and Army Group Center a single, final chance to get to Moscow. The German October advance beyond Vyasma had been halted by the autumn, mud-producing rains on the unpaved Russian tracks disguised as roads. But had Army Group Center been favored by the miracle of an absolute autumn drought, it probably would have continued toward Moscow on the roads of summer. The fictional miracle suggested for October would have been little different from the nonfictional miracle that occurred in late November and favored the Red Army.

As 1941 turned into 1942 and the German army groups survived the Soviet winter offensive, Hitler still held the initiative in World War II. Notwithstanding the momentary Soviet recovery, he had freedom of strategic maneuver to launch any offensive, anywhere, and with any objective. We are presented with one final opportunity to break the code of Hitler's thoughts by examination of his last theater-dominating offensive of World War II. He could have—and probably should have—launched an offensive toward Moscow in order to bring the bulk of the Red Army into battle, destroy it, and seize the capital. Instead, he would cement the interpretation of himself as siege Fuehrer wedded to the proposition that German wars were fought to secure strategic resources. For Hitler, the oil fields of the Caucasus had been the foremost objective of his planning after the thwarted but nevertheless considerable territorial successes of Barbarossa. There can be no doubt that Hitler himself conceived the plan for the summer offensive.[41] The plans for Operation Siegfried (later Blau) had been drafted by Halder and his assistants in OKH according to detailed instructions received from Hitler. In his overall plan for the Russian theater he would note that all available forces would have to be concentrated for the principal operation in the south in order first to destroy the enemy forces in the Don River bend and then to seize the oil resources of the Caucasus. The Soviets continued to hold the great naval base of Sevastopol in Crimea, and Hitler timed the beginning of the great offensive in the south to the fall of the city. The final complete conquest of the peninsula so vital to Hitler because of its potential as a great air base for attacks against the Romanian oil fields took place roughly on the same day—June 28, 1942—that the main concentration of the attacking German armies in Russia struck out for the Caucasian oil fields. There are lots of oil fields and considerable strategic space in this picture. We seem to have Hitler nicely in focus in the same picture.

The German offensive would gain enormous territory from the southeastern Ukraine into the Caucasus between late June and September. Both Hitler and OKH saw the necessity to secure the area around Stalingrad as strategic level protection for the armies moving into the Caucasus, and they assigned two German Armies to secure this area on the lower Volga River. As fighting developed there, however, Stalingrad lost its significance as flank protection for the Caucasus offensive and its seizure turned into an end in itself. Hitler became consumed by a compulsion to take the place, committed the Sixth Army to the task, but positioned two weak Romanian armies on either side. The Soviet High Command would flexibly and decisively take advantage of the situation to drive through the weaker forces on November 19, 1941, and eventually, by early February 1942, destroy the encircled Sixth Army. The Battle of Stalingrad would be treated by the Soviets as the turning point in the war. The British would ascribe similar importance to the Battle of Britain and El Alamein. The Americans would attribute their dominating contribution to the Normandy landings as a great final turning point. But according to Manstein, in his memoir, "In point of fact not one of these individual events should really be treated as decisive. The outcome of the war was decided by a wealth of factors, the most significant of which was probably the hopelessly inferior position in which Germany found itself vis-à-vis her opponents in consequence of Hitler's policies and strategy."[42] By the turn of 1943 and Stalingrad, Hitler had placed Germany in a war with three major powers with combined overwhelming superiorities in crude oil, iron ore, and coal production and resultant overwhelming production of ground weapons, aircraft, and ships.

The concept of a hopelessly inferior position brings into focus the course of the war at the time of Stalingrad and the Caucasus. Hitler by that time had placed Germany in a war that it could not win, and that the localized outcome of even a great battle could not affect. The main concentration of the Red Army would have remained largely untouched and invincible to German arms under the conditions of the hopelessly inferior overall position of Germany in 1943. The situation had not always been as such; in June 1940, Hitler had placed Germany in a hopelessly *superior* position in the war with the West. The situation of transition from a superior position to a hopelessly inferior one suggests that Hitler conducted a strategy that led Germany through accumulated mistakes to the hopeless position of January 1943 both in the east and west—the unfolding of El Alamein, Stalingrad, Kursk, and Normandy. And advocates of the predestined defeat of the Germans in Barbarossa would add the Battle of Moscow at the end of 1941. In revisionist retrospect, however, Hitler had placed Germany in its strongest position of the war in the summer of that year—America not in the war, Britain off the continent, neither autumn rain nor winter snow in Russia. And most important for the events of June 1941, Hitler seemed to have inserted Germany into a war that the conventional wisdom has interpreted as two-front in which Germany automatically would be placed in a hopelessly inferior position. But reevaluation of the Barbarossa summer shows the German army, in a "blitz blitzkrieg," would have translated in the event of its success into final victory in the opening stages of the war. As such, the eastern campaign would not have continued as an ordinarily understood lengthy war with its different rules for success. With immediate German success, the eventual Russian trumps of numbers of mobilized men and weapons, industrial production, and strategic resources would not have been brought into play in the absence of a usual lengthy war.

Analyzed from the viewpoint of having put Germany in a campaign that, if it were won quickly, the Germans would win World War II, Hitler must appear as an able strategist. Analyzed from the viewpoint of Army Group Center having the clear and present capability on August 14, 1941, to advance through every Soviet field army between it and Moscow and seize the capital, Hitler comes off as the strategic genius of the century. But in a master irony, Hitler would divert Army Group Center into the Ukraine with the intent to win the campaign against Soviet Russia but with the result of losing it. Hitler would have the intent and the opportunity to win the entire war at no other time before or after Barbarossa, and victory in the campaign would have placed his remaining opponents in a hopelessly inferior situation. Nothing that the Red Army could have accomplished in August would have been capable of saving it from destruction by Army Group Center. Yet it was saved. Hitler's historical stature lies significantly in his putting Germany in position in August to win World War II. Hitler's interpretation as world-historical personality lies in his decision to *lose* World War II. The decision was single, lonely, and influenced by no other man. The Allies did not win the war; Hitler lost it.

Hitler would plan in detail the 1942 campaign and enforce his will on OKH in Operation Blau to execute it. In Barbarossa, Hitler intended to topple the Soviet government by seizing the strategic resources of the western half of European Russia. In Blau, he would have more limited intent enforced by Germany's hopelessly inferior situation. Hitler, of course, would not acknowledge such a situation but press toward a strategic resource that would allow Germany to endure a vast siege of indefinite length on the defensive. In Blau, Hitler set its objective as a nicely concentrated but eight-hundred-mile distant oil producing area. The objective would have taxed the mobility of any army to reach and the strength to defend its resulting exposed flank. The point, though, for comprehending the course of World War II is that even if Hitler had achieved his own objective, he would have won neither the Russian campaign nor World War II. The Battle of Stalingrad and the vast Soviet counteroffensive in the north along the Don River and farther south in the Caucasus would present mortal danger to the German position in the Soviet Union. But the German army would prove strong enough not only to survive but also to launch a counteroffensive in March 1943 that would firmly stabilize the Russian front east of

Kharkov to the advantage of the Germans. Stalingrad cannot be interpreted as the turning point of either the campaign in the east or World War II.

In the other half of the war, Hitler would face disaster in the October 1942 El Alamein battle, an Allied victory that would attract powerful American ground forces to North Africa. At the turn of 1943, Hitler would face the strategic nightmare of a ground campaign out of Africa and onto some location on the European continent. With the German defeat and surrender in May 1943 in Tunisia, the Western Allies would bring the war to the continent in the campaign in Sicily in July and August. Strategy for Hitler by this time would consist almost entirely of reaction to Allied moves, including the landings at Salerno in early October 1943 and at Anzio near Rome in January 1944. Hitler would show acute sensitivity to the Italian disaster. He would set up Mussolini in an alternate fascist republic in northern Italy that helped the German occupation authorities. And he would commit just enough trusty German divisions to maintain a campaign effective enough to keep the Turkish government neutral and the polyglot Allies at bay—Indians, New Zealanders, French, Americans, Texans, and so on. But shortly after the beginning of the Allied landings in Sicily on July 10, Hitler would order a strategic move devastating for the Germans in the Russian campaign. On July 13, when the Kursk battle was at its climax and the issue apparently at hand, Hitler announced to the two German army group commanders that the Allies had landed in Sicily. Citadel, the German operational name for the Kursk battle, would have to be broken off. The commander of German Army Group South would point out that "the battle was now at its culminating point, and that to break it off at this moment would be tantamount to throwing a victory away."[43] But Hitler, in a move of bizarre strategic ineptitude, would take elite mobile divisions out of the Citadel battle and direct them to Italy. Through the vagaries of the overall strategic situation, not one of those divisions would arrive in time to have any effect in Sicily. Most would be diverted to other areas as fresh crises arose, for example, in Army Group Center in Russia.

On the eastern front, thanks to the brilliance of the commander of Army Group South, the operational capabilities of Hitler's army and corps-level commanders, and the tactical prowess of his divisions, the German army had actually seized the initiative again in March 1943 after Stalingrad. Hitler accordingly would face strategic-level opportunity to stabilize the situation in the east. Victory in the campaign in Russia had become a distant impossibility. He would be given, however, the opportunity to launch an offensive at a time and place of his choosing. And as a corollary, he would be presented with at least the distant possibility to batter the Red Army effectively enough to keep it at bay in 1943 and force a stalemate afterward. Opportunity beckoned, and Citadel was born out of it. An enormous bulge had been pressed into the German lines between Orel in the north and Belgorod farther south, and Hitler sensed an obvious opportunity to encircle the Soviet forces in it and retake significant territory. The concept was unimaginative and realistic but would depend for assured success on being executed immediately—by no later than late April. The Soviet forces would still be relatively weak and psychologically off balance, and the battered Soviet strategic reserves attracted to the battle would be capable of being roughly handled. Hitler, however, could not bring himself to order the attack until July 4, with the result of attracting the entire, largely recovered Soviet strategic reserves to the battle. The Soviets would also have had three months to prepare field fortifications thirty-five miles deep and lay more than one-half million land mines. The southern wing of the German advance would get thirty-five miles into the prepared Soviet positions but be halted irretrievably on July 13 by a bizarre combination of Soviet strength and Hitler's order to disengage divisions for transfer to a new Italian front. Citadel was Hitler's last serious hope for at least a stabilization of the eastern front.

After Citadel, Hitler moved through unrelieved strategic disasters in the east. Given the preponderance of the Soviets, Hitler had virtually no strategic options for forcing a stalemate, and none for victory. His intrepid commander of Army Group South would suggest that he turn over command on the eastern front to one military leader whose strategy would be to conduct superior mobile operations designed to force a stalemate. Hitler would reject the suggestion. After July 1943, the German army would manage several successful ripostes but not one major eastern offensive through war's end. Given Germany's hopelessly inferior situation, Hitler would not have been able to enforce any strategy, in the conventional sense of coordinated large-scale military operations, to achieve German objectives in World War II. After the turn of 1944, Germany could have no more wartime objectives except for the pathetic one of a possible dictated but leniently imposed surrender.

Yet even under these conditions, Hitler would astonish us with the iron consistency of his direction of the war in terms of the central importance of strategic resources. After Citadel, Hitler would demand that Army Group South hold the Donetz Basin with its massive metallurgical industries and iron ore and coal production. But when disaster threatened to destroy the entire southern front, he allowed a withdrawal of approximately two hundred miles back to the Dnieper River by the turn of October 1943. As the war continued along the Dnieper, Hitler would imperil the entire German position in the south, the decisive area of the entire war on the Russian front, by demanding that the manganese producing area around Nikopol on the Dnieper be held. He would also demand holding of the Crimea to prevent it from being used for air attack against the Romanian oil fields. These vast strategic details show Hitler pacing the war in the east to the holding or protection of pathetically reduced strategic space and industry.

By the middle of 1944, however, with the enormous Soviet advances and the Western Allied landing in Normandy, Hitler became a war leader without a strategy. By that time in the war, the trail grows cold for much more understanding of him as German war leader. As often had been the case in his life, he would reveal consistency in purpose and refusal to accept defeat, even in an approaching bitter end. He would conceptualize in September and launch in December 1944 the Ardennes offensive with the objective to seize the Allied port facilities around Antwerp. In the case of success and the holding of the area and destruction of its facilities, he would have severely dislocated the British and American advance in the west. Possibilities for lengthening a lost war would have been reasonable. "This was his thinking in autumn 1944. In Speer's view, Hitler knew he was playing his last card."[44] It would not be a trump.

*   *   *

During the course of World War II, Hitler would drive to achieve German destiny in Europe. The drive would be obscured by conventional historical views of diplomacy and war fighting in Europe. The older conventional views would represent diplomacy as the adjustment of balances of power and wars fought to reflect minor exchanges of territory but appropriate adjustments in balances. Hitler would arrive on such a scene, especially in October 1939, with his order for an attack in the west. Hitler would arrive as from a different universe of diplomacy. Hitler was not interested in balance. He was interested in a German state secure in its destiny through large enough space and resources. He would argue so as early as 1925: "If without extension of its soil a great nation seems doomed to extinction the right to extend that soil becomes a duty."[45] The words are all in place—*extinction, right, duty*. There is little overly new in the words above, but the equating of German destiny with the seizure of agricultural, industrial, and mineral resources at the expense of conventional military victory is both new and startling. Hitler's war-fighting style at the highest level of consideration might be characterized as forward far enough on the offensive, not one step back on the defensive.

The question of what man conducted the war, the power-hungry tyrant of the great biographers or another man associated with overdue revision, remains open. It seems almost inconceivable that a power-hungry dictator, no matter how hungry, would launch Barbarossa against the world's largest land power. But Hitler was other things besides the easily attributed dictator so well known. He had been a painter of talent in water and oil colors but can hardly be seen, because of that, to be compelled to dominate the European continent. But Hitler was an aspiring, potentially brilliant architect acknowledged by Paul Ludwig Troost to be superior to him in the theoretical aspects of that fine art. And with his fascination for the heroic themes of grand opera and its stage settings and directorship, he edges into view possibly as the conductor of theater set to music as World War II. These things entertain our imagination but stretch our credulity. Yet these talents and interests existed and were leavened into his character. We are left with the usual revisionist suspects to aid in breaking the code of Hitler as war leader. As messiah, with the *de rigueur* baggage of a mission, Hitler must be considered as focused on that mission. Having saved his people from the German Marxists and the peacetime French, he had now in war to save the Germans from an unwanted combination of French, British, and Russians. But how does a racial messiah save the Germans from such a racial potpourri? Hitler would subdue—not destroy—the British and French tribes of equivalent culture but displace— destroy—the Russian tribe of allegedly lesser culture. The center point for the whole business in terms of assuring German existence for historical eternity would be the German seizure of Russian resources. What comes into focus for World War II is yet another irony: Hitler as German messiah clearly focused on strategic resources but suffering them widely scattered over Europe and European Russia.

The suspect, however, that most pulls together Hitler through war is the historical man. He was in the sphere of a momentous collision between existing laws and rights and contingencies adverse to the existing system. Victory over his opponents in France, Britain, and Russia would have secured him not the mere "conquest" of

Europe but rather the setting in place of a new historical reality. In the face of such a situation, the great biographers may have become historical valets unable to acknowledge Hitler to be in the category of the hero in history—but not because he was no hero, but because they were valets. Yet Hitler was not a moral man, and as the mighty form he had become would trample down many an innocent flower, crush to pieces many an object in his path.[46] But ascribing to Hitler the attributes of world-historical personality still does not explain a strategy centered on the seizure of strategic resources, space, and the setting in place of barrier lines to secure it. Hitler had an astonishing memory for numbers that was fundamental to the realities of achievement and political–military power. His "endless recitation of production figures" may have been less obfuscate rambling and more germane to war-fighting strategy than we give it credit—a kind of mathematics of strategy that has been missed to the present day.

And in the midst of this immense drama in the second half of 1941, Hitler, by his own logical predilection and the surrounding influences of Nazis working toward him, began to embrace a final solution to the Jewish problem. After having not referred much to the Jewish problem in Europe for several years before and during the war, he began to mention it with increased frequency and virulence. He would make the deadly, imaginative analogy that, "I feel like the Robert Koch of politics. He found the bacillus of tuberculosis and through that showed medical scholarship new ways. I discovered the Jew as the bacillus … of all social decomposition."[47] And to complete the analogy, he would say that he had proved that a state could live without Jews. He would present the theme that they were not needed in Europe and had never produced a true musician, thinker, or artist. The final step toward outright genocide was the September 1941 decision to deport Jews eastward from everywhere in Europe under German control. Hitler, impelled partly by Stalin's August decision to deport the Volga Germans, approved deportations, which soon expanded. By January 1942 they had merged into an unimaginatively cruel systematic killing of European Jews.

Hitler would argue that the Jews had been responsible for the outbreak of both world wars and prophesize that they would not survive the second, notwithstanding how it turned out for Germany. Such reasoning and finality fit comfortably under the cloak of a dark messiah. Such reasoning and deed added to the giant cataclysm of World War II would also fit the presence of an equally dark world-historical personality.

NOTES

INTRODUCTION

1. The publication dates for Maser and Fest are those for the English language versions of their biographies.

2. See, for example, Ian Kershaw, *Hitler, 1889–1936, Hubris* (New York: W. W. Norton, 1999), p. xxi.

3. Ibid., p. xxiv.

4. Yet even Kershaw notes, quoting Wolfgang Sauer, "In [Hitler] the historian faces a phenomenon that leaves him no way but rejection.... There is literally no voice worth considering that disagrees on this matter. ... [but] does not such fundamental rejection imply a fundamental lack of understanding?"

5. Albert Speer, *Inside the Third Reich: Memoirs by Albert Speer* (New York: Macmillan, 1970), p. 143.

6. Ibid., p. 80.

7. Ibid., pp. 67, 68.

8. A.J.P. Taylor, *The Origins of the Second World War* (New York: Atheneum, 1961).

9. This author's quote in counterpoint.

10. David Cesarini, *Literary Review* and Gordon A. Craig, *New York Review of Books*; as noted in Ian Kershaw, *Hitler, 1936–1945, Nemesis* (New York: W. W. Norton, 2000).

11. Richard J. Evans, Cambridge University; as noted on the back cover of Kershaw, *Hubris*.

12. Kershaw, *Hubris*, p. xxiv.

13. Ibid., p. xxvi.

14. Ibid., in which the author acknowledges his debt to Max Weber and Hans-Ulrich Wehler in works of 1972 and 1983, respectively, for the ideas.

15. Ibid., p. xxix.

16. Ibid.

17. *Journal of Roman Studies* quote on cover of Christian Meier, *Caesar: A Biography* (New York: Basic Books, 1993).

18. As noted and quoted in ibid., p. 24.

19. Ibid., p. 479, quoting the formidable Prussian historian Leopold von Ranke.

20. Ibid., p. 17.

21. Mommsen as paraphrased from ibid.

22. Burckhardt as quoted in ibid.

23. Kershaw, *Hubris*, p. xxv.

24. Ibid., p. xx.

25. Ibid., p. xix.

26. Ibid., p. xxiii. The author notes: "an autodidact whose only indispensable talent was one for stirring the base emotions of the masses."

27. Ibid., p. 170. The author comments: "Politics to Hitler—and so it would remain—*was* propaganda." Note that Kershaw's use of italics here was one of only a handful in the entire copious volume.

28. See in Sir John Glubb, *The Life and Times of Muhammad*, (New York: Stein and Day, 1971), p. 72.

29. Ibid.

30. Thomas Mann, "That Man Is My Brother, and If Genius Is Madness Tempered with Discretion, This Sly Sadist and Plotter of Revenge Is a Genius," *Esquire*, March 1939, pp. 31, 132, 133.

31. Ibid.

32. Adolf Hitler, *Mein Kampf*, trans. Ralph Manheim (New York: Houghton Mifflin, 1943), p. 107.

33. Kurt G. W. Ludecke, *I Knew Hitler* (New York: Charles Scribner's Sons, 1937), p. 8.

34. Ibid., p. 13.

35. Ron Rosenbaum, *Explaining Hitler: The Search for the Origins of His Evil* (New York: Random House, 1998), p. iv.

36. Ibid., p. 80.

37. Kershaw, *Hubris*, p. xxix.

38. Hitler, *Mein Kampf*, p. 199.

39. Ibid., p. 163.

40. Mann, "My Brother," p. 31.

41. Hitler, *Mein Kampf*, p. 205.

42. Ibid.

43. Ibid.

44. Ernst Neuman, *Wagner as Man and Artist*, (New York: Garden City, 1937), p. 272.

45. Hitler, *Mein Kampf*, p. 22.

46. Mann, "My Brother," p. 31.

47. See the photograph in Reichspropagandaleitung der NSDAP, *Ich kaempfe* (Munich, Ger.: F. Eher Nachf., 1943), p. 13.

48. Hitler, *Mein Kampf*, p. 88.

49. Ibid., p. 381.

50. Mann, "My Brother," p. 132.

51. Ibid., p. 133.

52. For the word picture see Ernst Juenger, *Storm of Steel* (London: Penguin, 2003).

53. Speer, *Inside the Third Reich*, p. 114.

54. Ibid., p. 115.

55. Ibid.

56. Hitler, *Mein Kampf*, p. 357.

57. Ibid.

58. Ibid., p. 491.

59. Ibid., p. 501.

60. Kershaw, *Hubris*, p. xxiv.

61. See, for example, John L. Snell, ed., *The Nazi Revolution: Germany's Guilt or Germany's Fate?* (Boston: Heath, 1959), p. vii.

62. Mann, "My Brother," p. 31.

63. Hermann Balck, *Ordnung im Chaos: Erinnerungen 1893–1948* (Osnabrueck, Ger.: Biblio-Verlag, 1980), pp. 635–36.

64. Roland Auguet, *Cruelty and Civilization: The Roman Games* (Paris: Flammarion, 1970; New York: Routledge, 1998), pp. 13–15. Citations refer to Routledge publication.

65. Ibid., p. 14.

66. Adolf Hitler, *Hitler's Secret Conversations, 1941–1944*, trans. Norman Cameron and R. H. Stevens, (New York: Farrar, Straus, and Young, 1953), p. 595.

67. Ibid., p. 395.

68. Hitler, *Mein Kampf*, p. 55.

69. Ibid.

70. Ibid., p. 64.

71. Ibid.

72. Speer, *Inside the Third Reich*, p. 131.

73. Ibid.

74. Ernst Hanfstaengl, *Hitler: The Missing Years* (London: Eyre and Spottiswoode, 1957), p. 45.

75. August Kubizek, *The Young Hitler I Knew* (New York: Tower, 1954), p. 13.

CHAPTER 1: HITLER'S ATTRIBUTES REASSESSED

1. Adolf Hitler, *Mein Kampf*, trans. Ralph Manheim (New York: Houghton Mifflin, 1943), p. 9; as noted in Bradley F. Smith, *Adolf Hitler: His Family, Childhood and Youth* (Stanford: Hoover Institution 1967), p. 73.

2. Billy F. Price, *Adolf Hitler: The Unknown Artist* (Houston: Billy F. Price, 1984), p. 7.

3. Smith, *His Family, Childhood and Youth*, p. 96.

4. Ibid., p. 103; Smith cites August Kubizek, *The Young Hitler I Knew* (New York: Tower, 1954) p. 84.

5. Kubizek, *Young Hitler*, pp. 54–55.

6. Ernst Hanfstaengl, *Hitler: The Missing Years* (London: Eyre and Spottiswoode, 1957; New York: Arcade, 1994), p. 40. Citations refer to the Arcade edition.

7. Ian Kershaw, *Hitler, 1889–1936, Hubris* (New York: W. W. Norton, 1999), p. 91.

8. Hanfstaengl, *Missing Years*, p. 206.

9. See in Price, *Unknown Artist*, p. 104, for the test paintings and compare them with the noticeably superior other work of the period 1907 through 1918.

10. See in Kershaw, *Nemesis*, p. 183.

11. Thomas Mann, "That Man Is My Brother, and If Genius Is Madness Tempered with Discretion, This Sly Sadist and Plotter of Revenge Is a Genius," *Esquire*, March 1939, p. 31.

12. Ibid.

13. Kubizek, *Young Hitler*, pp. 6–7.

14. Ibid., p. 7.

15. Ibid., pp. 187–88.

16. Ibid., p. 189.

17. Ibid., p. 190.

18. Ibid.

19. Hanfstaengl, *Missing Years*, pp. 26–27.

20. Ibid., p. 303.

21. Ibid., p. 194.

22. See in Kershaw, *Hubris*, p. 43.

23. Kubizek, *Young Hitler*.

24. Hanfstaengl, *Missing Years*, p. 195.

25. Ernst Neuman, *Wagner as Man and Artist*, (New York: Garden City, 1937), p. 24.

26. Joachim C. Fest, *Hitler* (New York: Harcourt Brace Jovanovich, 1974), p. 31.

27. Kubizek, *Young Hitler*, p. 201.

28. Ibid.

29. Ibid., p. 200.

30. Ibid., p. 193.

31. Ibid., p. 194.

32. Ibid., p. 209.

33. Ibid.

34. Kurt G. W. Ludecke, *I Knew Hitler* (New York: Charles Scribner's Sons, 1937), p. 82.

35. Hitler, *Mein Kampf*, p. 548.

36. Ludecke, *I Knew Hitler*, p. 81.

37. Kubizek, *Young Hitler*, p. 201.

38. Hitler, *Mein Kampf*, p. 550.

39. Ludecke, *I Knew Hitler*, p. 90.

40. Kershaw, *Hubris*, p. xxvi. Kershaw applies the quality of "playing

the role" to Hitler as political fuehrer. Hitler was probably more likely playing the role of distant, fate-delivered messiah.

41. Ron Rosenbaum, *Explaining Hitler: The Search for the Origins of His Evil* (New York: Random House, 1998), p. 86. Lord Bullock speaks the words in the context of defining Hitler as the personification of evil: "If not he, then who." Hitler probably personified an intense messiah more than a disembodied abstraction identified as evil.

42. Col. James E. Mrazek (Ret.), *The Fall of Eben-Emael: Prelude to Dunquerque* (Novato, CA: Presidio Press, 1970), pp. 29–33.

43. Ibid., p. 30.

44. Albert Speer, *Inside the Third Reich: Memoirs by Albert Speer* (New York: Macmillan, 1970), p. 28.

45. Kershaw, *Hubris*, p. 41.

46. Ibid.

47. Fest, *Hitler*, p. 38.

48. Kershaw, *Hubris*.

49. Speer, *Inside the Third Reich*, p. 79.

50. Kubizek, *Young Hitler*, p. 91.

51. Hannah Arendt, *Origins of Totalitarianism* (New York: Harcourt, 1951), pp. vii–ix.

52. Kubizek, *Young Hitler*, p. 91.

53. Hitler, *Mein Kampf*, pp. 98–101.

54. Ibid., pp. 39–41.

55. Fest, *Hitler*, p. 41.

56. Konrad Heiden, *Der Fuehrer: Hitler's Rise to Power* (New York: Houghton Mifflin, 1944), pp. 36–76.

57. Fest, *Hitler*, p. 40.

58. Heiden, *Der Fuehrer*, p. 49. Grades for the *Staatsrealschule* in Steyr issued on September 16, 1905, as the last school report of the fourth class.

59. Adolf Hitler, *Hitler's Secret Conversations, 1941–1944*, trans. Norman Cameron and R. H. Stevens, (New York: Farrar, Straus, and Young, 1953), p. 321.

60. Heiden, *Der Fuehrer*, p. 51.

61. The more complete Latin sometimes used was *ceterum censeo carthaginem esse delendam* (but I declare that Carthage must be destroyed).

62. See in Fest, *Hitler*, p. 49, as part of a quote from Mann, "My Brother."

63. Kubizek, *Young Hitler*, p. 16.

64. Ibid., pp. 13–14.

65. Ibid., p. 25.

66. Ibid., p. 26.

67. Ibid., p. 201.

68. Ibid.

69. Ibid., p. 195.

70. Werner Maser, *Hitler: Legend, Myth and Reality* (New York: Harper and Row, 1973), especially pp. 77–109 and appendix A, pp. 322–25.

71. Juenger, *Storm of Steel*, p. 198.

72. Ibid., p. 235.

73. In exceptionally heavy concentrations against unprotected eyes or breathed into the lungs, the effects, of course, would be almost immediate.

74. Kershaw, *Hubris*, does not even mention that Hitler was wounded in the left upper arm by fragments; nor does Fest, *Hitler*, or Toland, *Pictorial Documentary*.

75. Fest, *Hitler*, p. 68.

76. Kershaw, *Hubris*, pp. 89–97.

77. Ernst Juenger, *Storm of Steel* (London: Penguin, 2003), p. 93.

78. Price, *Unknown Artist*, p. 189.

79. Ibid., p. 193.

80. Plutarch, *The Lives of the Noble Grecians and Romans*, The Dryden Edition (Chicago: William Benton, 1952), p. 541.

81. See in Hitler, *Secret Conversations*, pp. 235–36, night of January 22–23, 1942.

82. Ibid, p. 236.

83. Kershaw, *Hubris*, p. 93.

84. Ibid., p. xxvii.

85. As recounted in Maser, *Legend, Myth and Reality*.

86. See in Dr. Johannes von Mullern–Schoenhausen, *Die Loesung des Raetsels Adolf Hitler: Der Versuch einer Deutung der geheimnisvollsten Erscheinung der Weltgeschichte* (Vienna, Aus.: Verlag zur Foerderung wissenschaftlicher Forschung, [1959?]), a controversial collection with several similar such comments claimed for Hitler.

87. Maser, *Legend, Myth and Reality*, p. 84.

88. Smith, *His Family, Childhood and Youth*, p. 127.

89. Firm statistics from World War I show approximately 1.8 million German soldiers were killed in action or died of wounds. A reasonable, conservative figure for significantly wounded would be twice that figure; hence, a total of approximately 5.4 million young men largely from ages seventeen to thirty—the prime of life.

90. This generalization to the effect that Linz was Hitler's "home town" is supported in Evan Burr Bukey, *Hitler's Hometown: Linz, Austria, 1908–1945* (Bloomington: Indiana University Press, 1986), p. 1.

91. Hitler, *Mein Kampf*, p. 8.

92. Ibid., p. 21.

93. Kershaw, *Hubris*, p. 60.

94. Hitler, *Mein Kampf*, p. 51.

95. Ibid.

96. Ibid., p. 52.

97. Ibid.

98. Ibid., p. 56.

99. Ibid.

100. Ibid.

101. Ibid., p. 56.

102. Ibid., p. 57.

103. Kershaw, *Hubris*, p. 61.

104. Hitler, *Mein Kampf*, p. 113, as noted within the context of the Germans and religion.

105. Ibid., p. 125.

106. Ibid., p. 113.

107. Ibid., p. 210.

108. Ibid., p. 212.

109. Ibid., p. 63.

CHAPTER 2: HITLER AS A PRODUCT OF HIS TIMES

1. René Albrecht-Carrié, *A Diplomatic History of Europe Since the Congress of Vienna* (New York: Harper and Row, 1959), p. 462. Notwithstanding the author's name, he was professor of history at Barnard College, New York, NY.

2. Koppel S. Pinson, *Modern Germany: Its History and Civilization* (New York: Macmillan, 1954), p. 349, quoted in Ernst Juenger, *Der Kampf als inneres Erlebnis*, 4th ed. (Berlin, 1929), pp. 2–3, 76–77.

3. Arthur Bryant, *Unfinished Victory* (London: Macmillan, 1940), pp. 3, 26.

4. As noted in Hermann Lutz, *German–French Unity: Basis for European Peace* (Chicago: H. Regnery, 1957), p. 71. See also Thomas A. Bailey, *Woodrow Wilson and the Lost Peace* (New York: Macmillan, 1944) p. 305.

5. Lutz, *German–French Unity*, p. 71.

6. Ibid., p. 70.

7. Ian Kershaw, *Hitler, 1889–1936, Hubris* (New York: W. W. Norton, 1999).

8. Alma Luckau, *The German Delegation at the Paris Peace Conference* (New York: Columbia University Press, 1941), "Document 30," pp. 223–24.

9. Words to this effect can be found in numerous works on the subject by authorities such as Stephen King-Hall, Gilbert Murray, Sisley Huddleston, Robert Strassz-Hupé, and Stefan T. Possony. See, for example, Lutz, *German–French Unity*, pp. 60, 212 (note 72 for chapter 2).

10. Lutz, *Germany–French Unity*, p. 242.

11. See, for example, Pinson, *Modern Germany*, p. 5.

12. Sarah Wambaugh, *Plebiscites Since the World War, With a Collection of Official Documents* (Washington, DC: Carnegie Endowment for International Peace, 1933), pp. 133–34.

13. In Robert G. L. Waite, *Vanguard of Nazism: The Free Corps Movement in Postwar Germany 1918–1923* (New York: Harvard University Press, 1952), p. 228, as quoted by the author from House of Commons debates.

14. The south Baltic coast was only thinly inhabited at the turn of the first millennium. In Pomerelia, the region of the 1919 formation of the Polish Corridor, documents show the beginning of organized colonization by Germans with the establishment of approximately 342 villages between 1280 and 1320 CE. See in F. L. Carsten, *The Origins of Prussia* (Oxford: Clarendon, 1954), pp. 59–60.

15. Lutz, *German–French Unity*, p. 73.

16. R. W. Seton-Watson, *Britain and the Dictators: A Survey of Post-War British Policy* (Cambridge: Cambridge University Press, 1938), pp. 76–77.

17. See, for example, Lutz, *German–French Unity*, p. 93.

18. Herbert Hoover, *The Memoirs of Herbert Hoover: Years of Adventure, 1874–1920* (New York: Macmillan, 1951), pp. 461–62; as noted in Lutz, *German–French Unity*, pp. 38–39.

19. See in Lutz, *German–French Unity*, p. 47.

20. J. C. Smuts, *Jan Christian Smuts* (London: Cassell, 1952), pp. 228–29.

21. Harold Nicolsen, *Peacemaking 1919* (New York: Houghton Mifflin, 1939), p. 359.

22. Ibid., p. 350.

23. See as reproduced in Lutz, *German–French Unity*, pp. 52–54. The author was a German émigré of 1948 to the United States who was encouraged to write a book on German diplomacy under Hitler and did so in the period 1952–1957 at the Hoover Institution in Stanford, California.

24. See in Bailey, *Woodrow Wilson*, pp. 240–41.

25. Sir Raymond Beasley, *The Road to Ruin in Europe, 1890–1914* (London, 1932), pp. 1–3, 6–7, as noted in Lutz, *German–French Unity*, p. 60.

26. See, for example, Waite, *Vanguard of Nazism*, p. 239.

27. See in Nigel H. Jones, *Hitler's Heralds: The Story of the Freikorps, 1918–1923* (London: John Murray, 1987), p. 226.

28. As generalized and quoted by William L. Langer, ed., *An Encyclopedia of World History*, (Boston: Houghton Mifflin, 1972), p. 1123.

CHAPTER 3: OUT OF THE DESERT, 1919–1922

1. See, for example, Edward Hallett Carr, *The Twenty Years' Crisis, 1919–1939* (New York: Harper and Row, 1964). This work was originally published in 1939 with a second edition in 1946. The thesis is in the title.

2. Adolf Hitler, *Mein Kampf*, trans. Ralph Manheim (New York: Houghton Mifflin, 1943), p. 206.

3. Koppel S. Pinson, *Modern Germany: Its History and Civilization* (New York: Macmillan, 1954), p. 389, as noted in this Left-oriented— although beautifully written and researched—history.

4. Ian Kershaw, *Hitler, 1889–1936, Hubris* (New York: W. W. Norton, 1999), p. 110.

5. Ibid.

6. Ibid.

7. Ibid., p. 58.

8. Joachim C. Fest, *Hitler* (New York: Harcourt Brace Jovanovich, 1974), p. 52.

9. Hitler, *Mein Kampf*, pp. 39–40.

10. Ibid., p 40.

11. Kershaw, *Hubris*, p. 46.

12. See in August Kubizek, *The Young Hitler I Knew* (New York: Tower, 1954), p. 150.

13. See, for example, John Toland, *Hitler: The Pictorial Documentary of His Life* (Garden City, NY: Doubleday, 1978), p. 21.

14. Ibid., p. 17.

15. See in Thomas Mann, "That Man Is My Brother, and If Genius Is Madness Tempered with Discretion, This Sly Sadist and Plotter of Revenge Is a Genius," *Esquire*, March 1939.

16. Kershaw, *Hubris*, p. 48.

17. Ibid., p. 40.

18. Hitler, *Mein Kampf*, p. 223.

19. Ibid., p. 125.

20. Ibid., p. 223.

21. Ibid.

22. Ibid.

23. Kershaw, *Hubris*, p. 127.

24. Ibid., p. 128.

25. As quoted in ibid., p. 129, within the context of Hitler as an emerging "beerhall agitator."

26. Ibid., p. 280.

27. Ibid., p. 281.

28. Ibid., p. 280.

29. Ibid., p. 282.

30. Ibid., p. 276.

31. Toland, *Pictorial Documentary*, p. 277.

32. Kershaw, *Hubris*, p. 277.

33. Ibid., p. 276.

34. Hitler, *Mein Kampf*, p. 353.

35. Ibid., p. 329.

36. Ibid., pp. 346–47.

37. Ibid., p. 346.

38. Ibid., p. 352.

39. As quoted in Konrad Heiden, *Der Fuehrer: Hitler's Rise to Power* (New York: Houghton Mifflin, 1944), p. 150.

40. Kershaw, *Hubris*, p. 121.

41. Fest, *Hitler*, p. 4.

42. Ibid., p. 50.

43. Ibid.

44. Ibid.

45. Kubizek, *Young Hitler*, p. 13.

46. Ibid.

47. Ibid., pp. 12–13.

48. Hitler, *Mein Kampf*, p. 165.

49. Ibid.

50. Toland, *Pictorial Documentary*, p. 172. The American professional army officer Captain Truman Smith could remark about a public parade of "storm troopers" that he experienced "twelve hundred of the toughest roughnecks I have ever seen in my life pass in review before Hitler" in the street outside the new NSDAP headquarters in Munich in late 1922.

51. Hitler, *Mein Kampf*, p. 536.

52. Ibid., pp. 536–37.

53. Ibid., pp. 346–47.

54. See especially the unaltered color reproduction in Toland, *Pictorial Documentary*, Color Section VI, pp. 18–25.

55. Hitler, *Mein Kampf*, p. 346.

56. Ibid.

57. Ibid., p. 354.

58. Ibid., p. 355.

59. The then-independent *Muenchener Beobachter*.

60. Hitler, *Mein Kampf*, p. 355.

61. Ibid., p. 358.

62. Ibid.

63. Ibid., p. 356.

64. Ibid., p. 347.

65. Ibid.

66. Ibid., p. 359.

67. Ibid., p. 364.

68. Ibid., p. 363.

69. Ernst Hanfstaengl, *Hitler: The Missing Years* (London: Eyre and Spottiswoode, 1957; New York: Arcade, 1994), p. 33. Citations refer to the Arcade edition.

70. Ibid., p. 36.

71. Kurt G. W. Ludecke, *I Knew Hitler* (New York: Charles Scribner's Sons, 1937), p. 97.

72. Hitler, *Mein Kampf*, p. 491.

73. Hanfstaengl, *Missing Years*, p. 89.

74. Hitler, *Mein Kampf*, p. 480.

75. Ibid., pp. 480–81.

76. Ibid., p. 230.

77. Ibid., p. 227.

78. Ibid., pp. 233–34, 317.

79. Ibid., p. 456.

80. Ibid., p. 380.

81. Ibid., p. 490.

82. Ibid.

83. Ibid.

84. Ibid., p. 586.

85. Fest, *Hitler*, 144.

86. Hitler, *Mein Kampf*, p. 505.

87. Toland, *Pictorial Documentary*, p. 114.

88. Hitler, *Mein Kampf*, p. 504.

CHAPTER 4: SETBACK, PERSEVERANCE, AND INFALLIBILITY, 1923–1929

1. John Toland, *Hitler: The Pictorial Documentary of His Life* (Garden City, NY: Doubleday, 1978), p. 108.

2. Ibid., p. 113.

3. Ibid.

4. Adolf Hitler, *Mein Kampf*, trans. Ralph Manheim (New York: Houghton Mifflin, 1943), p. 552.

5. Ibid.

6. Franz Neumann, *Behemoth: The Structure and Practice of National Socialism* (Toronto: Oxford University Press, 1942), p. 75.

7. Nikolai Tolstoy, *Night of the Long Knives* (New York: Ballantine, 1972), p. 156.

8. As quoted in Joachim C. Fest, *Hitler* (New York: Harcourt Brace Jovanovich, 1974), p. 163.

9. See, for example, ibid.

10. Hitler, *Mein Kampf*, pp. 680–81.

11. Ibid., p. 680.

12. Ibid., p. 682.

13. Ibid., p. 683.

14. Ibid.

15. Fest, *Hitler*, p. 161.

16. Konrad Heiden, *Der Fuehrer: Hitler's Rise to Power* (New York: Houghton Mifflin, 1944), p. 55.

17. Ibid., p. 74.

18. Ibid., p. 34.

19. Ibid., p. 35.

20. Kurt G. W. Ludecke, *I Knew Hitler* (New York: Charles Scribner's Sons, 1937), p. 14.

21. Ibid., p. 15.

22. Ibid., pp. 91–92.

23. Ibid., p. 92.

24. Ibid.

25. Ian Kershaw, *Hitler, 1889–1936, Hubris* (New York: W. W. Norton, 1999), p. xxvii.

26. Ludecke, *I Knew Hitler*, pp. 92–93.

27. Ibid., p. 93.

28. Ibid.

29. Fest, *Hitler*, p. 238.

30. Hitler, *Mein Kampf*, p. 580.

31. As quoted in Fest, *Hitler*, p. 174.

32. Ibid., p. 177.

33. Hitler, *Mein Kampf*, pp. 579–86.

34. Ibid., p. 579.

35. Ibid., p. 182.

36. Ibid., p. 184.

37. As cited in Dietrich Orlow, "The Conversion of Myths into Political Power: The Case of the Nazi Party, 1925–1926," *American Historical Review* 72, (1967): 907.

38. Kershaw, *Hubris*, p. 252.

39. Ibid.

40. Ibid., p. 253.

41. Ibid., p. 250.

42. Heiden, *Der Fuehrer*, p. 97.

43. Mann, "My Brother," 31.

44. Kershaw, *Hubris*, p. 251.

45. Ibid., p. 253.

46. Hitler, *Mein Kampf*, p. 216.

47. Ibid., p. 217.

48. Ibid., p. 580.

49. Ibid.

50. Ibid., p. 437.

51. Gordon A. Craig, *The Politics of the Prussian Army, 1640–1945* (Oxford: Oxford University Press, 1956), p. 337.

52. Fest, *Hitler*, p. 190.

53. Kershaw, *Hubris*, p. 211. Note that Kershaw has designated "a foot to the right," oriented in a revealing way as if he had fired the police carbine.

54. As quoted in Charles Bracelen Flood, *Hitler: The Path to Power* (Boston: Houghton Mifflin Harcourt, 1989), p. 556.

55. Toland, *Pictorial Documentary*, p. 172.

56. Ibid., p. 182.

57. Ibid.

58. Ibid.

59. Flood, *Path to Power*, p. 571.

60. August Kubizek, *The Young Hitler I Knew* (New York: Tower, 1954), p. 200.

61. Hitler, *Mein Kampf*, p. 534.

62. Kershaw, *Hubris*, xxvi.

63. Heiden, *Der Fuehrer*, p. 359.

64. Hitler, *Mein Kampf*, 122.

65. Ibid.

66. Ibid., p. 455.

67. Ibid., p. 456.

68. Kershaw, *Hubris*, p. 240.

69. Ibid.

70. Toland, *Pictorial Documentary*, p. 198.

71. Fest, *Hitler*, p. 199.

72. Alan Bullock, *Hitler: A Study in Tyranny*, (New York: Harper and Row, 1962), p. 382.

73. Georg Wilhelm Friedrich Hegel, *The Philosophy of History* (New York: Encyclopedia Britannica, 1952), p. 167.

74. Hitler, *Mein Kampf*, p. 182.

75. Hegel, *Philosophy of History*, p. 166.

76. Ibid.

77. See all of this in ibid., p. 167.

78. Ibid., p. 163.

79. Ibid., p. 168.

80. Kershaw, *Hubris*, p. xxvii.

81. Bullock, *Study in Tyranny*, p. 384.

82. Hitler, *Mein Kampf*, p. 581.

83. Ibid., p. 585.

84. Ibid., p. 468.

85. Ibid., p. 467.

86. Ibid., p. 465.

87. Ibid., p. 466.

88. Ibid.

89. Kershaw, *Hubris*, p. 341.

90. Ibid., p. 281.

91. Ibid., p. 299.

92. Ibid., p. 341.

93. Ibid.

94. Ibid., p. 702.

CHAPTER 5: OLD FIGHTERS, NEW CONVERTS, DECISIVE SUCCESS, 1929–1932

1. Joachim C. Fest, *Hitler* (New York: Harcourt Brace Jovanovich, 1974), p. 297.

2. John Toland, *Hitler: The Pictorial Documentary of His Life* (Garden City, NY: Doubleday, 1978), p. 264.

3. Ibid., p. 281.

4. Ibid., p. 282.

5. Ibid.

6. Ibid., p. 261.

7. Fest, *Hitler*, p. 304.

8. Presented in ibid., p. 311.

9. Ibid., p. 166.

10. Ibid., p. 168.

11. Ibid.

12. Ibid., p. 327.

13. Ibid.

14. Ibid., p. 328.

15. Ibid., p. 320.

16. Ibid., p. 328.

17. Ian Kershaw, *Hitler, 1889–1936, Hubris* (New York: W. W. Norton, 1999), p. 294.

18. Ibid., p. 295.

19. Ibid.

20. Ibid.

21. Fest, *Hitler*, p. 327.

22. Ibid., p. 312.

23. Ibid.

24. Frederic V. Grunfeld, *The Hitler File: A Social History of Germany and the Nazis 1918–1945* (New York: Bonanza, 1979), p. 112.

25. Kershaw, *Hubris*, p. 313.

26. Toland, *Pictorial Documentary*, p. 318.

27. Ibid., p. 278.

28. Ibid., p. 191.

29. Adolf Hitler, *Mein Kampf*, trans. Ralph Manheim (New York: Houghton Mifflin, 1943), p. 465.

30. Ibid., p. 470.

31. Ibid., pp. 470–71.

32. Ibid., p. 471.

33. Fest, *Hitler*, p. 316.

34. Kershaw, *Hubris*, p. 361.

35. Fest, *Hitler*, p. 317.

36. Hitler, *Mein Kampf*, p. 546.

37. Ibid.

38. Ibid., p. 547.

39. Ibid.

40. Werner Maser, *Hitler: Legend, Myth and Reality* (New York: Harper and Row, 1973), p. 247.

41. Fest, *Hitler*, p. 156.

42. Hitler, *Mein Kampf*, p. 552.

43. Ibid., p. 550.

44. Ibid., p. 548.

45. Maser, *Legend, Myth and Reality*, p. 247.

46. Kershaw, *Hubris*, p. 178.

47. Fest, *Hitler*, p. 156.

48. Hitler, *Mein Kampf*, p. 551.

49. Kershaw, *Hubris*, p. 320.

50. Fest, *Hitler*, p. 294.

51. Ibid.

52. As constructed from Richard F. Hamilton, *Who Voted for Hitler* (Princeton, NJ: Princeton University Press, 1982), pp. 64–100.

53. Fest, *Hitler*, p. 295, as quoted in Albrecht Tyrell, *Fuehrer befiehl… Selbstzeugnisse aus der Kampfzeit der NSDAP* (Dusseldorf, Ger.: Droste, 1969), p. 297.

54. Hitler, *Mein Kampf*, p. 490.

55. Ibid., p. 491.

56. Ibid., p. 417.

57. Ibid., p. 534.

58. Fest, *Hitler*, p. 50.

59. Hitler, *Mein Kampf*, p. 180.

60. Ibid., p. 185.

61. See in Toland, *Pictorial Documentary*, pp. 317–18, for both quotations.

62. Ibid., p. 317, quoting the young Hanfstaengl.

63. Fest, *Hitler*, p. 5.

64. Toland, *Pictorial Documentary*, p. 497.

65. Maser, *Legend, Myth and Reality*, photo numbers 17 and 18 following page 178.

66. Norman H. Baynes, ed., *The Speeches of Adolf Hitler, April 1922–August 1939*, 2 vols., (London: Oxford University Press, 1942), 1:139.

67. Ibid., p. 137.

68. Hitler, *Mein Kampf*, p. 52.

69. Ibid.

70. Toland, *Pictorial Documentary*, p. 145.

71. Albert Speer, *Inside the Third Reich: Memoirs by Albert Speer* (New York: Macmillan, 1970), pp. 286–91.

CHAPTER 6: TRIUMPH OF A MESSIAH WITHIN GERMANY, 1933–1934

1. Ian Kershaw, *Hitler, 1889–1936, Hubris* (New York: W. W. Norton, 1999), p. 449.

2. Ibid., p. 450.

3. Norman H. Baynes, ed., *The Speeches of Adolf Hitler, April 1922–August 1939*, 2 vols., (London: Oxford University Press, 1942), 1:974.

4. Ibid.

5. Ibid., p. 961.

6. As noted and quoted in John Toland, *Hitler: The Pictorial Documentary of His Life* (Garden City, NY: Doubleday, 1978), p. 297.

7. Louis Leo Snyder, ed., *Third Reich Documentary History* (Chicago: Nelson-Hall, 1981), pp. 106–107.

8. Kershaw, *Hubris*, p. 476.

9. See for example, Snyder, *Third Reich Documentary*, pp. 95–105.

10. Kershaw, *Hubris*, p. 459.

11. Toland, *Pictorial Documentary*, p. 306.

12. Kershaw, *Hubris*, p. 468; Toland, *Pictorial Documentary*, p. 307; see also Joachim C. Fest, *Hitler* (New York: Harcourt Brace Jovanovich, 1974), p. 408.

13. See as quoted in Fest, *Hitler*, pp. 408–409.

14. Ibid., p. 409.

15. Kershaw, *Hubris*, p. 468.

16. Fest, *Hitler*, p. 409.

17. Kershaw, *Hubris*, p. 468.

18. Ibid., p. 408.

19. Ibid., p. 547.

20. Ibid., p. 541.

21. As quoted in Alan Wykes, *Himmler* (New York: Ballantine, 1972), pp. 85–86.

22. Ibid., p. 84.

23. *Organizationsbuch der NSDAP* (Munich, Ger.: [Zentralverlag der NSDAP?], 1938), p. 417.

24. Kershaw, *Hubris*, p. 471.

25. Ibid., pp. 471–72.

26. Ibid., p. 472.

27. Ibid., p. 473.

28. Ibid., p. 473.

29. Hermann Lutz, *German–French Unity: Basis for European Peace* (Chicago: H. Regnery, 1957), p. 100. For the authorities, see footnote 18.

30. Ibid.

31. Franz von Papen, *Memoirs* (New York: Dutton, 1953), p. 203.

32. Ibid., p. 204.

33. Baynes, *Speeches of Adolf Hitler*, 2:1089.

34. Papen, *Memoirs*, pp. 259–60.

35. Ibid., pp. 297–98.

36. Fest, *Hitler*, p. 452.

37. B. H. Liddell Hart, *The German Generals Talk* (New York: William Morrow, 1948), p. 308 (third sentence from the end of the book).

38. Fest, *Hitler*, p. 454. Hitler's comments recorded as part of the minutes of the meeting.

39. Konrad Heiden, *Der Fuehrer: Hitler's Rise to Power* (New York: Houghton Mifflin, 1944), p. 720.

40. Ibid., p. 755.

41. Ibid., p. 758.

42. Toland, *Pictorial Documentary*, pp. 332–33.

43. Fest, *Hitler*, p. 459.

44. Ibid., pp. 333–34.

45. For the impression as quoted, see Toland, *Pictorial Documentary*, p. 333.

46. Heiden, *Der Fuehrer*, pp. 720.

47. For this unique picture, the author is indebted to the words and insight of ibid., p. 719.

48. Ibid., p. 731.

49. Toland, *Pictorial Documentary*, p. 460.

50. Baynes, *Speeches of Adolf Hitler*, 1:301.

51. Toland, *Pictorial Documentary*, p. 335.

52. Fest, *Hitler*, p. 335.

53. Ibid., p. 466.

54. Hieden, *Der Fuehrer*, p. 772.

CHAPTER 7: ARRIVAL OF A WORLD-HISTORICAL PERSONALITY IN EUROPE, 1935–1936

1. Ian Kershaw, *Hitler, 1889–1936, Hubris* (New York: W. W. Norton, 1999), p. 532.

2. Ian Kershaw, *Hitler, 1936–1945, Nemesis* (New York: W. W. Norton, 2000), p. 234.

3. Sarah Wambaugh, *Plebiscites Since the World War, With a Collection of Official Documents* (Washington, DC: Carnegie Endowment for International Peace, 1933), 1:413.

4. Ibid., 1:414–15.

5. Kershaw, *Hubris*, p. 547.

6. Wambaugh, *Plebiscites*, 1:415.

7. Norman H. Baynes, ed., *The Speeches of Adolf Hitler, April 1922–August 1939*, 2 vols., (London: Oxford University Press, 1942), 2:1196.

8. Gordon Wright, *France in Modern Times: 1760 to the Present* (Chicago: Rand McNally, 1960), p. 427.

9. Ibid.

10. Joachim C. Fest, *Hitler* (New York: Harcourt Brace Jovanovich, 1974), pp. 483–510. Chapter entitled "Age of *Faits Accomplis*."

11. Alan Bullock, *Hitler: A Study in Tyranny*, (New York: Harper and Row, 1962), p. 322.

12. Ibid., p. 327.

13. Wright, *France in Modern Times*, p. 493.

14. Baynes, *Speeches of Adolf Hitler*, 2:1228.

15. Fest, *Hitler*, p. 199.

16. John Toland, *Hitler: The Pictorial Documentary of His Life* (Garden City, NY: Doubleday, 1978), p. 368.

17. Ibid., pp. 368–69.

18. Russel Henry Stolfi, "Reality and Myth: French and German Preparations of War 1933–1940" (Ph.D. diss. Stanford University, 1966), pp. 108–109a.

19. Baynes, *Speeches of Adolf Hitler*, 2:1288.

20. Wright, *France in Modern Times*, p. 497.

21. See, for example, Bullock, *Study in Tyranny*, p. 342.

22. Baynes, *Speeches of Adolf Hitler*, 2:1235. Specifically the Reichstag speech of May 21, 1935.

23. Kershaw, *Hubris*, p. 585.

24. Baynes, *Speeches of Adolf Hitler*, 2:1270.

25. Wright, *France in Modern Times*, p. 496.

26. Kershaw, *Hubris*, p. 589.

27. Fest, *Hitler*, p. 499.

28. Kershaw, *Hubris*, p. 589.

29. Baynes, *Speeches of Adolf Hitler*, 2:1307.

30. Kershaw, *Hubris*, p. xxv.

31. Ibid.

32. Billy F. Price, *Adolf Hitler: The Unknown Artist* (Houston: Billy F. Price, 1984), p. 7.

33. Ibid.

34. Ibid., p. 15.

35. Baynes, *Speeches of Adolf Hitler*, 1:586.

36. Ibid.

37. Ibid., p. 588.

38. Ibid., p. 571.

39. Ibid., p. 572.

40. Ibid., p. 575.

41. Ibid., p. 588.

42. Oswald Spengler, *The Decline of the West: Form and Actuality*, (New York: Knopf, 1926), 1:40.

43. Ibid., 1:44.

CHAPTER 8: REDEEMER OF THE GERMANS, 1937–1939

1. Sarah Wambaugh, *Plebiscites Since the World War, With a Collection of Official Documents* (Washington, DC: Carnegie Endowment for International Peace, 1933), 1:546.

2. John Toland, *Hitler: The Pictorial Documentary of His Life* (Garden City, NY: Doubleday, 1978), p. 421.

3. See Ian Kershaw, *Hitler, 1936–1945, Nemesis* (New York: W. W. Norton, 2000), p. 47, for the first quote and Joachim C. Fest, *Hitler* (New York: Harcourt Brace Jovanovich, 1974), p. 539, for the second.

4. Fest, *Hitler*, p. 541.

5. Ibid., p. 543.

6. See Albert Speer, *Inside the Third Reich: Memoirs by Albert Speer* (New York: Macmillan, 1970), p. 12, as cited there from Heinrich Tessenow, *Handwerk und Kleinstadt* (Berlin: Bruno Cassirer,1920), the concluding lines.

7. Fest, *Hitler*, p. 541.

8. Ibid., p. 546.

9. Franz von Papen, *Memoirs* (New York: Dutton, 1953), p. 407.

10. Ibid.

11. Ibid., p. 392.

12. Ibid.

13. Ibid., p. 425.

14. Toland, *Pictorial Documentary*, p. 443.

15. Heinz Guderian, *Panzer Leader* (Washington, DC: Zenger, 1979), p. 50. Reprint of original 1952 edition.

16. Toland, *Pictorial Documentary*, pp. 433–34.

17. Charles Bracelen Flood, *Hitler: The Path to Power* (Boston: Houghton Mifflin Harcourt, 1989), p. 220.

18. Fest, *Hitler*, p. 465.

19. Papen, *Memoirs*, p. 426.

20. *The Diplomats 1919–1939*, eds. Gordon A. Craig and Felix Gilbert, 2nd vol., *The Thirties* (New York: Atheneum, 1963), p. 538.

21. Toland, *Pictorial Documentary*, p. 449.

22. Papen, *Memoirs*, p. 428.

23. Ibid.

24. Fest, *Hitler*, p. 546.

25. Norman H. Baynes, ed., *The Speeches of Adolf Hitler, April 1922–August 1939*, 2 vols., (London: Oxford University Press, 1942), 2:1416–17.

26. Baynes, *Speeches of Adolf Hitler*, 1:1423–25.

27. Ibid., p. 1422.

28. Ibid., p. 1423.

29. Fest, *Hitler*, p. 547. Hitler, as quoted years after the Austrian crisis.

30. Ibid., pp. 550–51.

31. See, for example, Baynes, *Speeches of Adolf Hitler*, 2:1271.

32. Ibid., p. 1457.

33. Ibid.

34. Ibid., pp. 1457–58.

35. Ibid., p. 1457. Letter read in Linz on April 7, 1938, but written to the commandant of the *Vaterlaendischer Schutzbund* in upper Austria fourteen years earlier.

36. Ibid., p. 1346.

37. Ibid., p. 1490.

38. Ibid., p. 1488.

39. Baynes, *Speeches of Adolf Hitler*, 1:411. June 1937 in a speech at Wuerzburg.

40. Baynes, *Speeches of Adolf Hitler*, 2:1409.

41. Telford Taylor, *Munich: The Price of Peace* (New York: Random House, 1980), p. 391.

42. Ibid.

43. Baynes, *Speeches of Adolf Hitler*, 2:1493.

44. Ibid., p. 1494.

45. Ibid., p. 1494.

46. Ibid., p. 1495.

47. Fest, *Hitler*, pp. 552–53.

48. Toland, *Pictorial Documentary*, p. 464.

49. Ibid., pp. 472–74.

50. Kershaw, *Nemesis*, p. 92.

51. Toland, *Pictorial Documentary*, p. 480.

52. Ibid., p. 490.

53. Ibid., p. 497.

54. Baynes, *Speeches of Adolf Hitler*, 2:1497.

55. Toland, *Pictorial Documentary*, p. 473.

56. Ibid., p. 474.

57. Kershaw, *Nemesis*, p. 91.

58. Baynes, *Speeches of Adolf Hitler*, 2:1457.

59. Toland, *Pictorial Documentary*, p. 471.

60. Fest, *Hitler*, p. 521.

61. Baynes, *Speeches of Adolf Hitler*, 2:1509.

62. Ibid., pp. 1526–27.

63. Ibid., p. 1520.

64. Ibid., p. 1523. The translation is inaccurate at the critical beginning of Hitler's listing of fugitives: "We see the appalling figures: on one day 10,000 fugitives, on the next 20,000" should be: "on one day 10,000 fugitives, *by* the next 20,000." (Italics mine.)

65. Ibid., p. 1518.

66. Ibid., p. 1519.

67. Ibid., p. 1488.

68. Adolf Hitler, *Mein Kampf*, trans. Ralph Manheim (New York: Houghton Mifflin, 1943), p. 653.

69. Toland, *Pictorial Documentary*, p. 497.

70. Speer, *Inside the Third Reich*, p. 75.

71. Ibid., p. 74.

72. *Webster's New International Dictionary*, 2nd ed., s.v. "chimera." The dramatist was Lord Lytton.

73. Peter Adam, *Art of the Third Reich* (New York: Harry N. Abrams, 1995), p. 255.

74. Speer, *Inside the Third Reich*, p. 43.

75. Ibid., p. 74.

76. Baynes, *Speeches of Adolf Hitler*, 1:583–84.

77. Ibid., p. 588.

78. Ibid.

79. Angela Lambert, *The Lost Life of Eva Braun* (New York: Saint Martin's, 2007), p. 12.

80. Toland, *Pictorial Documentary*, p. 252.

81. Ibid., p. 253.

82. Kershaw, *Hubris*, p. 388. Angela Lambert, however, states in her

authoritative biography of Eva Braun that she "aimed at her jugular," a less likely interpretation of events than aiming for the heart. See in Lambert, *Eva Braun*, p. 134.

83. Heinrich Hoffman, *Hitler* (London: Burke, 1955), p. 160.

84. Ibid., pp. 163–64.

85. Ibid., p. 484.

86. Ibid., p. 484.

87. Toland, *Pictorial Documentary*, pp. 88–89.

88. Baynes, *Speeches of Adolf Hitler*, 2:721.

89. Speer, *Inside the Third Reich*, p. 112.

90. Fest, *Hitler*, p. 115.

91. Ibid.

92. Baynes, *Speeches of Adolf Hitler*, 1:729.

93. Ibid., p. 733.

94. Speer, *Inside the Third Reich*, p. 127.

95. Ibid., p. 131.

96. Ibid.

97. Taylor, *Munich*, p. 808.

98. Ibid., p. 810.

99. Ibid., p. 809.

100. Ibid., p. 815.

101. Ibid., p. 883.

102. Ibid.

CHAPTER 9: THE SIEGE OF GERMANY

1. Field-Marshal Erich von Manstein, *Lost Victories* (Chicago: H. Regnery, 1958) p. 99.

2. Ibid., p. 97.

3. Charles Burdick and Hans-Adolf Jacobsen, eds., *The Halder War Diary* (Novato, CA: Presidio, 1988), p. 68.

4. Klaus Gerbet, ed., *Generalfeldmarschall Fedor von Bock: The War Diary 1939–1945*, (Atglen, PA: Schiffer, 1996), p. 88.

5. Ibid., pp. 74–75.

6. Burdick and Jacobsen, *Halder War Diary*, p. 149.

7. Ibid., pp. 149–50.

8. Ibid., p. 182.

9. Earl F. Ziemke, *The German Northern Theater of Operations 1940–1945*, Department of the Army Pamphlet No. 20-271 at 9 (1959).

10. Burdick and Jacobsen, *Halder War Diary*, p. 103.

11. Ziemke, *German Northern Theater*, p. 22.

12. Ibid., p. 65.

13. Heinz Guderian, *Panzer Leader* (Washington, DC: Zenger, 1979), p. 30. Reprint of original 1952 edition.

14. Ibid., p. 92.

15. Nicolaus von Below, *At Hitler's Side: The Memoirs of Hitler's Luftwaffe Adjutant* (Wiesbaden, Ger.: Hase and Koehler, 1980), p. 47.

16. Ibid., p. 46.

17. Manstein, *Lost Victories*, p. 153.

18. William Green, *The War Planes of the Third Reich* (Garden City, NY: Doubleday, 1970), p. 547.

19. Manstein, *Lost Victories*, p. 165.

20. Matthew Cooper, *The German Army 1933–1945: Conquest*, vol. 2 (New York: Kensington, 1979), p. 137.

21. Cooper, *Conquest*, p. 137.

22. Ian Kershaw, *Hitler, 1936–1945, Nemesis* (New York: W. W. Norton, 2000), p. 308.

23. Ibid.

24. Ibid., p. 305.

25. Burdick and Jacobsen, *Halder War Diary*, p. 180.

26. Kershaw, *Nemesis*, p. 305.

27. Ian Kershaw, *Hitler, 1889–1936, Hubris* (New York: W. W. Norton, 1999), p. 307. See also George Blau, *The German Campaign in Russia: Planning and Operations (1940–1942)*, Department of the Army Pamphlet No. 20-261a at 4 (1955).

28. Ibid., p. 23.

29. Kurt Meyer, *Grenadiers: The Story of Waffen SS General Kurt "Panzer" Meyer* (Mechanicsburg, PA: Stackpole, 2005), p. 51.

30. Kenneth MacKsey, *Kesselring: The Making of the Luftwaffe* (New York: David McKay, 1978), p. 82.

31. As noted in R. H. S. Stolfi, *Hitler's Panzers East: World War II Reinterpreted* (Norman: University of Oklahoma Press, 1991), p. 20.

32. Burdick and Jacobsen, *Halder War Diary*, pp. 323–24.

33. Ibid., p. 424.

34. Ibid., p. 437.

35. Heeresgruppe Mitte, *Aufmarchweisung "Barbarossa,"* Records of German Field Commands: Army Groups, Microcopy T-311, Roll 216, Fr. 000649, US National Archives.

36. Burdick and Jacobsen, *Halder War Diary*, p. 515.

37. Paul Carell, *Hitler Moves East, 1941–1943* (Boston: Little, Brown, 1964), p. 126.

38. Burdick and Jacobsen, *Halder War Diary*, p. 514.

39. Ibid.

40. The number does include Jews of the final solution.

41. Blau, *German Campaign in Russia*, p. 121.

42. Manstein, *Lost Victories*, p. 289.

43. Ibid., p. 449.

44. Kershaw, *Nemesis*, p. 733.

45. Adolf Hitler, *Mein Kampf,* trans. Ralph Manheim (New York: Houghton Mifflin, 1943), p. 54.

46. Georg Wilhelm Friedrich Hegel, *The Philosophy of History* (New York: Encyclopedia Britannica, 1952), p. 168.

47. Kershaw, *Nemesis*, p. 470.

INDEX

Dates are presented first and in chronological order within each entry.